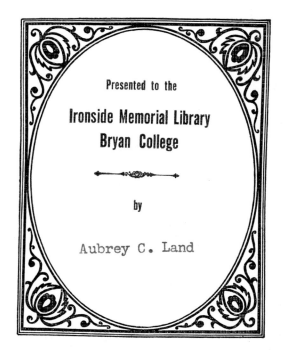

Leander Perez

LEANDER PEREZ

Boss of the Delta

GLEN JEANSONNE

LOUISIANA STATE UNIVERSITY PRESS

Baton Rouge and London

LIBRARY OF CONGRESS CATALOGING IN PUBLICATION DATA

Jeansonne, Glen, 1946–
  Leander Perez, boss of the Delta.

  Bibliography: p.
  Includes index.
    1. Perez, Leander Henry, 1891–1969. 2. Politicians—
Louisiana—Biography. 3. Judges—Louisiana—Biography.
4. Louisiana—Politics and government—1865–1950.
5. Louisiana—Politics and government—1951–
6. Plaquemines Parish, La.—Politics and government.
7. Louisiana—Race relations. I. Title.
F375.P45J42   345′.763′01 [B]   77-4486
ISBN 0-8071-0191-5

Publication of this book was assisted by the American
Council of Learned Societies under a grant from the
Andrew W. Mellon Foundation.

To Stephen A. Webre
and William Ivy Hair

Contents

Illustrations

Preface

In researching this book I have developed an affection and admiration for several close friends and relatives of Leander H. Perez. I have also developed an admiration and affection for several men who were his bitter opponents. The book could not have been written properly without contributions from both sides.

It is difficult to be objective about Perez. His talents were considerable; his faults, glaring. He was at once bigoted and humane, unscrupulous and generous. Those who knew only his kindness or his wrath will find a new Perez here—a many-sided individual capable of both good and evil.

Perez had many admirable characteristics: audacity, an indomitable spirit, and a sense of humor. He also had a torrid temper and a streak of vindictiveness. He felt that he had to dominate his environment totally, and usually he did. After his first few tumultuous years in office, he had enough genuine support in his judicial district that he did not need to resort to electoral trickery to keep himself and his group in power. Yet he persisted, just to make sure. When he could not dominate, he fought his futile battles to the end.

Some of the things he did are unpardonable. He siphoned off a great deal of mineral revenues, which should have gone to the state or parish, into his own pocket. He ruthlessly crushed political opponents. He oppressed blacks. He manipulated the local judiciary.

But Perez was loved by the overwhelming majority of the people of Plaquemines. He ruled with an iron hand, but efficiently. The physical condition of the parish when he died, compared with its condition when he gained power, is impressive proof of remarkable progress, despite periodic setbacks from hurricanes. Many of the residents of

Plaquemines are convinced that it is the finest place in the world. Others have moved away in disgust.

Perez is most frequently criticized for his racism, for that is what made national headlines. But I am convinced that his racial philosophy was entirely sincere. Sincerity does not excuse bigotry, but perhaps bigoted does not properly describe Perez. He believed that enforced segregation was best for Negroes as well as for whites. It goes without saying that he had no empathy with blacks. But it is perhaps presumptuous to assume that other whites, who consider themselves enlightened, can completely understand Negro problems from the Negro's point of view. Realizing this, one still is obligated to try. If Perez can be morally condemned for his racial views, it must be primarily because he did not really make that effort, so sure was he of the rightness of his own views.

I have dedicated this book to William Ivy Hair, without whom it would not have been written, and to Stephen A. Webre, without whom it would not have taken its present form. Professor Hair, as my major adviser at Florida State University, encouraged me to attempt what we both knew would be a difficult and risky dissertation. Many of the sources I would have to use were closed and might never be made accessible. Yet Professor Hair's encouragement and his excellent judgment on style and organization saw me through to conclusion. I also wish to thank the rest of those who sat on my dissertation committee for their prompt reading and helpful suggestions: William W. Rogers, Richard A. Bartlett, James P. Jones, and Elston Roady. I owe special thanks to Professor Bartlett, who goaded me into not being satisfied with the dissertation until it was in publishable form.

During the rewriting of the manuscript I realized that it needed many stylistic improvements. I went to the best writer I knew, my friend Stephen Webre, and we reworked the final draft together in about four months. I must thank Stephen not only for his stylistic help, but for his moral support at a time when my spirits were low.

My parents provided me with financial support during the second of the two years I took to research the book. My first year of research was financed by the Woodrow Wilson Foundation. The Perez family, particularly Chalin O. Perez and Leander Perez, Jr., permitted me to use an extensive collection of uncataloged private papers. I also want to thank all of those who permitted me to tape interviews with them. For reading the manuscript and suggesting revisions I express appreciation to Herbert M. Levine and Albert L. Boudreau, Jr. The entire staff of the Louisiana State University library was most helpful, especially John Price, Margaret Fisher, and Stoney Miller. Background information was furnished by David Baldwin, Mrs. Edith Bowden, Secretary of State Wade O. Martin, Jr., and the Public Affairs Research Council. My heartfelt thanks go to my typist, Mrs. Berta Terry, who helped me meet many deadlines, and to my editor, Marie Carmichael, who labored patiently on the manuscript. I also wish to thank Juanita Terry for her meticulous proofreading and indexing.

Prologue

"Do you know what the Negro is? Animals right out of the jungle. Passion. Welfare. Easy life. That's the Negro. And if you don't know that, you're naive."[1] The speaker was Leander H. Perez, a fiery segregationist who did not believe in sugarcoating his words. He traced the movement to desegregate schools and public facilities "back to all those Jews who were supposed to have been cremated at Buchenwald and Dachau but weren't, and Roosevelt allowed two million of them illegal entry into our country."[2]

Leander Perez was more than simply another Neanderthal segregationist. He was a political boss who held absolute power in Plaquemines Parish,[3] Louisiana, to an extent unsurpassed by any parish leader in Louisiana's history. He was something of a social reformer, a political figure of national stature, and an oil tycoon worth millions of dollars. He was known to one and all, including himself, as the Judge, although the office he held for most of his career was that of district attorney for the judicial district comprising St. Bernard and Plaquemines parishes. Perez got his political start in the early 1920s, when Huey Long was beginning to attract statewide attention. But, even after Long was gunned down in 1935, the Judge continued to dominate life in the lower delta of the Mississippi River for thirty-four years, until he died from a heart attack in 1969. His enemies in the Governor's Mansion and in the White House were sometimes able to defeat him on the state and national levels, but they were never able to shake his hold on Plaquemines. His grip on the parish was partly economic and partly political, and it was enforced by an iron will stronger than the will of any other man in the lower delta.

After being appointed district judge in 1919, Perez used his office to build a political machine probably unmatched by any rural county or parish in the United States. His bailiwick was characterized by elections in which his candidate won 90 percent or more of the votes cast, uncontested offices, and hundreds of people on the parish payroll. Plaquemines became famous for its lopsided voting totals for Perez's favorite, but in the early 1930s neighboring St. Bernard was even more notorious. In 1930, when Governor Huey Long ran for the U.S. Senate, St. Bernard had only 2,454 registered voters, yet recorded 3,977 votes for Long. There were even 9 votes left over for his opponent, incumbent Joseph E. Ransdell. Ward 2 of St. Bernard had a total population of 912 men, women, and children, white and black, but its final tally showed 913 votes cast. In Ward 7, Precinct 3, the voters were recorded as having marched to the polls in alphabetical order. Perez's henchmen in St. Bernard even had a sense of humor. At one time the registration rolls contained the names of such noted personages as Herbert Hoover, Ben Eagle, Will Crow, Clara Bow, Babe Ruth, Jack Dempsey, and Charlie Chaplin, not one of whom was ever known to have set foot there.[4]

Perez's supporters have praised him as a defender of the southern way of life, and his liberal opponents have condemned him as a vicious demagogue. Much of the Judge's oratory certainly falls into the category of demagoguery. He made all of the stock appeals to the Founding Fathers, flag, and feminine purity. He pandered to the prejudices and played upon the emotions of his audiences. But he was not a typical demagogue. For one thing, he did not lack principle. For another, he was not a "man of the people." Rather he was an aristocrat who handed down decisions from on high. He did not follow public opinion; he plunged boldly ahead and dared the public to follow. Another mark of the demagogue is unlimited ambition. Perez, however, never sought a political office higher than district attorney of his judicial district. Although often urged to run for governor by his segregationist supporters, he never seriously considered it. He would have been ill at ease stumping the state, kissing babies and slapping backs. He was an elitist and preferred to maintain a tighter control over a smaller area.

Above all, Perez relished power. He was an anachronism in the twentieth century, an old-time political boss who preferred manipulating others to holding high office himself. Although he was notorious for the vehemence and extravagance of his oratory, the essence of his power lay in his skill as a backroom power broker and in his personal friendships with such right-wing ideologues as J. Strom Thurmond, Ross Barnett, Lester Maddox, Orval Faubus, and George Wallace.

The tremendous mineral wealth discovered during the thirties and forties gave rural and isolated Plaquemines the potential to play a role in state and national politics totally disproportionate to its size and population. A political and financial magician of brilliance, resourcefulness, and unyielding determination, Judge Perez personally oversaw the development of oil, sulphur, and natural gas extraction in the lower delta and through finesse and inside knowledge became a millionaire many times over. Secure in his own territory, he played a prominent role in every reactionary campaign from the Dixiecrat adventure to the George Wallace uprising. At his death in 1969 he was still at the peak of his power, and he passed along the rule of this last redoubt of feudalism to his sons.

Leander Perez

ONE

Coming of Age

Plaquemines Parish is the end of the line—a narrow, fertile peninsula more than a hundred miles long, stretching out into the blue waters of the Gulf of Mexico. It is a land built gradually over the eons by the silt-laden Mississippi River as it empties into the open sea. A hot, muggy, swampy region, it has been called nature's compromise: half land, half water. Along either bank of the river lie, protected by earthen levees, two extremely narrow ribbons of high land where the majority of the delta's folk live and work. Not far from the river, in places just a few hundred yards, this dry ground disappears. Beyond lie hundreds of square miles of trembling grass prairie afloat in the water—the vast and desolate marsh once known only to trappers, smugglers, and pirates.[1]

No one really knows how the Perez family first came to Plaquemines. One legend has it that the first Perez to view the lush swamp that became the parish of Plaquemines was a sea captain from Madrid, Spain. Sometime during the early eighteenth century he supposedly steered his galleon through the narrow passes at the mouth of the Mississippi and sailed up the muddy waterway. He did not find the thriving cities or Indian slaves he sought, but instead he discovered a subtropical paradise overrun with luxuriant vegetation and teeming with infinite varieties of wildlife. He was so delighted that he sent his crew back to Madrid and remained behind to colonize the verdant utopia.[2]

Except for the development of the oil and sulphur industries, Captain Perez would find Plaquemines today much like the subtropical marsh that captured his imagination. Gray green swamp covers more than 90 percent of the total area of Plaquemines. Seen from

1

the air, flying into New Orleans from the south, the first coffee brown traces of the Mississippi appear far out in the Gulf. Following the river upstream, one finds it almost impossible to distinguish where the sea ends and the land begins. The Father of Waters appears to flow free and unbounded in the open marsh—a watery expanse laced with a puzzling maze of bayous, canals, cutoffs, and ditches.[3]

No bridges cross the Mississippi below New Orleans. A single highway runs down either bank to serve the small settlements lining the river. It is impossible for the motorist to take a wrong turn in Plaquemines Parish; there are no byways or back roads. The last ferry crosses the river forty miles below the Crescent City near the old brick courthouse and small cluster of buildings known as Pointe a la Hache, the parish seat. On the east bank the blacktop ends just past Bohemia, a tiny community about four miles below the ferry landing. On the west side the highway continues another forty miles to the south before a superfluous stop sign announces its abrupt termination. Beyond that there is only water. The lower reaches of the parish are accessible only by boat or helicopter.

If Captain Perez is in fact a myth, it is conceivable that the family ancestors journeyed to Louisiana overland from California, a possibility suggested by another family story. The Perez family's ethnic derivation is as obscure as its geographic origin. Leander Perez once stated that he was descended from no less than five Caucasian nationalities. His adversaries have rumored that the family line includes Negro blood—a fascinating speculation completely unfounded in fact. Although the name Perez is Spanish, the family tree bears more French names than Spanish. Leander's earliest tongue was French; he did not learn English until he started school at the age of six. He rarely spoke French after entering grammar school and ultimately lost his original fluency.[4]

By the time Leander Henry Perez was born on July 16, 1891, the Perezes were established as one of the oldest Catholic families in Plaquemines. Leander's father, Roselius E. ("Fice") Perez, a blue-eyed, mustachioed gentleman-farmer, owned two plantations totaling seven hundred or eight hundred acres. This would have been only a moderate-sized farm in north Louisiana, but in the incredibly fertile delta it was enough to provide the family with a comfortable, though not ostentatious, standard of living. The family home, an unpretentious white frame house, was at Star plantation, on the west bank of the Mississippi about ten miles below the town of Belle Chasse. Fice earned a substantial income from his crops of rice and sugarcane, but most of it was needed to support his large family.[5] Not an intellectual, he was a hard-working planter and an amateur politician. It is probably from his father that Leander got his capacity for hard work, as well as his interest in politics.[6]

The head of the Perez clan earned a reputation as a kindly person, but as a man who was fiercely partisan in public affairs. He served as a member of the Lafourche Levee Board for thirty-five years and as a Plaquemines Parish police juror for twenty-four years. In his youth, Fice had actively worked to overthrow the carpetbag Republican rule in Plaquemines. It was a protracted struggle; not until the election of 1896 did the Plaquemines Democrats succeed in ousting the Republicans. Along with Captain Horace Harvey, Leander's father also pioneered the construction of the Gulf Intracoastal Waterway.[7]

Fice Perez married Gertrude Solis, who was from a large, Catholic, upper middle-class delta family. The Solis family had dwelt in St. Bernard Parish nearly as long as the Perezes had inhabited Plaquemines. Leander's mother, a year older than his father, was the disciplinarian. She was not a "soft" woman, but rather a stern and devout person who considered raising a family to be a serious responsibility. Of the union there were thirteen children, two of whom died in infancy. Taught not to question the authority of their parents, the Perez children idealized them. Even today, when speaking of their parents, members of the family do so with almost reverence. They insist that their parents were kind, but admit that they were firm. Leander's father was concerned with his own dignity as head of the household and made certain that his children did not disgrace the family name. The stress was on middle-class values: hard work, sobriety, good grades, and politeness in public. Leander worked hard for the approval of his parents; he was a "good" child, rarely rebellious.[8]

Leander apparently had a happy youth. He was not particularly witty, although he indulged in the usual childish pranks. Even as a youngster he showed a passion for order. His younger sister remembers that he was the only child in the family who kept a neat room. His appearance was also neat—immaculate but not flashy. Young Leander was an impatient, compulsive doer. He was an active, cheerful child, not much given to quiet contemplation but happiest when he was busy at some tangible project, such as fishing for sunfish or hunting ducks or building a hideaway in the marshes. He grew up believing that idleness, including "idle" curiosity, was a sin—a sort of puritan ethic in a Catholic family. But even so, he did not like physical labor and was willing to use his brains to evade it. He would not work on the farm, but Fice could afford to employ enough laborers to perform the manual labor. Besides, Leander believed that there was no future in farming. He early demonstrated tenacity; he did not like to be denied what he sought after and in fact seldom was. When he was only six, his three-year-old sister died of pneumonia. It was a shattering experience for him, because he and his little sister had been closer than any of the other children. He grieved for her for more than a year, an unusual amount of time for a child of his age.[9]

Leander grew up in a home in which there was much love, but also in an intellectual atmosphere that put a premium on conventionality and conformity. He was taught to conform by the church, the home, and the school. He grew up in a closed society in which Christianity and its moral code were regarded as absolutes and deviations were frowned upon and punished. He was free to decide little for himself; his personal values were those of the home and the church. Rather than rebel against this fixed nature of things, he reveled in it. He was adventurous in a physical but not in a mental sense; his heroes were conventional ones such as Napoleon and Frederick the Great, authoritarian figures rather than dissenters such as Martin Luther or men of science such as Louis Pasteur. His emphasis was on strength of will and inflexibility of purpose rather than on broad tolerance or original thoughts. Ideas were not as important as physical empires.[10]

Leander's parents were devout Catholics who made certain that all of their children received religious instruction. Young Perez, or

Lelé, as he was nicknamed, was sometimes compelled to study catechism as a punishment for misbehavior. He did not object, but he did the memorizing in record time. Later his remarkable memory would help him keep track of enough details to occupy several normal men.[11] Perez's religious convictions were not products of a deep emotional experience or independent thinking; they were something he grew up with. Being Catholic was the thing to do to please parents and friends and fit in with society in the delta. He went to church because he was expected to. His religion was dogmatic and conventional rather than reflective and mystical. It was something that gave order to life. To young Perez, religion was a bulwark of the status quo. When it later became a force for progress, urging mixing of the races, he rejected it.

Plaquemines was an isolated, underdeveloped parish during Leander's boyhood. The nearest city was New Orleans, which could be reached only by railroad or boat. There was not even a dirt road for carriages between Plaquemines and the city, although horses could be ridden atop the levee. Because travel was so difficult, parish families often lived in semiseclusion on remote farms and plantations. Their contacts with the outside world were minimal, and they learned to fend for themselves. Physical isolation bred provincialism and suspicion of outsiders. Even within the parish, society was rigidly organized, and clannishness was a way of life. The jambalayalike population of English, French, Negroes, Dalmatians, Italians, Germans, Spanish, Indians, and mulattoes rubbed elbows daily but eyed one another with suspicion. Whites and blacks may have worked together and their children may have even played together, but adults never mixed socially. The mulattoes, disdaining association or intermarriage with darker blacks, demanded segregation from them in schools and churches.[12]

The poverty-ridden, sparsely settled parish furnished few diversions for children and a limited social life for adults. The Perezes' nearest neighbors, a Negro family, lived several miles away. The desolate environment served to strengthen family ties. Frequent visits from relatives and family excursions became gala events. The family consisted of more than the parents and siblings. There were aunts, uncles, cousins, brothers, and sisters-in-law all living nearby.

The children played, attended school, and socialized with their relatives. Family gatherings were the chief social outlets for the older children. There was always plenty to eat, hunting and fishing stories to listen to, and sometimes dancing. Leander experienced only superficial relationships with those outside his family; at best he was on casual, friendly terms. The Perez children were taught to be proud of their family and loyal to it. Family came first and family could rarely be wrong. To the children the family was a secure, homogeneous group, and the world outside their family-oriented society was strange and chaotic.[13]

Although neither Fice nor Gertrude Perez had attended college, they encouraged their children to obtain an education. So firmly was the value of home life implanted in the children, however, that several of the girls refused to leave home to attend school. They preferred to help out around the house until they married local boys, then remain in the parish to become homemakers and mothers. Leander received his first formal education in a one-room schoolhouse his father had constructed in a pasture on Star plantation. The teacher was his eldest sister, who taught twenty-eight white children in the first through eighth grades. After completing the eighth grade the Perez boys left home to attend classes in New Orleans, because there were no high schools in Plaquemines. Leander and his brother Roselius, Jr., enrolled in Holy Cross College, a Catholic secondary male academy for boarding and day students. Leander proved an exemplary but unimaginative scholar. He had no preference for any particular subject but instead seemed indiscriminately to study whatever was placed before him. His classes emphasized repetition and retention, not creativity. He seems to have been quite satisfied with this type of learning and memorized with great ability. Leander was thoroughly competent in the material assigned, but he demonstrated little intellectual curiosity. His son later said that he could never remember his father reading a book for pleasure.[14]

Lelé's grades were solid if not spectacular, and he was cited for virtuous conduct and punctual attendance. He participated in extracurricular activities as a substitute left fielder on the junior baseball team and as an officer in the League of the Sacred Heart, a religious society. But the constant grind bored him. Leander believed that he was wasting his time and talent in school while wealth and distinction awaited him in the world of business. With such ambition in mind, he left Holy Cross without a diploma during the summer of 1906, declaring that his formal education was complete. He found a summer job as a handyman at a New Orleans bookstore and wrote home that he was now a "bookkeeper." But by the following fall Leander had tired of "keeping" books and was ready to resume studying them. He enrolled at Louisiana State University as a subfreshman, a special category for university students who had not completed high school. In addition to disillusionment with menial labor, his decision to resume his education was inspired by an offer of financial aid. The Plaquemines Parish Police Jury, probably persuaded by Fice Perez, awarded Leander a partial scholarship.[15]

Young Perez, fresh from provincial Plaquemines and briefly seasoned in cosmopolitan New Orleans, did not overawe his classmates or professors at Baton Rouge. In his first semester, he earned excellent grades in English, received mediocre marks in math, and dropped Latin. Many years later, when he was Plaquemines district attorney, Perez confessed to a gathering of local high schoolers that he had had difficulty adjusting to the strain of college until he had read that "you learn mathematics to develop thinking, and you learn language to give your thinking expression." He explained that his comprehension of that inspirational passage had been a turning point in his life. He added, "Without self-discipline you will miss the boat." The expression was apt; persons who missed the boat in Plaquemines were truly stranded.[16]

Stricken with an unusual malady, Leander dropped out of LSU in 1907–1908. He had visited a Baton Rouge dentist to have three teeth pulled. After extracting each tooth, the dentist placed it on Perez's lower lip. When he turned to remove the teeth, the dentist found only two; Leander had swallowed one of them. Lelé developed a hacking cough and returned home where his mother could care for him. Her remedy was to gorge him with olive oil. According to his sister, Leander coughed up the tooth about a year later, and all of the symptoms promptly vanished.[17]

Returning to LSU for the 1908–1909 academic year, Perez decided to major in law, which then could be taken at the undergraduate level. Before beginning the second semester, he resolved to acquire a more diverse background and changed to a general arts and sciences curriculum, without a specific field of specialization. Leander did not abandon his ambition to become an attorney, but he reasoned that he would be better equipped for his chosen profession by first obtaining a liberal education. Perez himself might have expressed his intentions differently, because the word *liberal* subsequently became anathema to him. His grades improved during the second semester except for a failing grade in, of all things, political science; theory was never his forte. Leander had successfully adapted to his milieu by his sophomore year. He received superior grades for the next three years and was graduated class salutatorian.[18]

At LSU Perez was known as a serious scholar but not a recluse. He was gregarious but discriminating in those he associated with. His sister-in-law remembers, "He liked people—the right kind of people." His principal extracurricular activity was participation in the marching military band, in which he played the French horn. Leander's musical talent was limited; one schoolmate alleges that Perez just "carried that horn." But he parlayed his band membership into free trips to football games and other social functions. Leander became a personal friend of the band director, a blind musician whom he daily led around the practice field. In his senior year Cadet Perez was promoted first lieutenant, the highest-ranking officer in the band. The students alluded to him as "Perez of the band" to distinguish him from other Perezes on campus.[19]

In the early 1900s LSU was an austere military institution. A few co-eds attended classes, but they were far outnumbered by male cadets. The cadets were required to wear their uniforms to class. Those with acceptable grades were permitted to saunter to downtown Baton Rouge, which offered a few dingy taverns and primitive moving pictures, for dates once a week. Leander occasionally finessed an additional excursion by attending services at the local synagogue with a comely Jewish girl he dated,[20] an irony in view of his later anti-Semitism.

Perez was reputed to be quite a ladies' man. The inscription beneath his photograph in the senior yearbook reads, "He is a paralyzer of the female heart."[21] He was a handsome and moderately vain young man. When he returned home to court his local girlfriend, Leander was meticulous in preserving a fastidious appearance. His favorite ensemble included white pants, a black coat, white shirt, and a diminutive black tie. His girlfriend's home could be reached only by riding horseback atop the muddy, twisting levee path. Perez protected his clothes by wrapping himself, his horse, and the saddle in three separate sheets. Upon reaching his destination, he led his horse to the barn, where he carefully removed the wraps before appearing at the home resplendently attired.[22]

Perez was a muscular youth, but he was not athletic. He competed on the class football team but demonstrated more ability as an athletic administrator than as a participant. He served as secretary of the LSU Athletic Association, a student organization that assisted alumni in boosting school spirit. But even in his college days Leander had a streak of physical belligerence and stubbornness. His classmates remember him getting into fistfights with his peers—a not unusual occurrence at LSU at that time. Although small in stature, Leander was proud of his stocky, sturdy physique and then, as later, he was no physical coward. Perez also joined a debate club but manifested none of the fiery eloquence that subsequently distinguished him. He did not pledge a social fraternity at LSU and never actively participated in campus politics. His fellow students remember him as amiable and complaisant, neither aggressively forward nor uncommonly shy.[23]

But Leander always thought big. Many LSU cadets earned extra money by working during the summer in the Kansas wheat fields. Although he scorned manual labor on his father's plantation, Perez spent two summers in Kansas harvesting wheat with his classmates. The part-time workers slept in bunkhouses or barns on the farm, but Perez believed that such quarters were not elegant enough to impress his friends and relatives back home. After a strenuous day in the hot fields he sometimes tramped to pretentious hotels in town, where he wrote letters home on their stationery, informing his correspondents that he was enjoying his sojourn. During another summer vacation Leander worked as a deckhand on a luxury steamer touring the Caribbean. Now he penned letters on the captain's stationery to demonstrate his intimacy with the ship's commander. When he returned to Plaquemines he brought his parents gifts of pineapples and coconuts, which, he claimed, were sent with compliments of the captain.[24]

Perez also delighted in teasing his younger siblings. Once he came home from LSU to baby-sit while his parents attended a performance of Mrs. Wiggs of the Cabbage Patch in New Orleans. On the day of the theatrical, Leander arose before dawn and paddled into the swamps to hunt birds. Before returning, he beheaded all of the catch. That evening, he prepared the birds in two separate containers, putting only two or three in a little kettle and numerous birds in a larger pot. At dinner, he served his plate from the small pot and the other plates from the larger one. After everyone had eaten, he asked if anyone had noticed something strange about the birds. Then he informed the children that the birds in the big pot were cranes and explained that it had been necessary to cut off their heads and necks because the cranes had had snakes down their throats. Another time when his parents were absent Leander passed around a lighted cigar, which the children puffed until they became dizzy. Fice Perez disapproved of smoking, and Leander never smoked in his father's presence.[25]

Perez studied law in his final year at LSU and upon graduation in 1912 obtained summer employment as secretary to the Appropriations Committee of the Louisiana House of Representatives. He became so fascinated with the operation of the state assembly that from then on he never missed a regular or special session of the legislature until his death more than half a century later.[26]

The following fall Leander entered Tulane University Law School with advanced standing, thanks to the law courses he had taken as an undergraduate in Baton Rouge. At Tulane, he demonstrated none of the drive and determination that later made him the political boss of Plaquemines. His grades were better than average but not outstanding. He blended into the collegiate background while more aggressive schoolmates attracted most of the attention. His former classmates are without exception amazed that he became an influential public figure. One is astonished that Perez had even earned his law degree. "Just average" and "mediocre" are how his Tulane contemporaries describe him. In later life he was a compulsive striver—an overachiever—but in his youth he seems to have acquiesced in mediocrity. His very lack of sophisticated academic training later led him to hold scientific training in contempt. Leander's part in a moot court murder case was typical of his college career; he played the victim.[27]

Perez attended Tulane during the same years when a number of other men destined for prominence in Louisiana public affairs were earning their degrees there. Among them were Frank James Clancey, future sheriff and political monarch of Jefferson Parish; Allen J. Ellender, who served in the U.S. Senate from 1937 until his death in 1972; W. J. O'Hara, Jr., and George P. Platt, who became state judges; and Herbert Waguespack, later involved in a sulphur transaction with Perez. Although he had not affiliated with a social fraternity at LSU, he pledged Pi Kappa Alpha at Tulane, becoming a fraternity brother of Waguespack and Ellender. Perez's senior yearbook shows him stiffly posed with the class of 1914. His hair was dark, thick, and luxuriant, and he wore the same type of rimless glasses he would always use. Then unaccustomed to being photographed, Leander stood with his chin resting uncomfortably on a high collar. He wore buttoned shoes and sported a stickpin. The 1914 yearbook also includes a section entitled "What the '14 Law Class Likes." According to the editor, who seemingly possessed the gift of prophesy, Clancey "likes the Codes," Waguespack "likes to study," and Perez "likes politics."[28]

Perez received his law degree in 1914 and at the age of twenty-three began his practice in New Orleans and the adjoining parishes. The first political job he ever held in Plaquemines was the restoration and cataloging of water-damaged records in the clerk of court's office. The courthouse had been inundated when a severe hurricane had struck the parish in 1915. The task was accomplished during summer vacation with his cousin John R. Perez, who was a few years older.[29]

Leander displayed no exceptional ability as a young lawyer; in fact he struggled to earn a subsistence income. His salary averaged less than a dollar a day during his first year of practice. As attorney for a New Orleans collection agency, Perez brought payment suits for sums as small as five or ten dollars and for a while supplemented his income by clerking for a Louisiana Supreme Court justice. He stretched his financial resources by regularly dining at a New Orleans bar and restaurant that offered a weekly special of a free lunch with the purchase of a five-cent beer.[30]

In 1916 Perez made his first foray into practical politics as a candidate for the state House of Representatives, campaigning as a reformer against the reigning boss in Plaquemines Parish, John Dymond, Jr. Bossism was nothing new in the lower delta. For over a hundred years there had been sheriffs, district attorneys, or judges who, through political savvy, skillful dealing, and a good command of popular psychology, had managed to build personal regimes reminiscent of a machine-run northern city or a Caribbean banana republic. They had been aided greatly by the ignorance and poverty of their constituents, since it took only a little learning to give the astute politician an advantage over the unsophisticated locals. To the poor man, the benefits to be enjoyed as a reward for his vote were a powerful inducement, and the sanctions to be incurred for disloyalty, a sobering threat.[31]

Leander had little financial backing, but he possessed much free time and an abundance of nerve, which he needed. Any opponent of the local regime risked physical injury or worse, especially when campaigning in the sparsely settled bayou country. Perez trudged the levee roads and railroad tracks along both banks of the Mississippi, wending his way from house to distant house to deliver his message to distrustful farmers, fishermen, and trappers. He declared that the Dymond machine stifled all opposition, refused to recognize the rights of citizens, and rigged elections. Leander failed to loosen the machine's grip on Plaquemines, receiving only a dozen or so votes, but he established a reputation as a reformer—albeit a hopelessly idealistic eccentric.[32]

By the time he enrolled at Tulane, Leander had already begun to date his future wife. His grandfather had married twice, and the second group of children included a daughter Beatrice, about the same age as Leander. While attending Dominican College in New Orleans, Perez's young aunt befriended vivacious Agnes Chalin and invited her to visit in Plaquemines. There Agnes met Leander, and

from their first date the hitherto romantically mercurial Perez became a one-woman man. Agnes belonged to an upper middle-
class New Orleans family. Her father owned a sash, door, and blind
business, but after he died in 1909 the family income was derived
primarily from real estate. Agnes' suitor was impressed by the electric lights at the Chalin home because no family in Plaquemines
had electricity or telephones.[33]

During their courtship, one of their dates nearly ended in tragedy. While they were sailing with friends on Lake Pontchartrain
one September, a storm suddenly struck, hurling the tiny boat
against a piling. The boat was smashed, and its occupants were
plunged into the turbulent water. Agnes crawled atop a piling, and
Leander and the others clung to floating debris while the best
swimmer among the men fought his way to shore for help. Luckily, he reached the beach. After five frightening hours in the lake,
the party was rescued.[34]

After courting more than five years, Agnes and Leander decided
to marry in 1917. The wedding was so unpretentious that Agnes'
own sister did not learn of it until the afternoon of the event.
Before leaving for her home on Bayou Lafourche after a weekend
visit in New Orleans, she asked Agnes why she had been sewing
all day. Agnes replied that she was making a dress for her wedding
that afternoon. Her sister was incredulous, but their mother confirmed the statement. With the sister among the half dozen guests,
Agnes and Leander were married on May 12 in the huge, stately
Mater Dolorosa Church in New Orleans. Two days later, the ceremony received five lines in the society section of the New Orleans
Item.[35]

Agnes and Leander Perez were to have two sons and two daughters, who by 1973 had produced nineteen grandchildren. Leander
dearly loved and somewhat pampered his offspring. His two boys
became his law partners after graduating from Tulane Law School.
The children remained close to their parents, geographically and
spiritually; all four continue to live in the Plaquemines–New
Orleans area. Leander's wife was as concerned with dignity and
status as her husband. Her sister remembers, "She was outgoing
to a point. But never forward."[36]

The newly wed Perezes moved in with Agnes' mother while

Leander labored to build a profitable law practice. He spent most of his time in New Orleans but retained his official home in Plaquemines for voting purposes. About four months after the marriage, Perez was inducted into the army to fight in World War I and was admitted to officer training school in Texas. However, less than three months later he was honorably discharged and sent home. He stayed in Texas during his brief tour of duty and never thereafter left North America.[37]

Perez's quick release from active duty aroused suspicion among his acquaintances. During an obstreperous political campaign in 1920, an opposing candidate claimed that Leander had employed every devious device available to avoid fulfilling his military obligation: he had suddenly married in 1917 because he realized that single men would be the first drafted, and he had used family influence to have himself appointed selective service registrar for his home precinct in Ollie. His opponent also insisted that as registrar Perez had altered the military records of other eligible males to place them above himself on the draft list. The charge that Leander had been a "slacker" during the war was repeated in subsequent local primary contests in the 1920s. Perez never directly denied the accusation but asserted that it was irrelevant. The probable causes for Leander's abrupt release were his position as a parish official and his preferred status as the sole support of his wife.[38]

The soldier returned from his brief army tour to his profitless law practice. He might have remained in obscurity had not fate intervened. On December 4, 1919, Robert Emmet Hingle, judge of the then Twenty-ninth Judicial District, which encompassed Plaquemines and St. Bernard parishes, drowned while on a fishing trip. Because less than a year remained of his term, Governor Ruffin G. Pleasant had to appoint an interim successor. Since the judge and the district attorney were traditionally selected from different parishes and the incumbent district attorney resided in St. Bernard, custom dictated that the appointee be a native of Plaquemines.[39]

Pleasant asked governor-elect John M. Parker to recommend someone. Parker was a progressive reformer with few supporters in Plaquemines. One of his backers, however, was John R. Perez, Leander's older cousin, who had been elected an Orleans Parish

state representative on the Parker ticket and would soon become the governor's floor leader. He reminded Parker that his young cousin, a promising attorney, had challenged the anti-Parker Plaquemines bosses in the 1916 election. That was enough for the incoming governor, because Plaquemines was overrun with neither bright lawyers nor Parker partisans. So John R. called Leander and asked, "'Lelé,' how would you like to be appointed judge?"[40]

Before Hingle's funeral was held, Leander Perez had received his commission from Governor Pleasant. Getting appointed was one thing; taking office proved a taller hurdle. In the 1919 primary in which Parker had been nominated, an anti-Parker slate had overwhelmingly carried Plaquemines. The triumvirate that dominated the parish was headed by John Dymond, Jr., a zealous supporter of Parker's opponent and a recently elected Plaquemines representative to the state legislature. He had no intention of accepting a Parker progressive as district judge. He argued that more, not less, than a year remained of Hingle's term and that the chief justice of the Louisiana Supreme Court, not the governor, was therefore constitutionally authorized to appoint a temporary successor. Furthermore, Dymond contended that, because Perez lived with his mother-in-law in New Orleans, he was not a bona fide resident of Plaquemines and was therefore ineligible for the appointment.[41]

Dymond took his case to the home of Chief Justice Frank Monroe in New Orleans. Siding with the Plaquemines boss, Monroe named Judge Hugh C. Cage of Division A of the Orleans Parish Civil District Court to replace Hingle. Plaquemines and St. Bernard officials, following Dymond's lead, recognized Cage as interim judge and locked Perez out of the courthouses in both parishes. Parker's appointee had himself sworn in on the courthouse lawns at Pointe a la Hache and Chalmette, then prepared his case for a hearing before the state supreme court. The issue turned on the date on which a regularly elected successor to Hingle could have qualified for office and had no precedent in state judicial history. At first it seemed that the decision would go against him, but at the last minute one of the justices changed his vote, allowing Perez to squeak into office by a one-vote margin.[42]

TWO

The Judge

Perez took office despite the opposition of nearly every public official in the Twenty-ninth Judicial District. For over thirty years a tightly knit political machine composed of most of the parish officials and allied with the New Orleans Ring, or Old Regulars, had controlled Plaquemines. These politicians considered Perez a brash upstart and a pest. The ruling triumvirate of Plaquemines comprised, besides Dymond, Simon Leopold, a state senator, and Frank Mevers, a former sheriff. St. Bernard was dominated by District Attorney Nemours H. Nunez and Sheriff Albert Estopinal, Jr. The interests of the two parishes were inextricably intertwined. The district attorney served as legal adviser to both police juries and to every board and commission in the two parishes, and the Lake Borgne Levee Board had jurisdiction over both parishes. At that time, St. Bernard was by far the richer of the two. The Plaquemines school superintendent reported that the total assessed valuation of his parish was less than the assessed valuation of just the American Sugar Refining Company in St. Bernard. In Plaquemines taxes were heavy, educational facilities were miserable, and illiteracy was high.[1]

The twenty-seven-year-old Perez began his term as judge knowing that within a year he would have to face a machine-backed opponent in the Democratic primary. Democratic nomination was tantamount to election because the Republicans, what few there were, rarely bothered to run candidates in Louisiana local elections. In the hot summer of 1920 Perez launched his campaign. His chances of winning seemed remote because his entrenched Old Regular rivals customarily delivered 90 percent majorities to their candidates. The ambitious young judge aligned himself with the New Regulars, a nascent Democratic reform faction, which had been organized in the New Orleans area to endorse gubernatorial candidate John Parker. Leander initiated a clean-government crusade in the complaisant delta parishes by cracking down on gambling and vice. But he played the political game with finesse; stacking a grand jury with New Regulars, he had indictments returned against his rivals, including District Attorney Nunez.[2]

The Old Regulars selected Milton Schaefer to run for district attorney, with Nunez as their candidate for judge. The New Regulars endorsed Perez for judge and Philip R. Livaudais, a mild-mannered St. Bernard attorney characterized as a "gentleman" even by the opposing faction, for district attorney. The heated campaign first brought out the charges that Perez had been a slacker during the First World War. Schaefer claimed to have seen the precinct draft cards that Perez had altered while serving as selective service registrar. According to Schaefer, he had written on the backs of the cards statements to the effect that the statements made by the other registrants were untrue. There was no notation on Leander's own card. Schaefer said that he had called Perez a slacker to his face and that the two had engaged in a fistfight, in which Leander had slapped him first and he had then punched Perez in the jaw. Schaefer charged that Perez had had Nunez indicted so that he could say, "Yes, I am a slacker, but my opponent is a crook." Defending his release from the army, Perez produced a letter from the district board of appeals stating that he was entitled to exemption under draft board regulations. Leander said, "My war record is as clean and legal as any of the married men in this state."[3]

This election was the most hotly contested local primary on record for the district. The St. Bernard Parish Democratic Executive Committee met in Chalmette and declared that the Perez-Livaudais ticket had carried the parish by a razor-thin margin. But the Twenty-ninth Judicial District Committee, meeting in Point a la Hache, after tabulating the returns of both parishes, proclaimed that Nunez had been elected by three votes and Livaudais by one vote. Thereafter, reports of victory alternated. From Baton Rouge the secretary of state promulgated returns showing that Perez had received a majority of three votes and Livaudais a majority of sixty votes. Both factions filed suit but the Perez-Livaudais faction withdrew theirs on the basis of the secretary of state's returns. The case was settled by an ad hoc judge in the district court, who ruled Perez the victor by three votes, although he had failed to carry his native parish. Since all returns showed that Livaudais had polled a majority, the suit against his election was dismissed. Oddly, the Ring candidates did not appeal the decision. The Perez-faction candidates for the lesser offices in both parishes were all defeated.[4]

Once elected, Perez used the power of the court to reward his friends and render impotent his political opponents. Obstructing his ambition to dominate Plaquemines was cunning John Dymond. The initial confrontation between the upstart judge and the Ring boss occurred in 1921 over the selection of an official parish printer. Two weekly newspapers, the *Plaquemines Protector* and the *Lower Coast Gazette,* were published in sparsely populated Plaquemines.[5] Perez's father was a part owner of the *Protector* and Dymond's brother owned the *Gazette;* each paper needed the parish printing business to survive. At the Plaquemines Parish Police Jury meeting convened to designate an official printer, Leander spoke in behalf of the *Protector,* but the Dymond-dominated police jury chose the *Gazette.* Perez jumped up, dashed toward the table at which the jurors were seated, and denounced them as "dummies" who had no "guts" and had purposely selected the highest-bidding printer. He threatened to bring legal action to nullify the selection but instead, summoning a mass meeting of his faction, started a recall petition against the seven jurors who had chosen the *Gazette.* Leander said that to file suit to annul the printing contract would be useless as long as the police jury was controlled by the same man who had assigned the contract. A battle of words ensued in the rival newspapers, with Leander penning invective articles for the *Protector* and Dymond replying in kind in the *Gazette.* The *Gazette* remained the public printer, but the embattled judge refused to concede; he personally solicited advertisements of judicial sales for the *Protector.* Plaquemines Sheriff Ernest Alberti testified that he had switched judicial advertisements from the *Gazette* to the *Protector* because he feared that Perez might assign the sales to an independent auctioneer, causing the sheriff to lose his commissions on the sales.[6]

Leander's experience with the printing contract convinced him that he would have to destroy Dymond to gain political control of the parish. Dymond was vulnerable because his regime was riddled with nepotism and corruption. Perez had Dymond's brother William, the school board president and the road district superintendent, indicted for payroll padding. Next he issued an *ex parte* order to compel the presentation of all parish drainage district books, then used the books to compile evidence against John Dymond. Perez discovered that Dymond had made a practice of having his political cronies name him special attorney for parish boards and districts, in place of the district attorney, to earn lucrative legal fees. The former district attorney had conveniently stepped aside because he and Dymond were political allies, but the new district attorney, Livaudais, refused to consent to this arrangement. Dymond attempted to bypass Livaudais by introducing a bill in the state legislature that would authorize the drainage districts to employ special counsel without the permission of the district attorney or state attorney general. Perez took the Dalcour Drainage District minute book to Baton Rouge, where he appeared before a legislative committee to denounce the bill as a scheme to enrich the corrupt Plaquemines boss. Although Dymond withdrew the bill, Perez pressed the attack. He had Dymond and seven associates indicted for certifying bonds for payment of a drainage system that had never been constructed. He also charged that Dymond, in return for a $500-per-month position as president of the Business Men's Racing Association, had used his influence as a legislator to defeat a bill that would have outlawed betting on horse racing. Dymond insisted that, although he never played poker or bet on horses himself, he opposed all blue laws on principle.[7]

The rival politicos also engaged in an acrimonious struggle for control of the Plaquemines Parish School Board. The Dymond faction tried to change the board's printing contract from the *Protector* to the *Gazette,* but the vote deadlocked five to five, and the *Protector* kept the contract. Afterwards, Perez asserted that Dymond had submitted a four-hundred-dollar bill for the "imaginary work" of organizing a special school district in Wards 1, 2, and 3. Dymond waited two months to reply, then protested that the only bill he had ever charged to the school board was a thirty-five-cent phone bill. He declared that Perez had personally disrupted school board meetings so often that the board had been compelled to adopt bylaws preventing interference in meetings by outsiders. Dymond also alleged that Perez had slipped notes to his brother Elridge, a school board member, advising him how to vote. Elridge insisted that he had enough sense to know how to vote without his brother's advice.[8]

Perez determined to break Dymond's stranglehold on the parish by unseating the boss himself and his Ring allies in the local Democratic primary of 1922. To accomplish this, it would be necessary for Perez to register all of his followers. Unfortunately, the Plaquemines registrar, Emile Martin, Jr., was a devout Old Regular. It was customary for the registrar to tour the parish enrolling families in their homes rather than to remain at his headquarters in the parish courthouse, a practice that continued even after Perez had supplanted Dymond. A partisan registrar could thus bypass the homes of factional foes and establish substations at locations that favored his own faction. Perez demanded that Martin keep his office at Pointe a la Hache open and threatened him with criminal prosecution if he did not comply. Leander consulted the state attorney general, who agreed that the registrar was required by law to keep his office open. Martin conferred with his personal legal adviser, John Dymond, who told him that he was bound to adhere to the traveling schedule for registration published in the official journal. When Martin announced that he would make his rounds as usual, Perez had an affidavit sworn accusing him of violating state law but told the registrar that if he would enroll certain Perez supporters the affidavit would not be filed. When Martin refused this condition, Perez had him indicted by the parish grand jury. Martin protested that Leander had personally prepared the affidavit signed by a prosecution witness, upon which the indictment was based.[9]

Perez also worked among the Plaquemines fur trappers, who constituted a substantial voting bloc in the parish. The trappers were accustomed to taking furs in the marshes without paying rent, but recently the Delaware-Louisiana Fur Trapping Company had attempted to charge them a fee for trapping rights. When the trappers had balked, the company had initiated legal proceedings to compel payment, and John Dymond had represented the landowners against the local men. Perez then told the trappers that Dymond was their enemy and, as judge, ruled in their favor. The company appealed to the state supreme court, which overruled Perez. The legal victory brought little comfort to Dymond, who had become a villain in the eyes of his constituent trappers. He also complained that Perez had masterminded a poison-pen letter allegedly composed by Dymond's own nephew and published in the *Plaquemines Protector*. Dymond said that he did not think that his nephew, who lived in Texarkana, Arkansas, even knew that such a paper as the *Plaquemines Protector* existed unless he had been told by Perez or a Perez emissary. The upshot of these political machinations was that Dymond was defeated by about one hundred votes in his bid for reelection to the state House of Representatives. He attributed his defeat to losing the trapper vote.[10]

Perez and the New Regulars also determined to conquer St. Bernard. Leander attempted to compel the Ring-backed registrar of voters to appoint a deputy to enroll Italian farmers in Ward 2 who favored the New Regular ticket. The registrar declined upon advice from the attorney general that he had no right to appoint such a deputy. Despite failing to enroll their Italian supporters, the New Regulars triumphed at the polls. They celebrated with a parade in St. Bernard including sixty-eight vehicles and a brass band; Leander and Dr. L. A. Meraux rode in the lead car, followed by other autos decked with streamers reading Liberty and Down with Bossism.[11] After the New Regulars had obtained a majority on the police jury, a host of incumbent parish officials were dismissed and replaced with New Regular appointees, who received salary increases though the expense accounts of some Old Regulars were slashed.[12]

The New Regulars in St. Bernard were ably led by a physician, L. A. Meraux. He is representative of a professional class, the country doctor, that once held considerable political power in Louisiana. As he motored the dusty roads of the parish to treat his patients, Meraux dispensed medical prescriptions and political advice with equal expertness. The St. Bernard rustics respected the political counsel of their doctor because they considered him enlightened, sagacious, and benevolent. Public affairs was originally a hobby, but before long he became a full-time politician and a part-time physician. He began canvassing in 1920 in the gubernatorial campaign for progressive Democrat John M. Parker. Four years later, in his first bid for public office, Meraux won election as sheriff of St. Bernard. The doctor was wealthy, and he triumphed as only the rich could in St. Bernard politics. In addition to his medical practice and public career, Meraux dabbled in real estate, banking, and the leasing of trapping lands. But money was not his only asset; he was brilliant, pragmatic, and thoroughly schooled in the rough-and-tumble techniques of factional infighting. Allied with Perez, he reigned as benevolent dictator of St. Bernard until his death in 1938. Although he did not command Perez, Meraux acted as the young jurist's political mentor. Throughout the twenties it was Meraux's bailiwick of St. Bernard rather than Plaquemines that provided the greatest numerical margins for New Regular candidates.[13]

After gaining strength in Plaquemines and St. Bernard in the 1922 election, Perez resolved to install permanently the New Regulars as the dominant political force in the two parishes. The next two years witnessed the pitiless power struggle of a dynasty-in-the-making. Leander used his position as judge to chastise offenders who were his political opponents but went to extreme lengths to protect his friends and allies.

The flickering political squabble in the two-parish judicial district was ignited by the sensational "rum murders" of two deputy sheriffs. During Prohibition the lower delta served as a haven for bootleggers and moonshiners. Easily accessible to Cuba, Central America, and the West Indies, the delta offered a climate suitable for year-round operations, as well as innumerable water inlets that made close surveillance impossible. "Mother" ships, loaded with booze, anchored offshore in international waters and smaller fishing boats relayed the cargo through the narrow inlets to a secret rendezvous in the swamps. Freight trucks, oil trucks, or passenger cars then completed the run to New Orleans. Sometimes the liquor was disguised as molasses, canned vegetables, or fruit juices. At least once a funeral coach was packed with illegal whiskey rather than a corpse. The natives were happy to cooperate, especially for minimum fees of $100 to $500 to transfer the contraband from an offshore ship to an inland destination. Local officials usually ignored bootleggers, and many, including St. Bernard Sheriff Meraux, were rumored to be involved. Although the local residents considered bootlegging an honorable and profitable profession, it could be dangerous. Bootleggers were often waylaid by hijackers, who stole cash as well as the illicit cargo. Hijackers became so bold that they once stole 1,500 quarts of impounded liquor from the St. Bernard Parish jail. Bootleggers and hijackers were judged on entirely different standards. The *St. Bernard Voice* explained: "Of course, the authorities are not overlooking the bootleggers, who are also violators of the law, but they are not in the same category as the high-jackers, who are bold and dangerous and are a menace to decent citizens." Some outraged bootleggers even went to court to prosecute hijackers.[14]

At about 5 A.M., April 17, 1923, two rumrunning trucks sped toward New Orleans through St. Bernard. Sheriff Estopinal, who had been tipped off that a shipment of booze was scheduled to arrive, posted three deputies at the Violet bridge: his brother Joseph, August Esteves, and Joseph Guerra. Halting the first truck, Deputy Guerra ordered two Negroes, one the driver, to get out. As he approached the second truck, a Ford touring car suddenly appeared on the other side of the first truck, and one of its occupants fired shotgun blasts at Estopinal and Esteves. The first officer's left side was torn away; the other's face and brain were riddled with buckshot.[15]

Although St. Bernard citizens were normally apathetic about Prohibition violations, the "rum murders" enraged them. Judge Perez quickly convened an extraordinary session of the St. Bernard grand jury and delivered a strong charge to the jurors. Several suspects were arrested, but no one wanted to talk. Angry mobs of armed men milled about the courthouse. Someone shouted, "Get a rope!" Hearing that, one of the prisoners broke down and recited the names of those involved. Implicated was J. Claude Meraux, former Tulane football star, wartime aviator, rising young attorney, and secretary of the Lake Borgne Levee Board. He was also a brother of Dr. L. A. Meraux. Claude Meraux was indicted as an accessory after the fact. Evidence was produced showing that his yardman, under instructions from Meraux, had ferried one of the alleged murderers across the Mississippi River in a rowboat several hours after the shooting.

The jury returned a verdict of guilty without capital punishment against the accused murderer Gus Tomes, alias Dutch Gardner, sparing his life because he claimed to have mistaken the deputies for hijackers. Tomes, a former prizefighter, was pardoned in 1930 by Governor Huey Long. Claude Meraux fled to parts unknown, apparently to Europe, two days after his indictment. Accompanied by his lawyer he returned in July, surrendered to a deputy sheriff, and posted bond. Perez refused to summon a special session of the St. Bernard grand jury at that time because he feared that there was sufficient evidence to indict Meraux for a more serious crime, possibly murder. Soon the charges against Meraux were dropped, and a year later he was elected district judge on the Perez ticket.[16]

A spate of indictments for Prohibition violations followed the rum murders, but few convictions resulted. Several months after the murders, the following account of a case in Judge Perez's court appeared in the *St. Bernard Voice:* "Martin Terwilliger, who was charged with having liquor in his possession, was acquitted and his whiskey ordered returned to him."[17]

District Attorney Livaudais' attempts to obtain convictions in cases relating to the rum murders were frustrated when the trial dates were set so close together that he had no time to collect evidence. Perez scheduled seven murder cases to be heard on the same date. On July 11, 1923, he set twenty-seven cases for trial during the week of July 23–28. He gave as his reason for the hectic scheduling "heavy expenses upon the parish." Livaudais argued that the only expense involved was the guarding of four lots of seized liquor connected with seven of the cases in question. In all, Livaudais was compelled to discontinue prosecutions in forty criminal cases. Perez even had the district attorney indicted for alleged brutality in obtaining confessions from three suspected murderers. Livaudais, protesting that the grand jury had been stacked against him, said that he had photographic copies of a list of men to be selected for the grand jury that had been prepared beforehand and checked off in red pencil by someone higher up. The indictment against Livaudais was quashed by the judge of an adjoining district after Perez had been forced to disqualify himself from hearing the matter.[18]

Perez and Livaudais had been elected on the same ticket, but now

Livaudais became convinced that Leander was intent on erecting a more ruthless dictatorship than had ever existed under the Old Regulars. He split with Perez, joined the opposition, and filed impeachment charges against his erstwhile ally. Livaudais also broke with his own brother, Oliver S. Livaudais, who would serve as Leander's cocounsel in the impeachment trial.[19]

Livaudais and fifty others signed the petition. Seven of the signers, including the St. Bernard sheriff, bore the family name Estopinal. Three others, who were illiterate though politically active, marked the document with hand-drawn X's. John Dymond signed the petition, as did the Plaquemines registrar of voters, Emile Martin. Perez could hardly restrain himself when discussing Dymond. During the impeachment controversy he walked up to his friend Herman Schoenberger and asked, "Herman, do you want to do me a favor?"

"Sure," said Herman.

"Then tell John Dymond I said he is a crook, a grafter and an s.o.b."

According to Dymond, Perez's elder brother interceded, suggesting that Schoenberger omit the obscenity. Schoenberger, however, delivered the message verbatim. Quizzed by newsmen about the incident, Leander admitted making the statement but insisted that he could prove that Dymond was a crook and a grafter. When this account appeared in the press, Dymond quickly added a criminal libel suit to the charges against Perez.[20]

The twenty-one page impeachment petition charged that Judge Leander Perez was "unfit to exercise and discharge with an open and unprejudiced mind the high duties and functions of the office." One of the accusers exclaimed, "He tried to put us in jail because we're against him politically."[21] Twenty-three specific charges were made. Some were petty, but others were serious. Among them were the following: (1) Perez had kept a pearl-handled revolver nearby as he presided over court; (2) he had hunted up and interviewed witnesses, had witnesses summoned before grand juries, and had personally directed investigations by grand juries; (3) during a grand jury hearing he had told the jury that District Attorney Nemours H. Nunez had committed an indictable offense, summoned witnesses to appear against him, and then, when the jury made its findings, disregarded them and ordered the jury back to reconsider while he instructed Philip R. Livaudais, then an attorney of the court, to go to the grand jury room and prepare another indictment against Nunez; (4) Perez had ordered that a St. Bernard petit jury, which customarily dined at the establishment of a political enemy, be taken to an eating place operated by a political supporter; (5) he himself had tried four political allies accused of making false election returns, instead of submitting the case to a jury as the law required, and had acquitted them; (6) Perez had instructed a St. Bernard constable not to serve a trespassing warrant against a friend of his; (7) he had refused to swear out a search warrant to examine the home of a factional ally accused of possessing stolen property; (8) he had rushed cases to trial before the district attorney was prepared to present them; and (9) he had shielded J. Claude Meraux in the case of the rum murders.[22]

The trial finally began on May 12, 1924. Perez charged that the impeachment petition had been instigated by Philip Livaudais, an announced candidate to succeed him as district judge, and had been drafted in John Dymond's office. He denied that he was "an active agent or accorded leader" of any political faction. He said that upon taking office he had found the district overrun with graft and corruption, so he had closed gambling houses and sent corrupt officials to jail. Leander, who had imprisoned the president of the St. Bernard school board for "operating a banking game," claimed that he had purchased an automatic pistol to protect himself from gamblers who were plotting to murder him because he threatened to shut down their illicit operations. One of Perez's attorneys, St. Clair Adams, claimed that a judge's keeping a handgun was not unusual and was done all the time. In fact, Judge J. W. Jones of Natchitoches not only carried a sidearm but had shot a man down on the street. The state supreme court had refused to unseat Jones, so Adams could not see how Perez could be faulted for merely having a weapon handy. The young judge stated that he had sent jurors to dine at the restaurant of a political ally rather than that of a factional foe to save time and because his friend had better accommodations. He admitted that he had made "an honest mistake of judgment" in permitting four indicted friends illegally to waive a jury trial and then in acquitting them, but he asserted that the defense attorney had presented persuasive arguments and that the district attorney had failed to point out that a jury trial was required by law. Perez explained that he had instructed a St. Bernard constable not to arrest Anthony Salinovich, charged with trespassing, because Salinovich had already posted bond to appear for a similar offense. Leander continued that he had subsequently dismissed the charges against Salinovich because the land on which he had been accused of trespassing had not been posted. Perez stated that he had refused to sign a warrant to search the premises of a political ally because at the time he was busy with the trials resulting from the rum murders. He contended that he had scheduled an unusually large number of cases arising from these murders on the same day because they all involved substantially the same evidence. The fact that he had refused to summon a grand jury at the same time that Claude Meraux had surrendered as a fugitive from justice was purely coincidental, Perez insisted. He maintained that political considerations had influenced none of his decisions and contended that all of his mistakes had been due to inexperience and benevolent intentions. To satisfy Livaudais, Leander asserted, he would have had to decide all cases against his political allies and in favor of his political enemies.[23]

Adams called the charges against his client "frivolous, ridiculous, and scandalous." The case dragged on through May with no end in sight. The courtroom was packed with curious spectators; business in St. Bernard and Plaquemines practically came to a standstill as people flocked to the trial. For the first time in half a century (and only the second time in Louisiana history), the supreme court sat as a court of original jurisdiction. Not since the justices had tried and removed Judge Henry Lazarus in 1887 had the high court heard an impeachment case against a district judge. The proceedings revealed a chaotic, graft-ridden atmosphere in the deep delta parishes. Perez's attorneys, Oliver Livaudais, Adams, and John Perez, frequently digressed for long discussions of John Dymond and his nefarious schemes for defrauding the parish. Adams, opening a black notebook, brought out "inside" information on Dymond's election as president of the racing association and the subsequent defeat of two antiracing bills pending before the legislature. Former gov-

ernor John M. Parker, questioned about Leander's trips to Baton
Rouge to secure appointments for political allies, admitted that
Perez had made such trips, but only as part of a delegation. Parker
testified that he considered the New Regular leader an honorable
man and "an indefatigable worker." The prosecution came closest to
proving one of its serious charges in testimony concerning the rum
murders and the involvement of J. Claude Meraux. District Attorney Livaudais testified that he had visited his brother Oliver shortly
after the murders. When he arrived, Oliver and Perez were engaged
in an animated conversation. Oliver told Philip that he and Perez
were afraid that, in his confession, suspect Tom Favalora had said
that Claude Meraux had killed one of the deputies. The district attorney testified that Leander had asked him whether Favalora had
actually confessed and what the Meraux family should do. The defense maintained that Perez had merely stopped at Oliver
Livaudais' house to ask for a ride to the courthouse and had never
even discussed Claude Meraux. Concerning other charges, the prosecution showed that in two cases in which Leander had had a direct,
personal interest he had failed to disqualify himself. The defense
was rather lame. Once, it was explained, Perez had mislaid the recusation petition, and the other time he had simply been too busy to
bother with it.[24]

Perez's most effective defense characteristically consisted of an attack on his accusers. He later quipped, "I always take the offensive.
The defensive ain't worth a damn."[25] Leander subpoenaed records,
collected documents and witnesses, and prepared to launch an all-
out assault on his impeachers. If he could not prove his own innocence, he might equally incriminate his enemies.

On the morning of June 4, 1924, the prosecution appeared ready
to begin its final day of testimony. But, before court convened, the
prosecuting attorneys and justices closeted themselves for an hour
in the judicial chambers. Then Chief Justice Charles O'Neil
emerged from his office and signaled defense counsel St. Clair
Adams to join the conference. Both sides returned aglow with amiable expressions and overflowing with congenial exchanges. The
prosecution had agreed to drop all charges. District Attorney Philip
Livaudais, sobbing openly, and his brother Oliver effected an emo-

tional reconciliation. A letter from Perez was distributed to newsmen, stating that he retracted the statements he had made about John Dymond "in the heat of controversy of a political campaign." Chief Justice O'Neil, joining the love feast, announced, "I now desire to address myself to Judge Perez and to say that he has made some mistakes but I must say that these mistakes were mistakes of judgment. All of the members of the court are of the same opinion."[26] A witness quipped, "It was quite an ending. It reminded me of the courtship dance of the whooping cranes."[27]

After escaping removal from office, Leander redoubled his efforts to become the political czar of Plaquemines and St. Bernard. He retired as judge and ran for district attorney; the opposition did not enter an opponent.[28] Although he never again occupied the bench after 1924, Perez was called Judge by every parish resident, including himself, for the rest of his long life. There were many judges but only one Judge. Potentially, the district attorney is the most powerful local official in Louisiana, especially when allied with the district judge. He investigates and prosecutes—or does not prosecute—whom he chooses and nearly always has incriminating evidence in reserve to bludgeon his potential or actual foes. He serves as legal adviser to grand juries, police juries, and parish boards. As a judge, Perez had not been permitted to practice law, but as district attorney he could quickly build a lucrative practice in civil law.[29]

Already firmly in control of Plaquemines, Perez concentrated on St. Bernard in the local Democratic primaries of 1924. The *St. Bernard Voice* described the contest between the Old and New Regulars as the hottest political conflict in parish history. Both Democratic factions offered a full slate of candidates. The New Regulars gained an edge by having the Old Regular registrar of voters, Lawrence D. St. Alexandre, removed from office. He had allegedly misled potential voters by telling them that if they left their party affiliation blank they could vote in all elections, whereas actually this disqualified them from voting in Democratic primaries. He was also accused of asking "irrelevant questions of elderly ladies" and keeping the registration books closed to the public to conceal his discrepancies. Perez appeared before the Louisiana Board of Registration as the only witness against the registrar.[30]

The New Regulars geared themselves for an all-out effort in the campaign. In nominating Perez as the New Regular candidate for district attorney at a factional caucus, a partisan declared, "St. Bernard needs more order and less notoriety."[31] Claude Meraux, nominated as Perez's running mate for district judge, asserted that District Attorney Philip Livaudais had trumped up charges against him relating to the rum murders in order to destroy him politically. Learning of the attempts to persecute him and ruin his good name, Meraux explained, he had taken the advice of his mother, relatives, and friends and had briefly absented himself from the parish, which any man would have done under the circumstances.[32]

Leander's reconciliation with District Attorney Livaudais proved short-lived. Livaudais ran for district judge on the Old Regular ticket but was defeated by Claude Meraux. Afterward, claiming that he had been defamed in the campaign, Livaudais filed a $30,000 libel suit against Perez and his allies and the editor of the *Plaquemines Protector*. On the day that he filed suit, he and Perez engaged in a fistfight in the St. Bernard courthouse. Leander reportedly received a black eye and Livaudais some "hickeys" on his face, but witnesses gave the edge to Perez.[33]

The New Regulars won every important parish office and a majority of the police jury seats. Dr. L. A. Meraux received almost double the votes of incumbent Albert Estopinal, Jr., in the contest for sheriff, and Joseph Gravolet defeated Ring incumbent Simon Leopold in the race for state senator. The triumphant New Regulars were not satisfied with swamping their rivals only in the Democratic primary. Several Old Regular parish candidates had edged their New Regular opponents for the Democratic nomination in the primary, but three of these nominees were defeated by New Regular write-in candidates in the general election. The defeated faction contested one police jury seat in court, but the challenge was dismissed on the technicality that the Old Regulars had filed their charges too late. The newly elected police jury promptly wielded its political ax, and numerous Old Regular appointed officials lost their jobs or had their salaries reduced. Estopinal was indicted for irregularities in tax collections by a grand jury that he claimed was packed with Perez partisans.[34]

The New Regulars fared less well in the statewide elections. For governor they supported John M. Parker's lieutenant governor, Hewitt Bouanchaud, a small-town, anti-Klan Catholic. (Huey Long, an ambitious, crusading, upstate attorney who ran as an anti-Parker candidate, was eliminated in the first primary, although he showed surprising strength in the rural parishes.) Bouanchaud and Henry L. Fuqua, head of the state penitentiary at Angola during the Pleasant and Parker administrations, entered a runoff for the Democratic nomination. Fuqua had the support of the New Orleans Old Regular machine of Mayor Martin Behrman and had relied on his many New Orleans votes to get him into the second primary. The *Plaquemines Protector,* which supported Bouanchaud, accused Fuqua of taking money for his campaign from Standard Oil, the telephone company, and the carbon black companies. Although Bouanchaud carried St. Bernard and Plaquemines in both the first and second primaries, Fuqua triumphed statewide. Nonetheless, the local elections had been satisfying to Leander. The Old Regulars would never again be a potent force in his judicial district. He was the undisputed chief of Plaquemines and was firmly allied with L. A. Meraux, the dominant political figure of St. Bernard. A new dynasty now emerged to supplant the defeated and discredited Old Regular clique.[35]

THREE

The Trappers' War

By the mid-1920s, Judge Perez had become the undisputed political boss of Plaquemines. But power demands a financial as well as a political base, and the Judge began work early on his. There were several avenues an enterprising resident of the delta could follow to wealth. Gambling and bootlegging were both major industries of the day, but by far the most promising—and legitimate—was fur trapping. The lower delta was teeming with fur-bearing animals, primarily muskrat, but also mink, otter, and raccoon. Although trapping is normally associated with a cold climate, during the twenties Louisiana produced more furs than any other state and more muskrat than all other states combined. The territory of Alaska, thirteen times larger than Louisiana, sold only one-third as much value in pelts in 1925.[1]

This is not to say that Louisiana fur trappers usually grew rich or that, if they did, they were able to stay that way. For one thing, the demand for muskrat pelts was limited. During the nineteenth century, Europe had been the major market for all kinds of furs, but sales were confined to the elite, the aristocracy, and the monied classes, who preferred furs more prestigious than "rat" and could obtain these from northern suppliers. Also, trapping was not a year-round vocation but was restricted to a ten- to twelve-week season in the late fall and early winter. To supplement their incomes, most lower-coast trappers labored, logged, fished, farmed, or worked in shipyards nine months out of the year. When the cold months came, they would take their traps and heavy clothing and set out into the bleak and trackless marsh. Many trappers were *isleños,*

32

Spanish-speaking emigrants from the Canary Islands, and their sons and grandsons. Their educational level was dismally low and many were illiterate, but these tough and independent men knew the swamp and its inhabitants. Each had a territory he traditionally trapped, and his father had usually trapped it before him. This was no place for a tenderfoot. An expert could walk across the marsh stepping on clumps of grass roots and solid spots no larger than his foot; one wrong step and a man could find himself treading muck. Life in the swamps in muskrat season was unrelieved drudgery. The trapper holed up in a flimsy hut, ate out of tin cans, and spent every day from sunup to sundown making the rounds of his traps.[2]

During the twenties, prosperity rolled across the country on a wave of hot air and paper. Automobiles, radios, bootleg liquor, and fur coats became the rage. Now, not only wealthy society ladies could afford to wrap themselves in the luxury of animal skins, but housewives and working girls too. Although northern fur areas had been overtrapped, the Louisiana delta was looking forward to some of its best yields yet. Muskrat pelts, given more impressive names and made into coats, suddenly were in great demand. Prices paid to the trappers soared. The boom rocked the marsh. In 1925–1926, a few energetic trappers reported taking as many as 150 muskrats a day, worth $1.30 apiece, at the beginning of the 75-day season. Outside trappers, attracted by the bonanza, descended in such numbers that, by the end of the season, the average operator was snaring only 30 or so pelts per day. Incomes varied widely, depending upon the trapper's experience and the territory he worked. An expert muskrat man in a choice location could earn $3,000 or $4,000 in a season, but others might net as little as $800 or $900. Still, it was more than they had ever made. In the late twenties, a normal year's pelt yield from Plaquemines Parish alone was worth several million dollars. With all this cash floating around in the delta, the middlemen and the parasites could not be far away. The *isleños,* unused to handling money, proved easy marks for slick-tongued salesmen, who appeared out of nowhere hawking everything from automobiles to rubber boots. Fortunes were dropped on the roll of dice or the turn of a card. But the hucksters and the gamblers were only small fry. The real professionals in the game of part-the-boob-from-his-money made up a breed the *Plaquemines Protector* called the "land grabbers."[3]

Until now, no one had given much thought to the fact that the marsh must actually belong to someone. The muskrat men trapped where they wished, and their right to roam the swamps at will was never questioned. Titles to many acres of soggy wasteland were undefined because the owners had never thought it worth their trouble. If the poor and ignorant *isleños* could make anything out there in all that muck, they were welcome to it. Under the Swamp Act of 1850, the U.S. government had transferred thousands of acres of wetland to the states. Louisiana had sold much of its share to individuals at pennies an acre, but many had neglected to pay their property taxes, allowing the lands to revert to the state. Some of the state land had been granted to local school and levee boards as revenue property. Once the trapping boom was in full swing, many of the old, neglectful landowners suddenly wanted to reclaim their property. An obliging legislature adopted a law permitting original title-holders to redeem their lands by paying back taxes. The clerks of court in Plaquemines and St. Bernard were kept busy recording redemptions. Where land was not claimed by individual owners, it was gobbled up by land companies, many organized solely to exploit the fur trade. Titles and leases to trapping lands were obtained by means both foul and fair: through purchase and redemption and through chicanery and liaison with corrupt officials and judges. By 1926, some marshland was worth more than dry ground.[4]

The owners and land companies moved in. Property was staked off and posted. The trappers were told that henceforth they would have to pay for the privilege of working their old territories. Outsiders from neighboring parishes and even neighboring states began to crowd the swamp with their traps. The local marshmen were confused. They had no understanding of titles, rents, leases, or rights. They could not even read the No Trespassing signs.[5]

One of the "land grabbers" who began purchasing large tracts of good trapping land was Leander's cousin, John R. Perez. In 1924, he leased almost 100,000 acres of muskrat-rich swamp from a New Orleans concern, the Phillips Land Company. Strangely enough, the company's secretary was Leander's old nemesis, John Dymond, Jr., who had evidently found new and profitable interests since being expelled from delta politics. John Perez obtained the trapping rights on the property for ten years at $3,000 per year; he also reserved an option to buy the lands should the company receive an offer. Most of the Phillips lands were in Plaquemines, but a smaller tract was located in St. Bernard. The new leaseholder, of course, did not intend to trap the marsh himself. He subleased it to a man named E. P. Brady, representing the Delaware-Louisiana Fur Trapping Company, who demanded that the local trappers pay him for the right to trap on his land. When they refused, he imported outsiders to put them out of work. Armed with court orders and shotguns, company guards and deputies patrolled the area. But no one knew the backwaters like the *isleños,* and the labyrinthine marsh was almost impossible to police. The locals continued to trap, disappearing into the tall grass when they heard the telltale putput of a patrol boat. The scab trappers were fired upon and harassed wherever they ventured. They often returned to their camps to find their tar-paper shacks demolished and to read painfully lettered signs that warned, "Bettr Be Gon Wen We Get Back." Eventually, 150 delta men were cited with contempt of federal court for trying to trap where they always had.[6]

The local trappers badly needed a champion, and they found one in Judge Leander Perez. In November, 1924, he called them together at the district courthouse to discuss their rights against the land companies and explained how, by jointly leasing the lands, they could guarantee themselves a place to trap. Almost singlehandedly, he organized the St. Bernard Trappers' Association and a smaller companion group, the Plaquemines Parish Protective Association. Each trapper paid fifty dollars for a share in the association, plus annual dues. The subscribing members could then lease trapping rights from the association for an additional fifty dollars a year. In staking out individual territories, the charters specified that the marshmen would abide by "the custom of the trappers on the Prairies"; in other words, each man would trap the area that was traditionally his. Disputes would be arbitrated by the president of the association. The shareholders, buying out Brady's sublease for

1924–1925, enjoyed an exceptionally lucrative season. The next one, everyone predicted, would be even better. It was a beautiful solution to the problem. For a small investment, the trappers were able to stay within the law and to keep their traditional lands.[7]

A president and board of directors were named in the charters, but in reality Perez, as the attorney for both associations, conducted most of the business. Although most of the trapping lands were in Plaquemines, the St. Bernard association was by far the stronger organization. No accurate records were kept, but the stock ledger of the St. Bernard group showed 467 members. The 9 directors took little interest in the association's business. Several of them were illiterate, one could speak only Spanish, and none understood the functioning of a corporation. Most of the members did not know, or care, who sat on the board of directors. Among the delta trappers, an educated man like the Judge enjoyed a status much like that of a witch doctor in a primitive society. He knew the legal chants and spells that permitted them to tend their traps unmolested. They liked his medicine and were willing to pay for it; but they did not pretend to understand it, being satisfied contentedly to work their familiar marshlands as long as profits were high.[8]

The St. Bernard trappers so thoroughly trusted Perez that they allowed him to function as the entire association. From the founding of the corporation in December, 1924, until August, 1925, no meetings of the board of directors were held. The Judge arranged for John R. Perez's lease to be transferred from Brady to the association, collected dues from the trappers, and paid John Perez, all without holding a board meeting. The association did not even have a bank account until August, 1925. The Judge, putting the shareholders' money into his own account, simply paid the bills when they came due. Even after meetings began to be held, he totally dominated the proceedings because no one else understood what was going on. The association minute book was merely a bundle of loose-leaf pages clamped together, to which sheets could easily be added or removed. Leander drew up resolutions, submitted them for nominal approval, and then filed them in the minutes. At meetings, the association's secretary, Bennie Harris, took rough notes, then brought them to Perez's law office in New Orleans. After the Judge had written the final draft of the minutes and had had it typed, Harris discarded his originals. If this seemed a bit irregular, Harris explained that he was not as intelligent as Perez and needed his help—presumably with grammar, spelling, and punctuation—in completing the final copy.[9]

John R. Perez profited handsomely from his arrangement with the two organizations. After Brady gave up his rights, Perez subleased the Phillips lands to the St. Bernard Trappers' Association and Plaquemines Parish Protective Association for a total of $6,500 for the 1925–1926 trapping season and $8,000 for the 1926–1927 season.[10] But he thought he saw a way to make still a larger profit. Since the price of muskrat skins had reached an unprecedented height, with a little subterfuge the naïve marshmen might be induced to pay even more for the privilege of trapping. Apparently, their own trusted attorney, Leander Perez, was in on the scheme from the beginning.

The plan called for a figurehead trustee to whom John R. Perez could transfer his lease. The trustee could then demand an enormously increased rental without seeming to involve the Perez cousins. Chosen for the role was J. Walter Michel of New Orleans, who had been best man at Leander's wedding. Michel was unknown to the trappers, and he agreed not to reveal for whom he was acting. A contract was drawn up transferring the seven remaining years of John R.'s lease to Michel for $10,000 per year. The former still reserved his option to purchase, which meant that he could cancel Michel's lease at any time by buying the Phillips lands; and, as an extra added attraction, he was now relieved of all tax obligations on the lands. Although John R. had already leased the property to the St. Bernard association for the 1926–1927 season, the two Perezes soon devised a plan that they hoped would result in the board of directors voluntarily transferring its rights to Michel.[11]

The first meeting of the St. Bernard Trappers' Association board had been on August 16, 1925. The only action taken had been to authorize the treasurer Leon Meraux to transact all association financial business, including the borrowing and lending of money and the signing of checks. Acting under this authorization, Meraux then lent substantial sums to himself and Judge Perez. The Judge used the money to buy into a real estate deal with his political ally, St. Bernard Sheriff L. A. Meraux, Leon's first cousin. When questioned as to the propriety of this action, Treasurer Meraux explained, "The Association authorized me to do whatever I wanted with the funds." Meanwhile, Perez accused his critics of "making a grandstand play to the newspapers." Of course, it is highly unlikely that the scarcely literate directors understood the scope of the authority they were granting Meraux; indeed, it is quite possible that they were unaware that they had "authorized" anything at all.[12]

According to its charter, the association was required to hold its annual stockholders' meeting in September. The 1925 meeting appears to have been on either September 10 or 25; much about it is obscure. State law provided that a list of shareholders eligible to vote should be posted before the meeting, but the corporation did not even possess such a list. The law also specified that each stockholder be notified personally of meetings at which directors were to be elected. The method used to notify the trappers was unique. A number of notices were printed and sent to the Meraux & Leon Bakery with instructions to wrap one with each loaf of bread sent out in that day's delivery. A deputy sheriff left additional dodgers at St. Bernard stores where trappers were known to congregate. Corporation secretary Bennie Harris explained that the bakery turned out between 1,500 and 2,000 loaves of bread a day and that it was frequented by nearly everyone in St. Bernard. Just the same, shareholders who were illiterate, did not buy bread, or resided outside the parish had no way of knowing about the meeting. The corporation had investors in the parishes of Orleans, Jefferson, Plaquemines, and Lafourche who were never notified. At the mysterious meeting, all but two of the original nine directors were reelected. Although Louisiana law made the ownership of stock a qualification for membership on the board of directors of a corporation, only four of the nine directors were stockholders. Harris testified that he could not say whether the treasurer Leon Meraux or even he himself held any shares. Most of the members were indebted to Leander Perez either through blood or patronage: some held parish jobs; others were relatives of political allies.[13]

In April, 1926, the *St. Bernard Voice* published reports of a rumor

going about the marsh of an upcoming deal involving large tracts of
the best trapping lands in the delta. The *Voice* tried vainly to learn
who the supposed principals were but was able to report only that
they represented an unnamed corporation. Rumors of this sort were
bound to cause excitement, especially since the demand for trapping
territory in the delta during the previous season had been so great
that it could not be satisfied.[14] Rumor aside, however, there *was* a
big land deal shaping up in the spring of 1926, and it involved the
Perez cousins, the Phillips lands, and considerable mystery of its
own.

Only four directors of the St. Bernard Trappers' Association attended the board meeting held March 7, 1926. A fifth, Brooks
Molero, the president, did not arrive until after the last resolution
had been passed. At this session, the directors took the extraordinary action of transferring the trappers' lease on the Phillips lands
for the coming season to J. Walter Michel. As the association's attorney, Leander excused himself prior to consideration of the proposal, "because my cousin, John R. Perez, stood to make some money
out of it." John R. Perez and Stanley Ray, serving as attorneys for
Michel, explained the lease transfer to the board. One of the directors, Domingo Gonzales, poorly understood English and had to
have the contract explained to him in Spanish. The trappers were
told that they were getting a splendid bargain: in return for turning
over their season's lease to Michel, they would receive first consideration for a sublease on the Phillips lands for a period of eight
years. The directors thus were led to believe that they were simply
exchanging a one-year lease for an eight-year lease. They would be
given sixty days following the close of each trapping season to sign
up for the next year. Eyewitnesses later testified that the written
resolution recorded in the minutes did not correspond to the resolution adopted at the meeting. The final copy of the statement, drafted
of course in Judge Perez's law office, obligated the muskratters to
trap on Michel's terms, if they trapped at all, but it in no way bound
Michel. He was required only to give preference to the association
trappers. An additional clause provided that each trapper who desired to lease must be "personally acceptable" to Michel. To top it off,
the entire deal depended on the goodwill of John R. Perez, who could

cancel all arrangements at any time simply by exercising his option to purchase.[15]

Again, it is doubtful whether any of the directors clearly understood the transaction. Most appear to have assumed that, since their attorney Leander Perez approved of the deal, it was in their best interests. A review of testimony in subsequent litigation indicates that few, if any, of the association members were aware of the right reserved to Michel to refuse to lease to particular trappers. They seemed to think that they would automatically be able to lease land under the contract. St. Bernard Deputy Sheriff Clem Nunez, who had explained the contract in Spanish to Gonzales, admitted later that he had not fully understood what he had been called upon to translate. This had not bothered him, he said, because "whatever the board done I expect was all right; the board was running the corporation." Nunez also endorsed the plan before a number of other trappers who were present. He was sure that whatever had been done was proper, because it had been done by men he trusted. Nunez was obviously uneducated and only somewhat literate in English. But he was a deputy sheriff and a conservation officer and, therefore, looked up to by the other muskratters. It did not take much book learning to command respect in trapper society. One St. Bernard justice of the peace was a semiliterate who could read only with great difficulty and hesitation.[16]

After the board had surrendered the association's lease, Michel promptly raised the rent. Previously, the trappers had paid $50 each for a year's trapping rights. He now informed them that they would have to pay $150. Ignorant of the board's transfer of their lease to Michel, they had already staked out and taken possession of their territories when told that the ante had tripled.[17]

Although many trappers assumed that the deal was in their best interests, others knew something about arithmetic. A group of dissatisfied muskratters approached fellow association member Manuel Molero, a well-to-do, educated general merchandiser who lived at Delacroix Island, a St. Bernard fishing, trapping, and rumrunning community on Bayou Terre aux Boeufs. Agreeing that the deal looked suspicious, Molero promised to have his lawyer Oliver S. Livaudais investigate. Livaudais concluded shortly that a fraud had been perpetrated. Assuming that Michel was acting for the Perezes, what John R. had in fact done was to transform his old one-year lease to the association into an eight-year lease with broad discretionary powers reserved to him, at triple the price. Livaudais calculated that the trustee could potentially collect $150 per trapper from 500 trappers the first year, for a total of $75,000. Michel had paid John Perez only $70,000 for the entire seven-year lease (he had paid nothing for the year transferred to him by the association directors); therefore, he would net a $5,000 profit the first year and a clear profit of at least $75,000 each year thereafter. And, of course, there was nothing to stop him from raising the rent again. If the local men balked at the terms, Michel was free to lease to outside trappers, many of whom were willing to pay huge sums to work the delta. The deal appeared even shadier when Michel steadfastly refused to reveal for whom he was acting as trustee. But Livaudais, at least, was certain that he was nothing more than a faithful steward for the Perez interests. John R., who sold the lease, was acting as attorney for Michel, and Leander was busy collecting the $150 rental fee. Trapper John Dunn later testified that Judge Perez had informed him of the terms, executed an agreement with him, and accepted payment, all without even mentioning the name J. Walter Michel until it came time to make out the check. When Dunn received the canceled check through his bank, the endorsement on the back showed that it had been deposited to the credit of Leander H. Perez. The Judge did not deny that he had received money from Michel's collections, but maintained that he had not done so as Michel's attorney; he did not elaborate.[18]

Livaudais explained what he had discovered to Molero and his uncle Brooks Molero, the nominal president of the association. The three decided to call a special meeting to discuss the situation. On April 12, 1926, about eight hundred grim-faced trappers assembled at the St. Bernard Parish courthouse. The crowd was in an ugly mood, and there was much shouting and shoving to get a place in the packed and stuffy courtroom. Immediately, Judge Perez asked that a closed-door meeting of the board of directors be held in the basement, but Livaudais insisted on including all the trappers, saying that surely there could "be no harm in holding the meeting open and above board." President Molero opened the meeting by introducing his nephew Manuel, who was elected chairman. Perez violently objected, calling the younger Molero a "usurper and impostor" and demanding that he step down, but was overruled. Livaudais and Manuel Molero then set out patiently and carefully to explain the Michel sublease to the trappers. Livaudais told them that they could have bought the entire seven-year lease from John R. Perez for less than they would now have to pay Michel for the first year. Judge Perez attempted to address the meeting, citing his own record as a defender of the trappers, but was angrily shouted down. He insisted that he was not the principal for whom Michel was acting, but refused to identify Michel's shadowy partner.[19]

A fistfight nearly broke out when Perez accused Livaudais and Manuel Molero of sour grapes because John R. had beaten them to the Phillips lands. "These two men here were among those who had planned to buy the trapping lands outright," he shouted, whirling and pointing. "You're a liar!" Molero cried and started toward him. They would surely have come to blows had not some of the burly trappers moved between them.[20]

Livaudais continued his case against Perez and the Michel lease. He charged that the Judge had the association's money and books in his personal possession. Perez retorted that the money was in the Whitney National Bank in New Orleans and that the books were in the hands of the corporation secretary, Bennie Harris. Harris, for his part, claimed that the books were with the auditors. Having heard enough, the indignant trappers loudly approved a resolution calling upon President Brooks Molero to file suit in the name of the corporation to nullify the Michel agreement. Another resolution, which also passed with great enthusiasm, demanded that Leander Perez remove himself as the trappers' attorney. But the Judge haughtily refused, asking, "What are Mr. Livaudais and Manuel Molero going to do about it?"[21]

Following the heated assembly, the board of directors gathered in secret and adopted resolutions supporting Perez and upholding the Michel sublease. A statement issued by the directors charged that Livaudais had misrepresented the facts in the case and that the eight hundred trappers present at the meeting did not speak for the membership of the association.[22] The Perez-controlled board "denounced and officially repudiated" Livaudais for "attempting to agitate trappers over a matter in which he has no actual concern only . . . to stir up litigation for reasons best known to himself." Five days later, President Brooks Molero filed suit in Orleans Parish Civil District Court to annul the Michel agreement. Livaudais was engaged to serve as attorney for the shareholders, and Manuel Molero agreed to foot the bill. During the trial, Perez repeated the charge that Livaudais had fabricated the entire incident solely to earn an attorney's fee.[23]

On April 20, three days after filing the suit, Brooks Molero, bedridden and exhausted by the controversy, resigned as president of the association. He sent word to the board of directors that he was ill, could not attend a scheduled meeting, and wished to step down. With amazing dispatch, the St. Bernard Parish clerk of court appeared at Molero's bedside with a typewritten resignation, which the old man dutifully signed. He later claimed that he had resigned only with the understanding that his action would not affect his suit to overturn the Michel contract. The board of directors, however, quickly accepted the resignation, installed a successor, and, voting to withdraw the suit against Michel, announced that there was no longer any authority to press the action. The directors maintained that only they could speak for the association. They moved to retain Perez as corporation counsel. Brooks Molero, once his condition improved, ran a notice in the New Orleans *Times-Picayune* telling the trappers that his resignation had been improperly handled by the board and that he still intended to pursue the Michel case. When the suit finally came to trial, he was still referring to himself as the lawful president of the St. Bernard Trappers' Association.[24]

As a parish political leader and through his alliance with St. Bernard's powerful sheriff, Dr. L. A. Meraux, Judge Perez easily controlled the board of directors. Bennie Harris, the secretary, was a deputy sheriff. Director Charles Rodriguez, Harris' father-in-law, was also a deputy, as was Louis Serpas. Treasurer Leon Meraux was the sheriff's first cousin. Casimer Sylveria was a police juror. Victor

Morales, Jr., elected president to replace Molero, was an assistant janitor at the parish courthouse. Throughout the litigation, the board consistently upheld Perez's position.[25]

The legal battle arising from the trappers' attempt to throw out the Michel contract was lengthy and complex. Although at least five major cases involving the dispute were pending at one time— including actions filed in the Plaquemines–St. Bernard local district court, the federal district court, and the Louisiana Supreme Court—attention focused on the suit brought by Brooks Molero in the Orleans Parish Civil District Court. From early morning until late at night the courtroom and corridors were crowded with hundreds of unshaven, muddy-booted trappers and their sympathizers. Bitterness was in the very air; no attempt was made to conceal the hostility between the opposing sides. Several times, fights broke out in the hallway. At one point, two uniformed policemen from the Third Precinct were detached to the courtroom to preserve order. Interest in the case was certainly not diminished by the continued appearance in the *St. Bernard Voice* of rumors of still more mysterious land transfers. The paper predicted that competition for trapping lands would be tremendous during the coming season. As the litigation dragged on, Leander Perez, unable to travel into the rural areas of the parish because the trappers had sworn to kill him, appeared to be the most hated man in St. Bernard.[26]

From the beginning, the affair was darkened by the menacing shadow of official harassment. On May 24, 1926, deputies from St. Bernard arrested Benito Molero, a nephew of Brooks Molero, outside the New Orleans courtroom where the trappers' case was being heard, and charged him with "assault, beating and wounding." The accusation stemmed from an incident the previous Sunday when Molero had been attacked by three men wielding knives and bottles. Oliver Livaudais had to go to St. Bernard to bail him out of jail. Apparently no charges were ever brought against Benito's attackers, who were known to be supporters of the Michel lease.[27] Even more serious was the matter of John Dunn. A friend of Manuel Molero's, he had testified against Judge Perez in court. As a consequence, he claimed, he had been arrested and taken to the St. Bernard jail, where he had been beaten by Chief Deputy Sheriff Celestine F.

("Dutch") Rowley. According to Dunn, Rowley had knocked him to the floor and had allowed the other deputies to kick him while he was down. When friends had tried to help him, the trapper said, they had been beaten up too. Dunn showed reporters cuts, bruises, and a split lip. Sheriff Meraux did not deny that Dunn had been roughed up but made light of the matter. He claimed that the trapper had been arrested on a warrant sworn by a local woman, charging him with entering her home, abusing her, using obscene language, and making threats. When Dunn had been brought to the jail, he had been loud and insulting, Meraux said, adding that he did not blame Rowley for hitting him. Some of his prisoner's friends had come to the courthouse to "start a rumpus," the sheriff acknowledged, but they "ran like yellow rabbits." What had scared them so was not specified.[28]

A particularly acrimonious episode occurred during the trial when Livaudais attempted to compel the association's minute book and stock ledger to be produced for inspection by the court. Previously, Livaudais had tried to introduce as evidence copies and excerpts made from the documents by accountants, but Perez had always objected, saying that the books themselves were the best evidence. When the Judge was told to produce them, however, he steadfastly refused, maintaining that a New Orleans court could not subpoena the records of a corporation domiciled in another parish. Finally, Livaudais and Manuel Molero filed suit in the local court on behalf of almost 150 members of the association to force the officers to open the books for inspection within St. Bernard. Perez reacted by filing charges against Livaudais, Molero, and the trappers who had signed the petition, claiming that the suit contained libelous allegations against him.[29]

Two sheriff's deputies went to Livaudais' home about 9 P.M. on May 7, 1926, to arrest the attorney on the criminal libel charge. Not finding him at home, they waited for him at a nearby intersection. Once they had Livaudais in custody, they allowed him to continue home for supper as it was his fifty-third birthday. After supper, Livaudais, his son, and his bondsman A. P. Perrin tried to find District Judge J. Claude Meraux but were unsuccessful. Driving along the highway, they were suddenly passed by Meraux, speeding in the opposite direction. Livaudais later said that he had turned around and given chase but had been unable to overtake the judge, "although my car can go 60 miles an hour." Enraged, he charged that Meraux, brother of the St. Bernard sheriff, had deliberately fled the parish to avoid setting bail, hoping thereby to force him to spend the night in jail. Taken finally to the jail, Livaudais joined Manuel Molero, who had been arrested earlier by deputies at the community of Violet. Sheriff Meraux later released both men upon learning that their lawyers had asked the state supreme court to set bail. He denied that there had been any conspiracy to keep Livaudais and Molero in jail on the misdemeanor charge. He asserted that they had never even been put in a cell; they had merely been held in "constructive custody" for a couple of hours.[30]

The next day, Judge Perez, as district attorney, ordered deputies to arrest all the trappers who had signed the offending petition. Eventually, 103 trappers were rounded up and incarcerated. Judge Meraux released them all on bonds of $500 each, some of which were signed and others of which were accepted by the court on its own recognizance when the formalities of posting bond for so many defendants threatened to keep the court in session past the judge's bedtime.[31]

At length, Mark M. Boatner, the presiding judge in the suit against Michel, issued a subpoena for the company books, which were brought to Orleans Parish and placed in a vault in the office of the clerk of court. However, upon going to examine them, Livaudais discovered that two office associates of Perez had been allowed to remove them for the ostensible purpose of preparing an income tax return. The attorney traced the books to accountant Edward J. deVerges' offices, which adjoined those of Judge Perez in the Hibernia Bank Building. When Livaudais appeared at deVerges' office and demanded to see the records, the accountant stalled him while he sent next door for advice. Neil A. Armstrong, Jr., one of the men who had taken the books from the court, instructed deVerges to tell Livaudais that he would need a special court order from Judge Boatner if he wished to see anything. When word of this reached Boatner, he was annoyed, since he had sent Livaudais to deVerges' office in the first place. He ordered the books returned to the custody of the court, and this was done the following day.[32]

The battle of the books did not end here, but erupted anew during the trial. During questioning of trapper Alex Menesses about the dodger distributed in the bread loaves to announce the September stockholders' meeting, Perez showed the witness a copy of the dodger that had been pasted in the minute book. Attorneys for the trappers exchanged surprised looks, and Livaudais rose to charge that the notice had not been in the book previously and that, consequently, the minutes must have been altered, perhaps during their trip to the Hibernia Bank Building. Perez characterized the suggestion as "outrageous." Judge Boatner ruled that the charge was serious and merited close examination but directed Menesses to continue with his testimony. Perez then rushed to the bench and shoved the book at the judge, urging him to examine it for himself. Annoyed at this breach of decorum, Boatner silently picked up the book and hurled it to the floor, at which Perez backed away, growling something at Livaudais. "He called me a dirty cur," Livaudais charged. "I heard him," Boatner replied grimly, "and am going to take action." Perez apologized profusely to the court but was fined $25 for contempt. Other contempt actions during the trial were a $10 fine against Livaudais for belittling Judge Perez as "that party" and a $2.50 fine against Bennie Harris for giving a sarcastic reply to a question from Livaudais.[33]

The personal acrimony between Livaudais and Perez continued to surface throughout the proceedings. After the "dirty cur" incident, Livaudais told the court, "For months there has been bitter feeling between Perez and myself and I do not want to engage in any further trouble until after this case has been settled." Earlier he had attempted to assure a witness for Michel that he had no personal feeling against him. "The feeling is all there," he had said, indicating Leander Perez. "The feeling is mutual," Perez had replied.[34]

The trappers split into two factions during the trial. Most of them supported Livaudais, but a substantial number, siding with the Perezes, signed a petition stating that they wished to uphold the Michel sublease. The Judge also had the Plaquemines Parish Protective Association, its president Louis Cappiello, and Leon Meraux, the treasurer of the St. Bernard Trappers' Association, file motions in support of Michel. Meraux and Cappiello maintained that, since their signatures appeared on the original lease agreement, they each held a quarter interest in the property. Perez argued therefore that, even if the St. Bernard association wished to void the Michel arrangement, it could not do so, because the matter involved several other parties. Of course, the two organization officials had signed in just that capacity—as officials, not individuals—and they actually had no personal interest in the case.[35]

The trial presented some bizarre legal complications. Both Perez and Livaudais claimed to represent the St. Bernard Trappers' Association, the former through the board of directors and the latter through the suit filed by President Brooks Molero on behalf of the shareholders. Adding a new dimension to corporate ethics, Perez argued that the board had acted properly in ignoring the interests of the trappers, since a director's true responsibility was to the corporation and not to the shareholders. He showed that the board, by signing over its lease to Michel, had increased the company's projected revenue over an eight-year period: first, whereas it had previously collected only $50 a year per member for trapping rights, that figure would now be tripled; second, the corporation was guaranteed the receipt of dues from shareholders for eight years instead of one, adding up to $35,000 for the tenure of the lease. Perez suggested that the directors would have been irresponsible had they not acted to cut their corporation in on this bonanza. This argument may be valid when applied to the usual type of corporation that derives its revenues from selling goods or services to the public and, then, if business is good, pays a dividend to the stockholders, who at the risk of their cash investments had capitalized the operation. In the case of the St. Bernard Trappers' Association, however, the corporation's only source of income was the dues paid to it in return for a service by its own investors—its clientele and its ownership were identical. The board of directors had acted in the best interests of the corporation, Perez argued, because it had increased revenue, and he deemphasized the fact that the increased revenue came directly and exclusively from the stockholders. Of course, the St. Bernard Trappers' Association paid no dividends and few, if any, salaries, and it made no capital improvements. Where the money went is unclear. A certain amount, of course, was needed to pay for the leases obtained for its members, but the trappers themselves made additional payments each year to cover this. Some of the corporation's money was lent to Perez and his allies, and a good deal, no doubt, went for attorneys' fees. Increasing the income for the association simply meant collecting more money so that more money could be paid to J. Walter Michel and his mysterious partner.[36]

Though John R. Perez was nominally the attorney for J. Walter Michel, his cousin Leander handled most of the legal work. Never content with a single line of attack, the Judge developed many stratagems for use during the trial, one of the most imaginative and ultimately successful being his attempt to insinuate himself into the role of plaintiff. Through Perez, the board of directors declared that the suit against Michel was its own suit, since it had been filed in the name of the corporation by its president, Brooks Molero, and only the board of directors could legally speak for the corporation. Molero had resigned his office, and the board now wished to withdraw the suit, a right guaranteed the plaintiff by established jurisprudence. Judge Boatner, however, recognized the individual trappers as the true plaintiffs and ordered the case to be heard on its own merits. Perez's argument would be treated with more respect by the state supreme court.[37]

In his effort to undermine the plaintiffs' case, Judge Perez pulled an astounding coup by calling a surprise witness, none other than Brooks Molero. The old man testified that he had thought it over and was now satisfied with the Michel sublease. He and members of his family, he said, had paid Bennie Harris their $150 for trapping privileges during the coming season. Livaudais, furious, charged that Molero had sold out in return for a choice trapping concession. Though embarrassed by his uncle's defection, Manuel Molero stuck by the suit.[38]

In testimony, Michel at first stubbornly refused to reveal for whom he was acting. Later he offered the information that he had bought John R.'s lease on behalf of a certain Ferdinand Schultz of Fort Totten, New York. If Michel had been shadowy, Schultz was positively ectoplasmic; no one had ever heard of him or had any idea why he was interested in delta trapping. He never appeared to testify and took no part in the litigation. It was eventually learned that, two days after Brooks Molero had filed his suit, the elusive

Schultz, acting again through Michel, had transferred his sublease on the Phillips lands to the Canadian Land and Fur Company, an obscure Wilmington, Delaware, corporation, in return for one thousand shares of no par value common stock. It developed later that the president of Canadian Land and Fur was the same Ferdinand Schultz and the secretary none other than J. Walter Michel. The directors of the St. Bernard Trappers' Association subsequently entered into a supplemental agreement with the new leaseholder.[39]

In court Livaudais had been emphasizing the clause in the original sublease that required leasing trappers to be "personally acceptable" to Michel. In his capacity as secretary of Canadian Land and Fur, Michel wrote the trappers' association, explaining that this reservation meant simply that the men must obey state conservation laws. Judge Boatner ruled that this letter could not be considered part of the contract and agreed with Livaudais' contention that the lease agreement as it stood endowed Michel with an absolute veto over who would be allowed to trap the Phillips lands and therefore with the authority to impose any conditions he might choose upon the members of the association.[40]

The intrusion of Canadian Land and Fur into the affair made it possible for Livaudais to take the case into federal court. In the name of trapper Miguel Perez—apparently no relation to Leander—he filed suit to nullify the Canadian Land and Fur sublease on the grounds that the original Michel sublease was invalid. Federal District Judge Louis H. Burns granted a temporary restraining order against the Delaware company. When arguments came to be heard, Livaudais contended that the lease should be voided because it was the product of a conspiracy among Leander Perez, Leon Meraux, J. Walter Michel, and others. Burns ruled this to be the case. Ironically, however, his ruling posed a difficulty. If the proper parties of the defense were Louisianians like the trappers, there was no diversity of citizenship, and therefore the matter had no business being in a federal court. Although conceding the correctness of the plaintiff's argument, Burns was forced to throw the case out of court.[41]

Following Judge Burns's decision, the center of battle swung back

to civil district court, where Judge Boatner was still hearing arguments. On July 26, he handed down a lengthy decision, written over
the weekend, in which he annulled the Michel sublease on the
grounds that Michel had paid nothing for it. The jubilant trappers
celebrated that night at Delacroix Island. Leander Perez announced
that he would appeal to the state supreme court. Because the court
would not convene until October, however, a final decision might not
come until the trapping season, which would begin November 20,
was already underway.[42]

In the aftermath of the Boatner decision, the two factions of the
St. Bernard Trappers' Association completely split apart, each
claiming to be the authentic organization. At the September stockholders' meeting, held at the St. Bernard courthouse, Perez stationed
armed deputies outside the courtroom as an unofficial "credentials
committee" to pass on the qualifications of trappers wishing to attend
and on the validity of any proxies they might hold. Oliver Livaudais
convened a rump meeting in the police jury room of those who were
turned away. The two factions went on to elect separate slates of
directors and company officers. Although the Livaudais group far
outnumbered the Perez group, Leander had no difficulty in obtaining
a local court order from his old friend, Judge J. Claude Meraux,
prohibiting his foes from functioning as the association or using association books or property.[43]

Meanwhile, John R. Perez had been busy. Within weeks of Judge
Boatner's decision, he announced that he had exercised his option
and bought all of the Phillips lands for $600,000. In short succession,
he concluded a spectacular series of deals. The American Land and
Fur Company, of which he was president, purchased ten thousand
acres known as the Swift lands for $125,000. He also bought the
Finkle lands, encompassing eight square miles in Plaquemines, and
the Schwab lands, a fifteen-thousand-acre tract adjoining the Phillips and Finkle lands in the two parishes. The territory thus amassed
was described by the New Orleans States as "one of the greatest
trapping empires in the world." The Swift lands, acquired from the
Chicago meat-packers, made up one of the richest areas in the delta;
some trappers during the previous winter had taken as many as
six thousand muskrats apiece there. A recent hurricane was said to

be a harbinger of a bountiful season. Heavy rains had swollen the bayous and cutoffs, thus preventing salt water from entering the marsh. The grass upon which the muskrats fed had been at seed when the high winds hit, and the seeds had been scattered throughout the area, promising plenty of food for the animals. John R.'s inspectors reported that no muskrats had drowned in the storm. Meanwhile, in preparation for what everyone looked forward to as one of the greatest fur seasons Louisiana had ever known, the Canadian Land and Fur Company assigned its sublease on the Phillips lands to another misty Delaware corporation, Louisiana Muskrat Ranch, Inc., whose president, not surprisingly, was John R. Perez.[44]

As the 1926–1927 muskrat season approached, there was considerable confusion over who had the right to trap what land. Attorneys for the trappers held that John R. Perez's purchase of the land, though voiding the eight-year Michel lease, did not affect trapping privileges in the coming season because they had been agreed to in a lease signed with John R. himself before anyone had heard of J. Walter Michel. The Perez interests, however, argued that the terms of the Michel lease were still valid pending a supreme court decision. Louisiana Muskrat Ranch, Inc., which now owned the Michel lease, sought to exercise it and began moving in outside trappers to displace the locals who had refused to pay again for rights under a contract voided by a court of law. The marshmen represented by Livaudais were so confident that Judge Boatner's decision in their favor would be affirmed by the high court that they began to stake off trapping territory and to prepare for the season. John Perez filed suit in federal court—in the person of his Delaware corporation— for an injunction to prohibit the association trappers from trespassing on his land. Meanwhile, some of his company employees went about destroying camps belonging to the locals. One trapper swore that he had seen a man he recognized as a deputy sheriff, accompanied by a group of strangers, knocking down several camps with axes. The trapper was told that his own cabin would be next if he did not take it down himself. The Perezes claimed that Livaudais and Manuel Molero were stirring up the locals and encouraging them to trespass and, presumably, to poach.[45]

On November 2, 1926, the state supreme court reversed Judge Boatner and upheld the validity of the Michel lease. The case was decided not on its merits, but on a technicality. The court ruled that, although the Perez board of directors was not legally constituted, it was the de facto governing body of the association and that, being so, it had the authority to dismiss any suit filed on the association's behalf. The justices admitted that the case presented some "unusual features," especially since the board was appealing a judgment rendered in favor of the corporation it was supposed to represent. Nonetheless, the court ruled, the board, not the association membership, was the true plaintiff and a plaintiff had the right to withdraw his own suit at any time—even if it was someone else's to begin with. The Perezes also won their case in federal district court when the judge issued an injunction prohibiting trappers belonging to the Livaudais-Molero faction from trespassing on lands controlled by Louisiana Muskrat Ranch, Inc.[46]

When John R. Perez had first announced his purchase of the trapping lands, he had told the newspapers that his policy would be to give first refusal on subleases to Plaquemines and St. Bernard trappers. However, he said, if these men did not wish to avail themselves of this advantage—he might have added, on his own terms—the lands would be leased to outsiders. He soon found that not many locals were willing to play ball. The St. Bernard trappers were angry and armed, and it began to look as though the Perezes' marsh was going to go untrapped this season. Leander journeyed to Orange, Texas, and Cameron Parish to recruit trappers and guards. More than two dozen gunmen were brought in; some were given commissions as conservation agents, others as deputy sheriffs. When news reached St. Bernard that Perez was out of state hiring muscle, it did nothing to calm the already seething indignation among the trappers. The Louisiana Muskrat Ranch began constructing camps in the swamps, and a number of private fishing cabins were bought to serve as trapping outposts. The Perezes planned to systemize muskrat trapping throughout the lower delta. The trappers, traditionally free and independent minded, would now be required to remain in their camps all season and to report on their catches daily. Trapping would be on a fifty-fifty basis, and each trapper would be charged by the company one dollar a day for his board and keep and would be penalized five dollars for any day he was unable to work. These conditions drove the Plaquemines Parish trappers, previously loyal to the Perez cousins, into the ranks of the discontented. Association members who sought to exercise the trapping rights they had already paid for were chased off by company guards. Tempers grew short, and an ugly mood descended upon the local muskratting communities. Sporadic violence broke out. Amid rumors that public order in the delta was rapidly deteriorating into outlawry, Leander Perez met reporters and scoffed at the idea of a trappers' war. If there were a trappers' war, he said, he would be its most popular target, but as it was he went about day and night quite safely. Everything in St. Bernard, he said, was peaceful.[47]

However, even before the supreme court decision, the fear of violence and assassination seems to have been uppermost in the minds of Perez and his political allies. These fears were certainly not groundless. The trappers were a tough and simple lot, who, lacking the lawyers' glib tongues and talent for obfuscation, tended to express themselves directly and brutally. In the weeks before the season opened, a wave of violence swept the delta, leaving acres of prairie burnt over, several houses—including that of Sheriff L. A. Meraux—in rubble and ashes, one man dead, and several injured. The Perez courthouse ring was quick to attribute it all to the unruly trappers, though some violence was undoubtedly the work of rumrunners, another roguish element of delta society. The dead man was Robert Brehedt, an elderly fisherman from Shell Beach known in the community as the "Old Dutchman," whose body was fished out of the brackish waters of Lake Borgne. Two autopsies failed to produce any evidence of foul play, and it was theorized that he had simply fallen from his boat and drowned. Suddenly, however, the case was reopened by District Attorney Leander Perez and Sheriff Meraux. Two trappers, Vito Molero and Rufino Guerra, were charged with Brehedt's murder. Molero, a cousin of Brooks Molero, charged that Meraux was persecuting him because he was a political opponent. Both trappers denied any knowledge of the killing, but Meraux announced that he had full confessions. The sheriff also declared that he was about to make some arrests in the recent arson cases. Several trappers were subsequently hauled in and held in-communicado. The New Orleans *States* noted that all those arrested for murder or arson during this period were political foes of the Meraux-Perez clique. Nothing much ever came of the Old Dutchman case. If, in fact, he did not meet his end by accident, his death was much more likely to have been the work of bootleggers than of trappers. The night before he died, Brehedt had rented his motor launch to Prohibition agents, who had used it to capture the booze-laden *Miss Shell Beach.* [48]

While the rounding up and jailing of Perez opponents continued apace, events moved inexorably toward a dramatic conclusion. By the week preceding the opening of the season on November 20, ill feeling had grown to a fever pitch, and more cases of arson and assault were reported. On Sunday, November 14, some trappers belonging to the Molero-Livaudais faction went to the Perez camp to complain about pelts being taken prematurely by the imported hirelings, but they were turned away by armed guards. The following evening a large group of angry muskratters held a war council at Delacroix Island, the center of trapper opposition, and decided to attempt a negotiated peace with the company guards but to keep the guns loaded just in case. [49]

Most of the outsiders who signed on to trap for the Perezes probably had no idea that they were being used to squeeze out the local independents or that their lives might be in danger because of it. One such was Cutoff Cherami of Houma, in the south Louisiana bayou country, who along with thirteen friends had been induced to come by promises of excellent trapping and good prices for the pelts. On the same evening that the Molero trappers were holding their meeting, Cherami, his friends, and his oyster lugger *Dolores* were suddenly drafted into the trappers' war. About 11 P.M. a small motorboat full of heavily armed strangers tied up to Cherami's launch at Camp Mandeville, one of the Perez trapping stations. The men in the boat had apparently been drinking. Their leader, who wore a deputy's badge, identified himself as Captain J. H. Asher. A former Texas Ranger from Dallas who had been hired by the Perezes as a guard, he told Cherami that he and his companions were going to Delacroix Island to "make Spanish soup" out of the trappers there and were commandeering his boat for that purpose. When Cutoff protested, he was told that Asher was the law and that he had to obey him. The raiding party left in the *Dolores* about thirty minutes later. Young Edward Marlbrough, one of Cutoff's crewmen, was conscripted to handle the engine. "Captain Asher told me the same thing about him being the law and I had to obey it," he declared later. "Well, I didn't want to go but when he put it that way I went; I had to. He told me there would be no trouble; everything would be all right."[50]

During the night, about four hundred armed trappers had gathered at Delacroix Island. At sunrise, Tuesday, November 16, a number of them were watching vigilantly along the levee, expecting some action from the Perez forces but not knowing what. About eight o'clock, the *Dolores* came chugging into view bristling with rifles and shotguns manned by deputies with set jaws and narrowed eyes. The helm was flanked by two mounted machine guns. The trappers hoisted a flag of truce. Aboard the lugger, Marlbrough spotted the white flag on the levee and pointed it out to Asher. "Don't stop," he was told. "We'll leave 'em have it when we get there."[51]

No one knows who fired the first shot, but the crisp November air soon was filled with lead. One of the machine guns was manned by thirty-year-old Samuel Gowland, the former "marrying justice of the peace of Arabi," impeached for hijacking an illicit liquor shipment back in 1923. Gowland opened fire and was immediately shot dead by the trappers. The coroner later found seventeen bullet holes in his badly torn body. Hearing the shots, hundreds of trappers came running to the levee with their weapons. When Gowland fell, Marlbrough tried to man the second machine gun mounted on the other side of the wheel. He pulled the cover off but could not get the weapon to range properly, and the bullets popped the still waters of the bayou far short of the bank. In panic, he raised his arms in surrender and was hit in the head, the back, and the left hand. "I'll tell you the truth," he told newsmen later from his hospital bed, "I don't know who fired the first shots. It wasn't any of my fight and I don't know anything about it, except about a million shots were fired and three of 'em had to hit me; that's my luck, and as soon as I get out of this hospital I'm going back to Houma."[52]

Its pilot seriously wounded, its gas tank punctured, and its hull riddled with bullet holes, the *Dolores* began to take water and to drift out of control, finally beaching on a sandbar on the opposite side of the bayou. The fusillade from the levee continued unabated. Finally, the company guards, most of whom had been shot at least once, were forced to jump into the chilly waters and swim for their lives—directly into the withering fire. When they came ashore, they were surrounded by enraged trappers, who beat them with gun butts and threatened to kill them. Captain Asher, dropping his gun belt, pleaded for the lives of his men. After extracting signed statements from them that they, not the trappers, had fired the first shots, the marshmen dispatched a large automobile to take them to a New Orleans hospital. The dictated confessions collected from the company raiding party showed the singleness of purpose, if not the literary brilliance, of the defenders of Delacroix Island:

> Judge Perez sent us here to protect his estates and shoot to kill, but my men fired first on the men on the island. We fired with our machine gun first.
>
> . . . .
>
> Judge Perez sent us here with guns to protect his estate and said shoot to kill.
>
> . . . .
>
> Judge Perez sent us here with machine gun. We acknowledge that he sent us here to murder.

Most of the men from the lugger quickly repudiated the statements once they were safely away. When Cutoff Cherami learned of the battle and the fate of the *Dolores,* he and his friends headed for home. They were to have plenty of company.[53]

The trappers at Delacroix Island dug in and waited for retaliation. According to reports, the place looked like the German army had been through it. Lines of bullet holes made by the machine gun slashed the fronts of houses and outbuildings along the waterfront. Gowland's riddled body still lay on the deck of the boat at midafternoon. Inside the cabin were found a machine gun—its mate had apparently been dropped overboard—a Colt .45 automatic pistol, three repeating rifles, three double-barreled shotguns, one automatic shotgun, a .45-caliber revolver, a huge stock of ammunition, and three large folding knives. As word of the violent confrontation spread through the swamps, muskratters picked up their shotguns and headed for the island. By boat and by car they came. By nightfall, trappers were confidently predicting that they would have a thousand armed men to fight the company guards and sheriff's deputies should they dare to attack. All roads leading into the village were under trapper guard. Women and children were evacuated "from the danger zone" to the safety of New Orleans and surrounding communities. Still, spokesmen for the trappers insisted that this was not an indiscriminate rebellion against public authority. "If the Perez men come to get us," one said, "there will be trouble. But if the governor sends militia, we will lay down our arms and submit." Others stated emphatically that they would respect any law but "Meraux law."[54]

By the same afternoon, Sheriff L. A. Meraux had already completed his investigation of the shoot-out. He announced that there were four hundred suspects and that he had warrants to arrest them all. The only problem was that he, Perez, and his deputies did not dare to go anywhere near Delacroix Island. Instead, they stretched a rope across the road at the parish line and searched all cars bound for New Orleans. Meanwhile, with local law enforcement paralyzed, the delta trappers ran wild. Down in Plaquemines, two hundred former members of the association invaded the swamp, forcing outsiders to leave. James Wilkinson, an attorney who had worked with Oliver Livaudais on the trappers' case, happened to be on a bus going from Pointe a la Hache to New Orleans the day of the *Dolores* incident. All along the road, he said, imported muskratters were climbing aboard empty-handed, in a hurry to get clear of the delta. "We heard the guns shooting," one said, "and about fifty of us came out." Company guards were chased down, disarmed, and expelled from the marsh. Many did not wait to be told but hurriedly abandoned their camps, leaving firearms, ammunition, traps, and provisions behind. A group of local men moved on Leander Perez's Plaquemines home intent upon lynching him, but the Judge, forewarned, managed to escape with his family across the Mississippi in a rowboat.[55]

By Wednesday morning, the siege atmosphere at Delacroix Island had begun to relax. As the thrill of open rebellion wore off, the trappers went home and hung up their weapons. Women and children began to return. All of this was happening unbeknownst to Perez and Sheriff Meraux, who were desperately appealing for outside intervention. When Meraux sought federal aid, he was told by U.S. Marshal Victor Loisel to handle the situation himself. "I'm not going to appoint a crowd of special deputies to police St. Bernard parish," Loisel said. "It's not the business of the marshal to guard every muskrat catcher in the country." Perez had no better luck when he approached the New Orleans police superintendent for help. Finally, Meraux asked Governor Oramel H. Simpson to declare martial law and send in state troops. Simpson, an Old Regular and therefore a factional opponent of Perez and Meraux, was intrigued by descriptions of what was happening in St. Bernard. He decided to take a personal look at the town the sheriff of the parish was afraid to enter. The defenses had already come down by the time the governor reached Delacroix Island Wednesday. The *Dolores* was still tied up at the village store, but Gowland's body had finally been removed by the coroner. Simpson and two aides drove through the wet streets of the town, stopping in front of an establishment where a number of trappers had gathered because of the rain. No one recognized the governor, and he poked about the building unchallenged, opening doors and checking rooms. He found no firearms or evidence of any kind of the previous day's battle. The town was quiet, almost abandoned. Returning from his inspection, Simpson wrote Meraux a scathing letter, in which he all but accused the sheriff of cowardice and hysteria in failing to perform his duty and refused even to consider a request for military aid.[56]

No indictments were ever returned in the shooting of Gowland and the other men. Shortly after the battle, John R. Perez sold the Phillips and Swift lands to Manuel Molero, as purchaser for the local muskratters, for $800,000. Considering what he had spent to buy the empire, erect trapping camps, and pay for his original lease, John R. lost from $30,000 to $40,000 on the deal. However, he recouped some of his losses and possibly even made a profit by keeping the money that individual trappers had paid him for 1926–1927 trapping rights, even though those rights had subsequently become worthless. One of the conditions of the purchase was that both sides would discontinue all litigation. The trappers undertook to pay for the land by pledging a certain percentage of each year's catch until the obligation was retired. Oliver Livaudais announced that a new trappers' association, including trappers from both St. Bernard and Plaquemines, was being formed.[57]

Just as had been predicted, the muskrat catch for the season that opened November 20, 1926, was a big one, but the trappers' felicity was to be short-lived. When the Great Depression hit in the early thirties, the bottom fell out of the fur market. The marshmen found it harder and harder to make the payments on the lands they had bought. The independent trappers disappeared, to be replaced by company debt slaves. The muskrat population of the swamp was severely reduced by poachers. One observer, noting that he found trappers in the marsh who were literally starving, concluded that they were "little better off than the animals they hunt." Leander Perez, however, had moved on to bigger and better things: oil was discovered in Plaquemines Parish in 1928.[58]

An interesting footnote to the trappers' war was the impeachment of District Judge J. Claude Meraux, who was accused of showing favoritism to the Perez cousins in the trapping cases that came before his court and in two other civil cases. Perez served as one of Meraux's defense attorneys and also testified for more than two hours in behalf of his friend. The trial accomplished little except to air the proverbial dirty linen of lower delta politics. The prosecuting attorneys, maintaining that gambling was rampant in the lower delta, pointed out that the defendant's brother, Sheriff L. A. Meraux, was under federal indictment for conspiracy to violate the national Prohibition laws. Sheriff Meraux testified that with his small salary and staff he could not patrol the marsh, the Gulf, and the highways and, at the same time, assist federal officers; he even had to pay two deputies out of his own salary. "You have to have money to be sheriff of St. Bernard," he concluded, "or you have to rob a whole lot."[59]

For his own part, Judge Meraux testified that any mistakes he had made were due to honest poor judgment rather than malicious intent. St. Bernard Chief Deputy Dutch Rowley testified that he, not

Judge Meraux, had been responsible for releasing prisoners before their terms were up. The trial lasted six days, but the state supreme court took only ten minutes to acquit Meraux unanimously. After the verdict, the defendant was carried in triumph from the courtroom by his jubilant friends. Perez's alliance with the Meraux brothers of St. Bernard and his personal hold on Plaquemines remained intact, despite the setback of his losing the trappers' war.[60]

FOUR

The Judge and the Kingfish

The 1930s were relatively quiet in Plaquemines Parish after the spectacular bootlegging and trapping wars of the twenties. Local politics became overshadowed by Huey Long's flamboyant state machine and the national depression, and Perez's domination of Plaquemines met only token resistance. It was said that, before official police jury meetings, the jurors would meet informally with the Judge, who would tell them what he wanted done; they then would convene formally and rubber-stamp the resolutions dictated by Perez. "There's hardly ever a dissenting vote," Leander explained. "We work together 100 per cent."[1]

In 1924 Perez had met a rising young politician named Huey Long. Like Leander, Huey had struggled to eke out a subsistence living from his meager law practice before entering politics as a reformer. In 1918, at the age of twenty-four, Long had been elected to the Railroad Commission from his north Louisiana district, just a year before Perez had been appointed interim judge of his judicial district. Both men had campaigned for gubernatorial candidate John M. Parker in 1919, but following Parker's election Long had broken with him for compromising on Huey's pet project, a pipeline regulation bill intended to harness Standard Oil. The feud had become so heated that in 1921 Parker had sued Long for criminal libel.[2]

In 1923, at the tender age of thirty, Long audaciously entered the gubernatorial race against two better-known, better-financed, and more experienced rivals, Hewitt Bouanchaud and Henry L. Fuqua. Bouanchaud, a short, spare, French-speaking attorney from the small south Louisiana town of New Roads, was Parker's lieutenant governor and his handpicked successor. With Parker's blessing and New Regular support, he made abolition of the Ku Klux Klan in Louisiana the principal issue in his campaign. His insurmountable handicap was that he was a Catholic and stood to gain few votes in fundamentalist Protestant north Louisiana, where the Klan was strong and anti-Catholic sentiment was widespread. Fuqua, the paunchy and balding former president of a Baton Rouge hardware company, had been appointed head of the state penitentiary at Angola by Governor Ruffin G. Pleasant and reappointed by Governor Parker. Fuqua enjoyed the support of the New Orleans Old Regulars and many powerful rural leaders. A Protestant, he too denounced the Klan, but less vociferously than Bouanchaud. Long characterized both Fuqua and Bouanchaud as Parker henchmen, who had been put into the race to defeat the only true champion of the people—himself. He sought New Regular support, but the New Regulars decided to back a candidate who would take a stronger stand against the Klan. Long, who as governor was to adorn the campus of Louisiana State University with numerous pretentious buildings, denounced Parker in the 1923 campaign for moving LSU from its old campus to a new agricultural plant designed to teach newfangled methods of farming. During the campaign, Huey, like Leander, was accused of being somewhat less than patriotic during the First World War. Bouanchaud, carrying both St. Bernard and Plaquemines, led the first primary but lost the runoff to Fuqua, who picked up most of Long's north Louisiana support. Although polling only thirty-nine votes in Plaquemines, Huey ran surprisingly strong in most rural parishes.[3]

From the minute he was eliminated in the first primary in 1923, Long became a candidate for governor in 1927. This time he was better known, better organized, and better financed. One of Long's two major opponents also entered the fray early; Governor Simpson became a candidate practically from the day he succeeded Fuqua, who had died in office in 1926. Unimaginative and moderately conservative, Simpson had few friends or backers outside his own immediate area of New Orleans and lacked even the support of his hometown Old Regulars. The great flood of 1927, in which the Mississippi inundated nearly two million acres in Louisiana and other states, thrust into prominence and into the gubernatorial contest the chairman of the U.S. House of Representatives Committee on Flood Control, Riley Joe Wilson. A stocky, rugged person of medium height, Wilson was a self-made man who had overcome an impoverished childhood to become successively a district attorney, a state judge, a state legislator, and finally a congressman in 1914. He sincerely echoed the standpat philosophy of the Old Regulars, who endorsed him for governor. Long, with the support of the New Regulars and also the best-financed campaign of any of the candidates, amassed a huge first-primary lead over his principal rivals. Because Wilson barely edged Simpson to qualify for the runoff, the Old Regulars decided not to back him in a hopelessly uphill second primary, and he withdrew from the race. Apparently Perez did not take a firm stand in the primary, because Plaquemines split between Simpson and Long, with Simpson carrying the parish, and St. Bernard went for Long. Wilson received only twenty-nine votes in Plaquemines and twenty-eight in St. Bernard.[4]

Long possessed an uncanny talent for luring talented men to his side. Allen Ellender, who had fought him bitterly in 1927, became one of his staunchest supporters by the following year.[5] Perez also converted shortly after Long's election. It was a symbiotic relationship: Huey got a talented lawyer and a small number of guaranteed votes; Leander got a voice in public appointments and in the awarding of state contracts and the prestige that came from identification as a member of Long's inner council. He publicly praised Long's virtues and privately admitted his faults. He even considered the governor a physical coward because of his fear of being shot.

A comparison of the two men indicates some striking similarities, as well as some differences. At this time, Perez's economic views were not fully formed, and Long's were appealingly obscure. Both were brilliant lawyers and indefatigable workers who created authoritarian empires; both believed in paternalistic public works programs and would stop at nothing to achieve their ends; both were ambitious, but their aspirations were divergently channeled. Long wanted to be president. Perez, on the other hand, did not even desire a statewide elective office, although he no doubt could have been elected to such a position with Huey's help. He was content with tighter control over a small area; Long was a more flexible politician with broader appeal. Huey operated in the limelight; Leander, in the backrooms. Huey never resorted to race-baiting, and Leander, simply because it was then assumed that blacks had no role to play in government, was not the outspoken racist that he later became. Long was anathema to the oil industry, but Perez was its partisan champion. Huey depicted himself as the champion of the "little man," but Leander preferred the company of right-wing millionaires. Both were men of action: Perez was better educated, but neither man was well read. Long, like Perez, pursued opponents to the grave, but both men at times concluded unlikely alliances. Each used the tactic of the undated resignation with their political appointees. Huey was the most powerful liberal politician and Perez the most powerful reactionary politician that twentieth-century Louisiana has produced, yet during the 1930s the two were firm allies. Leander doubtless has reservations about Huey's Share the Wealth program, but he never opposed Long openly. Long, like Perez sometimes a puritan, sent the National Guard to raid gambling houses in Jefferson and St. Bernard parishes, but he never touched Plaquemines. Long's career was brief and dramatic; Perez remained firmly entrenched in his local power until his death, nearly thirty-five years after Long's assassination. Harvey Peltier, a Longite state legislator who knew both men intimately, comments, "In my opinion Huey Long was the smartest man that I met during my lifetime (and I'm now seventy-two years old and I've met a lot of people), and Leander Perez was second."[6]

In the first session of the state legislature under his administration, Long pushed through bills providing for cheap natural gas for New Orleans, a bond issue to underwrite highway construction, free textbooks for the state's school children financed by an increased severance tax on natural resources, and improvements in state hospitals funded by an additional levy on the manufacture of carbon black. The increased severance tax cleared the federal courts but was temporarily nullified by the U.S. Supreme Court. Unalarmed, Long summoned a special session of the legislature to provide a five-cent-per-barrel tax on refined oil and to tend to other matters that he mysteriously did not specify.[7] Feverish opposition to the oil tax developed at the session, which was to meet from March 18 to April 6, 1929. Huey's opponents, who had been seeking an opportunity to impeach him, beat down a Long attempt to suddenly adjourn the House and launched impeachment proceedings.

Perez, who hitherto had not been close to Long, rushed to Baton Rouge to offer his services. At that time the Judge was relatively unknown outside his own bailiwick, and he saw the impeachment as an opportunity to establish a statewide reputation and to cement a friendship with the governor. Huey was grateful for help from any quarter. Stunned and helpless at the outset of the impeachment proceedings, he moped around his Baton Rouge hotel for days in a depressed state. Perez helped to bolster his sagging ego and convince him that he could win. Once activated, Long became a whirlwind. He papered the state with truckloads of circulars blaming his impeachment on Standard Oil and took to the stump in his own defense. Millionaire Long partisan Robert Maestri helped finance the counterattack. The circular campaign alone cost at least $40,000.[8]

An eight-man battery of lawyers, including Perez, went to work to save the governor. Setting himself up in Long's law library in the Louisiana National Bank Building, Leander began his legal research. Nightly strategy sessions were held in the governor's suite in the Heidelberg Hotel. Long himself presided over these meetings, but Perez was the most active attorney. Leander was considered the best political tactician and John H. Overton the best lawyer on the defense team.[9]

Huey's chances looked dismal at the outset. Only six legislators attended the first strategy meeting organized by Long's advisers. The number gradually increased as the Long defense gained momentum. Perez busied himself writing legal memoranda for Allen Ellender and Harvey Peltier, Huey's House floor leaders, and also made personal contacts in Huey's behalf. He collected the proceedings and decisions of major impeachment cases from other states, as well as articles of the Louisiana constitutions dealing with impeachment going as far back as 1812. The material in Perez's file suggests that he purposefully worked out a strategy of delay, raising legal technicalities to slow the House debate. If the debate could be prolonged past April 6, the date set for adjournment, the charges considered would be voted by an illegally convened body. After that date, Perez explained, "the legislature would stop being a lawmaking body and become just a crowd of men."[10] Peltier discovered an old statute that permitted the governor's defenders to cross-examine witnesses appearing before the House. Upon learning of the statute, Huey became so excited that he locked Peltier in a hotel room for several days because he feared Peltier might tell someone else about it.[11]

During the time-consuming debate, Representative George Delesdernier of Plaquemines delivered a speech entitled "The Cross of Wood and with [sic] Shackles of Paper," in which he compared the impeachment of Long to the crucifixion of Christ. When the opposition realized the drift of his remarks, cries of blasphemy arose, but the Plaquemines representative droned on. At the conclusion of his speech, Delesdernier, no doubt carried away by his own eloquence, fainted and collapsed on the floor. He lay there until the vote was taken to convict Huey on the first charge and was then carried away by friends. It is likely that Delesdernier's speech was composed by someone else, because it was included in Huey's first antiimpeachment circular before being delivered in the House.[12]

Despite the delaying tactics, the House managed to vote on one charge before April 6. This charge alleged that Long had tried to blackmail Douglas Manship, the publisher of the Baton Rouge *State-Times* and *Morning Advocate,* who had published a series of front-page editorials denouncing the proposed oil tax. Huey had informed Manship that, unless his editorials were made more moderate, he would publicize the fact that the publisher's brother was a patient at the state mental institution at Jackson. The threat had the opposite effect; Manship took the offensive with a front-page editorial entitled, "This, Gentlemen, Is the Way Your Governor Fights." The Manship allegation was the weakest of the eight charges eventually returned against Huey by the House, but was the only one that actually came to a vote in the Senate.[13]

The Senate trial opened with a general demurrer against the second through the eighth charges. John Overton argued that these should not be considered because they had been voted on after the eighteen-day special session had expired. The next morning the

Senate voted twenty to nineteen against sustaining the demurrer. It was actually a victory for Huey, because a two-thirds vote was needed for conviction. Following the vote, Perez argued an exception to the Manship allegation, emphasizing that the incident was a personal, not an official, affair. He contended that the commitment of the publisher's brother was a matter of public record and that Huey had violated no state law in publicizing it. The Senate voted twenty-one to eight to sustain the Perez exception and thus dismissed the Manship charge. The only charge that the Long forces admitted was legal had been thrown out.[14]

Huey had an even better reason to feel confident at this point. He had, locked in a bank vault, a round robin signed by fifteen state senators, declaring that they would not vote to convict because the charges were legally faulty and had been voted on after the date set for the adjournment of the House. Thus, with the votes of more than one-third of the Senate assured, Huey's acquittal was guaranteed regardless of the evidence presented. When the Manship charge was defeated, the phrase declaring the charges legally faulty became unnecessary, and a condensed version of the round robin was drafted and the original destroyed. The new version was signed by the same fifteen senators. On May 16, Philip Gilbert presented the document to the secretary of the Senate. Stunned, the anti-Long forces now realized that it would be futile to continue the case, and they allowed the Senate to adjourn *sine die*. [15]

The signers of the round robin and Huey's attorneys were well rewarded for their loyalty. Some of the signers became judges; others received lucrative legal fees and state public works projects for their constituents. Among the attorneys, Overton and Ellender were elected to the U.S. Senate. Perez was offered an appointment to the Louisiana Court of Appeal for the district including Plaquemines Parish, but he declined. As a judge, he would have been unable to practice law or take the lead publicly in partisan politics. But he continued to perform other legal duties for Long and was designated to represent several Long appointees in intrusion-into-office suits against incumbents who had refused to yield their offices.[16]

Perez also took advantage of Huey's friendship in ways that would help his parish. After the discovery of oil in Plaquemines in 1928, he had realized that under the vast and lonely expanses of swamp lay fortunes in oil, sulphur, and natural gas. Much of this mineral wealth was on lands owned by the levee boards, which had originally been created by the state to construct and maintain levees in flood-prone districts. There were only sixteen levee board districts in the entire state, and six of them were wholly or partially within low-lying Plaquemines Parish. By the 1930s the boards were already anachronistic, because the U.S. Corps of Engineers had taken over most of the levee work. But, in the days when flood protection had been handled locally, the state had deeded thousands of acres of swampland to the levee districts. The boards, whose members were appointed by the governor, were authorized to lease the land to finance flood control. The assignment of the lands meant little at the time because they were considered practically worthless. Presumably, any revenues above those needed to maintain levees would be returned to the state.[17]

In 1932 Perez pushed through the legislature a constitutional amendment permitting a police jury to assume the bonded indebtedness of any levee district located wholly within its parish. The police jury would also receive the assets of the levee district as long as it remained in debt. Initially this seemed a philanthropic gesture, since the levee boards were chronically in the red, and for the first few years the indebtedness was indeed greater than the revenue. But soon mineral royalties began to pour in, making Plaquemines the richest rural parish in the state. Although the new revenues were more than enough to retire the deficits, Perez devised a plan by which the levee boards were intentionally kept in debt by the periodic levying of new bond issues. The levee board commissioners did not object, because they had been appointed by a governor allied with the Plaquemines boss. Perez's utilization of the riches beneath state lands was also facilitated by friends in the State Land Office. He had the state apply for federal swamplands, which in turn were granted to the local levee boards. Some of the mineral wealth was under school board property, which Perez could easily exploit through his control of the parish school board. He used the bonanza from royalties to implement an impressive program of public works and to increase the parish payroll. Between 1932 and 1950, Perez was able to halve the taxes paid by the ordinary citizen.[18]

In 1938 he obtained more revenue for his parish by masterminding the passage of Act 80, which created a state royalty road fund. This law dedicated 10 percent of the royalties from mineral production on state-owned lands to the parish from which the minerals were extracted. The money was disbursed by the state Highway Commission for specific road construction projects requested by the parish. Later, use of this fund was broadened to include bridges, tunnels, and the purchase and operation of ferries. By the 1960s more than $2,000,000 per year was being deposited to the credit of Plaquemines Parish, which received so much money from the royalty road fund that it agreed to share some of its bounty with St. Bernard.[19]

Perez also attempted to personally cash in on his friendship with Long. Shortly after helping the governor escape impeachment, he was retained by Harry Bovay, a Memphis financier, to obtain a state franchise for a bridge across the Mississippi River at Baton Rouge. Perez was to receive $150,000 or one-third of the stock in Bovay's bridge company. His principal recommendation as an attorney was his potential influence with Huey Long. Bovay hoped to turn a large profit by erecting the $10,000,000 structure as a toll bridge, which would become free in twenty-five years. Since the Long administration was committed to a program of free bridges, Leander's efforts to secure the franchise through the Highway Commission chairman, O. K. Allen, were unsuccessful. A number of companies had been competing for this franchise, and two more attempts in the 1930s to gain approval for a toll bridge also failed. Finally, a project for a combination highway and railroad span was approved by the administration of Governor Richard Leche in 1936 and was completed in 1940 as a free bridge.[20]

The Judge was always happy to return the favors of his state allies. In 1930 Huey Long decided to run for the U.S. Senate while still governor, although he promised that he would not take his seat until his term as governor expired two years later. In the senatorial election, Plaquemines returned the lopsided total of 1,913 votes for Long to 131 for his aged, goateed opponent, Joseph E. Ransdell.[21]

Huey would have been elected senator regardless of this reassuring display of "popular" support in Plaquemines. But the vote of Plaquemines and St. Bernard did alter the outcome of the election for the U.S. House of Representatives seat from the First Congressional District. The race pitted Joachim O. Fernandez—known as "Bathtub Joe" because he got rid of unwanted callers by using the excuse that he was taking a bath—against James O'Connor. O'Connor had the support of the New Orleans Old Regular machine of Mayor T. Semmes Walmsley, and Fernandez had the backing of the Long apparatus. Early returns from the Orleans wards indicated that O'Connor had been elected with 23,030 votes to 19,944 for Fernandez. O'Connor was rejoicing prematurely when he was told the totals from the lower parishes. Fernandez received 3,652 votes in St. Bernard to 295 votes for O'Connor. In Plaquemines the total was 1,873 to O'Connor's 160. O'Connor and the general public took for granted that the totals from the delta parishes were fraudulent, and he announced that he would contest the results in court. But, immediately following the election, the Long-Walmsley machines merged. O'Connor dropped his protest and was appointed an assistant attorney general for the state.[22]

Three years later Earl Long, who had broken with his brother, testified about the Fernandez-O'Connor election before a U.S. Senate committee. He swore that he had been in Huey's room in the Roosevelt Hotel in New Orleans around noon the day following the election. Huey was stretched out on his bed looking at the St. Bernard tally sheets and discussing the number of votes O'Connor should be allowed to have.

"They agreed to let him have 250 votes," Earl testified.

One of the Senators exclaimed: "They couldn't fix the tally sheets there."

"You don't know St. Bernard," Earl answered.

"Did you hear Huey telephoning anybody?"

"Yes, something about Plaquemines parish."

Huey interrupted at this point: "There isn't a telephone in the parish," he protested.

"I said about Plaquemines parish," Earl continued. "I can fix you on that—the Plaquemines leader is supposed to live in the parish but doesn't. He lives here (in New Orleans). . . .

"He (Huey) wanted everything fixed so the election would stand a contest if one was brought. He seemed to be afraid of St. Bernard and if anything happened he wanted the results bullet-proofed with Plaquemines."[23]

In the January, 1932, gubernatorial primary, St. Bernard turned in an even more suspicious total. The count was 3,152 votes for Long-machine favorite O. K. Allen and 0 for four opponents. A unanimous vote was recorded for all seven members of the Allen ticket. Those who protested that they had voted for the opposition were told that they must have placed their ballots in the wrong box.[24]

About two months before the senatorial primary of 1932, the state legislature had killed a bill providing for specific penalties for anyone convicted of fraudulent election practices; thus, in Louisiana, fixing elections became a crime for which there was no punishment. The Senate race pitted incumbent Edwin S. Broussard against John Overton, who ran with the support of the Long-Walmsley machine. Overton carried Plaquemines with 2,137 votes to 189 for Broussard, and in neighboring St. Bernard Overton received 3,080 votes to only 15 for Broussard. In the congressional election held concurrently, St. Bernard returned an even more lopsided total. Bathtub Joe Fernandez received 3,085 votes to only 6 for his opponent, Augustus G. Williams. The 1930 census showed that there were only 2,310 white men and women above the age of twenty in St. Bernard.[25]

For governor in 1936 Perez backed the Long protégé Richard Leche, who would later go to federal prison for using the mails to defraud. Leche polled almost 98 percent of the votes in Plaquemines and slightly more than 98 percent of the votes in St. Bernard. In a third of the Plaquemines precincts not a single vote was cast against him. The ultimate in political unanimity came in 1938, when the electorate in St. Bernard and Plaquemines voted on certain amendments to the state constitution. Plaquemines voted 5,361 to 3 in favor of the amendments. In St. Bernard absolutely no votes were recorded against any of the amendments, although 3,806 persons reportedly went to the polls.[26]

Judge Perez also flexed his political muscles in local elections. Perez-Meraux candidates, from the top to the bottom of the ticket, consistently ground out victories in all local contests. In 1935, eleven St. Bernard candidates who tried to run against the Perez-Meraux machine were disqualified by the parish Democratic executive committee. The anti-Perez candidates carried their appeal all the way to the state supreme court but lost on a technicality. Leander himself was unopposed in his bid for a second term as district attorney in 1930, but in 1936 he received nominal opposition from Neil A. Armstrong, Jr. The incumbent carried Plaquemines by a vote of 4,092 to 75 and St. Bernard by a vote of 3,499 to 19.[27]

In 1938 the Judge lost a valuable ally when Sheriff Meraux died. There seemed to be no single leader capable of replacing Meraux in St. Bernard. Soon after the sheriff's death the St. Bernard Democratic Organization, which included nearly every voter in the parish, elected Judge J. Claude Meraux to succeed his late brother as factional chief. Dutch Rowley, who had served as chief deputy sheriff for fourteen years, was chosen sheriff without opposition. Both J. Claude Meraux and Rowley showed an independence in their new roles that disconcerted Perez. Within a year of Sheriff Meraux's death, they were quarreling with the Judge, and the quiescent period of delta politics had ended.[28]

FIVE

Small Stealing Is an Outrage

With the Long machine monopolizing Louisiana's political spotlight during the early 1930s and Perez's local machine grinding out electoral victories without serious opposition, the time was ripe for an enterprising politician to make money. After switching from judge to district attorney, Perez leaped into a frenzied and lucrative legal practice and also became involved in the oil, sulphur, banking, cattle, and real estate businesses. The machinery that poured wealth into his coffers was largely set up during the friendly state administrations from the late twenties to the late thirties. Thereafter, royalties and earnings from investments continued to increase his income. Once his wealth was established, he largely abandoned law as a money-making enterprise and devoted himself entirely to politics. In his later years his law practice included few paying clients, and Perez expended his energy arguing for state ownership of the tidelands and defending the state, Plaquemines, and other parishes against desegregation and voting suits. It was power, not money, that the Judge relished. He did not live ostentatiously and never flaunted his wealth, but, without his millions, he would never have been the political titan that he became. Money provided the leisure for politics and a potential lever for power.

Perez's total wealth has never been determined. His detractors like to inflate, and his admirers deemphasize, the extent of his fortune. Some Louisiana politicians estimate his worth to have been as high as $100,000,000, though Leander's family claims a more modest figure in the neighborhood of $300,000. But even his friends admit that he disposed of many of his assets before his death so that the succession records would not reveal how wealthy he actually was. Abundant evidence indicates that Perez was a millionaire many times over, and he probably transferred most of his holdings to his four children, who are all now millionaires.[1]

Leander's fortune was entirely self-made. When his mother died in 1944, she left only three small lots and a total estate worth slightly more than $2,000. Perez became a multimillionaire on a district attorney's salary that was never more than $7,000 annually and was less than $5,000 for much of his political career. He and his associates were extremely reluctant to discuss money matters, as *Fortune* writer Richard Austin Smith discovered. Smith commented that "Perez's normally torrential conversation has a way of drying up like a desert river at the first mention of personal finances."[2] In 1924, the year he became district attorney, Perez purchased a home at Dalcour, on the old Promised Land plantation, for $6,400, borrowing $1000 from his mother-in-law. Fifteen years later he confided to friends that he had made his first million.[3]

How did Perez become a millionaire? The answer lies in the rich mineral deposits of Plaquemines Parish. Realizing the potential of the natural resources before anyone else, the Judge moved swiftly to exploit his knowledge and position. His financial manipulations reveal a shrewd mind adept at devising complex legal stratagems.

Because most of the swampland in Plaquemines was once considered practically worthless, owners frequently neglected to pay taxes, which allowed the state to claim the land. The federal government also granted thousands of acres of swampland to the state, most of which, ignorant of its tremendous potential, the state subsequently granted to the local levee and school boards. While the swampland was being transferred to the local boards, Perez frenetically incorporated land companies to complete the final stage of the transfers. An amazing amalgam of land, realty, and oil companies operated in Plaquemines Parish, many of which had imaginative names and had been chartered in such states as Delaware, Texas, Oklahoma, Maine, Maryland, and Michigan. The operations of these companies were difficult to trace because of the out-of-state charters; to cover the trail even better, companies with the same name were often chartered in different states. Leases passed freely from company to company for nominal considerations such as one dollar or ten dollars; sometimes no monetary consideration at all was mentioned in the transfer. Some of the companies issued no stock or stock of no value, and the officers and stockholders remained anonymous. One Delaware company reported no assets at all on its tax returns except for a Delaware office rented for fifty dollars a month. Earl Long once said of Perez's Plaquemines corporations: "He's got companies down there nobody knows about."[4]

Manned by passive and cooperative associates of the Judge—relatives, friends, and parish officials—these dummy corporations possessed only one asset, a remarkable ability to obtain leases on oil land. These leases, acquired from levee boards and school boards for a nominal fee, were then subleased to oil or gas companies for a much larger fee.[5] A Plaquemines man explained to a Kansas City *Star* writer how Perez's financial manipulations worked by citing a theoretical deal. An oil company executive would tell Leander that his company wanted to lease some levee board land for drilling at ten dollars per acre. Perez would then inform him that the board would take it up at its next meeting, at which time the lease would be awarded at twenty-five cents an acre to a land company controlled by Perez. Then the oil company would lease the land from the land company for ten dollars per acre. Perez would also force the oil company to grant an overriding royalty to his company, usually $1/16$ or $1/32$ of all production, thus assuring that money would continue to pour in as long as production continued.[6]

Oil companies that refused to deal with the Judge had no chance of obtaining leases, and those that fell from favor found it impossible to operate effectively in the parish. His cooperation was necessary to obtain from the parish government the drilling and exploratory permits and the rights-of-way for pipelines and access roads. Perez demanded that industries operating in Plaquemines employ a high percentage of local people, contribute to parish projects such as parks, swimming pools, and the private school system, and lend equipment and personnel during natural disasters and the rebuilding that followed. One of Leander's chief parish officials rented boats to the oil companies. A company preferring to use its own boats often found that their fuel tanks had become clogged with sugar during the night and that, during the day, fishing boats blocked the canals leading to the oil rigs.[7]

Perez received the bulk of his income as an attorney for the land companies rather than from holding shares in them, thus avoiding both taxation on dividends and the necessity of being listed as a stockholder. Although insisting that he had no connection with the companies, he filed their tax returns and received copies of their correspondence; the offices of the dummy corporations were in the same building as his law office. Contracts were drawn up in his office, notarized by his associates, and witnessed by his secretary and the assistant district attorney. No quisling ever defected from Leander's financial empire; although there were occasional defections from his political legions, his financial partners always closed ranks. A defector would probably have incriminated himself, not to mention provoking the unrelenting wrath of Perez. Another reason for this solidarity is that the Judge was probably the only one who understood the involved process of redeeming and subleasing the valuable lands that also extended into other south Louisiana parishes.[8]

At first the local police juries and levee boards may not have realized what they were doing, but it is inconceivable that after the oil boom began they did not understand. Then, too, they were staffed with Perez partisans, who could not be elected or appointed without his favor and some of whom became indirectly involved in the subleasing schemes themselves. Perez himself was not directly connected with the actual transfers and thus was not legally accountable, but he so thoroughly mixed his public and private activities that in 1939 and 1940 his office telephone number and that of one levee board were the same. Bills for that number were paid by the levee board. When questioned about lucrative contracts obtained by his friends from the boards he dominated, Perez himself asked, "What reason would I have to object that my friends should have leases?"[9]

It is possible that Leander knew the law so well that he avoided any technical violations, but no investigation ever proceeded far enough to find out. His domination of the local courts and his friends in the state judicial system assured him of virtual immunity from criminal prosecution. The biggest danger came when an unfriendly governor sat in Baton Rouge. Perez's tensest moments came during the administration of Sam Jones (1940–1944) and during Earl Long's second elective term (1956–1960). At those times, the Judge's strategy was to tie up investigations in the courts with help from his judicial allies, while he found legal loopholes in the governor's means of attack. Injunctions were easy to obtain from the district court, and appeals took time. Leander was able to handcuff his would-be prosecutors until they went out of office. Fortunately for him, he was never faced with two successive unfriendly governors.

After he had broken with Perez, Governor Earl Long pinpointed the attempt of a Perez-dominated company to secure a lease on state land. Long said:

> In the recent regular session of the legislature they were attempting to deed 9,895 acres of levee land in the swamps of Louisiana to the Louisiana Land and Exploration Company. We got us up a bill to stop it and give it to the State. That had been going on for years. That outfit had been getting land for 8, 10, and 11 cents per acre that is worth a thousand and some of it a million an acre. Can you imagine that? When that bill got in they came and offered to compromise—some good friends of mine—if we would give them 700 acres. What do you think the Mineral Board leased that 700 acres for later? 3½ million bucks. We have got oil on it, we have got overrides, and we got royalty. We should now join in and most of them people with that Louisiana Land and Exploration Company are the *Times-Picayune* and Leander Perez buddies. Oh yeah, small stealing is an outrage, but when you get to where you can steal in millions you are a professional. You are to be honored.[10]

From time to time investigators tried to dig into Perez's finances. After *Collier's* writer Lester Velie penned a two-part article revealing some of Perez's financial manipulations, Representative Walter Ray introduced in the Mississippi legislature a resolution praising Leander and condemning Velie as a hack writer. Ray accused Velie of "half-truths which are more vicious than lies, impugning the motives, questioning the honesty and assassinating the character of Hon. Leander H. Perez." Salvador Chiapetta, a bitter local enemy of the Judge, wrote the speaker of the Mississippi House of Representatives that he had read the articles carefully and failed to find any "half-truths." Indeed, he said, there was much more that could be said. Shortly after the article appeared, Perez obtained an affidavit from the State Mineral Board stating that he had never attended a board meeting or represented anyone who did. He reportedly bought the *Collier's* issues by the truckload to prevent them from falling into the hands of Plaquemines natives.[11]

The most thorough published inquiry ever made into Perez's finances was undertaken by David Baldwin, an enterprising New Orleans *Item* reporter, who gained access to documents that had been subpoenaed by the Louisiana Crime Commission through an attorney for that body.[12] To avoid legal complications, Baldwin designated the Perez-dominated companies he discussed by magicians' names. However, the names of individuals and the figures are real.

The first was Mandrake, Inc., whose address was listed as "in care of L. H. Perez, New Orleans, Louisiana." It had been incorporated on April 7, 1926, by Ernest R. Perez, a cousin of Leander's. As of November 4, 1940, its officers were E. B. Pursglove, a relative of Perez's; C. P. Foret, another relative; and A. S. Cain, a notary in Perez's office. Foret testified before the Crime Commission that Perez kept all of the company books. When a commission member called the Plaquemines boss to ask him if he would respond to a subpoena in his capacity as the company's lawyer, Perez told him to go to hell. From 1937 through 1939 the company paid more than one-third of its income in attorney's fees, which amounted to $8,745.[13]

The Houdini Company had similar close ties to Perez. As of December 9, 1940, its president was Robert J. Lobrano, former chief deputy clerk of court in Plaquemines and a Perez partisan. Lobrano was holding three political jobs in 1940; he was a member of the Lake Borgne Levee Board, a member of the East Bank Levee Board, and a member of the Louisiana Tax Commission. He later played a major role in sulphur transactions.[14] Lobrano also personally received leases for oil on state land. On September 8, 1928, the Buras Levee Board voted to adopt a resolution granting him "a mineral lease on all of the lands which this board may own or in which it has or may have any right, title or interest in whole or in part, or to which it may be entitled under the provisions of Act No. 18 of 1894, Act No. 205 of 1910, or any amending laws of this state."[15] Lobrano paid only $500 for the lease, although Ernest Hingle, a Perez foe, later testified that the Gulf Refining Company would have paid $25,000. In 1930 Lobrano transferred the lease to Gulf in return for overriding royalties on oil and sulphur production.[16] The Houdini Company had been chartered in Delaware in 1932 and authorized to do business in Louisiana. Its first president was Jones T. Prowell of the law firm of Prowell and McBride in New Orleans. The company's business was listed as the "buying, selling, leasing and sub-leasing of land." In 1938 the company reported an income of $56,195.10, derived from sulphur royalties. Lobrano and Robert J. Chauvin, the company's secretary-treasurer, each received a salary of only $2,500 yearly for work described as "part time devoted to business." That same year the firm paid $10,000 in legal fees. In 1938 its stockholders, whose identities were a closely guarded secret, received two dividends totaling $17.50 per share on 1,000 shares of stock.[17]

Another company, Blackstone, Inc., dealt in oil leases. It showed a total income of $51,597 for the 1937–1939 period.[18]

The real name of possibly the most active company with which Perez was associated was the Delta Development Company. Perez was listed as attorney for Delta by the Louisiana Crime Commission. A Gulf executive commented, "Every oil company in the business holds leases from Delta Development. They (Perez and Delta) are pretty well synonymous; they're linked up together."[19] Delta was chartered as a Louisiana corporation in 1934. The incorporators were Chauvin and Lobrano. In 1941 this corporation dissolved, and its assets were transferred to the Delta Development Company of Delaware. The persons named in the second incorporation were only nominal parties. Chauvin remained president, O. A. Daigle became secretary, and Mrs. J. Douglas Eustis was vice-president.[20]

The case of *Richardson and Bass* v. *Orleans Levee District,* heard by the state supreme court in 1954, revealed some intriguing facts about the Delta Development Company. The case involved a dispute between the Orleans Parish Levee Board and the Grand Prairie Levee Board over oil-producing lands in Plaquemines Parish. The Orleans board claimed that the legislature had granted it the acreage in an act authorizing it to expropriate lands for the creation of the Bohemia Spillway. The Grand Prairie board refused to recognize the claim and in 1936 leased ten thousand acres of land to Delta, without bids or advertisements, for three cents per acre. The contract was witnessed by Perez's secretary. Delta subleased part of the tract to the Gulf Refining Company, which found oil and paid the company a handsome sum in royalties.[21]

The Orleans board claimed that Delta's lease was invalid for two reasons. First, the Grand Prairie board had no right to lease the land; second, Delta was a dummy corporation. Delta had paid only a nominal consideration, the Orleans board argued, and had acted in "bad legal faith." To ascertain the validity of the lease, the Orleans board attempted to learn some background information on the company itself. Robert J. Chauvin, president of Delta, refused to answer questions pertaining to employment of geologists for oil exploration, other leases acquired by the company, the negotiation of the July 20, 1936, lease, the person who served as Delta's attorney, the stock issued by Delta, or the identity of stockholders. Chauvin refused to say whether Delta had ever drilled an oil well and declined to reveal who had actually drawn up the 1936 lease. During this testimony, Leander Perez broke in to complain that the questioning was irrelevant and was delaying his lunch hour. Chauvin did testify that Delta now had offices in Room 2316 of the American Bank Building, the same building in which the Judge kept his law offices. When asked where the company had kept its records before leasing this space, Chauvin replied that he had carried them on his person. No doubt he cut an imposing figure strolling down Canal Street carrying a filing cabinet filled with oil leases. The case was eventually decided in favor of the Orleans board. After the ruling was given, apparently no one cared to pursue the intriguing question of how Delta had obtained the leases in the first place.[22] J. Ben Meyer, then a virulent opponent of Perez, but now a Perez partisan, claimed that Delta had secured a lease on thirty-five thousand acres of school board land for only five hundred dollars and within six months had made more than half a million dollars. Meyer also said that Delta and a number of other corporations controlled by Perez had never filed annual reports required by state law.[23]

As attorney for Delta, Perez's income varied proportionally with the company's. In 1937 Delta found itself in such a profitable state that it authorized the purchase of health, accident, and life insurance for its attorneys and officers. According to Louisiana tax records, in 1938 Delta paid out more than half its net income—some $89,000—in legal fees. In 1939 the company paid $76,400 in legal fees, which breaks down into $1,460 per week. Leander's income that year was $281,000. At the same time, the company's general expenses, rent, and telephone bills totaled $789, or less than $16 weekly. The 1939 state income tax returns for Delta were notarized by an office associate of Perez. The two officers listed on the return, Lobrano and Chauvin, owned only a fraction of 1 percent of the stock.[24]

On January 29, 1937, Perez accepted the position as attorney for the Creole Oil Company, a Louisiana corporation domiciled in New Orleans, although the company was not even chartered until three days later. On February 7 the Buras Levee Board leased to Creole, for three hundred dollars plus reservation of one-eighth oil royalties and fifty cents per ton on sulphur, the mineral rights to all lands possessed by the board or which it might obtain. For serving as attorney, Perez was to receive one-half of any stock dividends that the corporation's president might receive from the company.[25]

Leander also had intimate ties with Freeport Sulphur Company, which had sunk a $3.5 million investment in Plaquemines Parish.[26] After his break with the Judge, Earl Long remarked of these business deals:

> I'm informed that the levee boards in Plaquemines Parish, and some companies that a certain man is interested in, are receiving royalties from the Freeport Sulphur Company. I'm informed that that's not necessarily a voluntary contribution. . . . If you want to do well, you've got to stay with the King. I had a man the other day to tell me—he's a millionaire—that he swore he would not give an overriding royalty, I think of one-sixteenth. He stood out and stood out and finally his partners came to him and said, "Listen, we've got great investments. Everybody else in that part of the country has done it. Go ahead and do it and let's recover something on our investment."[27]

In 1936 Freeport learned the consequences of defying Perez when it brought in outside workers and laid off some Plaquemines men. The Judge, in Baton Rouge lobbying in the legislature when he learned of the action, immediately had a bill introduced to raise the sulphur severance tax from sixty cents to two dollars per long ton. Freeport's president, Langbourne Williams, rushed to Baton Rouge from Atlanta to implore Governor Richard Leche not to sign the bill. Leche assured him that he would veto it, but even before Williams had returned to Atlanta, he had signed it. The tax increase was ruinous for Freeport. Plaquemines Parish supplied over half the company's total output and contained the second largest sulphur mine in the world. Although Freeport cut back its Louisiana production by nearly a fourth and increased its Texas production by over a third, this could not provide permanent relief. The company was also harried by two lawsuits, one by Perez and the other by private parties. The suits involved payment of back and future royalties and Freeport's title to Fractional Section One, the source of sulphur for its biggest plant.[28]

The sulphur giant was ready to surrender by the time the legislature convened in 1938. The corporation made overtures to Perez, and he responded by becoming as effective an ally as he had been implacable an opponent. He managed to push through a bill reducing the severance tax from $2.00 to $1.03 per long ton, which Governor Leche obligingly signed. The measure was put in the form of a constitutional amendment so that a two-thirds vote of the legislature would be necessary to repeal it. As attorney for the levee board, Perez helped arrange a compromise settlement of the royalty suits. He induced the board to accept the offer of Freeport and the other interested parties, thus making secure Freeport's title to Fractional Section One. Leander also concluded a "gentlemen's agreement" between the company and the parish. The parish promised to keep the property-tax rate, which was thirty-five mills at the time, below twenty mills; in return, Freeport pledged to hire a certain percentage of local workers.[29]

In his second term, Governor Earl Long attempted to raise sulphur taxes again, but was blocked by Perez. The delta boss could not muster a majority vote, but he did sway enough votes to prevent the two-thirds majority necessary to repeal the constitutional amendment.[30]

Perez continued to receive oil and sulphur royalties for the remainder of his life. The mineral companies operating in the parish developed such an indebtedness to him that they had a vested interest in keeping him in power. Perez also kept labor unions out of the parish. His substantial income enabled him to devote most of his time to politics without having to worry about mundane financial matters.

SIX

Burying the Hatchet, Perez Style

By early 1940 Perez was engaged in the hottest local political duel since his battle with John Dymond twenty years earlier. In May, 1939, the tension between the Plaquemines district attorney and the district judge J. Claude Meraux erupted into an open break. When a levee board position became vacant, Leander and Meraux supported rival claimants for the appointment. Meraux, who had accompanied his favorite to the board meeting to be sworn in and taken an active part in the proceedings, resigned a week later as head of the St. Bernard Democratic Organization. Thomas W. Serpas, the police jury president and a Perez stalwart, was elected to succeed him. A spokesman for the Perez faction in St. Bernard explained that it was improper for a judge to take an active role in partisan politics, commenting that Meraux's selection had been "a sort of sentimental gesture" in the first place.[1]

St. Bernard Sheriff Dutch Rowley tried to remain neutral in the feud but soon found himself aligned with Meraux. Rowley said that the trouble between him and Perez had originated when Perez had demanded his undated resignation and he had refused. Like Perez, he was stubborn. He knew his constituents well and was the type of man who never subjected himself to another's leadership if he could succeed on his own.[2]

Resolving to unseat Rowley in the January, 1940, Democratic primary, Perez organized a rival slate of candidates to oppose the Rowley-Meraux ticket in St. Bernard. His candidate for sheriff was Manuel Molero, who had been his archenemy in the trappers' war of 1926. The campaign was the most bitterly fought since the Perez-Parker faction had ousted the Old Regulars. The Rowley-Meraux forces seceded from the St. Bernard Democratic Organization after Meraux was ousted and formed a rival group they called the Original St. Bernard Democratic Organization. The campaigning was spiced by a "bombing" incident in which Rowley supporters in planes dropped leaflets for their candidate on a Molero parade.[3]

During the campaign Perez resorted to a tactic he used every time he and Rowley feuded. As district attorney, he allowed commercial gambling to flourish in St. Bernard as long as he and the sheriff were on good terms; but, when he and Rowley became enemies, the district attorney suddenly cracked down. About ten days before the Democratic primary, Leander launched an investigation of gambling in St. Bernard. At an open hearing, one witness testified that Rowley had employed him to run a commercial gambling house and that the sheriff had collected all profits over seventy-five dollars per day. In return, Rowley had furnished rent, protection, and facilities. Perez accused Rowley of accepting payoffs from gamblers and using the money to buy votes and charged him with eleven counts of bribery. Judge Meraux's brother Charles was also implicated. One witness testified that Charles Meraux had accompanied a collection man who emptied slot machines at the Riverview Club; another testified that Charles Meraux owned or had formerly owned the Riverview Club. During the hearing, all gambling houses in the parish suddenly shut down. When Rowley deputies and Perez supporters met at the White Cottage Tavern, a fistfight erupted, with blows and uncharitable expressions being exchanged.[4]

The Perez faction challenged the registrations of more than 150 Rowley supporters, many being removed from the rolls on the grounds that they were not parish residents. Meanwhile, Rowley claimed that the location of several voting places had been changed to favor the Perez faction.[5]

Encouraged by reform-minded gubernatorial candidate Sam Jones, Rowley's partisans organized a ticket to oppose the Perez candidates in Plaquemines Parish. The revolt against the Judge in Plaquemines was led by J. Ben Meyer, a former parish assessor who had broken with Perez; Walter Blaize, a Buras garage owner who had never sided with Perez; and Salvador Chiapetta, who had once been given a job by Perez. The most outspoken of the group, Meyer had once been editor of the *Plaquemines Gazette* and a firm Perez ally. But during the 1940s he edited an opposition paper called the *Challenger* ("dedicated to the abolition of dictatorship"), in which he repeatedly denounced Perez as "Our Great Dictator" and compared him to Adolf Hitler, claiming to have been beaten by the dictator's hired thugs. Many years later Meyer reconciled with Leander and was appointed the official parish historian upon the boss's recommendation. He thereupon penned a fawning biographical sketch in which he referred to Perez as "Our Hero" and compared him to Hercules and "Leander, stalwart lover who nightly swam the Hellespont."[6]

Five days before the Democratic primary, Meyer published a letter in which he claimed that vote stealing had been occurring in Plaquemines for years. Stating that the Plaquemines registration book was a loose-leaf binder to which pages could be added or deleted, he claimed that page 23 consisted almost entirely of persons who had moved to Alabama 12 years previously. Meyer further charged that in Perez's home ward there were 604 persons registered, but only 60 houses in which white people lived, and asserted that another ward had 400 names on the rolls, although there were no more than 139 persons qualified to vote.[7]

The Plaquemines election was only a sideshow, because the anti-Perez ticket had little chance of winning. The chief struggle was in St. Bernard. On election day Sheriff Rowley arrested ten Perez "canvassers," confiscating eight pistols and six blackjacks, charged them with intimidating voters at the polls, and detained them in the new but unheated St. Bernard jail. The state supreme court ordered the men released on bond because they might have died of exposure if forced to spend the winter night in the damp and frigid cells. The Meraux-Rowley faction won most of the contested positions in St. Bernard, Rowley himself winning an easy first-primary victory over Molero. But in Plaquemines the entire Perez ticket was elected by overwhelming majorities except for one police jury seat, for which the Perez candidate was elected by a single vote.[8]

Following the election, the Perez-Molero faction filed eight suits contesting the returns of the Rowley nominees, but Rowley won six of the eight. At the general election in April, five Rowley candidates were written in as independent candidates against the Democratic nominees belonging to the Perez faction. The temporary district judge Paul Debaillon ordered the election commissioners not to count the write-in votes, but they did so anyway. The state supreme court overruled Debaillon, and three of the write-in candidates were allowed to take office.[9]

On January 31, in the wake of Rowley's victory, an ouster suit was filed against Perez. The brief petition was signed by twenty-six citizens of St. Bernard. Perez claimed that few of them paid property taxes in the parish and that eleven were illiterates who had signed their X's without witnesses. He also charged that Judge J. Claude Meraux had instigated the impeachment proceedings to protect his brother Charles, whom Perez was investigating for gambling.[10]

About two weeks later a similar impeachment petition was filed by thirty-two citizens of Plaquemines Parish, charging that Perez had "diverted to his own private gain, through subterfuge, all of the mineral wealth of the various public levee boards and the school boards of Plaquemines and St. Bernard parishes." The petition also charged that Perez had built a political dynasty "saturated with crime and corruption."[11]

The main charge in the St. Bernard petition was that Perez had deliberately frustrated the prosecution of the murderer of Angela Treadaway. Treadaway, a fifty-two-year-old black woman whose husband was blind, was employed at the Dunbar-Dukate Shrimp Packing Plant in the community of Violet, where she was paid 22.5 cents an hour. She, along with several hundred fellow women workers, belonged to the Seafood Workers Association of the Gulf Coast of Louisiana, which in August, 1939, went on strike protesting a management scheme to organize a company union and demanding a 2.5-cent wage increase. The Delacroix Corporation, in the person of its president, wealthy retailer Manuel Molero, undertook to supply the Violet plant with the scab labor necessary to keep it operating. Judge Perez, who saw organization of labor as a threat to his power, threatened to cut off from parish relief any striker who would not return to work.[12]

Tensions continued to mount at the strike scene until Wednesday, August 23, when tragic violence erupted. About 150 women strikers and their supporters were picketing the plant under the watchful eyes of armed agents of Molero's Delacroix Corporation. As the guards patrolled the picket area in automobiles, a rumor swept among the strikers, some of whom, according to later testimony, were themselves armed, that a gang of hired toughs was coming from New Orleans to break the strike. What happened now is unclear. Apparently shooting broke out between company agents and supporters of the strikers. Provoked or not, a group of Molero's men, possibly Adam Melerine, Peter Guerra, and Sylvero Molero, leaped from their car, weapons in hand, and began to fire into the picket line. At this point the strikebreakers from New Orleans entered the scene. These shady types, reputedly members of a mysterious seamen's union quartered on Chartres Street, were known only as the Chain Gang and had come armed with three carloads of firearms, ammunition, ax handles, baseball bats, and chains. The Chain Gang seems to have entered the fray without much regard for which side was which. One witness testified that he saw one of the strangers pull a revolver and fire at Adam Melerine, one of the Delacroix guards. In the ensuing melee, Treadaway fell, seriously wounded in the abdomen. A black Packard belonging to the Chain Gang was commandeered for the harrowing fifteen-mile race to Charity Hospital in New Orleans, where the unfortunate woman died the following Saturday.[13]

Witnesses' reports were confused. Many locals thought the killing was the work of the obscure and distasteful strangers who had lurked about town making the rounds of bars before disappearing later in the afternoon. It was soon bruited about that the seamen, one of whom was said to be called Kentucky Red, were a cadre of Bolshevists, or at least AFL members, who for some unexplained reason went about the countryside suppressing strikes. Others were sure the responsible party was Adam Melerine. An unsavory character, he had an ambiguous record that included two indictments for murdering deputy sheriffs and two unsuccessful races for the office of sheriff of St. Bernard. He was known to be a heavy drinker, easily angered and intemperate in behavior, who nonetheless enjoyed the confidence of Leander Perez.[14]

Melerine was among a number of suspects named when the case came before the grand jury on August 29, in a special session called by Perez in his capacity as district attorney. For two days the jurors took testimony from more than fifty witnesses, then, deciding that the evidence was too hopelessly confused and contradictory, adjourned without returning an indictment. Perez stated his intention of pursuing the investigation and of calling the grand jury back into special session should any fresh evidence come to light. The St. Bernard grand jury met again on October 5, 1939, to consider further the Treadaway killing. This time its attention was focused on the shadowy seamen from New Orleans. Three St. Bernard deputies dogged the streets of the French Quarter for days searching for clues to their identities and whereabouts, but apparently the mariners had disappeared as quickly as they had come. A fair-skinned fellow named Midlow Dinaski was finally arrested and detained but, upon convincingly protesting his total innocence, was set free. The grand jury stated that, since the principals in the shooting were outsiders who were totally unknown and could not be brought to justice, there was no point in continuing the inquiry.[15]

The Treadaway family was not satisfied with the conduct of the investigation. They claimed that Perez had an interest in obscuring the facts in the case, that he had ordered Sheriff Rowley not to make arrests in the case, that he had neglected to call known eyewitnesses before the grand jury, and that he himself had drafted the jury's statement that evidence was insufficient to return an indictment. The family further claimed that the district attorney had refused to submit the question of the Treadaway killing to the new grand jury that had been impaneled following the expiration of the old one.[16]

Feeling that they had been denied justice by the derelictions with which they charged Perez, members of the Treadaway family, possibly at the prompting of the Judge's political enemies, had their attorney prepare impeachment proceedings against him. The petition was not filed until sometime after the election in which incumbent Sheriff Rowley beat Manuel Molero, ostensibly because the family wished to avoid having the suit involved in partisan politics. At any rate they brought their petition to court when it became known, in January, 1940, that Perez had interceded to obtain a permit for Adam Melerine (still regarded by many as a prime suspect in

Treadaway's death) to carry a pistol and had appointed him special investigator for the district attorney's office.[17]

Unfortunately for Perez, the motion for impeachment caught him in the middle of his feud with Judge J. Claude Meraux. He could not afford to have Meraux hear the case, so he demanded that the judge disqualify himself. Meraux refused and appointed attorney Richard Dowling to undertake the prosecution. Desperate as the situation seemed, Perez was not easily intimidated; taking the offensive, as he had done before, he filed impeachment proceedings of his own— against Meraux.[18]

Now Meraux was really angry. He invited Governor Jones to investigate Perez's financial transactions involving mineral leases in Plaquemines Parish. Meraux said that an examination of the records in Plaquemines would reveal that mineral leases on most of the land owned by the Buras Levee Board had been granted to "an individual absolutely controlled by" Perez. Meraux continued, "An examination of the public records will, likewise, disclose that the Grand Prairie levee district made a mineral lease of all of the lands owned or to be owned by that board to this same individual above referred to or to the same corporations above referred to, likewise controlled or owned by Judge Perez." Meraux claimed that the parish school board had leased every one of its sixteen sections "to one of these same corporations so controlled by Judge Perez for a very small or inconsequential consideration." Meraux contended that Leander had a stranglehold on all Plaquemines officials, that he held undated resignations from every officer and board member, that he countersigned all checks paid by public boards and by the police jury, that he kept a large number of deadheads on the parish payroll to keep them politically pliable, and that resolutions, contracts, and minutes for public boards were prepared by Perez and simply presented to the members for their signatures. According to Meraux, the members often did not even know what they were signing.[19]

Leander brought numerous charges of his own against Meraux; the impeachment petition, filed in the Judge's name, was forty-six pages long. Among the charges were the following: (1) Meraux had charged personal purchases at the L. T. Fontenelle Store and Bar to the police jury account; (2) he had had his hunting guide released from jail after serving only thirty minutes of his thirty-day sentence; (3) he had illegally suspended sentences of prisoners and had not sentenced some convicted persons at all; (4) he had ordered a collection from St. Bernard gambling houses to buy himself a Lincoln Zephyr automobile, then had exchanged the Lincoln for a Ford sedan and kept the difference in cash; (5) he had deliberately concealed himself so that it would be impossible to locate him to try election suits; (6) he had beaten a Negro to extort a confession; (7) he had refused to excuse himself in trying registration cases in which he had a political interest; (8) he had operated a divorce mill in St. Bernard in collusion with certain attorneys.[20]

Meraux decided not to wait for the state authorities to investigate Leander. He appointed five implacable Perez opponents as jury commissioners and instructed them to select a venire from which grand and petit juries would be chosen. Meraux intended to use the grand jury to probe voting irregularities in the recent Democratic primaries. The commissioners proceeded to select a venire loaded with Perez opponents. The two witnesses to the venire list were Perez men who refused to sign it, thus temporarily blocking operation of the jury. Undaunted, the commissioners called in two outside witnesses who were allowed to sign. Judge Meraux then impaneled a grand jury composed entirely of Perez foes. The foreman was J. Ben Meyer, who requested that Leander be superseded as legal adviser to the grand jury; Perez, in turn, asked the state supreme court to supersede Judge Meraux. The court reacted to the charges and countercharges by superseding both Perez and Meraux in Plaquemines.[21]

Judge Paul Debaillon of Lafayette was appointed to replace Meraux. In early April, Debaillon heard testimony concerning the legality of the Plaquemines venire and the grand and petit juries selected. The individual grand jurors were called to the stand, and each testified that he had not pledged to indict anyone. Pointing out that all of the Meraux commissioners were defeated candidates from the last Democratic primary, Perez complained that Meyer, the foreman of the grand jury, had been charged with libel and that juror Ernest Hingle had been charged with disturbing the peace and carrying a concealed weapon. He also claimed that the two official witnesses had not been in constant attendance when the names for the general venire list were selected. A Perez witness testified that, before the petit jury venire had been drawn, one of Meraux's commissioners had withheld a stack of name cards when the box was shaken up. He had then handed them to another commissioner, who had placed them on top; the venire had then been drawn from the cards on top. The Judge's mouthpiece, the *Plaquemines Gazette,* reported that Meraux had told witnesses in the courtroom that he was going to get even with Perez through the new grand jury.[22]

The great investigation Perez feared did not materialize. The grand jury adjourned on April 7 after returning only two routine indictments, neither of which concerned Perez. The grand jury also submitted a supplemental report, which Judge Debaillon termed "innocuous" and ordered burned. Debaillon then dismissed Meraux's commissioners and ordered a new three-hundred-name venire selected, instructing his jury commissioners to exclude parish officeholders from the list.[23]

Judge Debaillon's new Plaquemines grand jury proved even less active than its predecessor. After investigating for six months, it reported that it had "no report to make at this time on the investigation of any criminal matters." The jury did state that the jail needed to be painted and the toilets cleaned and that the fan in the grand jury room needed to be repaired. As for the parish government, it was doing a commendable job.[24]

As the Perez-Meraux conflict intensified, local officeholders were forced to choose sides. The Plaquemines officials stuck with Perez, but most of the St. Bernard people sided with Rowley and Meraux. One such was Carmella LeClerc, the new registrar of voters for St. Bernard. Formerly a deputy registrar affiliated with the Rowley faction, she was willing to talk about the operation of the Perez machine, and in October, 1940, she consented to a newspaper interview. She produced a registration book that she claimed had "approximately 700 names of fictitious characters which were protested by the Rowley administration." LeClerc said that the book had been compiled under the direction of Registrar of Voters Mathias Reuter, a Perez stalwart, and that when she had refused to destroy the book she had lost her job.[25]

Judge Debaillon had originally been appointed to supersede Judge Meraux only in Plaquemines, but the order was soon extended to cover St. Bernard. Debaillon impaneled a St. Bernard grand jury, instructing it to clean up the parish. When the jurors proved curiously lethargic, meeting only three days in more than three months, Debaillon called them before him and derided them in open court, accusing them of not cooperating, threatening to cite them for contempt if they did not do their job, and asserting that they seemed to be afraid to investigate certain conditions in the parish. He also told the jury that he suspected that there was a leak in the secret proceedings. After Debaillon's tongue-lashing, the grand jury became hyperactive, meeting for seven hours without even taking time out for lunch. The suddenly serious jurors then requested that Perez be superseded as its legal adviser. Perez objected vehemently, but the state supreme court upheld the right of the attorney general to supersede the district attorney.[26] The jurors did not persist in their newfound industriousness. After six months of investigating rumors of gambling and political corruption in St. Bernard, the grand jury adjourned without returning a single indictment. It reported incidentally that the courthouse and the toilet bowls in the jail were dirty and that there was a large hole in the flower bed in front of the courthouse. A collateral report submitted at this time maintained that there was insufficient evidence to return any criminal indictments, but three members of the grand jury refused to sign it. The report enraged Judge Debaillon, who told the jury: "But for anyone who has been in session for six months ... to come into Court and practically admit, that this Parish is free from crime, free from irregularities, and free from all the other things which seem to infest it, is beyond comprehension. ... My efforts have been futile. Your efforts have been fruitless. The people are just where they were before."[27]

While the grand juries in Plaquemines and St. Bernard deliberated, Perez waged a court battle to prevent the suit for his impeachment from coming to trial. He filed an exception contending that the impeachment petition was invalid because the charges were not specific. Judge Debaillon upheld Perez's exception and ordered the suit dismissed, but the state supreme court overruled him and ordered the proceedings to continue. Perez then filed an exception maintaining that not enough payers of property tax had signed the petition, claiming that the homeowners who received homestead exemptions could not be counted as taxpayers. Judge Debaillon again upheld Perez's exception and dismissed the case; this time his ruling was sustained by the supreme court. The Perez impeachment case would never come to trial.[28]

Court recessed for the summer without hearing the Meraux impeachment case. In June an explosion destroyed Perez's speedboat when an employee started the motor. Everyone initially assumed that it had been an attempt to assassinate the Judge, but an investigation revealed that it had been caused by collected gas. In August, 1941, Judge Debaillon held his last court session in Plaquemines Parish. Debaillon, who had ruled in favor of Perez in every case that had come before his court (sometimes on questionable legal grounds) and had rendered numerous rulings in St. Bernard that had embarrassed Judge Meraux, said that he had received excellent cooperation from Plaquemines officials and had found conditions in the parish "rather good." Complimenting the grand jury on its investigations, he said that he would respect their opinion that there was insufficient evidence to return any indictments. Perez's assistant district attorney and the parish clerk of court presented the outgoing judge with a silver plaque commemorating his work in Plaquemines.[29]

In October, 1941, Meraux's impeachment came to trial. Serving as Meraux's chief attorney was silver-haired St. Clair Adams, who had defended Perez in 1923. He and Perez indulged in angry exchanges in court, and at one point Adams offered to take Leander outside to settle things physically. The Plaquemines Parish Police Jury advanced a thousand dollars for attorney's fees to finance Meraux's impeachment, and the balance of the cost was collected by Perez from parish employees. He also used some of the money to hire an investigating agency to collect evidence against Meraux.[30]

Special Commissioner Benjamin Y. Wolf collected 1,350 pages of testimony in the case, then turned the testimony and briefs over to the state supreme court for a decision. In early testimony Adams placed Assessor Dewey Cognevich on the stand to prove that most of the 131 signers of the petition held political jobs or were relatives of persons holding political jobs. Cognevich admitted that he could not name a single signer who did not have a political job. When Cognevich would admit that a petitioner operated a place of business in the parish, Adams would invariably ask if the petitioner had slot machines in his establishment. And Cognevich would reply, "I don't play slot machines. I shoot craps."[31] Perez supporters who took the stand refused to admit that the Judge was the political leader of Plaquemines Parish. They maintained that power was divided among several officials. As Clerk of Court Allen Lobrano said, "Perez has no more power than any of us." John Alphonso, a trapper put on the stand to substantiate the charge that Meraux had suspended sentences without waiting for a request from the defendant, testified that he had not even known his sentence was suspended until he was told he could leave. Defense attorney Adams demanded of Alphonso, "You came here to take Judge Meraux's job away from him, didn't you?" Alphonso replied, "I ain't got enough education to take Judge Meraux's job." Given the nature of Plaquemines–St. Bernard politics, he evidently regarded it as a serious possibility.[32]

Portions of the trial resembled comic opera. Testimony proved that Meraux had sentenced his personal hunting guide to thirty days for possession of immature furs out of season. When he had recognized the man, Meraux had rescinded the sentence, having failed to identify him at first, he explained, because he had never seen the guide with a clean shave.[33]

Meraux's defense was unconvincing. He claimed that the impeachment suit had been brought by "politicians actuated by political motives." The state supreme court agreed, but stated that this had no bearing on the merits of the case. Meraux said that the charge that he had used police jury funds for his personal account at L. T. Fontenelle's store was a frame-up by Perez and Fontenelle. He further claimed that he had failed to sentence some prisoners because District Attorney Perez had not fixed the cases for sentencing. Meraux admitted to not reading most of the petitions in the divorces he granted, but denied profiting personally from the cases.[34]

In July, 1942, the supreme court ordered Meraux removed from office, principally on the grounds that he had operated a divorce mill, holding that one wrongful act might be considered an error in judgment, but not a series of wrongful acts. The court nullified about a hundred divorces and annulments granted by Meraux and warned third parties against marrying the concerned parties. Not content merely to remove Meraux from office, Leander sought to have him disbarred. The justices balked at this and dismissed the proceedings.[35]

Governor Sam Jones appointed one of Perez's most acrimonious enemies, sixty-eight-year-old Oliver S. Livaudais, to succeed Meraux temporarily until the 1942 election. Perez contested the appointment, but the state supreme court held that the appointee was entitled to the seat. In the ensuing election, the Rowley faction backed Livaudais for judge and Richard Dowling for district attorney. J. Claude Meraux also entered the race for district attorney against Perez. Leander filed a suit to disqualify Dowling on the grounds that he lived in New Orleans rather than in the Twenty-fifth Judicial District, and Dowling filed a similar suit against Perez. They compromised, and both suits were dropped.[36]

Perez's running mate for district judge was Albert Estopinal, Jr. Years earlier, in 1924, Estopinal had been sheriff of St. Bernard and a leader of the Old Regulars. After Leander had exposed him for protecting a gambler and had engineered his defeat by Dr. L. A. Meraux, he had had the former sheriff indicted for misuse of tax collections. The present sheriff, Dutch Rowley, said that he had pleaded with Perez to make peace but that Perez had declined. He explained that he had offered to support a compromise candidate for judge but that Perez had insisted on Estopinal. Rowley concluded that he knew the only way Perez could support Estopinal was to hold his undated resignation.[37]

The campaign was unusually bitter, even for the deep delta. Among the charges the *Plaquemines Gazette* leveled against the Rowley faction were the following: (1) Richard Dowling carried a gun while campaigning for district attorney; (2) the St. Bernard draft board drafted Rowley opponents and gave deferments to his supporters; (3) the Rowley faction collected huge sums of tax money with nothing to show for it but deadhead jobs; (4) the levee boards appointed by Governor Sam Jones and endorsed by Oliver S. Livaudais neglected storm protection; (5) Rowley intended to put up a big gambling casino near Port Sulphur in Plaquemines; (6) Rowley deputies had warned Plaquemines slot machine owners that if they did not vote for Rowley candidates they would not be allowed to continue operations.[38]

When the *Gazette* was not lambasting Rowley it was describing the public improvements Judge Perez had brought to Plaquemines. Among these were new and enlarged school buildings, sidewalks, athletic fields, school buses, an extra month's salary for schoolteachers and bus drivers, reduction of property taxes, and college scholarships for "unlimited numbers" of local high school graduates.[39]

After the balloting, state police tried to impound the Plaquemines ballot boxes on an order from Judge Livaudais, but Leander refused to recognize the order. "I ordered the state police away and they were glad to leave when they saw the crowd of about 150 aroused citizenry around the courthouse," Perez boasted. The Rowley candidates carried St. Bernard, but Perez and Estopinal received such top-heavy majorities in dependable Plaquemines that both were elected. Leander remained firmly in control of Plaquemines, but Rowley dominated St. Bernard.[40]

Rowley and Governor Jones attempted to organize opposition to the Judge in Plaquemines, but their efforts met little success. In 1943 a number of Perez foes went to the Pointe a la Hache courthouse to participate in planning the 1944 primaries. They found the courthouse dark and empty. The meeting, it turned out, had been shifted thirty miles up the river, and only Perez supporters had attended. Asked why a suit had not been brought, one delta native explained to writer Lester Velie, "By the time the court gets around to it, the election's been held."[41]

Leander tried to dethrone Sheriff Rowley in 1944 by backing Dr. Nicholas P. Trist for sheriff. Manuel Molero, whom Perez had supported in 1940, also ran for sheriff, but this time on his own. Rowley, however, rolled to a comfortable first-primary victory over all five opponents. J. Claude Meraux also gained a measure of revenge against Perez, being elected state representative from St. Bernard on the Rowley ticket. Following the election, Molero merged his faction with Rowley's. Perez complained to a friend: "We had everything pretty well lined up in St. Bernard but for Mr. Manuel Molero. Manuel got mad because we would not support him and go down in defeat with him, so he teamed up with Dutch (Rowley) and his gang."[42]

Rowley also dominated the gubernatorial election in St. Bernard. The Perez-Long candidate, little-known Lewis Morgan, easily carried Plaquemines, but in St. Bernard ran a poor second to James H. ("Jimmie") Davis, backed by Sam Jones and Rowley. Davis garnered more votes in St. Bernard than all seven of his opponents combined. The St. Bernard election was still characterized by peculiarities; although more than 6,500 votes were cast for the gubernatorial candidates, only 3,008 were counted in the sheriff's race. In the second primary in St. Bernard the Rowley faction swept the field in the local contests, and Jimmie Davis more than doubled the vote of Perez's candidate Morgan, in the governor's race. Davis also won statewide.[43]

Perez and Rowley finally buried the hatchet before the 1948 elections. "I'm all for it," Rowley quipped, "as long as you don't bury that hatchet in my head." Perez also reconciled with former judge J. Claude Meraux, who, regaining the trust of St. Bernard residents, became president of the St. Bernard Bank and Trust Company.[44]

In 1948 Sheriff Rowley won another easy victory in St. Bernard, this time with Perez's backing. The Perez-Rowley ticket lost only four St. Bernard offices, one of which was parish coroner, to which an independent, Dr. Trist, was elected. Judge Albert Estopinal, Jr., retired as district judge, and one of Perez's assistant district attorneys, Bruce Nunez, was elected to succeed him.[45]

In Plaquemines, Perez opponents had difficulty even getting on the ballot. An anti-Perez candidate for the police jury was denied a qualifying form because, he was told, none remained. If he wanted a form, he would have to drive to Baton Rouge, more than a hundred miles away. Another Perez foe claimed that he had been given deliberately misprinted registration forms at the parish courthouse. If he had filled them out, he complained, he would have been disqualified for improper registration. This determined candidate obtained proper forms directly from Baton Rouge, but was then disqualified for failing to post the proper fee. "I couldn't find out what it was," the office seeker protested through his lawyer. Twenty-four other opposition candidates were disqualified on the same technicality. Somehow, none of the Perez candidates experienced any difficulty in qualifying. The disqualified candidates fought their cases to the Louisiana Supreme Court. Most of them qualified, only to be beaten by the usual landslide.[46]

After the mending of the Perez-Rowley and Perez-Meraux feuds, partisan politics on the local level subsided. Leander was not seriously challenged in his own bailiwick again until the mid-1950s. This allowed him more leisure to participate in state and national politics.

SEVEN

The Carrot and the Stick

Machiavelli, the philosopher of pragmatic politics, wrote that it is more advantageous to be feared than loved. Leander Perez recognized that fear was a more reliable way of holding allegiance, but he also craved love; thus there were two components in his particular brand of bossism—the carrot and the stick, a blend of threats and benefits.

The Judge's autocratic domination of his native parish prompted one Louisianian to characterize Plaquemines as the only unconstitutional monarchy in the United States. Political scientist V. O. Key termed Plaquemines an "autonomous principality." Perez himself liked to tell newsmen that the parish was the only true democracy in the state, but he had an unusual definition of the term, claiming that "the word democracy was coined by Joe Stalin who said he had the most perfect democracy in the world."[1]

Perez was utterly unwilling to compromise with his local opponents, even when they posed no real threat to his ascendancy. Never satisfied with the simple defeat of an enemy, he always tried to totally annihilate his foe. The Judge had an almost pathological fear of uncertainty. He tried frantically to order his world so that no unmanageable, unexpected, or unfamiliar dangers would ever appear. He tried to plan for every possible contingency and to make certain that no new contingencies occurred. He sought to maintain his equilibrium by avoiding the unfamiliar and the strange. In the limited environment of Plaquemines he was usually able to do this, but he would not have been so secure on a larger stage. If, through no doings of his own, something unexpected did occur in his tiny kingdom, he panicked, as if this unexpected occurrence constituted a grave danger.

Although Perez relished adulation and publicity, expediency compelled him to accomplish his most important tasks in private: hammering out political deals, persuading legislators to adopt bills favoring his interests, plotting the downfall of his political enemies, and executing the oil leases of his mysterious dummy corporations. The fact that there was a public Perez, who posed as the "Father of Plaquemines," and a private Perez, who systematically defrauded the parish, must have disturbed his conscience. Instead of realistically accepting himself for what he was, the Judge utilized the psychological mechanism of projection as a means to transfer blame for his own faults to others. Thus, he saw pathetically weak local opponents as threats to the parish welfare, and he saw blacks as threats to the American way of life. Through some intricate mental gymnastics, Perez was able to reconstruct reality in a manner designed to enhance his own ego—hence his intense concern with his own dignity and his high regard for the fawning admiration of his political henchmen.

Such a conversion of his own guilt feelings caused Perez to virtually seethe with repressed emotion. When given the opportunity to address the public, especially before television cameras, Perez's pent-up emotion found a ready outlet. His statements were commonly so explosive as to attract widespread attention. His prose crackled with snappy, pugnacious sentences that seemed to defy contradiction. He wielded a verbal machete rather than a rapier. Such flamboyant oratory served two purposes: it gained him the attention that he incessantly craved, and it allowed him to turn his condemnation outward rather than introspectively blaming himself.

The key to Perez's local power was his domination of every arm of government in his own two-parish judicial district. All important political officeholders in Plaquemines—the tax assessor, sheriff, clerk of court, voter registrar, police jurors, school board members, and district judge—were Perez backers. As district attorney, Leander was legal adviser to every governing body in the judicial district. The most important one was the parish police jury, which in Louisiana governs road, drainage, sewerage, water, and light districts. It authorizes all expenditures, including the salaries of most parish officials, and is empowered to levy taxes and borrow money for the boards it controls. Paid only for meeting days, jury members receive no annual salary. Perez proved singularly successful at electing his own men to the police jury. From his law office in New Orleans he drew up most of the resolutions, including appropriation measures adopted by it, and nearly all of his handiwork was approved unanimously and without debate. "There's hardly ever a dissenting vote," Leander boasted. "We work together 100 per cent."[2]

The Judge also controlled the judicial system of Plaquemines and St. Bernard, since he served as legal adviser to the parish grand juries, which seldom indicted Perez allies but never neglected to subject political opponents to microscopic investigations. As district attorney he intimidated cronies and foes alike by holding criminal charges over their heads. Sometimes he filed the charges but allowed them to languish in court. Other accusations remained unfiled, under the threat that they could be resurrected at any time.[3]

The judgeship of the Twenty-fifth Judicial District was an elective position, and every man chosen to fill it during Leander's career eventually ended up as a Perez supporter. The most convenient stepping-stone to the office of district judge was the post of assistant district attorney under Perez. The judge, sheriff, and district attorney, all Perez men, sometimes acted in concert to harass political opponents. The following was a common occurrence: a man would be arrested on a trumped-up charge; it would be difficult to arrange bail because the persons authorized to sign for him were unavailable and no local attorney would represent him; or perhaps bail would be set at an inordinately high figure; this could be reduced, but it took a higher court order, which required time; finally the accused would be released after wilting in jail for several days, no doubt having learned that opposition to The Judge amounted to self-flagellation.[4]

Those adversaries who managed to register to vote deserved an award for patience and fortitude. Until 1954, the Plaquemines registrar traveled throughout the parish registering, in their own homes, people already on the rolls. Substations were set up in outlying sections of the parish, but people who had not previously registered usually had to go to the registrar's home. To the Perez foes who attempted to enroll, the registrar was away on important business or visiting a sick friend; the well-traveled official must have seemed a whirlwind of activity. But Perez partisans always found the registrar at home and more than willing to help. One man remembered registering in the grocery store belonging to the brother of Registrar Frank Giordano. The registrar, who was Perez's nephew, had not been present at the time, the man testified; in fact, he did not even know who the registrar was. Another man, who had opened a grocery store in competition with Giordano's brother, found it impossible to register. Following the *Brown* school desegregation decision, Louisiana adopted a constitutional interpretation test designed to disqualify potential black voters. Leander's foes complained that in Plaquemines the test was used to disenfranchise not only blacks but all Perez opponents.[5]

Walter Blaize, one of Perez's few persistent opponents who did not leave the parish, fought the Judge for more than forty years by running for office, campaigning for Leander's foes, and serving as Sam Jones's appointee for sheriff during the "little war" of 1943–1944. Blaize managed to serve on the police jury for six years back in the 1920s. In 1958 he was called to testify in a voting suit against Registrar Frank Giordano. While Giordano's attorney was examining him, Blaize explained what it was like to belong to the anti-Perez faction: "I never miss an election and I never miss voting. Of course I lose all the time but I don't quit. For forty years I've been opposing that faction. I just don't like the system, none of the system. I just don't like the way the parish handles our funds." Giordano's lawyer interrupted, "Well, let's don't get into a long lengthy discussion." Blaize continued, "Well, I want to explain to you, beings you want to know something about it. I'll tell you. It's a matter of record. You know it is, just as well as I do. You just can't register down there unless you're on the right side. You know that."[6]

The classic example of a Perez opponent who unsuccessfully tried to register is that of Salvador Chiapetta, a man almost as stubborn as Perez himself. Chiapetta began his political involvement as a Perez partisan in the early 1920s. He worked as an assistant road maintenance superintendent during Governor Oramel Simpson's administration and had himself appointed to the Plaquemines

Parish Board of Supervisors of Elections, on which he used his position to help the Huey Long faction. In 1936 Chiapetta was a unit chief for the Louisiana Highway Commission on the east side of the Mississippi River in Plaquemines. Later, claiming that Perez had double-crossed him and prevented him from getting a better state job, he further charged that he and his men had been instructed by his immediate supervisor to build a park and fish pond on Perez's estate and that the road crew had done the work, at a cost to the state of six thousand dollars. Chiapetta offered to supply a grand jury with the pertinent information, but none of the local grand juries even took up the matter. After breaking with Perez, he found it almost impossible to register to vote. During one eight-month period he made six trips to the parish courthouse to try to register, but Frank Giordano was conveniently absent every time. Chiapetta wrote Giordano a registered letter asking when he could register; he received a receipt for the letter but no reply. Chiapetta then wrote Perez. Again there was no reply. He wrote to the United States attorney in New Orleans, who said that he could not act without authorization from the Justice Department. Chiapetta next wrote the state attorney general, who replied that the affair was a parish matter. Finally, in desperation, Chiapetta wrote President Harry S. Truman. The president, through an assistant attorney general, said that it was a state matter.[7]

Chiapetta found it equally hard to find employment. Local businessmen were afraid to hire a known enemy of Perez's. Once, he thought he had obtained a job with a contractor whose main offices were in New Orleans, but before he could report for work, he was notified that he had been discharged. Suspecting that Perez was behind the dismissal, Chiapetta asked the Judge's old adversary, New Orleans Mayor deLesseps S. ("Chep") Morrison, to intervene in his behalf. Morrison called the contractor, who explained that if Perez did not want him to hire Chiapetta then that was the way it must be. Otherwise, there would be little chance for any contracts in Plaquemines or St. Bernard in the future.[8]

Even if they managed to register, some Perez opponents still found it impossible to vote. Louisiana author Harnett T. Kane tells about one Plaquemines man who spent an entire election day in a futile attempt to cast a ballot. Approaching the usual polling place, he found that the voting booth had been moved and that no one, it seems, could tell him its new location. Finally he discovered that it had been set up far back among some interconnecting marsh lakes. After frustrating delays he managed to procure a boat and make the long trip through the winding bayous. Upon arriving he was told that the polls had been closed for the day—before the time set by law.[9]

Leander's partisans had no such trouble in registering or voting. No evidence of registration was required when they reported to the polls, and no checklist was maintained to prevent their reappearance. In 1950 five Plaquemines election commissioners were convicted of vote fraud on evidence gathered by the Federal Bureau of Investigation (FBI), but, when their attorney pleaded for leniency, they were given suspended sentences. Leander mellowly explained what had happened, as he puffed on a cigar: "Some of these Plaquemines folks don't have any way of getting to the polls, so they used to ask their friends to cast their votes for them. That's all that happened."[10]

Adversaries of Perez who tried to qualify for office had even more trouble getting on the ballot than they did voting, because the Judge completely dominated the party machinery. In Louisiana the Democratic party is subject to the rule of the state central committee and similar district and parish committees, which are responsible for determining who is qualified to run for office. Perez was a member of all three committees and for many years was chairman of the parish committee, which routinely disqualified all anti-Perez candidates. It was futile to challenge a committee decision in the courts, because the local judge always ruled in favor of Leander. If the opposition candidate decided to appeal, Perez could tie up the case with legal delays until the election had ended and the lawsuit had become pointless. In 1931 a group of anti-Perez candidates who tried to get on the ballot in Plaquemines could not locate the parish Democratic committee or even find out the name of its chairman. After the filing deadline had passed, it was revealed that Leander's father was the chairman; yet, the senior Perez had not even been notified that he had been named chairman until after the election. The dissidents sued their way onto the ballot, but lost by the usual landslide.[11]

Adolph E. Woolverton, a Plaquemines restaurateur, once attempted to run against a Perez candidate for the state legislature. Woolverton was supplied with misprinted forms that would have disqualified him if he had used them. After he went to the trouble of obtaining the proper forms, the parish committee disqualified him anyway on a technicality.[12]

Preventing all rivals from voting or running for office must have been a point of pride with Perez, because the opposition slate had no chance of winning anyway. He easily had enough genuine supporters to dispense with such electoral trickery as disqualifying rival candidates for technical reasons, but the old habits persisted. The Judge rarely demonstrated grace or mercy in victory. Intensely vindictive, he never quit until those who had dared oppose him had been chastised. Perez once had two men locked in jail without bond for tearing his picture from the bulkhead of a ferry. It took the signatures of four state supreme court justices to free them.[13]

While Leander himself was chairman of the parish Democratic committee, all candidates had to qualify personally at his home. He was frequently away when opposing candidates sought to file their papers, but friendly candidates seldom had trouble finding him. Perez controlled elections on voting day through his election commissioners and poll watchers. State law required each candidate to submit a list of qualified electors from which commissioners would be selected. A master list was then compiled, and each elector was assigned a number. Numbered balls were then put into a shaker, mixed, and drawn. The larger the number of Perez entries on the list, the better was the chance of Perez supporters being picked as commissioners. To stack the odds in their favor, the Perez faction sometimes nominated an entire slate of dummy candidates whose only purpose in running was to submit a list of commissioners to be drawn. Opposition poll watchers occasionally did not receive their commissions by mail, which disqualified them from serving.[14]

The value of friendly commissioners and poll watchers became evident on election day. In the early years of Perez's rule, such crude practices as "voting the list" were employed. This involved preparing marked ballots by copying the names of voters from the registration rolls onto the ballots. Voting the list was made possible because the law did not require that voters sign up as they voted, and through the years there have been charges of "the muskrats voting down there." Perez didn't like strangers nosing about his territory and reportedly hired a private detective to keep check. A newsman once decided to check door to door in Plaquemines to determine how people had actually voted after an unusually lopsided election. By the time he had reached the fourth door, the sheriff had learned of his mission.[15]

The election machinery was easier to rig before voting machines came into use in the 1950s. By placing a cardboard box inside the regular ballot box to catch the ballots, they could be checked, altered, or spoiled before being placed in the main box. Another method of ensuring huge majorities was by intimidation. The law specifies that only the illiterate, crippled, or blind may receive aid in the voting booth, but the physically sound were frequently given unrequested assistance, often by large, tough individuals.[16]

Speaking before a Senate committee in 1965, Leander described the venerable Louisiana practice of selling votes. He explained that some voters sold their votes for two dollars, others for five dollars, and yet others (constituting a sort of elite) charged ten dollars. He continued, "As a matter of fact it was so well established that they knew each other, the $5 and $10 voters would not ride in the same automobile with the $2 voters when they are being brought to the polls. It was beneath their dignity. A $10 vote would not ride in the same car with a $2 vote."[17] When Senator Hugh Scott of Pennsylvania asked him directly, "You segregated the voters according to how you paid them, then," Perez unabashedly replied, "Yes sir." Scott referred to the buying of votes in Louisiana as "the current Louisiana Purchase."[18]

Such efforts were unnecessary in Perez's later years because the overwhelming majority of the parish's white population consisted of genuine Perez supporters. But even when the outcome of the election was not in doubt, Leander liked to keep his territory shipshape by turning out a maximum percentage of voters. After one election, a barbecue was given for the ward turning out the highest percentage of voters. The parish official representing the ward with the lowest percentage of total registration was allowed to attend, but was served only beans.[19]

Photo courtesy Baton Rouge *State-Times* and *Morning Advocate*

Although never a member of the state legislature, Leander Perez journeyed to Baton Rouge to attend every session for more than thirty years. He actively lobbied for his own projects and never hesitated to tell the legislators what they should do.

Perez, along with two of his granddaughters, dedicates the new ferry at Pointe a la Hache in 1968. He took great pride in the material improvements he brought to Plaquemines Parish.

Heah com'
de
JUDGE

The Judge celebrates his birthday at a party given by employees of the Louisiana Highway Department. He was appointed by the governor to the Board of Highways in 1968.

Photo courtesy Baton Rouge *State-Times* and *Morning Advocate*

Perez (right) actively supported the presidential campaigns of George C. Wallace (left) with both money and time.

Photo courtesy Baton Rouge *State-Times* and *Morning Advocate*

Three leaders of the southern resistance (left to right): Perez, George C. Wallace, and Louisiana con-

Photo courtesy the New Orleans *Times-Picayune*

The Judge walks the ramparts at Fort St. Philip, which he renovated as a stockade for civil rights demonstrators. The fort, constructed by the French in 1724 and rebuilt later by the Spanish, was in the middle of a marsh prairie and could be reached only by helicopter or boat. Although no outside agitators were incarcerated here, the very existence of the fort served to intimidate those who might have considered invading Perez's territory.

Photo courtesy Baton Rouge *State-Times* and *Morning Advocate*

Leander Perez was a registered Democrat, but his principles were stronger than party loyalty. He opposed every Democratic presidential nominee from Harry Truman in 1948 to Hubert Humphrey in 1968.

Photo courtesy New Orleans *Times-Picayune*

The Judge provided a smooth transition of power to his two sons, Chalin O. Perez (left) and Leander H. Perez, Jr. (right). Chalin is president of the parish commission council, and Lea is district attorney for the Twenty-fifth Judicial District.

Leander Perez died of a heart attack in March, 1969. Eight of his grandsons serve as pallbearers to carry the casket from the Holy Name of Jesus Church on the Loyola University campus. Although he had been excommunicated as punishment for his stand against integration, it was revealed after his death that he and the Catholic church had become reconciled, and he was permitted a requiem mass.

Perez's supporters praised him as a defender of the southern way of life, and his detractors condemned him as a demagogue. Yet no one ever accused him of lacking principles. He did not follow public opinion, but plunged boldly ahead and dared the public to follow.

From time to time the federal government sent observers and agents to investigate voting in Plaquemines. In 1961 when two FBI agents went to Plaquemines to check voter registrations, the Plaquemines police jury ran an advertisement in the local and New Orleans newspapers urging residents not to cooperate. The ad advised, "Answer NO questions. Tell them they are not welcome."[20] Perez, claiming that the agents were engaged in "gestapo-style" tactics, blurted, "The federal government can go to hell and that goes for whoever gives the F.B.I. their orders—straight up to Washington."[21] In 1966 Perez had several direct confrontations with federal voting observers sent into the parish by the Justice Department. He instructed election commissioners that they must not "even give 'em a glass of water or a crumb of bread." At Belle Chasse he pointed out a federal observer and told newsmen to "take a picture of that federal spy."[22] The Judge charged that "some bad Negroes" were threatening other blacks in Plaquemines to force them to register. This prompted the parish council to offer a five-hundred-dollar reward for information leading to the arrest and conviction of anyone who threatened any Negro or compelled him to register against his will.[23]

Candidates backed by the "parish administration," what Perez and his supporters habitually called themselves, were selected at a parishwide caucus. Perez said that he would write about two hundred people telling them to come to the caucus and bring their friends but that he would never invite his political opponents. Sometimes eight hundred people would show up. Frequently a brass band would play, and barbecue, beer, and soft drinks would be served. The Judge would then make a speech, "suggesting" nominees for parish posts. These recommendations would immediately be rubber-stamped by the compliant caucus, which would then break up into ward caucuses. Perez would speak before each of these smaller caucuses, which would then approve his handpicked candidates. "Can you find anything more democratic?" he asked. When questioned if the caucus had ever endorsed one of his opponents, he replied, "There aren't even half a dozen [in the parish] who knock the administration. We could easily have them with us if we gave them political favors."[24]

Leander seldom found it necessary to campaign actively for his candidates, but when he did the parish was carefully organized and the activities lavishly funded. Ward captains were appointed to contact voters and transport them to the polls. Each voter was approached before election day in an effort to get every potential supporter to the polls. Every registered voter also received a letter from each administration candidate. The Judge himself said that he had been elected to office many times without opposition, although he had never made a political promise.[25]

Once Perez partisans were elected, they seldom deviated from his orders. The Judge's opponents claimed that he held undated resignations of most of the elected and appointed officials in Plaquemines. Perez could rid himself of recalcitrant local officials merely by sending their resignations to a friendly governor in Baton Rouge. The practice of holding undated resignations probably was superfluous after Perez's machine became firmly entrenched.[26]

Industries, like individuals, found it easier to appease Perez than to oppose him. Businesses operating in Plaquemines needed licenses, building permits, and rights-of-way for roads and canals. Oil companies needed drilling and blasting permits, pipeline permits, and approval of leases from the parish governing authority and State Mineral Board. Leander was selective about the industries he allowed in, once remarking, "We could have 100,000 people easily in this parish, but we don't want 'em."[27] Instead, the Plaquemines population never exceeded 24,000 during his lifetime. Perez explained that more residents would strain the parish's school system and social services. But probably the real reason he chose to keep the population sparse was that an influx of newcomers with no ties to the parish administration would dilute the voting rolls. This had happened in St. Bernard, where his influence declined as new people and new industries moved into the parish, although he never completely lost control there.[28]

Leander's opponents never had luck in finding jobs with parish industries. A former resident tells the story of a particularly vociferous adversary who frequented a Buras grocery owned by a Perez stalwart nicknamed Rooster. The Perez hater annoyed Rooster by launching into anti-Perez tirades in his store. Finally Rooster decided to retaliate. Hiding a tape recorder beneath the counter, he taped a sample of the man's outbursts, which he then carried to Perez. Listening to the tape, Perez became enraged. Calling the man's employer, the operator of a fish-processing plant with head-quarters in Plaquemines, Perez insisted that the offender be out of the parish the next day. When the employer objected, Leander threatened to prosecute the company for violating antipollution laws. The following day the anti-Perez man had been transferred to Cameron Parish. About a year later he was finally forgiven and allowed to return to Plaquemines, where he owned a home.[29] Occasionally, Perez even chastised his own relatives. In 1951 he forced the dismissal of parish school board superintendent Patrick Olinde, who was his nephew by marriage. Olinde moved out of the parish.[30]

Such power plays brought Perez and Plaquemines Parish an outpouring of unfavorable publicity. Except for the *Plaquemines Gazette,* the Shreveport *Journal,* the Shreveport *Times,* and some Mississippi newspapers, the Judge uniformly received a bad press. The New Orleans *Times-Picayune* was usually hostile, except for a brief period after 1956 when Perez and the *Picayune* were both fighting Earl Long. The most revealing study of Perez was David Baldwin's articles written in 1950 for the New Orleans *Item,* which dug into Leander's finances and his power politics. While the series was running, the *Item* newsstand outside the Plaquemines courthouse was moved inside, where it could not be patronized by the public. Although Baldwin was unsuccessful in obtaining an interview with Perez, *Collier's* writer Lester Velie had a different experience. Velie had tried to contact Perez for an interview for his two-part article, but the Judge was always busy. Soon, however, he discovered that Velie was making numerous other inquiries, among opponents as well as friends. He strolled into the Roosevelt Hotel, inquired the number of Velie's room, and went up. When Velie opened the door the Judge announced, "I'm Leander Perez. What the hell do you want?"[31] The notoriety Perez evoked prompted the Plaquemines police jury in 1959 to appoint a committee to consider employing a public relations firm to counteract some of the bad publicity the parish was receiving.

Perez was able to saturate his own stronghold with favorable propaganda through his mouthpiece, the *Plaquemines Gazette,* the consolidated successor to the old *Plaquemines Protector* and *Lower Coast Gazette.* The *Gazette,* which was the official parish journal, sometimes neglected to mention anti-Perez candidates at all, until news of their defeat appeared. In the unlikely event that one was elected, he might again be skipped over in the account of the swearing in. Exactly who owned the newspaper was never made public. At one time A. S. Cain, who worked in Perez's law office, was listed as a stockholder. Later the Judge's business associate, Robert J. Lobrano, was listed as president. J. Ben Meyer, editor of the *Gazette* until he split with Perez, later swore out an affidavit that "the paper was actually owned by Leander H. Perez, who issued all orders to me for the management thereof."[32] When a Perez opponent attempted to sue the *Gazette,* he found that no corporation such as the Plaquemines Gazette, Inc., existed.[33]

Whether Perez actually owned the *Gazette,* there is no doubt that he controlled it. The paper depended heavily on public printing for its survival. By 1961 it was receiving $450 quarterly as printer for the police jury, $500 each from the Buras and Grand Prairie levee districts, and $100 each from thirteen other parish agencies. Leander's photograph appeared on nearly every other page of the *Gazette,* showing him attending barbecues and public dedications and posing with Boy Scouts, national dignitaries, and Citizens' Council officials. Every Christmas the paper published a special edition outlining the accomplishments of the parish administration. Local industries periodically paid for advertisements simply to thank Perez for allowing them to be a part of Plaquemines. The *Gazette* also served Perez in more devious ways. In 1932 seven hundred acres of land forfeited to the parish for taxes came up for sale. According to law, such sales had to be advertised for a specified period of time in the official journal. The *Gazette* paid a Memphis firm, which handled some of its printing, to print one hundred extra copies of a special edition of the *Gazette* including an advertisement for the land. The copies of the *Gazette* sold to the public did not include the ad. The extra copies were hidden in Plaquemines for six weeks, then given to the sheriff to be placed in the files. The land was sold to Robert Lobrano without competitive bidding.[34]

Leander engaged in local, state, and national politics simultaneously while managing his own financial empire. Much of his time was
spent on the road, constantly shuttling from New Orleans to Plaquemines and St. Bernard, to neighboring southern cities to address
Citizens' Council groups, to Washington to appear before congressional committees to testify against civil rights legislation, and to the
capitol in Baton Rouge. At a testimonial dinner in his honor, Perez
was presented with a special certificate from Governor Davis en-
titling him to exceed the speed limit on his trips to and from Baton
Rouge.[35]

Although Perez's rule was frequently vindictive and always self-
serving, it was also sometimes paternalistic. No one was more spite-
ful toward opponents than the Judge, yet no one was kinder to
friends. His concern for the people of Plaquemines ran deeper than
political expediency. The public usually saw the irascible side of
Perez, but he also had a gentler nature. In informal conversation he
was charming as long as partisan politics was not discussed. An in-
gratiating host, the Judge liked nothing better than driving outsiders around in his air-conditioned Oldsmobile, sometimes with a
revolver in the glove compartment, proudly showing off his prize cattle and the many public improvements he had brought to
Plaquemines. He owned a small Lafitte skiff, but his real pride was
the *Manta,* an elegant seventy-foot vessel with a teakwood deck and
a mahogany superstructure bought by the parish for $75,000. The
stated purpose of the yacht was "to patrol the waters of Plaquemines
against seafood depredation," although this work was already being
done by state conservation agents. The *Manta* was used by the
Judge to entertain politicians and businessmen that "we think can
benefit the parish."[36]

Perez's positive attributes grew more evident after he became
safely entrenched in power; he seemed to mellow with the extinction
of his enemies. Leander gave generously to the Red Cross and the
American Cancer Society and sent Christmas boxes to servicemen
in Vietnam, as well as regularly supporting the Catholic church
until breaking with it over racial integration. He helped many of his
friends with patronage through his influence with Congressman F.
Edward Hebert, Senator Allen J. Ellender, and Senator James O.

Eastland of Mississippi.[37] He was able to secure postal appointments, nominations to Annapolis and West Point, visas, military transfers, and early releases from the armed forces through his contacts in Congress. Hebert, who often asked Perez to suggest appointees for federal posts in the lower parishes, always cleared potential appointees with him before acting. Hebert and Ellender were also instrumental in obtaining federal appropriations for flood protection, erosion control, bridges, locks, canals, and disaster relief. Occasionally, Perez even drafted legislation that Hebert introduced in Congress. The Judge also controlled considerable state patronage. Through cooperative governors he was able to get supporters appointed to the local levee boards, to the board of supervisors of elections, and to the position of attorney for the inheritance tax collector. Leander influenced the composition of the State Sovereignty Commission, Louisiana Department of Highways, State Mineral Board, and various other state boards, commissions, and regulatory agencies and the awarding of state contracts. Perez had a greater voice in the second Jimmie Davis gubernatorial administration (1960–1964) than under any previous governor. Leander was preeminently a political boss rather than a politician; although he never actually controlled the state, he did have a great deal to say about how it was run. He is, for example, credited with having named several of the members of Earl Long's state ticket in 1948.[38]

Judge Perez was able to find jobs for nearly everyone in Plaquemines who needed one. The parish unemployment rate was only 1.78 percent in 1972, one of the lowest rates in the United States. Plaquemines was and still is, in fact, a miniature welfare state. There were many jobs for front levee inspectors, back levee inspectors, brake tag inspectors, gasoline station inspectors, pump operators, maintenance men, clean-up men, and various other inspectors. For example, during the early 1940s Leander kept ten brake tag and license inspectors on the payroll at from twenty-five to fifty dollars per month each.[39] The parish is probably the most litter free in the state because a parish work crew cleans for forty or fifty feet on each side of the highways. The parish maintains a pension fund for indigent widows.[40] The Judge also helped Plaquemines natives find work in private industries. He asked firms doing business with the parish to submit a yearly report on man-hour employment and materials purchased locally. Yet Plaquemines remained firmly nonunion. Freeport Sulphur has operated in Plaquemines since 1933 without hiring union workers. No outsider can be employed by parish industries unless he is first fingerprinted and photographed. One delta resident said that a driller, on orders from Perez, was forced to lay off some outside workers to make room for Plaquemines men.[41]

People needing jobs, parish contracts, loans, pensions, legal aid, or medical care wrote directly to Perez, seldom bothering to go through a state or parish agency. Many of the messages were desperate pleas from local people in dire financial straits and unable to work or unable to earn enough money at their jobs. The writers frequently prefaced their letters with assurances of their political support. Some of the letters were written on the backs of circulars appealing for their votes, and one was written on the back of an invitation to a barbecue for the inauguration of parish officials. The Judge usually granted requests from his constituents as long as the person concerned voted "right." It was his meticulous attention to such favors, as much as his innate intelligence, that accounted for his success. The poor and semiliterate residents of the lower delta both needed and wanted a leader, someone of superior intelligence and education. They did not desire democracy because the concept was foreign to them. Such attitudes are not confined to Plaquemines—they permeated the enclaves of European immigrants in the great northern cities—but they endured longer in the isolated lower delta than elsewhere. Perez was brought up in such an environment, unconscious of either the theory or practice of democracy, but he had been taught that the wealthy and educated had a duty to lead. In the early 1920s, he would have found few in Plaquemines to disagree with him. But even in the 1960s, after many "outsiders," people with different backgrounds and more trenchant beliefs in democracy, had moved into Belle Chasse and especially neighboring St. Bernard, Perez persisted in his belief in benevolent despotism. He was utterly unchanging and uncompromising; his was the strength and provincialism of the single-minded.

Leander handled without compensation legal cases for indigent families. He arranged loans and sometimes personally advanced money to people in danger of losing their homes. Once he paid for dental work for the daughter of a farmer who was unable to pay the bill. On several occasions Perez even intervened to settle family squabbles in the parish. A quarreling household would send a delegation to Perez, who would hear both sides and give his opinion; the emissaries would return home with the feud ended. The Judge's decision stood.[42]

Returning from a hunting trip at the lower end of the parish, Perez would sometimes stop at each settlement along the way back, buy a round of drinks at a neighborhood bar, and sit in on a few games of poker. According to a close friend, Leander "played a mean game of poker. Name the game and he was ready!" By midnight he would have worked his way up to Port Sulphur. During the poker games, political cronies would pull up chairs and ask for advice on local problems, which Perez would freely give while playing his hand. By the following morning the word would be out that the Judge had been through the parish, and everyone knew what he had said.[43]

Plaquemines, rich in oil and sulphur, was easily able to devote huge sums to public works. When Leander first took office as district attorney in 1924, the parish budget was a mere $30,000. At the meeting at which he retired as president of the parish commission council, the 1968 budget, totaling $3,796,902.50, was unanimously adopted. Of his accomplishments, he said, "They tell you Perez is a boss, Perez is a dictator. The truth is, Perez is just a darn work horse."[44]

A Plaquemines Negro in his seventies told a Kansas City reporter that Leander could show kindness to blacks as well as to whites. He explained that on one occasion a black man who had tried to get a construction job had been told by the boss that Perez had given orders not to hire any Negroes. The black man then went to Perez himself and said that he needed a job. The Judge not only found him one but also got jobs for several of his friends who were out of work. The aged black man said that on another occasion three of his friends had been arrested for trapping out of season, fined thirty-five dollars, and sentenced to ten days in jail. One of them, seeing Perez in the hallway of the courthouse, asked if he could serve time for the others because they had to work to support families. The Judge told him that all three could go home without serving time. They did, and nothing more was ever heard of the matter.[45]

Leander was fond of describing the numerous improvements he had brought to the parish. "Mine is the life story," he once said, "of a man who's done more, I believe, than any other man in this country in a restricted area, in building up a community."[46]

Among Perez's achievements were the parishwide construction of roads, libraries, levees, water purification plants, and auditoriums. Between 1952 and 1962 the parish built eight public schools at a cost of more than eleven million dollars. Health and sanitation were improved by establishing a parish health department, systems of garbage collection and mosquito control, and an ambulance service and by the construction of a million-dollar hospital at Port Sulphur. Hospitalization and life insurance was provided for all parish employees. Scholarships were made available to all parish children, white and black alike, who sought a college education. Farmers were helped by land reclamation projects, the organization of cooperative marketing groups, and the construction of storage and marketing facilities. Rehabilitation funds were provided to replant orange groves destroyed by storms. Volunteer fire departments were organized and provided with modern equipment. Siphons and flumes were installed to furnish fresh water to rehabilitate wildlife areas and oyster beds. A parish employment office was created to serve as a clearinghouse for people seeking jobs in private industry. A historical research program was initiated, brochures were published, and several old forts were restored as tourist attractions. Parish parks, recreation grounds, and a wildlife preserve were created. Incinerator plants were built, and a parishwide emergency communications system was installed. Perez was especially proud of the two parish-operated free ferries across the Mississippi. The list is even more impressive when one remembers that Plaquemines entered the twentieth century as one of the most undeveloped sections of a backward state.[47]

For Plaquemines residents, the best thing about this plethora of benefits is that they are free. There is no sales tax, and property taxes are among the lowest in the country. Perez said that Plaquemines could be entirely without taxes but that he felt that token taxpaying gave the people a sense of participation in their government.[48]

Perez also provided a social life for his rural parish. Picnics, barbecues, fish fries, fairs, and dedications, sponsored by the parish administration, volunteer fire departments, chambers of commerce, and other civic organizations, were made gala events. Dances were held for teenagers and grown-ups. A summer recreation program was organized, and Perez helped plan the construction of swimming pools by private groups. There were fishing rodeos, pirogue races, donkey baseball games, comic womanless weddings, and muskrat judging contests. An annual Fourth of July celebration was held at renovated Fort Jackson, featuring a fireworks display, bathing beauty contest, and speeches by Perez. There was a little theater, barbershop quartets, and athletic teams for children. A parish physical fitness program was initiated. The social life of Plaquemines might have satisfied few urban dwellers, but the parish offered far more recreational opportunities than most rural regions. An inevitable participant and guest at parish social events, Perez never missed an opportunity to tell the people how parish "unity" made such good fellowship possible. He often served as chef at barbecues and sometimes donated one of his own steers for the occasion. At Christmas and Easter, he and his wife gave holiday parties, complete with gifts, for the white children of the parish.[49]

Periodically, semiaquatic Plaquemines was the victim of tragic hurricanes and floods. Perez galvanized the parish into action after such disasters, but was wary of outside help. After Hurricane Flossie struck in 1956, he spent thirty consecutive days in the courthouse, where he supplied the people with food, water, clothes, and medical help. A massive rebuilding program was begun after Hurricane Betsy flattened Plaquemines in 1965.[50]

The fact that Perez possessed considerable grass-roots support should not be dismissed lightly. Most Plaquemines residents considered anti-Perez leaders to be traitors to the parish. The Judge had a galaxy of articulate and vociferous opponents, but most of them lived outside the parish.

Leander was so busy in Plaquemines that he never seriously sought statewide office. He qualified to run for the Louisiana House of Representatives in 1967, but withdrew before the primary after deciding that attendance at the roll calls might interfere with his other activities. Although he received numerous letters urging him to run for governor, he was not interested in the position. He was, in fact, too ideologically rigid to compromise his political beliefs to please a cross section of the electorate. The Judge did not care personally to hold a high office as long as he could control those who did.[51]

The number of votes that Perez could deliver to a candidate running for state office was comparatively small, but his support was important for two reasons. His ability to deliver the vote was dependable, and he could produce it in enormously one-sided proportions. To make the best of his limited offerings in state elections, Perez sometimes withheld the totals until he found out exactly how many votes were needed to swing the election.[52]

Leander led the conservative faction in the Democratic state central committee. He was a master of parliamentary maneuver, his knowledge of the law sometimes intimidated his opponents. Perez succeeded in keeping the rural parishes in control of the state central committee when it was reapportioned. Many committee members followed the Judge's lead in voting, even when they were unaware of the issues involved. Perez had Plaquemines listed first on the roll call to help his friends follow his lead.[53]

Perez was also a power in the state legislature. Each year he rented a suite in a Baton Rouge hotel and lobbied for and against bills that concerned Plaquemines. He could seldom defeat legislation backed by a strong governor, but he could usually muster enough support to beat down tax measures, which required a two-thirds majority. Such was his strength that he was often referred to as the "third house of the legislature." Many legislators regularly asked Perez to prepare bills for them because they regarded him as an expert on the state constitution. In 1937 Governor Leche appointed him to a commission to prepare a code of oil, gas, and mineral laws for the state, a field in which his expertise was unmatched. A labor lawyer who heard Perez argue a case before the state supreme court termed him "the most brilliant constitutional lawyer in the state." Through the secretary of state, a personal friend, Perez was able to arrange where constitutional amendments would be placed on the ballot, which would improve the chances of those he favored and make it more difficult for those he opposed.[54]

Perez knew thousands of public officials and political workers throughout the state. Running something of a "farm system" for budding politicians, he recognized young men on the make, encouraged them, and backed them financially. Several prominent state politicians were put through law school by Perez.[55]

His influence declined somewhat as greater distance developed between him and the national Democratic party. State and congressional leaders, dependent on national patronage to an extent that the Judge was not, were also subject to party discipline. No section of the state other than Plaquemines could defy the national administration and not suffer financially.

Perez seemed to thrive on adversity. Although he suffered repeated setbacks in his forays into national politics, his power in Plaquemines remained undiminished, despite occasional challenges. One of these occurred in the early 1940s, and it was called the "little war."

EIGHT

The Little War of 1943

Perez's squabbles in the early 1940s with Claude Meraux and Dutch Rowley occurred at a most inopportune time. He already had his hands full fighting an anti-Long reform administration led by Governor Sam Jones.

Even after the assassination in 1935 of Huey Long, the Longite faction had kept its power, endorsing a ticket headed by Richard Leche in the 1935 gubernatorial primary. Leche, with Earl Long as lieutenant governor, won the election but resigned in 1939 after wholesale corruption was discovered in his administration. Eventually, more than 250 indictments resulted from the misappropriations that had bilked the state of an estimated $100,000,000.

One of the few prominent state officials to escape prosecution, Earl Long served as chief executive for eleven months, during which time he actively campaigned for a full term as governor in his own right. He tried to disassociate himself from the corrupt Leche administration by claiming that as lieutenant governor he had spent most of his time on his "pea patch" farm in Winnfield or practicing law in New Orleans.[1]

Emerging from the pack of anti-Long candidates as Earl's most formidable opponent in 1940 was Sam Houston Jones, a forty-two-year-old Lake Charles attorney who had never before waged a statewide campaign. Jones had worked his way through LSU waiting on tables for six dollars a month, then had enlisted in the army in 1917. After the First World War, he had returned to his birthplace, the small town of De Ridder, where he had worked in the law office of his father, the clerk of court, and studied law privately. He had been admitted to the bar in 1922 and shortly thereafter ap-

121

pointed a district judge. Two years later Jones had moved to Lake Charles, where he became an assistant district attorney and was elected state commander of the American Legion, a position providing him with political contacts throughout the state. Jones was serious minded, hard working, stubborn, and determined. He characterized himself as a liberal who had consistently opposed the Long machine because of its dangerous tendency toward dictatorship. As part of his reform program, he pledged to install civil service, reorganize the state government, abolish political assessments on state employees and deadheadism, reduce taxes, and balance the budget. Even Jones, however, refused to attack the sacrosanct name of the martyred Huey Long, admitting that "my pappy was for Huey."[2]

A wealthy Monroe oilman and state senator, James A. ("Jimmie") Noe, who apparently believed that he could become governor if his principal rivals were sent to prison, became the third major candidate in the race. His appeal was limited to disaffected members of the Long faction. The most colorful major candidate in the contest was James H. ("Jimmy") Morrison, a Hammond attorney and later United States congressman. Morrison spent most of his time entertaining the electorate by lampooning his opponents rather than stating his own qualifications. He was frequently accompanied to rallies by a pet monkey he called Earl Long, for which name he made a big show of apologizing to the creature.[3]

With his name, the remnants of his late brother's machine, and state patronage behind him, it seemed unlikely that anyone could defeat Earl Long. He also had the financial and political backing of Huey's faithful partisan, New Orleans millionaire Robert Maestri, who had been installed as mayor of New Orleans in 1936, upon the resignation of T. Semmes Walmsley.[4]

Perez did his best to ensure Earl's election. When Noe organized a ticket of local candidates in Plaquemines, the Judge had the parish Democratic executive committee disqualify twelve of them. Perez, chairman of the committee, explained, "Our attitude is that we'll do anything for our friends and to hell with our enemies."[5] Earl led the Democratic primary by a comfortable margin over Jones, who finished second, and Noe, who ran third. In Plaquemines Long polled a small majority over his combined opponents.[6]

Noe, who would make Earl his running mate for lieutenant governor in 1959, endorsed Jones against Long in the second primary. The campaign took on a menacing light when Jones's life was threatened and Governor Long was compelled to send state police to guard his rival. Before the second primary, Earl summoned the legislature into a special six-day session and drummed through popular measures intended to ensure his election: increased appropriations for free school lunches and welfare benefits, abolition of the state sales tax, and exemption of gasoline used in boats and farm equipment from the state gasoline tax. Feelings ran high at the special session, and the legislature refused to provide funds for the proposed expenditures since the state was already heavily in debt. Results of the second primary showed that, for the first time in recent state history, a Long had received a majority of the New Orleans votes but a minority of the votes cast outside the city. Even in New Orleans, the results were disappointing. Maestri had been expected to deliver a 25,000-vote majority, but the city gave Long only a 15,000-vote lead; the landslides expected in other former banner parishes also did not occur. Perez was able to deliver 67.6 percent of the Plaquemines vote to Earl, but it was not enough. Jones was the victor in the state by about 19,000 votes.[7]

The friendship of the man occupying the Governor's Mansion was important to Leander Perez. A congenial administration could greatly help him in his consolidation and exercise of local power; a friendly governor not only could cut the Judge in on the cornucopia of state patronage, but also could be invaluable in helping to win legislative concessions and to suppress embarrassing investigations. A state government that desired to do so could destroy him. Until now, Leander had had little to fear, since he had been an ally of every chief executive since the Kingfish. But suddenly, in the reformer Sam Jones, he had an enemy well worth worrying about. Right away, the defeated Long faction, led by Perez and Maestri, set out to ambush the new governor.

In the first primary campaign, Jones had vowed to do away with the 2 percent state sales tax. Long, seeking to win votes and to outflank the young reformer, had had his special legislative session pass a constitutional amendment repealing the tax. This popular measure had no trouble being ratified at the polls. The tax was thus swept from the books before Jones had even taken office. The new governor immediately faced a knotty problem: although he had favored the abolition of the tax, he had also promised to balance the budget, a project to which he gave top priority. Jones knew that with the sales tax gone the budget could not be balanced unless alternative sources of revenue could be found. Perez and the Longites, resolving never to allow this to happen, shot down every proposal the governor offered, including an increased income tax. Frustrated at every turn, he decided he would have to revive the sales tax. Thinking the politically unsophisticated Jones had stepped at last into their snare, the Judge and his allies sprang it. Leander, Maestri, and the other members of the Long machine pulled out all the stops in the battle to block readoption of the sales tax and to embarrass the governor in the process. It was not long, however, before they realized they were battling a foe of considerable mettle. Sam Jones jumped gamely into the fray by slashing the budget drastically. He cut off as much as he could of the appropriations going directly to New Orleans and even threatened to close Charity Hospital there as an economy move. The superintendent of the facility claimed that, if the governor had his way, six hundred patients would have to be ejected. Public pressure mounted as each side accused the other of callousness. Finally, Jones called a special session of the legislature, and a compromise was negotiated. He got a 1 percent rather than a 2 percent sales levy with certain items exempted from taxation.

The Perez-Maestri combine was even less successful in opposing the governor's pet civil service reform. It went through, but they repealed it when Earl Long became governor again in 1948.[8]

Jones gave Perez a hard run for his money on yet another front. As part of his reform program, the governor created the Louisiana Crime Commission. This body, intended to recover state funds that had been diverted through deception and fraud, was endowed with subpoena power, making it a potent investigative force. The commission set out to prove that Perez had "diverted to his own private gain, through subterfuge (involving dummy corporations), all of the mineral wealth of the various public levee boards and the school boards of Plaquemines and St. Bernard parishes."[9]

The Crime Commission scheduled an open hearing in Orleans Parish Criminal District Court to look into the mineral and trapping leases in the delta parishes. Subpoenas were issued for the company books and other records of five corporations: Suburban Coast Realty Company, Plaquemines Parish Development Company, Delta Development Company, Bird Islands Trapping Company, and Louisiana Coastal Lands, Inc. Although all of these companies were headed by Perez's close friends and relatives, the Judge himself denied that he owned or held stock in any of them; he did admit, however, that he was attorney for Suburban Coast Realty, Delta Development, and Louisiana Coastal Lands. The secretary of Suburban Coast Realty was Leander's brother-in-law, C. P. Foret. Robert J. Lobrano, a close friend, was secretary of both Delta Development and Louisiana Coastal Lands. Rudolph McBride, secretary of Plaquemines Parish Development, was an assistant district attorney under Perez. A Perez opponent pointed out that not one of the five corporations had filed an annual statement as required by law.[10]

Perez had no intention of giving ground. He and the corporation officials used every legal ploy imaginable to prevent the Crime Commission from securing the companies' records. The officers protested that presentation of their books for an indefinite period would tie up their businesses and constitute illegal search and seizure. Perez's lawyer argued that the alleged fraudulent procurement of oil, mineral, and trapping leases from public bodies was not a crime defined by any state statute. Company officers testified that all of their records were in the possession of Perez, who refused to produce them. The Judge was subpoenaed to appear before the commission but refused, telling its executive counsel, "You can go to hell with my compliments."[11]

While pressing the battle to force Perez to open the companies' books, the Crime Commission started to close in on him from another direction. It brought charges that he had "corrupted the office of district attorney by setting himself up as a political tycoon and by the use of fraudulent registrations and poll taxes had built up a dynasty saturated with crime and corruption." The commission claimed that in one election "5,361 votes were cast for certain constitutional amendments, with only 3 against. At this time not over 3,000 voters were existent in Plaquemines parish." The Judge was accused of abusing his position and public confidence, of political favoritism, of failing to prosecute in murder cases, election frauds, and fish and game violations, and of paying salaries to public officials who were no longer working. A Plaquemines opponent of Perez's wrote the Crime Commission that gambling was rampant in the parish and that the sheriff, district attorney, and grand jury were doing nothing about it.[12]

Unshaken, the Judge prepared his defense in his own time-honored fashion: he took the offensive. He launched an attack on the legality of the investigating body itself. Reeling from the barrage of writs with which Perez peppered the commission, state Attorney General Eugene Stanley declared, "Their number staggers the imagination." The spearhead of Perez's offense was an attack on the funding of the Crime Commission. He claimed that its $500,000 appropriation had been improperly taken from a fund dedicated to the payment of homestead exemptions. The state supreme court agreed, and the Crime Commission expired after ten months without completing its investigations.[13]

Although Governor Jones was unsuccessful in recovering levee board revenues that had already been drained off, he resolved to prevent a recurrence. Knowing that he would have to subvert Perez's control of the local boards, he appointed new members to those in Plaquemines and St. Bernard parishes. These newly reshuffled boards then passed resolutions to employ special attorneys to replace Perez as legal adviser. The Buras Levee Board authorized its new counsels, Thomas E. Furlow and William J. Blass, to file suits to recover part of the parish severance tax for the state and to try to secure for the state ten thousand acres of land, including an oil field in the lower area of the levee district. Furlow and Blass were also authorized to file suits against the parish to invalidate the bond assumption agreement between the Plaquemines police jury and the Buras Levee Board.[14]

The governor had now aimed a blow directly at the foundation of Perez's financial empire. When he learned that he was being supplanted as attorney for the levee boards, Leander quickly obtained a restraining order from the temporary district judge prohibiting Furlow and Blass from representing the boards or receiving payment from them. The three levee boards then adopted a second resolution employing the two, but Perez procured yet another local court ruling—he seldom found it difficult—which stated that he could not be replaced. He also filed suit against the state attorney general, Furlow, and three others, charging that they had conspired to defraud the levee boards by the employment of special attorneys. Meanwhile, plans lapsed to press the three revenue recovery suits on behalf of the boards; it would have been up to Perez to prosecute them.[15]

Although the political pyrotechnics set off by the battle over the sales tax, the Crime Commission investigation, and the matter of the levee boards kept Louisianians well entertained, the best was yet to come. The most spectacular confrontation between Governor Jones and Judge Perez is remembered in Louisiana history as the "little war," and it all started when Plaquemines Sheriff Louis D. Dauterive unexpectedly died in office. According to state law, the governor was entitled to appoint a successor if the remaining term of the deceased incumbent was less than a year. If more than a year remained, a special election would have to be held.[16]

It all seemed simple enough. Dauterive died June 1, 1943. A new sheriff was due to be elected in the general election on April 18, 1944, thirty days after which the governor would be authorized to issue a commission to the winner. Thus, according to Sam Jones, the sheriff-elect would be qualified to take office May 19, 1944, less than a year after Dauterive's death. Clearly, it was the governor's right and duty to appoint a successor to hold office in the interim. Down in Plaquemines, however, Judge Perez read the matter differently. He argued that Dauterive had not filed his oath of office with the secretary of state until June 14, 1940, which meant that his four-year term would not expire until June 14, 1944. Besides, he continued, even though the election for a successor was to be held on April 18, the governor might be tardy in issuing a commission to the incoming sheriff, thereby prolonging the incumbent's term beyond a year. It was Perez's opinion that a special election was required. Thus, while General Dwight D. Eisenhower's forces built up for an invasion of the Continent and U.S. Marines island-hopped in the Pacific, Leander Perez and Sam Jones prepared to lock horns over the question of who would be sheriff of Plaquemines Parish.[17]

Unfortunately for Perez, judicial precedent had determined that the remaining term in such cases was to be computed by figuring back from the earliest date a new regular term could begin, in this instance May 19, 1944. That precedent had been established twenty-four years earlier in a case involving the Judge himself, who had been appointed by the governor to succeed a district judge who had died in office with less than a year left to his term. Perez's right to the appointment had been contested but had been upheld by the state supreme court.[18]

The contradiction implicit in his present position was lost on Leander. He was not one to concede easily, either in law or politics. No matter how impossible a situation might appear to the casual observer, Perez's legal imagination, with its flair for the exotic and the *outré,* was capable of devising a stratagem to fit it. Once he had charted his course, he would plunge ahead with complete assurance. Often it was not at all necessary that a scheme be legally sound as long as it was complicated enough to delay and obstruct proceedings until the contested issue became academic. Although almost anyone would easily have granted the validity of the governor's claim, the political situation made it imperative for Perez to resist. He certainly did not want a Jones appointee snooping about his courthouse, making arrests, prying into records, and collecting taxes. Perhaps more crucial was the fact that a local election was approaching and an unfriendly sheriff probably would be on guard against voting irregularities.

The state constitution provided that, if the regular sheriff were unable to serve, the parish coroner would assume his law enforcement duties and state officials would assume his tax collection responsibilities. Acting under this provision, Perez had his coroner, Dr. Ben R. Slater of Belle Chasse, post bond as acting sheriff on June 2, the day after Dauterive died.[19]

On June 11 Governor Jones issued a commission to Walter Blaize of Buras to serve as sheriff and tax collector for the remainder of Dauterive's term. Blaize, an automobile repair shop owner and former police jury member, was a sworn enemy of the Judge. He was a never-say-die habitual anti-Perez candidate who never won but never gave up.[20] Dr. Slater, of course, refused to yield the office to Blaize.

Meanwhile, Perez began to erect both legal and physical defenses. A contingent of about twenty of Slater's deputies entrenched themselves in the sheriff's office; the parish courthouse was barricaded, and cots were moved in to accommodate the defenders. The coroner-sheriff told reporters variously that the barricades had been set up "to uphold the constitution of the state" and "for the benefit of the painters." No one saw any painters, however.[21]

While the barricades were going up in Plaquemines, Governor Jones was making some plans of his own. He intended to make a show of authority so awe inspiring that Perez and his supporters would quickly be intimidated into submission. When the Louisiana National Guard had been called overseas to help fight the Axis, the legislature, fearing that the regular police might prove inadequate in case of civil disturbance, had established the State Guard. Perez had opposed the guard on the grounds that it might be used as a "political weapon" against local officials. His fears appeared about to be confirmed. Within a week of Dauterive's death, Jones assembled the Baton Rouge and Lake Charles companies of the guard in the capital, amid rumors that they would be sent into Plaquemines. The guardsmen came armed and had been told to expect to be away from their homes for several days. The companies held formation in the yard beneath the crenelated, pseudo-Gothic Old State Capitol while five chartered buses lined up on a side street to take them to their unannounced destination. After a brief drill and roll call, however, the men were dismissed and sent home.[22]

If the governor's show of arms was meant to have a chastening effect on the Judge, however, it fell short of its mark. Perez reacted to the guard mobilization by having his police jury invoke a wartime ordinance authorizing local defense. Apparently he thought Jones had been watching too many newsreels; the governor, he charged, had "become so obsessed with the idea of conquered provinces that he was kidding himself into believing he could ignore the provisions of the state constitution and make a conquered province of Plaquemines parish." Perez called a mass meeting and urged "hundreds of men—and I mean men who can stand and fight for their rights" to attend. When newspapermen tried to find out when the rally was to be held, he replied that the time was a "military secret."[23]

The mass meeting was, in fact, never held. Instead, a group of perhaps a dozen citizens closeted themselves with the parish police jury to implement the next stage in the Judge's strategy. Perez— whom the New Orleans *States* dubbed "General Pipsqueak"—now wanted an army. Under a wartime ordinance that gave the parish the authority to call up its citizens in case of a public emergency, the police jury created a makeshift force christened the Plaquemines Wartime Emergency Patrol. The stated purpose of the patrol, com- posed of all able-bodied white men in the parish, was to protect Plaquemines' long and irregular coastline from German sub- marines; everyone knew, however, that it was really intended to intimidate Governor Jones. The proclamation announcing the mobilization of Perez's army specifically included the members of the local American Legion post. The state commander of the legion, J. Perry Cole, who was also executive officer of the State Guard, threatened to have the post's charter revoked and its commander expelled if he insisted on participating in a "political dispute." Ignor- ing the threat, the local commander, a Perez stalwart, declared that he and his Legionnaires would back the Judge all the way. Member- ship in the Plaquemines patrol was compulsory, and patrolmen were authorized to bear arms "concealed or openly" if the parish were threatened with the use of unlawful force, invasion, or sabotage. The police jury specified that no member of the patrol could be held re- sponsible for damages that might occur in the defense of the parish.[24]

Under these less than promising auspices, Walter Blaize and his attorney Richard Dowling set out from Baton Rouge on their way to Pointe a la Hache for the swearing-in ceremony. Just after crossing the Plaquemines Parish line, they found at Braithwaite a roadblock manned by armed deputies, who had stopped a car with an out-of- state tag and were telling the occupants that they could not continue because there was "trouble in the parish." Blaize and Dowling de- cided not to confront the deputies but went looking for District

Judge Albert Estopinal, Jr., in St. Bernard. The judge, however, was conveniently "out fishing." Blaize finally sent in his credentials by registered mail.[25]

With Perez and Slater holed up behind their armed guards and Blaize unready to shoot his way into the sheriff's office, the battle now shifted to the courts. The governor arranged a test case to confirm his appointment of Blaize. To bypass the Perez-dominated district court serving Plaquemines and St. Bernard, Jones brought suit against two of his own officials, the supervisor of public funds and the collector of revenue, claiming that the two refused to yield their positions as tax collectors for Plaquemines Parish to Blaize. Since the suit involved state officials in the capital, it could be tried in a Baton Rouge district court.[26]

Perez tried to intervene in the case on behalf of Wilson Dauterive, deputy tax collector and a nephew of the late sheriff, who claimed that he had never yielded the parish tax records to either official named in Jones's suit because the books were being audited. The case was pointless, he contended, because the state officials could not be compelled to turn over records they did not possess. The Baton Rouge court rejected this argument. If the situation was not now bad enough for the judge, Dauterive soon made it even worse when he secretly wrote Governor Jones requesting that he be appointed sheriff instead of Blaize or Slater in order to restore peace between the contesting factions. Eventually, Jones revealed the letter to the press. The would-be peacemaker quickly disclaimed it, but Perez disgustedly abandoned him, now deciding that Dauterive was not an officeholder at all because his commission had expired upon his uncle's death. "Sheriff" Slater, coming to Perez's support but unaware of the latest interpretation of Dauterive's employment status, announced he would fire the traitor. A few hours later Dauterive resigned, and the chaos was reduced to mere confusion.[27]

On June 18 the Baton Rouge district court ruled valid the governor's appointment of Blaize. To make the judgment final, the two state officials appealed to the state supreme court for writs setting aside the lower court ruling. Perez applied for a suspensive appeal on behalf of about eight hundred Plaquemines citizens, headed by the widow of the late sheriff. The Judge's suit charged that the lower court decision had been secured by collusion between the plaintiff and defendants and that Dr. Slater had not been made a party in the suit. Slater's deputies and the Plaquemines police jury also filed interventions on behalf of the defendants. On July 13, the supreme court, by a four-to-three vote, upheld the decision of the Baton Rouge court, stating, "There is no doubt that the Governor had the authority to appoint the plaintiff, Walter J. Blaize, to the office of sheriff, to fill the vacancy, caused by the death of Sheriff Dauterive on June 1, 1943, because, at that time the unexpired portion of the term of office was less than a year." The court also held that, even if there had been collusion between the plaintiff and the defendants in the lower court decision, this was not illegal in a test case.[28]

In his dissenting opinion Justice John B. Fournet, an old protégé of Huey Long's, seemed to be appealing to political reality rather than to law. "Even if Blaize," he wrote, "armed with this decision by the court, seeks to oust the coroner as the sheriff of the parish, the coroner could not be compelled to respect the same any more than he could be compelled to respect an order of the 'Zulu King.'"[29]

After handing down its decision, the Louisiana Supreme Court recessed for its summer vacation. Blaize's attorney announced that his client would now proceed to take office "regardless of any opposition by force or otherwise," but Dr. Slater continued to act as sheriff as though nothing had happened. Strangers were kept out of the well-guarded courthouse at Pointe a la Hache. A crudely lettered sign above the entrance to the sheriff's office warned, "Danger, For Deputies Only." Blaize still had not assumed his duties when the court reassembled in October. At this time motions for a rehearing offered by the Perez forces were denied. As far as the governor, Blaize, and the supreme court were concerned, the matter had been decided.[30]

Perez's supply of legal delaying tactics was quickly running out. He filed a petition on behalf of Slater in federal district court, but it was denied. Walter Blaize called at Slater's residence to request that he peacefully yield the sheriff's office, but the coroner was at Pointe a la Hache, protected by his deputies. Governor Jones wired both Perez and Slater to ask that they quietly step aside and allow his appointee to take office, but the Judge obstinately stood his ground, terming the message a "blood-curdling threat."[31]

It was more than apparent that Blaize would have to be installed by force if he was to be installed at all. The governor summoned his legal advisers and top officers of the State Guard to a war council, after which some four hundred guardsmen were called to active duty. The men borrowed uniforms, sidearms, machine guns, and ammunition from the Fort Polk army base and marshaled at Camp Pontchartrain in New Orleans. Many of them were elderly, and some had never handled firearms, so a preliminary maneuver was held to acquaint them with their equipment. The company from the town of Crowley refused to participate on the grounds that this was a political dispute, but other outfits soon arrived, bringing the effective force to about six hundred men.[32]

While the State Guard drilled and waited for orders, Judge Estopinal quickly supplied Perez with an injunction forbidding it to enter Plaquemines Parish. Another mass meeting was announced; residents were called upon to "stand up as American citizens . . . against attempted oppression." As it turned out, only twelve persons, five of them deputies, actually came. Meanwhile, reporters were being denied access to the courthouse yard. Perez had the parish grand jury summoned to investigate "complaints" that Governor Jones, Walter Blaize, and the entire State Guard were engaged in "an alleged conspiracy to incite a riot." He compared his antagonists to Hitler and Goebbels and exclaimed, "What do they think this is—Germany?"[33]

Anticipating an invasion,the parish defenders dug in. The doors of the courthouse and all gates surrounding it were locked and guarded, as was the driveway. The road in front was kept clear of traffic and bystanders. Food was taken into the barricaded building in large containers, as deputies worked in around-the-clock shifts. One of them told newsmen, "They will have to blow us off the map of Louisiana to get in here."[34]

Meanwhile, up the road at Braithwaite, other deputies were stopping cars on the road and making occupants produce identification before being allowed to continue. The only highway—in fact the only road—leading to Pointe a la Hache was blocked in front of Perez's home at Promised Land plantation; traffic was routed through the backyard, where unfriendly vehicles could be detained. With a dozen armed guards stationed there, the old house took on the aspect of a besieged fortress while Mrs. Perez unconcernedly served roast chicken inside. The Judge, denying reports that lawlessness and rebellion had broken out in the parish, announced, "Our court is in session, our grand jury is meeting, reporters are in the courtroom, the deputies are playing casino and everything is happy here. It is always peaceful down here."[35]

With good reason, Walter Blaize had by this time given up all hope of taking office peacefully. He wired the governor for assistance. At one minute past midnight on October 9, Jones placed Plaquemines Parish under martial law, explaining that the issue was whether one man or a group of men could defy a decision of the state's highest court. The State Guard commander, Brigadier General Thomas F. Porter, in civilian life a Lake Charles judge, was ordered to take physical possession of the sheriff's office and install Walter Blaize, to assure that the governor's appointee was not obstructed in the performance of his duties, and to suppress insurrection in the parish.[36]

The guardsmen at Camp Pontchartrain were awakened early and notified of their marching orders. Shortly after 7 A.M. they headed south fully armed in a convoy including thirty-one trucks, two command cars with mounted machine guns, and an ambulance. Blaize rode in the lead vehicle with General Porter and Colonel J. Perry Cole, Porter's chief of staff. The guard moved cautiously, mile by mile, scouting the levee for snipers. It took the column about five hours to travel the forty miles from New Orleans to Pointe a la Hache by the winding levee road.[37]

The state soldiers made their first contact with the Perez forces at Braithwaite, just across the Plaquemines Parish line. Three elderly deputies wearing sidearms halted the convoy and tried to serve the State Guard officers with the local court's injunction prohibiting them from entering the parish. The officers tore up the order, disarmed the deputies, arrested them, and placed them in their own paddy wagon. The prisoners were taken south with the caravan.[38]

The governor's army encountered a second obstacle in front of the Perez home. A trailer rig carrying oil-well pipe had been overturned in the middle of the highway, and trucks had been driven into the muddy ditches on either side of it. About two dozen Plaquemines deputies armed with rifles and shotguns were posted about three hundred yards down the road. The State Guard commanders, deciding to capture the deputies, sent one patrol behind the river levee, which ran along the road to the right, and another patrol behind the old railroad embankment, running for about two hundred yards to the left. Meanwhile, a machine gun was set up in the middle of the road. According to a participant, just as the patrol moving behind the levee came opposite the parish deputies, they came upon a Negro boy out hunting. When the lad fired at a rabbit, the deputies out on the road, thinking they were being attacked, scurried away.[39]

Tractors were brought up to move the overturned trucks from the road, and the convoy resumed its journey. The guard met no more resistance until reaching the outskirts of Pointe a la Hache. There, several truckloads of oyster shells had been commandeered at gunpoint, by Perez's men, dumped into the road, and soaked with war-rationed gasoline. As the state forces approached, a deputy ignited the shells and fled, melodramatically dodging a volley of imaginary bullets. The guardsmen waited until the fire had burned out, then brought up their bulldozer to sweep the shells from the road.[40]

As the column neared the parish seat, the Plaquemines defense forces melted away. A State Guard bomber menacingly circled the area, and, below at the courthouse, there was quite a commotion as workers moved out gasoline stoves, typewriters, adding machines, and other equipment. Perez's deputies, who had cheerfully taken up arms upon learning that only the State Guard and not the regular army was coming to enforce martial law, now had a change of heart; they began putting away their rifles and dismantling a machine gun that had been set up in the vestibule. The leader himself, dressed in hunting clothes, fled the courthouse shortly before the guardsmen arrived, withdrawing to the relative safety of the Pointe a la Hache ferry, which remained in the middle of the river because Perez feared that another column of invaders might have come down the west bank. Colonel Cole wanted to take a squad of men aboard the state conservation boat *Ruth* and capture the ferry, but General Porter feared that action taken on the river might involve a violation of federal law.[41]

Most of the defenses had been taken down by the time the state forces rolled into Pointe a la Hache. Perez's nephew Frank Giordano, who was standing outside the courthouse, was asked by guard officers if there were any armed men inside. He replied, "No, you can see that everything is quiet here." No casualties were sustained on either side, though a widowed mother of four later claimed that she had suffered a heart attack when advancing guardsmen had pointed their guns at her. The Judge charged that the state soldiers had arrested a number of innocent persons and that one little old lady had dropped dead upon seeing her employer taken away at the point of a bayonet. Dr. Slater, seated in the sheriff's office with two of his deputies when the first guardsmen arrived, refused to leave and was taken bodily from the building, but was not arrested. The deposed sheriff refused to shake hands with Walter Blaize, explaining, "I don't shake hands with a rat." He went on to declare, "I don't think we will be able to resort to the civil law in this case. I think from now on we will have to depend on the Ten Commandments." The only skirmish that occurred at the courthouse was among newsmen, who scrambled to use the one telephone connecting Pointe a la Hache with the outside world. All the while, Plaquemines natives manned their antiquated phones, turning the cranks, whistling into the mouthpieces, doing rousing renditions of old French fishing chanties—anything to tie up the line to keep news from reaching New Orleans. One reporter was interrupted during his dispatch by an indignant delta resident, who came onto the line to complain that the governor's trucks were scaring her dog. The general store, barber shop, and two saloons, the entire business district of Pointe a la Hache, were shut down by their owners. The grand jury that Perez had summoned to "investigate" the state conspiracy to incite riots within the parish was still in session when the State Guard occupied the courthouse. Undisturbed, the jurors filed out an hour later.[42]

Inside, the courthouse was a mess. All records had disappeared from the sheriff's office but were eventually found in a locked vault in the clerk of court's office. Drawers from desks and filing cabinets had been pulled out and left on the floor, and loose papers had been scattered about. Surveying the damage, Blaize joked wanly, "I guess I can file things in my pocket for awhile." One of Slater's ousted deputies said he thought Jones's man would need no permanent files. "I give Blaize two weeks in office," he said. "Then he will have to call the State Guard again."[43]

A token state force remained in Plaquemines Parish from October 9, 1943, until early May of 1944. After three days, all but about a hundred guardsmen were withdrawn from Pointe a la Hache. Shortly thereafter, all state soldiers were sent home except for fifteen men and a couple of officers. For the final three months the occupation force consisted of one officer and two men, who remained as symbols of state authority. Although Governor Jones had actually proclaimed martial law for the entire parish, guardsmen were stationed only at Pointe a la Hache. With few official duties to occupy them, they spent their time reading, sleeping, talking with those local people who didn't snub them, and occasionally riding the Pointe a la Hache ferry. The guardsmen walked about the community unarmed, took their meals at a local boardinghouse, and slept in the police jury room. The jurors, leery about conducting their business in a room occupied by state officers, met for the duration in the parish jail. The only physical suffering inflicted upon the soldiers came from swarms of hungry mosquitoes blown in from the marshes by easterly winds.[44]

Little was seen of Judge Perez by the state guardsmen. Occasionally he would call the officer in charge to ask when they intended to leave. He was usually to be found either in New Orleans or surrounded by armed guards at his home at Dalcour. Periodically, he issued statements attacking Governor Jones and the State Guard and once even made a statewide radio address entitled "The Truth About the Plaquemines Parish Situation," which was read into the *Congressional Record* by his friend, Congressman F. Edward Hebert. Charging that sending guardsmen into the parish was "the damnedest outrage ever perpetrated on an American people," Perez accused Governor Jones of "usurping the power of the president of the United States." He claimed that he had decided against meeting force with force because gunplay would only have resulted in the deaths of innocent members of the State Guard, many of whom had families at home who were worried about them. The *Plaquemines*

Gazette claimed that General Porter's order prohibiting the gathering of three or more persons meant that parish families would have to be disbanded.[45]

On the second day of the occupation, guardsmen searching for weapons came upon a cache behind the courthouse in a shack occupied by a Negro couple. The arsenal included a .45-caliber submachine gun, automatic, single-barreled, and sawed-off shotguns, a .38-caliber revolver, one blackjack, and ammunition. That same day the Pointe a la Hache ferry captain, saying a farmer had brought him word from the Judge to do so, tied up his boat and refused to transport the soldiers across the river; he later gave in after being threatened with arrest. Denying that he had ordered the ferry stopped, Perez accused the guard of interfering with free navigation on the river and threatened to take up the matter with federal authorities.[46]

Two days later a local opponent of Leander's informed officers that the Perez men had been stashing arms at a house across the river and were planning a surprise raid the following night. This was an easily believable report, because guardsmen were still trying to account for all the weapons and ammunition supposed to belong to the sheriff's office. A search of a residence near the courthouse had produced four machine guns tied to the springs beneath a bed; still missing were fifteen shotguns, several rifles and revolvers, and a dozen or more grenades. Colonel Cole took about thirty armed men aboard the state conservation boat *Ruth* and set out to investigate the story. Leaving ten men to guard the boat, the party approached the suspect house, owned by Perez's nephew Frank Giordano. The place was ablaze with lights, but no one was at home. The guardsmen searched the premises thoroughly but found no weapons. They did find, however, great piles of nickels and quarters; as it turned out, Giordano was the collector for slot machines in Plaquemines Parish. Later, he sued the officers in charge for breaking and entering and theft of his collections, but the case never came to trial.[47]

Once in office, Blaize found himself virtually paralyzed in performing his duties as sheriff. He had to bring locksmiths down from New Orleans to open his safes and was unable to find most of the equipment belonging to his office, including a patrol car. Actually, the new sheriff never tried very hard to recover the missing vehicle because he knew the tires were bad and did not think the ration board would allow him to get new ones. Blaize was also harassed by a flurry of lawsuits that consumed most of his time and attention. He was unable to pay his deputies because the funds deposited to the sheriff's office were tied up in litigation, and, in fact, he himself was never paid for the time he spent in office. When he tried to collect taxes, citizens refused to pay. At least one member of his staff was a spy for Perez. During Blaize's entire tenure, Dr. Slater operated a rival sheriff's office on a loan from the police jury, and the local district court conducted its business in Plaquemines through Slater rather than Blaize.[48]

Reversed but not precisely vanquished, Judge Perez went back to court and launched a volley of lawsuits—fifteen at one time. It was not unusual for him to stay up all night preparing his legal actions; some nights he slept on the table in his law library without even returning home.[49] The Jones administration responded with lawsuits of its own, including impeachment proceedings against Perez and Judge Albert Estopinal, Jr. Among the pending cases were: (1) A murder conspiracy suit by Perez against Jones; (2) a murder conspiracy suit by Jones against Perez; (3) suits by Slater and Blaize, both claiming the money deposited by the sheriff's office; (4) an Office of Price Administration investigation into the misuse of gasoline to create the fire barricade at Pointe a la Hache; (5) an injunction suit to prohibit the State Guard from continuing its occupation; (6) a Slater injunction against Blaize; (7) an intrusion-in-office suit against Slater; (8) writs by Blaize to prohibit "harassing" lawsuits that interfered with his duties as sheriff; (9) contempt of court charges against Perez and Estopinal; (10) contempt of court charges against Blaize for violating the local court injunction; (11) burglary charges in connection with the raid on Giordano's home; (12) kidnaping charges by a Perez constable who had tried to serve Blaize with injunction papers; (13) false arrest charges by the three deputies who had tried to serve the State Guard with injunction papers; (14) a libel and false arrest suit against State Guard officers by the captain of the Pointe a la Hache ferry.[50]

As usual, Perez quickly took the offensive. As he had done before with the Crime Commission, he attacked the legality of the State Guard itself. He declared that the use of regular army property by the guard was illegal and would be reported to federal authorities. Through the *Plaquemines Gazette,* he charged that Governor Jones had acted wrongly in declaring martial law in Plaquemines because civil authority was still functioning and there was no threat to public order. The *Gazette* expressed the fear that General Porter's restrictions on bearing arms would end the hunting in the parish. In his radio address, Judge Perez argued that Dr. Slater could not be expected to comply with the state supreme court's decision since he had not been made a party to the action and denounced Jones for calling in the military to discharge a responsibility that properly belonged to the local district court.[51]

Judge Estopinal was suspended pending the outcome of his impeachment, and Judge R. R. Reeves, a former Long partisan, was called in to serve as temporary district judge. Late in December, 1943, Reeves granted Dr. Slater an injunction to prevent Blaize from interfering with the coroner's duties as acting sheriff. Reeves upheld the governor's right to appoint Blaize, but ruled that the appointee had failed to qualify properly. Governor Jones then issued a second commission to Blaize and filed an intrusion-in-office suit against Slater. The day after he ruled for the coroner, Judge Reeves granted a suspensive appeal to Blaize, bringing the case before the state supreme court. Slater managed to have the intrusion-in-office suit delayed several weeks because Governor Jones was out of the state. Before the high court could rule on the matter, both a new sheriff and a new governor had been elected. It then refused to review all cases arising from the little war on the grounds that the substantive issues had become academic.[52]

When Dr. Slater was ejected from the courthouse by the State Guard, he told General Porter that Walter Blaize could not get ten votes in Plaquemines Parish. The Perez apparatus was prepared to guarantee, if not the exact figure, then at least the spirit of this prediction. Blaize tried to organize a slate of candidates to oppose the Perez ticket in the January 18, 1944, Democratic primary, but the party executive committee in the parish disqualified most of them. Sixty-eight election commissioners were chosen to represent the

Perez faction but only seven to represent the Jones-Blaize faction. Not surprising, the election returned a solid slate of Perez candidates, and Slater defeated Blaize by a four-to-one margin. Slater's candidacy conflicted with the ambitions of Perez stalwart Chester Wooten, who had been expelled from the legislature and now wanted to be sheriff. The two rivals signed an agreement by which Wooten withdrew from the 1944 race in favor of Slater and, in return, Slater promised to withdraw in favor of Wooten in 1948.[53]

On April 4, 1944, Judge Reeves ruled that Governor Jones's proclamation of martial law had been unconstitutional. On May 4, the governor rescinded the declaration, and the last guardsmen left Plaquemines. Five days later, Jones's term as governor expired. Judge Perez made peace with the new governor, easygoing country singer Jimmie Davis, who dropped the impeachment proceedings against Perez and Estopinal. In exchange, Perez dropped all of his suits arising from the little war, including the old actions against Furlow and others for serving as special counsel to the local levee boards. Thus, the episode called by the New Orleans *States* "the puff-ball putsch of the phony fuehrer of Plaquemines" passed into history.[54]

Sam Jones failed in his attempts to reform delta politics by legal action and by force of arms. When he went out of office, he left Perez, if anything, in a stronger position within his marshy empire. The Judge had defied the state courts, had taken up arms in rebellion against constituted civil authority (and this in wartime), and had been compared by a number of major state newspapers to Adolf Hitler; yet, when the smoke cleared, he had succeeded in stigmatizing his opponents and consolidating his already considerable local power. Governor Jones probably had the will, the wit, and the strength to destroy the Judge in Plaquemines, but he did not have the time. Had the state constitution allowed him to succeed himself, or had his successor been of similar mind, the little war would likely have been followed by other heated confrontations and Perez's eventual downfall. But the delta boss quickly established friendly relations with the new governor, and the struggle ended.

NINE

Politics as Usual

Judge Perez believed that he faced a crucial test in the Democratic gubernatorial primaries of 1944. A vigorous anti-Long (and thereby anti-Perez) successor to Sam Jones, determined to pursue Jones's efforts, might end Perez's personal domination of the lower delta. Unfortunately for him, the Long faction was internally riven by the ambitions of many competing politicians. By May, 1943, Jimmie Noe, Earl Long, and Ernest Clements, a state senator who styled himself the only true disciple of Huey, had announced their candidacies for governor. New Orleans Mayor Robert Maestri, now the dominant boss in the Long organization, vetoed Earl's candidacy because he felt that Long's erratic behavior had cost the faction the gubernatorial election of 1940. Earl, always a political realist, accepted second place on the Long faction's ticket behind Maestri's handpicked candidate, sixty-seven-year-old Lewis Morgan, a former state representative, district attorney, and congressman, who had retired from politics in 1917. The ticket was bottom heavy, and there were rumors that if elected the aged Morgan would resign, allowing Long to become governor.[1]

Governor Sam Jones did not openly endorse a favorite during the gubernatorial campaign, but worked quietly behind the scenes for Jimmie Davis, a tall, blue-eyed, drawling country singer, whose political career included stints as court clerk, public safety commissioner of Shreveport, and in 1942 public service commissioner, the same position Huey Long had used as a springboard to the governorship. Davis was an easygoing, easily dominated man, passive rather than assertive by nature. Although recognized as Jones's protégé, he had none of Jones's combativeness.[2]

Besides Morgan and Davis, the major gubernatorial candidates were Sam Caldwell, three-term mayor of Shreveport; Ernest Clements, former conservation commissioner under Earl Long; Dudley J. LeBlanc, the irrepressible "Hadacol man"; and Jimmy Morrison, Sixth District congressman since 1942. Jimmie Noe, withdrawing from the race in September, endorsed the Morgan-Long ticket.

In the first primary, Perez adamantly opposed Jimmie Davis, whom he considered a tool of Sam Jones, but was uncertain whom to support, failing to agree with Maestri on a common ticket. Perez mailed form letters to Plaquemines servicemen urging them to vote for either Caldwell or Morgan for governor, though Maestri endorsed Morgan. For lieutenant governor, the Judge endorsed Caldwell's running mate, Frank B. Ellis, but Maestri went all-out for Earl Long. Ellis, of St. Tammany Parish, had been president pro tempore of the Louisiana Senate for Sam Jones but had opposed Jones's effort to restore the sales tax in 1942, a fact that may have endeared him to Perez. The *Plaquemines Gazette* claimed that Jimmie Davis lacked the experience to be governor and attempted to link him with New Orleans gambling interests.[3]

The results of the first primary confirmed suspicions that Morgan was a weak candidate. He finished second, receiving only 131,682 votes, or 27.5 percent of the total, though Long, his candidate for lieutenant governor, topped all rivals, receiving 194,255, or 41.9 percent. Davis easily led the gubernatorial total with 167,434 votes (34.9 percent). Morgan handily carried Plaquemines, but Long, whom Perez had opposed, received only a handful of votes. In St. Bernard, where Leander was feuding with Dutch Rowley, Morgan finished a poor second to Jimmie Davis, who outpolled his combined opponents.[4]

When the Democratic State Central Committee met to certify the returns of the first primary and to elect officers, Perez attempted to dominate the proceedings to ensure that Davis supporters would not be elected to positions of power. Many committee members from the rural parishes where Davis was strongest had sent their proxies rather than make the long trip to Baton Rouge. Although he represented a rural parish himself and collected a large number of proxies before every meeting, the Judge insisted that the primary law adopted by the Jones administration in 1940 required that new officers of the state central committee be elected by a majority of the members present and voting. The chairman then submitted the question to a vote of the committee, and Perez was defeated fifty-seven to forty, proxies voting. Officers favoring Davis were then elected by the same vote, proxies included. W. H. ("Little Eva") Talbot, Davis' state campaign manager and a future Perez ally, claimed that less than one-fourth of the rural members of the committee supported Leander because they disliked his dictatorial tactics.[5]

Clements and Morrison endorsed Morgan in the second primary, LeBlanc backed Davis, and Caldwell remained neutral. Under Louisiana law, if one of the two gubernatorial candidates withdrew from the second primary, there would be no runoff, and thus the high man in the first primary would become the Democratic nominee. Had Morgan withdrawn, Earl Long, who had led the first primary voting for lieutenant governor, would have been automatically nominated. Earl brazenly attempted to persuade the Old Regulars to withdraw financial support from Morgan, compelling him to retire from the race, but Maestri blocked the move.[6]

In the second primary on February 29, 1944, Davis received 53.6 percent of the vote to 46.4 percent for Morgan. Long again outpolled his running mate, but finished second to Davis' candidate, Emile J. Verret, with 48.8 percent of the vote to 51.2 percent for Verret. In Plaquemines, Morgan swamped Davis with 73.8 percent of the vote, but in St. Bernard Davis received 68.2 percent of the ballots cast.[7]

After obstreperously fighting Davis throughout the first and second primaries, Perez became one of the first to visit the newly elected chief executive. After conferring privately with the governor, the Judge emerged smiling and satisfied. Davis had proved "reasonable." The feud ended. Perez had a new friend in Baton Rouge.[8]

When Jimmie Davis took office in 1944, good-government advocates believed that reform had finally taken root firmly in Louisiana through the efforts of Sam Jones. And, thanks to the painful pruning of wasteful expenditures by Jones, the new governor entered office with an inherited surplus of $12,000,000 rather than the customary huge deficit. Existing taxes promised to provide bountiful revenues from the buying binge that followed World War II. Davis, at heart a fiscal conservative, attempted to ensure an even larger surplus by increasing taxes, but the legislature defeated his proposals. Expenditures increased sharply throughout his administration, mainly at the instance of the legislators, though Davis managed by occasional vetoes and plentiful revenues to maintain a balanced budget. Reserved but genial, the governor acted as a conciliator among rival factions and spent much of his time traveling, frequently to Hollywood. He was absent from the state 44 days in the fiscal year 1944–1945, 68 days in 1945–1946, and 108 days in 1946–1947, causing the fund, which paid the lieutenant governor when acting as governor, to become exhausted twice.[9]

The most surprising electoral upset during Davis' administration occurred in the New Orleans mayoralty election of January 22, 1946. The Independent Citizens' Committee of New Orleans, supposedly a good-government organization inspired by Davis and Jones, decided to enter a candidate to unseat the omnipotent Maestri. With the inverted logic peculiar to Louisiana reformers, they selected a Ring politician, Joachim O. Fernandez, a Longite congressman from 1930 to 1940, on the theory that as "one of the boys" he would split the Ring vote. Fernandez proved to be indeed one of the boys by withdrawing from the race barely a month before the election and endorsing Maestri. The citizens' group, now desperate for a candidate naïve enough to believe he could defeat Maestri and respectable enough to appear gracious in defeat, selected deLesseps Morrison, thirty-four-year-old war hero, two-term state legislator, and floor leader for Governor Sam Jones in the Louisiana House. While campaigning in his army uniform, Morrison employed about 150 former servicemen to go around the city at night searching for holes in the streets, uncollected garbage, and other examples of official laxity. Into each pavement crevice and garbage heap the campaigners planted a cardboard sign reading, "Morrison will fix this." To the surprise of everyone, including himself, Chep eked out a 4,372-vote victory over Maestri from a total of 133,708 votes cast. Morrison went on to serve four terms as the progressive mayor of the state's largest city. He proved to be a liberal on racial and financial matters, a consistent supporter of the national Democratic party, and an interminable foe of Leander Perez, the friend of the man

Morrison had defeated and the champion of every cause that Morrison detested.[10]

As the 1948 Democratic primaries approached, it became evident that the contest would feature a rematch between Earl Long and Sam Jones. Jones's popularity had declined precipitously since 1940, partly because of the ambiguity of the reform movement under Jimmie Davis but more directly because of the vigor with which Jones had attempted to uproot corruption during his own administration. Many Louisiana politicians felt, with some justification, that Jones's Crime Commission had become an instrument of political persecution. They complained that, though it had pursued Jones's political opponents beyond the grave, it had investigated and indicted few of his backers. Even Jones admitted that some of his subordinates had overzealously indulged in political persecution. But the trouble was partly Jones's unbending, uncompromising personality, which inspired respect and admiration but generated little warmth and sympathy. Like earlier reformers, he had hesitated to supplant the machine he displaced with an efficient one of his own. Though an appealing candidate in a time of moral crisis and financial chaos, he was less attractive at a time when *reform* had become a hackneyed word and the state treasury overflowed. Earl Long, beaten in two previous campaigns but rich in political savvy and campaign funds, set up Jones as a prop for his own campaign by encouraging his followers to write Jones urging him to run in 1948. Such tactics were unnecessary; Jones had been planning to run for a second term even before his first term had expired.[11]

The other contenders were Congressman Jimmy Morrison and Circuit Judge Robert F. Kennon of Minden, a conservative reformer and a dark horse. The election inspired bizarre political pairings: F. Edward Hebert, elected to Congress for his investigative reporting that sent many of Earl's pals to jail, supported Earl Long for governor; W. H. Talbot, former campaign manager for Jimmie Davis, became Long's campaign manager; and Perez placed himself in the vanguard of Earl's stalwarts. Through Long and Maestri, Leander found himself in 1948 firmly allied with the Old Regulars,[12] whom he had uprooted from Plaquemines in the days of John M. Parker. As an adamant foe of Sam Jones, he vociferously opposed reform—a far cry from the days in which he had " exposed" John Dymond as a political pirate. Although himself a wealthy attorney for big oil companies, Perez sided with the candidate who attacked Jones for being a corporation lawyer. Finally, in Earl Long, Leander was championing a moderate on race at a time when racial issues were becoming more prominent and when Perez himself was growing more unyielding in his determination to deny economic and political opportunity to blacks.

In the first primary, Long made his usual bread-and-butter promises: higher pensions and homestead exemptions, more roads and hospitals, veterans' bonuses, and hot lunches for all schoolchildren. Kennon promised to stop waste, reduce taxes, and return government to the people. Jimmy Morrison ludicrously announced that his "majority" was approaching "landslide proportions." Jones, although philosophically opposed to a welfare state, emphasized that during his administration old-age benefits and homestead exemptions had doubled and the poll tax certificate had been abolished. [13]

Earl Long piled up a huge first-primary lead by polling 267,253 votes (41.5 percent) to 147,329 (22.9 percent) for Jones, who ran a distant second. Kennon finished a surprisingly strong third,[14] and Morrison finished fourth. In Plaquemines, Earl topped all three of his opponents with a whopping 70.9 percent of the vote, and in neighboring St. Bernard he tallied 57.0 percent. Sam Jones finished a remote second in both parishes. Jones, who by now realized that he had grown too unpopular to make his election likely, considered withdrawing from the second primary in favor of Kennon, but decided that the Minden judge was not well enough known statewide to defeat Earl Long.[15]

As the second primary neared, Jones became progressively more pessimistic and Earl grew increasingly more confident. Resorting to a tactic used by Earl against him in 1939, Jones announced that Governor Davis, who had endorsed him, had agreed to call a special legislative session to consider veterans' bonuses and welfare legislation if he were nominated. Meanwhile, the ebullient Long began sending invitations to the inaugural ball and promised the voters hot dogs, soda pop, cornbread, and buttermilk at his inauguration.[16]

Perez knew that Long would carry Plaquemines by a whopping

margin, but to make sure he devised a stratagem to deny Jones any commissioners at the Plaquemines polls. Judge Estopinal of the Twenty-fifth Judicial District had recently retired because of ill health, and Governor Davis had called a special election to fill the vacancy. Perez, as chairman of the Twenty-fifth Judicial District Executive Committee, set February 24, 1948, as the date for this special primary, the same date as the Jones-Long gubernatorial runoff. Although the local anti-Perez opposition, caught by surprise, was unable to enter a candidate for judge before the deadline, the Perez faction easily qualified two candidates, Perez's assistant district attorney Bruce Nunez and Perez's friend and office partner A. S. Cain, who was a dummy candidate. When the Democratic committee met to choose commissioners, both lists therefore had been submitted by Perez candidates. Supporters sent by Jones to witness the drawing were told that they had arrived too late. The committee announced that, to save money, the same commissioners and poll watchers would be used for both elections. Jones filed a lawsuit in protest but could not prevent the Nunez-Cain commissioners from serving in the gubernatorial runoff, thus depriving him of any representation. In the mock judicial election, Nunez overwhelmingly defeated Cain as had been planned.[17]

Leander's efforts to shut out Jones at the Plaquemines polls proved superfluous because Earl Long received 65.9 percent of the votes statewide. Nonetheless, the Judge's methods were efficient; they delivered 91.4 percent of the Plaquemines vote and 92.6 percent of the St. Bernard vote to the winning candidate.[18] In his third try for the governorship, Long had finally been elected at the age of fifty-two. Basking in the glow of victory, he told his supporters that he thought he would be a better governor than Huey and that he knew he would be a better governor than Leche. The enormous margin by which he had won relieved him of any obligation to a particular boss, such as Perez, and deprived the Judge of the claim to being a kingmaker. It was the last time Perez would support Earl Long for governor.[19]

In May, 1948, U.S. Senator John H. Overton died, and Earl appointed William Feazel, a wealthy oilman who had bankrolled his gubernatorial campaign, interim senator with the understanding that Earl's nephew Russell Long, soon to reach the legal age of thirty, would run for the seat in the August Democratic primary. Russell had no political record of his own, but he possessed the magic name Long and his uncle's efficient state machine. His opponent was Judge Robert Kennon of Minden, who was supported by New Orleans Mayor Chep Morrison and the New Orleans *Times-Picayune* and *Item,* which assured him of a majority in the Crescent City. New Orleans, which utilized voting machines, gave Kennon a 25,742-vote early lead, but, as returns trickled in from the rural parishes that still used paper ballots, his lead eroded. The most lopsided pro-Long vote came from St. Bernard, which recorded only 121 votes for Kennon out of more than 3,100 cast. Since the statewide race was decided in Long's favor by only 10,475 votes, Kennon was understandably angry. "They're phony and baloney!" he complained about the St. Bernard returns. "Why, I've got more than 121 personal friends in the parish who told me they voted for me." He did almost as badly in Plaquemines, where young Russell received 84.4 percent of the votes.[20]

In 1950 Russell Long faced election for a full term to the Senate seat he had held for two years. During his brief tenure, he had earned a reputation for independence and moderation, which made him a much better known and more popular candidate than he had been in 1948. However, by 1950 Perez had broken with Earl Long and had become alienated from Russell because of his moderate liberalism and support of the Truman administration. Russell's 1950 opponent was Malcolm Lafargue, an obscure United States attorney with no statewide organization, whose chief asset seemed to be that he was a French-speaking Cajun Protestant who resided in Shreveport, which presumably was calculated to appeal to both south Louisiana Cajuns and north Louisiana red-necks. Actually, Lafargue's appeal proved to be limited to Perez's Plaquemines Parish. He won 93.7 percent of the Plaquemines vote, against a candidate who had carried Plaquemines with 84.4 percent of the vote two years earlier, but failed to carry any other parish in the entire state.[21]

Governor Earl Long had managed to provide most of the benefits promised during his campaign at the 1948 regular session of the legislature, but the huge expenditures had necessitated increased taxation on a scale unanticipated by the voters. Louisianians now paid the highest tax rate in the nation, $97.66 per capita, compared with the national average of $59.59. Moreover, some of the taxes were most burdensome to the poor, especially the sales tax, which had been doubled. The governor became so desperate for revenue that he had the legislature levy a tax on slot machines, whose ownership and operation were illegal under state law. To satisfy the Long machine's demands for patronage, he had had the legislature repeal civil service during the special session of September, 1948.[22]

Midway through Long's 1948–1952 term, Perez and the governor began to quarrel. The first open animosity appeared at a meeting of the Democratic State Central Committee, which at the governor's request had ousted the national committeeman W. H. Talbot for supporting the Thurmond ticket. Perez had previously grown cool toward Long because of his refusal to back the Dixiecrat ticket, but the primary cause of the quarrel concerned local, not national, politics. Intimates of Long and Perez agree that the split occurred because Long reneged on some commitments he had made to Perez, but these persons are still reluctant to discuss the exact nature of these commitments.[23]

For many years an advocate of the Long tax-and-spend program, Perez recognized the value of fiscal frugality now that an unfriendly governor sat in Baton Rouge. Long, not satisfied with merely raising taxes and abolishing civil service, intended to consolidate all state power in his own hands by summoning a special convention to rewrite the state's constitution, an antiquated book-length document adopted in 1921. He planned to extend the governor's control over state agencies, increase his appointive power, and remove home rule from the city of New Orleans, controlled by his efficient young opponent, Chep Morrison. There were even rumors that Earl planned to include a provision extending his own term and that he did not even intend to offer the rewritten document for popular ratification. The people of Louisiana were "as good as any in the world," but unfortunately there was "much ignorance," explained the champion of the common man.[24]

Probably none of this would have bothered Judge Perez had he not previously broken with the governor, but, now with Earl a mortal enemy, Leander realized that one of the first acts of a Long-bossed constitutional convention would be to abolish the Perez-authored constitutional provisions that channeled the tax revenues from Plaquemines' mineral wealth into the parish coffers. Particularly in jeopardy was the 1932 constitutional amendment permitting the Plaquemines police jury to assume the bonded indebtedness and in return receive the revenues of levee boards located entirely within the parish. Earl might also tighten the governor's control over levee board appointees, regulate the leasing of state lands containing potential mineral deposits, and increase the taxes paid by Perez-sheltered companies, such as Freeport Sulphur. In mobilizing opposition to the proposed constitutional convention, Perez found himself allied with his hitherto adamant enemies, including Mayor Morrison, Sam Jones, and the New Orleans newspapers. The public outcry against Long's intended power grab, fueled by Perez and his newfound allies, finally compelled the governor to summon a one-day special session of the legislature in September to repeal the convention call.

Earl's hunger for power and his policy of heavy taxing made him increasingly unpopular during his last two years in office. Like previous governors, he discovered in 1952 that electing a chosen successor was an insuperable task for an incumbent, since a governor normally reached the nadir of his popularity near the end of his term and the state's voters rebelled against being instructed to vote for his "puppet." As his candidate, Earl selected District Judge Carlos Spaht of Baton Rouge, a World War II veteran and past president of the Louisiana State University Alumni Association. Spaht, relatively unknown at the outset of the campaign, was quickly tabbed "Earl's boy." Lieutenant Governor William J. Dodd, disgruntled at not receiving the governor's endorsement, stumped the state anyway, appealing to dissatisfied Longites. Judge Robert Kennon, determined to avenge himself for his successive defeats by Earl and Russell Long, based his candidacy upon opposition to Longism and promises of tax reductions. The most conservative candidate was James M. McLemore, a wealthy Alexandria cattleman sometimes known as "Cadillac Mac." Endorsed by the New Orleans *Times-*

Picayune, he spent most of his time denouncing "Trumanism" and assuring Louisianians that, if he were elected governor, President Truman would have no voice in running the state. At the outset, the most formidable anti-Long candidate appeared to be Congressman T. Hale Boggs, a liberal who attracted the support of Senator Russell Long, Mayor Morrison, Sam Jones, and Jimmy Morrison. Perez's initial choice for governor was Lucille May Grace (Mrs. Fred Dent), the registrar of the State Land Office. Miss Grace had broken with Long about the time Earl and Leander began feuding, because Long had proposed to exclude her office from the new state constitution he planned to write.[25]

Perez was far more interested in defeating Spaht, a Longite, and Boggs, a Trumanite, than he was in electing Miss Grace, a fact that she eventually discovered. Before the campaign began, Perez had met with other former Louisiana Dixiecrat leaders to fashion a coalition ticket that would ensure the defeat of both Spaht and Boggs. When they had been unable to agree upon a single candidate of their persuasion, Perez had then asked Miss Grace to enter the race for governor, promising that he would finance her campaign. The Judge knew that she stood little chance of winning, but he planned to use her to sabotage the campaign of Hale Boggs.[26]

Miss Grace believed that Perez considered her a serious candidate and naïvely thought that she had enough statewide support to wage a successful campaign. Before launching the campaign, Perez devised a strategy to disqualify, or at least discredit, Boggs by having Miss Grace file a challenge to Boggs's candidacy with the Democratic State Central Committee. She charged that (1) as a U.S. Congressman, Boggs was ineligible to campaign for a state office, and (2) as a student at Tulane University Boggs had belonged to a Communist-front organization, the American Student Union, thus violating a provision of the committee prohibiting members of the Communist party or Communist-front organizations from seeking office in Louisiana.[27]

The charge that a congressman was ineligible to run for governor was novel for Louisiana because a congressman had entered four of the preceding six gubernatorial campaigns. In fact, in 1948 Miss Grace herself had been a candidate on the ticket of Congressman

Jimmy Morrison. She explained that she had not insisted then that Morrison withdraw because "it was not an issue" but that the situation might have been different if he had been her opponent. The charge that Boggs had once joined the suspect American Student Union had been raised when he ran for Congress in 1940 but had never been proved or disproved. Boggs insisted that there had never even been a chapter of the organization at Tulane, but his fellow congressman, F. Edward Hebert, claims that Boggs had joined the leftist group as a youthful escapade. Whatever the truth, no informed person could have seriously doubted Boggs's patriotism.[28]

Both the New Orleans *Item* and *Times-Picayune* denounced the challenge to Boggs's candidacy as a smear tactic by Perez. Seven members of the U.S. House of Representatives defended their colleague, with Congressman Frank L. Chelf of Kentucky stating, "To say Hale Boggs is a Communist is to say that the American flag carries a hammer and sickle, Boston has no beans, and that Louisiana has no politics."[29] Boggs himself blamed Perez rather than Miss Grace for the charges, claiming that the Plaquemines boss feared his election because it would mean the end of gambling and crooked elections in the lower delta. Perez refused to say whether he had helped prepare the charges against Boggs, but commented, "I'd say that anyone would be glad to have had a part in it."[30]

Governor Long summoned a special session of the Democratic State Central Committee to rule upon the challenge to Boggs's candidacy, urging the committee members in the interest of fairness to allow Boggs to run, even though Long personally supported the candidacy of Carlos Spaht. The committee assembled in Baton Rouge for what the New Orleans *Item* described as "a rare political picnic." The most controversial and colorful political leaders in the state were prepared for an eyeball-to-eyeball confrontation, and no one wanted to miss the show. The proceedings were even going to be broadcast live over the radio. Spectators in a holiday mood packed the galleries, and all but fourteen of the one hundred committee members were present, milling about the crowded chamber, looking for seats. Earl Long, who stole the show, sported a necktie decorated with a hand-painted Confederate flag. Facing the speaker's rostrum was a long table, with Boggs, his attorneys, and Mayor Morrison at one end and Lucille May Grace at the other. Beside her were her attorney, Charles J. Rivet, and her running mate, W. H. Talbot. Attired in a black suit and red blouse and hat, she managed a tight-lipped smile as Dudley LeBlanc, a member of the committee as well as a gubernatorial candidate, stopped to wish her luck. Boggs's end of the table was crowded with well-wishers.[31]

The committee first considered the charge that Boggs was ineligible to run because he was a member of Congress and quickly adopted a resolution specifying that no candidate should be ruled ineligible because he was a member of Congress or a state official at the time of the Democratic primary. Perez then took the floor and delivered a long and technical speech that seemed not to interest the audience. When he was booed at one point, he commented, "I see Mayor Morrison has brought up a lot of New Orleans city workers." Next, Governor Long launched into a rambling speech in favor of fair play for Boggs. When Perez tried to interrupt him, he snapped, "You sit down. I refuse to yield. You have been talking all day," and continued, "Judge Perez has been making two-hour speeches to this committee for twenty years. This is one time for me." During his disjointed discourse, Long pulled a small bottle from his pocket and took a swig. Several spectators on the sidelines explained that his doctor had told him to keep a stimulant handy for his heart condition.[32]

Following Long's speech, Perez seized the microphone again to demand that the committee consider the charge that Boggs was ineligible to run because of his alleged affiliation with a Communist-front group. These remarks brought an angry Boggs to the microphone to demand an open hearing to clear himself of the charges. As cameras flashed, he added, "And I want to tell you, Mr. Perez, that you are just a big bag of wind." Perez regained the stand and became involved in a legal tangle that no one seemed to understand. By this time the committee and gallery had become bored. Suddenly, S. L. Digby, a state conservation commissioner and a Long supporter, moved to dismiss the charges on the technical grounds that they had been filed improperly with the secretary rather than with the chairman of the committee. Perez and Boggs both objected,

Boggs demanding the opportunity to clear himself. But Governor Long, firmly in control, urged the committee to adopt the motion. It did, by a vote of sixty-eight to twenty-four, and the meeting was abruptly adjourned. The Judge, who had dreamed up a technicality on which to base his case, had been defeated on a technicality. Boggs rushed forward to address the committee, thanking Governor Long for his support. Leander followed Boggs to the microphone. "You have just heard Hale Boggs taking advantage of some free radio time on the air," Perez said. When the crowd began making its way to the exits, he continued, "That's all right, leave if you want to. I've got some documents here showing that Hale Boggs advocated a world government which would have destroyed our freedom, which the Soviet Union would have had the votes to run. It would be committing national suicide."[33]

Perez and his candidate refused to abandon the effort to disqualify Boggs. Speaking over radio station WNOE (owned by Jimmie Noe), Miss Grace charged that a sinister conspiracy involving President Truman, Hale Boggs, Sam Jones, and Governor Earl Long had prevented the state central committee from hearing her charges against Boggs. The Judge next had Miss Grace take the case to court, where he served as her chief attorney. After a Baton Rouge district court dismissed the case, Leander appealed to the state supreme court, which ruled that it did not have jurisdiction. The case was finally heard by the state court of appeals. The only evidence Perez submitted against Boggs was a collection of fifteen-year-old newspaper clippings, but Boggs called so many prominent politicans as character witnesses that the affair threatened to become a pro-Boggs testimonial. Arguing before the court, Perez explained his version of how the Communists worked: Alger Hiss had denied having Communist connections; Hale Boggs had denied having Communist connections; therefore Hale Boggs was as dangerous as Alger Hiss. His voice trembling, Perez somberly warned, "A man who has held such ideas in his heart does not shed them as a snake does his skin when he's a candidate for public office. He cannot take an oath to support the constitution." The court of appeals dismissed the case, after which Boggs announced that he intended to sue Perez and Miss Grace for slander.[34]

After she had been used to perform Perez's dirty work on Boggs, Lucille May Grace was immediately eclipsed by the other candidates. Soon after the conclusion of the unsuccessful court battle to disqualify Boggs, Perez announced that she had "released" him from his commitment to support her and that he intended to campaign actively for James M. McLemore, the candidate endorsed by the Judge's old foe, the New Orleans *Times-Picayune*. Perez proudly added that McLemore was not a "psalm singer." A confused exchange followed. Miss Grace claimed that she could not release Perez from any commitments because he had never formally agreed to support her. From Shreveport, W. O. White, McLemore's campaign manager, said that his candidate had scorned Perez's support in the past and would again repudiate his endorsement. Leander promptly telephoned White and called him "an insulting s.o.b." McLemore himself, who was apparently out of contact with both Perez and his own campaign manager, insisted that he had made no deals with anyone and explained that, if Perez did support him, it was because of his opposition to the Truman administration and his fight for state ownership of the tidelands.[35]

The St. Bernard Parish leaders also dropped Miss Grace abruptly but refused to follow Perez in endorsing McLemore. Although the Judge made an hour-long speech for McLemore at a caucus of St. Bernard officials, he failed to sway them. After he finished his talk, St. Bernard Sheriff Dutch Rowley told him, "Well, Judge Perez, things are a little different in St. Bernard from what they are in Plaquemines. The governor's a pretty nice fellow and we have a precarious situation. I'd like to leave things alone, let the people vote like they want." State Representative Claude Meraux spoke in favor of Carlos Spaht, pointing out that Perez had waited until too late to back McLemore and that Governor Long, Spaht's sponsor, had provided old-age pensions and good roads.[36]

With so many anti-Long candidates in the race and only one Long candidate, it was conceded that Spaht would make the runoff; the only question was who would be his opponent. Spaht led the first primary, tallying 173,987 votes (22.8 percent) to 163,434 (21.5 percent) for runner-up Robert Kennon. Boggs finished a strong third,[37] followed by McLemore, Dodd, and LeBlanc. Miss Grace finished a pathetic next to last to Cliff Lyles. State Senator J. D. DeBlieux recalls that she received fewer votes statewide in the gubernatorial election than he himself received in his single senatorial district— and DeBlieux was soundly defeated. Perez proved that his vote-getting power in Plaquemines was undiminished by delivering 82.8 percent of the vote to McLemore against his seven opponents, by far McLemore's greatest majority in the state. Spaht led St. Bernard with 64.1 percent of the total vote, with McLemore a remote second. The voting in Plaquemines characteristically was not without peculiarities. In announcing its election results to the New Orleans *Item,* Plaquemines Parish reported returns from 15 precincts, although the Associated Press had only 14 precincts listed. An *Item* call to the secretary of state's office confirmed that there were only 14 precincts in the parish, but a call to the clerk of court in Plaquemines brought the equally firm reply that there were 15 precincts.[38]

Perez's remarkable ability to deliver the Plaquemines vote to the candidate of his choice—with less than two weeks' notice that he was switching from Miss Grace to McLemore—can perhaps be attributed to his control of the poll commissioners for the Democratic primary. Louisiana election laws provided that candidates for state or congressional posts could submit lists of proposed poll commissioners only if local offices were uncontested in the primary. Since most of the Perez choices for Plaquemines posts were expected to be unopposed, that meant that gubernatorial candidates would be allowed to submit lists of potential commissioners for almost every ward. On October 13, the day after the qualification deadline, Perez told a *Times-Picayune* reporter that none of the parish officials in Plaquemines, including L. H. Folse, his state senatorial candidate, would be opposed. Later, however, denying that he had made the statement, Perez announced that Folse would be opposed by Charles R. Fontenelle, a Pointe a la Hache café and grocery owner and a close political ally of the Judge. Fontenelle's candidacy was a surprise even to the secretary and member of the senatorial district committee that passed on the qualifications of Democratic candidates. Leander explained that Fontenelle had qualified with the committee chairman, who was Perez himself. There was no hint of a rift between Perez and either incumbent Folse or challenger Fontenelle. As a candidate for the Louisiana Senate seat, Fontenelle was entitled to three election commissioners in every ward in Plaquemines and St. Bernard, and his challenge meant that no gubernatorial candidate would be allowed to submit commissioners for any ward in the two parishes.[39]

Perez's attacks on Congressman Boggs probably hurt Boggs far less than they hurt Miss Grace. What really beat Boggs were his Catholicism, his image as a city slicker, his relative liberalism, and his moderate support of the Truman administration. With Boggs eliminated, the second primary was anticlimactic. Spaht remained low-key, but his mentor Earl Long provided some fireworks. Long, who was famed for giving away watermelons on the stump, said of Spaht's opponent Kennon, "I have never known a sillier man to offer for governor," and continued, "We don't need laughing and giggling in the governor's race."[40]

All the defeated candidates snubbed Earl by actively campaigning for Kennon, and Perez suddenly became one of Kennon's biggest boosters. In his mind, the Minden judge possessed all of the qualifications for an ideal governor: he opposed Earl Long; he opposed President Truman; he was disliked by Sam Jones; and he was a fiscal conservative. With most of the first-primary votes received by the defeated candidates certain to go to Kennon, the only real question to be settled by the second primary was the margin of victory. Perez did his best to make it as large as possible; his Plaquemines stalwarts counted 3,388 votes for the Minden judge to only 125 for Spaht, a 93.6 percent majority. St. Bernard stuck with Spaht, giving him, 2,805 votes (69.9 percent) to 1,203 for Kennon. Statewide, Kennon snowed under his fellow judge with 61.4 percent of the vote. For at least another four years Perez would be free from Earl Long, new constitutions, and executive interference in his delta domain.[41]

Perez continued to dominate Plaquemines, and St. Bernard was kept under control through his alliance with Dutch Rowley. In 1953 Dutch died suddenly of a heart attack at the age of sixty-one and was succeeded by Dr. Nicholas P. Trist who, running with Perez's support, polled more than sixteen times the votes of his seven opponents combined. A year after Trist's election, Perez himself and District Judge Bruce Nunez were each elected to another six-year term without opposition.[42]

In 1955, Leander and Trist began quarreling about St. Bernard political appointments. As had happened with previous St. Bernard sheriffs, Trist had become too independent to suit Perez. Trist insisted on appointing his personal legal adviser, Lawrence Bergeron, as secretary of newly created Sewerage District No. 2, but Perez supporters pointed out that Bergeron did not live in either of the wards included in the district. Trist next opposed ratification of a bond issue to provide revenue for the sewerage district. In retaliation, the Perez forces removed him as leader of the St. Bernard Democratic Organization, replacing him with the clerk of court, A. B. ("Tony") Nunez, a Perez stalwart whom they also endorsed as a candidate for sheriff opposing Trist in the coming Democratic primary. Most of the St. Bernard police jurors sided with Perez, but two joined the Trist faction.[43]

Now that Trist had become a political enemy, Leander suddenly found some irregularities in the sheriff's operation of the parish. He revealed that Trist's lawyer and confidant, Lawrence Bergeron, had been retained as associate counsel by the American Sugar Refining Company to break a 1953 strike at Chalmette, the parish seat. Trist allegedly had told a representative of the company that he would commission as many extra deputies as were necessary to remove pickets from the employers' property, break up mass meetings of unionized workers, and protect the scab workers bused in by the company. Sheriff Trist had also allegedly recommended "the organization of a group of deputies by a dummy, their commissioning by the Sheriff and their payment by the Company." The "dummy" turned out to be Bergeron, who had been paid by the company and in turn had paid the special deputies. The company also had paid some of Trist's regular deputies "to reimburse them for long hours and to stimulate their interest in affording protection to returning workers."[44]

Leander further charged that the sheriff had one hundred deputies on the parish payroll, most of whom were deadheads, including seventy-five who were not bonded as required by law. Perez pointed out that Trist had spent the entire surplus of more than $53,000 left in the sheriff's fund by his late predecessor and in addition had borrowed $30,000 to pay his numerous deputies. At Leander's instigation, the St. Bernard school board and a parish water board sued the sheriff for recovery of misappropriated funds, but Trist protested that he had only retained the deputies hired by his predecessors, Dutch Rowley and Dr. L. A. Meraux, and asked, "Why was it all right for a long period of years to retain these deputies and suddenly it is discovered that there is something wrong?" Calling upon Leander to make public the payrolls of other parish agencies, particularly the Lake Borgne Levee Board, Trist admonished, "Let Perez air his own linens." Leander, refusing to answer Trist's charges, had the St. Bernard police jury adopt a resolution taking the ambulance away from the sheriff's office.[45]

The Judge's accusations against Trist continued to roll out in a steady stream: the sheriff and his deputies were accepting bribes from gamblers for protecting their illegal operations; Trist had purposely withheld evidence of juvenile crimes to curry political favor with the parents of the offenders. Trist claimed that all of Perez's charges had been trumped up to force him out of the sheriff's race.[46]

As the political fight intensified, evidence of wrongdoing in the Perez camp also began turning up. The state auditor exposed a shortage of more than $15,000 in Clerk of Court Tony Nunez's office and recommended that Nunez forfeit one-half of his salary to make up the deficit. A report was sent to District Attorney Perez, but he took no action against Nunez, whom he was supporting for sheriff against Trist.[47]

The showdown in the Perez-Trist feud occurred in the St. Bernard Democratic primaries of 1955–1956. Qualifying for the parish offices were 125 candidates. On one side was Sheriff Trist, strongest in the upper, industrialized portion of the parish and supported by newly formed civic groups in that area. Opposing him was the Perez ticket, headed by Clerk of Court Nunez and backed by the majority of the St. Bernard police jury and the state legislative delegation. Perez's grip on St. Bernard had been considerably weakened by the construction of a large Kaiser aluminum plant in the parish just across the city line from New Orleans. This industry had been located there by Henry Kaiser under the prodding of New Orleans Mayor deLesseps Morrison, and other industries had soon followed, all accompanied by an influx of new workers. Perez had no hold on the new settlers, who did not owe their jobs to his political machine. Nunez estimated that 4,000 new voters would cast their ballots in the 1956 Democratic primaries in St. Bernard, and these voters were expected to constitute the balance of power in the Perez-Trist dispute. Shortly before the election the Perez-dominated police jury embarked upon a program of public works in the recently settled part of the parish: new roads, sewerage and drainage facilities, and outdoor lighting fixtures. During the campaign, a Perez-dominated grand jury reported that the St. Bernard jailer was using the jail as a private storeroom for Trist campaign material. The same jury, however, cleared Tony Nunez of responsibility for a $15,000 shortage in the clerk of court's office.[48]

Election day was predictably turbulent. Armed men claiming to be "probation officers" milled about near the polls, closely watched by Trist deputies, who were also armed. In the Seventh Ward, at Reggio, Perez commissioners refused to let Trist supporter Alex Nunez cast a ballot, saying that his name was not on the registration list. A Trist deputy who was also a commissioner announced that if Nunez could not vote, then no one could vote. He thereupon pulled the electric cord on the voting machine, and the Reggio precinct remained closed for the rest of the day. Perez claimed that his commissioners had been afraid to try to reopen the precinct because at least fifteen of Trist's deputies and three state troopers were in the vicinity.[49]

After the dust had settled, the election results seemed a standoff. Trist was reelected St. Bernard sheriff, but Perez supporters won five of the seven police jury seats in that parish. Perez's candidate for state senator, L. H. Folse, won reelection, though J. Claude Meraux, whom Perez had backed for state representative, was defeated by a Trist candidate. The Trist organization won nine of the twelve seats on the St. Bernard Parish Democratic Executive Committee. Typical of the perpetual factional shifts in the deep delta, the unsuccessful candidate for sheriff, Tony Nunez, broke with the Judge and joined the Trist faction shortly after the election.[50]

The Plaquemines boss had even less luck in the 1956 gubernatorial election, which was held concurrently with the local contests. Perez was reasonably satisfied with the Kennon administration, which had retained most of the Long welfare benefits yet had reduced the gasoline tax and increased state income tax exemptions. Because of his high regard for Kennon and, more important, because the two principal candidates, Earl Long and Chep Morrison, were his bitter opponents, Perez endorsed Kennon's choice of a successor, Fred Preaus. A forty-three-year-old Farmerville auto dealer, he was the head of the state highway board, a staunch segregationist, and a novice politician.[51]

The most formidable figure in the contest was Earl Long, three-time aspirant to the state's highest office. While his rivals concentrated on televised addresses, Earl stumped the state with a sound-truck and hillbilly band, making over five hundred speeches. New Orleans Mayor deLesseps Morrison, a long-standing enemy of Perez, was the most potent of the anti-Long candidates. He based his campaign on his record as a progressive mayor and promised to entice industrial plants to Louisiana. The dark-horse candidates included Colonel Francis Grevemberg, the head of the state police under Kennon, who was best known for his sudden raids on gambling houses. His credibility declined when it was revealed that he had once been part owner of a Mississippi Gulf Coast hotel that housed slot machines and sold liquor in defiance of state law. James M. McLemore, in his second bid for the governorship made maintenance of racial segregation his principal issue. He even went so far as to accuse Earl Long of encouraging blacks to register to vote. The Association of Citizens' Councils of Louisiana actively campaigned against Long on the grounds that he was too soft on the segregation issue.[52]

The balloting produced a smashing first-primary victory for Earl Long, who polled 51.4 percent of the votes. This was the first gubernatorial primary without a runoff in twenty years, and Long became the only man to that time to win two elective terms to the governorship. Morrison finished second, followed by Preaus, Grevemberg, and McLemore, respectively. Perez returned 61.4 percent of the

Plaquemines vote for Preaus, but in St. Bernard Earl Long thrashed all four opponents by a whopping margin of 57.4 percent, with Morrison finishing second.[53] In office for what would be his last term as governor, Long resolved to use his power to end the Judge's domination of the lower delta.

TEN

Saving the Country

Leander had been the political kingpin of Plaquemines and St. Bernard for nearly twenty years before becoming active in national politics, but when he finally joined the fray he did so in typical Perez fashion—engaging in a total war admitting of no compromise and no surrender. The Judge never lacked political enemies; for the first half of his career they were men like John Dymond, Dutch Rowley, Claude Meraux, and J. Ben Meyer. In the 1940s he added President Harry S. Truman, the United Nations, the U.S. Supreme Court, and the "international Communist conspiracy." Against these latter more formidable opponents Leander attempted to use the same brutal, bulldozing stratagems that had proved so successful against his provincial foes—tactics quite acceptable among the semiliterate lower delta trappers and fishermen but appallingly blunt and curiously anachronistic when applied to presidents and Supreme Court justices. Though lacking in finesse, the Judge possessed an unlimited supply of three indispensable assets: money, energy, and imagination. And he more than held his own against these new foes; he managed frequently to carry a majority of Louisianians with him.

Little in Leander's intellectual background prepared him for a presidential crusade; he was not well read on national issues, had little knowledge of the political climate outside the South, and had no expertise in foreign affairs. Such deficiencies, however, were not only unapparent to Perez, but they were also unnoticed (or at least unmentioned) by most of his political allies. Yet, what he lacked in experience and factual information he made up for in aggressiveness; Leander was never lukewarm in his feelings.

Perez relished the hearty backslapping and casual mingling with congressmen, senators, governors, lobbyists, and business executives, the whispered tactical exchanges, the boisterous news conferences, and the folksy, convivial strategy sessions over drinks and cigars with like-thinking politicians. The rustics back home were proud and impressed; there was their very own Judge photographed with Strom Thurmond and later with Ross Barnett, Lester Maddox, and George Wallace—the legendary defenders of the southern way of life. Perhaps the outcome of the southern struggle was not so important as the joy of the fight; the crusaders knew that they would be fondly remembered by their admirers as historic southern heroes regardless of success or failure. They were preeminently men of action, and Perez was at home among them.

Though both the wisdom and expediency of Leander's stand on particular national issues may be questioned, his sincerity cannot; his defense of states' rights was based on genuine conviction, albeit conveniently coupled with self-interest. Perez had become the boss of the lower delta by ruthless, pragmatic, utterly unscrupulous power politics. Once politically entrenched and financially secure, he became a man of principle—at least in national affairs. Those who came to know him solely in these national crusades understandably assumed that he had been a man of principle all along.

Like anyone who seriously aspired to political power in Louisiana, Perez belonged to the Democratic party; he was a member of his parish and district Democratic executive committees and a power on the state central committee. But, because conservative principles were more important to him than party loyalty, he opposed every Democratic presidential nominee from Harry Truman in 1948 to Hubert Humphrey in 1968. The Judge was further frustrated by finding the Republican party too liberal for his taste, although he reluctantly supported Eisenhower for president in 1952 and 1956 and somewhat more enthusiastically backed Barry Goldwater in 1964. His political dogma was simple, unchanging, and almost entirely negative: he opposed racial equality, federal ownership of tidelands oil resources, national welfare and public works programs, socialism in any form, and the mere existence of labor unions. Because the United States government, under both Democratic and Republican administrations, to some extent endorsed all of these, Leander became an indomitable foe of federal power in any form. Although he concentrated authority entirely in his own hands in Plaquemines, he denounced every vestige of centralized power in the national government. His antipathy toward Washington became so notorious that Earl Long once asked, "Whatcha gonna do now, Leander? The feds have got the atom bomb."[1]

Aside from civil rights, Perez's loudest and most prolonged confrontation with the federal government concerned jurisdiction over the tidelands—the name applied to the expanse of oil-rich submerged land stretching from the mainland to the edge of the continental shelf. Because the issue had not arisen before the development of offshore oil fields, it had never been legally determined whether the region lay within the domain of the individual states or the national government. Whoever won the right to administer the disputed territory would reap a bonanza from rental fees, royalties on production, and severance taxes. The greatest oil deposits lay off Louisiana's irregular coastline, about 38 percent of which is within the boundaries of Plaquemines and St. Bernard parishes.[2]

Shortly after the tidelands became a major point of contention in the late 1940s, Governor Earl Long appointed Perez to the post of unpaid special assistant attorney general to help prepare Louisiana's legal arguments. Plunging into the task with characteristic vigor, he quickly became the state's most erudite spokesman on the subject. He rummaged through dusty Washington bookshops for contemporary works on colonial America, reread Benjamin Franklin's autobiography, carefully examined the proceedings of the Constitutional Convention, and purchased from the Library of Congress a copy of every Louisiana coastal chart in their files. The Judge collaborated with Louisiana's attorney general and the State Mineral Board in writing the brief that was presented to the U.S. Supreme Court, but his name was omitted because Louisiana officials feared that it might needlessly antagonize the Court.[3]

Leander opposed federal tidelands jurisdiction on ideological as well as economic grounds. The state came closest to agreeing to a compromise in 1949, when the federal government proposed giving Louisiana all oil royalties and bonuses from fields within three miles of the shore and a 37.5 percent share from wells beyond that point. Louisiana's team of negotiators was on the verge of accepting when Perez rallied support to block the settlement; he stubbornly refused to assent to any agreement that did not recognize state ownership of the disputed area.[4] He consistently proved the most intractable state tidelands representative, claiming at one time that state authority extended into the Gulf as far as sixty or seventy miles.[5] In 1954 Perez masterminded a Louisiana legislative act asserting that the state's boundary extended three leagues, or ten and a half miles, into the Gulf. The law also established the coastline, or base line, at a point beyond all offshore lakes, bays, and inlets—a point dubbed the "Perez line" or "Leander's meander." The federal government had its own base line, which had been fixed by Secretary of the Interior Oscar Chapman in 1950. Although Perez carefully distinguished between the coastline and the shoreline,[6] Chapman defined the two as synonymous: the point at which the water lapped the land at low tide. Perez claimed that the Chapman line was so far inland that it would allow Russian submarines to cruise part-way up the Mississippi River and still be in international waters. More detached observers facetiously remarked that "the Chapman Line goes to Shreveport and the Perez Line goes to Venezuela."[7]

After the Judge broke with Earl Long in 1950, he lost his position as an assistant attorney general but continued on his own initiative to journey to Washington to represent the state. When he attempted to intervene in arguing Louisiana's case before the Supreme Court in 1957, Attorney General Jack P. F. Gremillion informed the justices that Leander had no official role in Louisiana's presentation, whereupon Justice Hugo Black, who was presiding, told Perez, "You have no position. Take a seat."[8]

The Judge detested Gremillion, a colorful and controversial figure in his own right,[9] even more than he hated Earl Long. He considered Gremillion incompetent and thought that he was becoming too cozy with the "federals." Gremillion, correctly arguing that he, not Perez, was the state's chief legal officer, insisted that, as long as Leander had anything to do with the bargaining, there was no chance of a settlement because "he is a diabolical enemy of the Supreme Court." Perez eventually persuaded his close political ally, Governor Jimmie Davis, personally to supplant Gremillion as Louisiana's chief negotiator and replace him as adviser to the governor with a five-member legislative tidelands committee.[10]

In May, 1960, the U.S. Supreme Court ruled that Louisiana's boundary should be limited to three miles seaward, but left unanswered the location of the base line from which to begin measuring.[11] Perez continued to fight; the 1962 Plaquemines budget included a ten-thousand-dollar appropriation for "expenses in defense of parish interest in tidelands."[12] At the time of his death the base line had not been determined.

Both on the national level and within his own bailiwick, Perez was a persistent and vehement foe of organized labor. Insisting that powerful leftist labor bosses controlled the Democratic party, he believed that unionization was but one step removed from outright socialism, and he never allowed unions of any type within Plaquemines. An honest worker could "live on a dollar a day," he told CBS newsman Dan Rather.[13] Along with fellow conservative William M. ("Willie") Rainach, the Judge was instrumental in having the Louisiana legislature adopt a state right-to-work law in 1954, during the friendly administration of Governor Kennon. A year later, when Earl Long, a friend of labor and an enemy of Perez, became a gubernatorial candidate, Leander joined a group of right-wing rural and New Orleans businessmen to incorporate the Louisiana Free Enterprise Association, a non-profit "educational" organization whose primary purpose was to prevent repeal of the right-to-work law. Their worst fears materialized when Long was elected governor and promptly had the law revoked. But the association was successful in defeating other Long-sponsored legislation, such as a proposed constitutional convention, a tax program placing the heaviest burden on the wealthy, and bills designed to guarantee unions the rights of collective bargaining, boycotting, and picketing. Even during the administration of his political ally, Governor John McKeithen, the Judge stubbornly fought legislation that required the state to pay workers the prevailing wage for all public maintenance and construction projects. Perez drew up and the Plaquemines commission council unanimously adopted legislation requiring local labor contractors to fingerprint and photograph all itinerant workers employed in the parish. Following passage of the ordinance, Leander boasted, "Bums are leaving Plaquemines parish by droves."[14]

About the same time that he helped organize the Louisiana Free Enterprise Association, Perez met with rightist leaders from ten other southern states at the invitation of Senator James O. Eastland of Mississippi to create a regional political action group called the Federation for Constitutional Government. The Judge was selected to be a member of a Louisiana advisory committee along with such inveterate state conservatives as Sam Jones, F. Edward Hebert, and Willie Rainach. Chairman of the federation's executive committee was John U. Barr of New Orleans, a veteran conservative activist who had formerly been the chief spokesman in the South for the National Association of Manufacturers. The federation had headquarters in the American Bank Building, where Perez then had his law office. The delegates resolved that the major purposes of the group should be the preservation of decentralized government, resistance to the nomination and election of liberal candidates, and opposition to socialistic platforms and court decisions that violated states' rights. At the suggestion of one of the delegates, maintenance of racial segregation was not mentioned in the official declaration of principles but was clearly intended to be among the organization's objectives. In May, 1956, the federation reprinted and mailed out thousands of copies of a militantly segregationist speech entitled "Where Is the Reign of Terror," which had been delivered by Mississippi Congressman John Bell Williams in the U.S. House of Representatives, terming the diatribe a "remarkable factual and undeniable collection of logic and truth." Williams, citing soaring Negro crime rates, claimed that the number of serious offenses committed by blacks was highest in racially integrated neighborhoods.[15]

The federation initially evoked an abundance of enthusiasm but lacked mass support and sustained financial backing. Although names of prominent persons headed the executive and advisory committees, those who did the actual work of the organization were not talented journalists or researchers. The AFL-CIO, branding the federation a coordinating committee of "neo-Klan" groups, demanded a federal investigation.[16]

Perez's views on foreign policy were dominated by an obsession with the international Communist menace. He believed that Kremlin agents had infiltrated the federal bureaucracy, the Supreme Court, and even the White House and dominated the national news media through the "Zionist Jews." He reasoned that an amorphous but sinister combine of Zionist Jews, Communist spies, and American civil rights leaders, working together for some unexplained reason, were plotting to destroy the "American way of life" by their advocacy of racial integration, higher corporate and individual income taxes, federal control of tidelands oil, and registration of black voters. He probably would never have become a crusader in national politics if federal policies had not intruded upon his vital interests. His conversion came suddenly, without extensive study or prolonged consideration; the sources he read only confirmed his prejudices. Although an avid reader of legal works and right-wing newspapers and magazines, the Judge never opened a book for pleasure. His reading was strictly limited to his own special interests and political views; his library was stocked with books about constitutional law, the testing of Negro intelligence, and the evils of communism. Perez also received voluminous material from such reactionary organizations as the Patrick Henry Society, Sons of Liberty, National Association for the Advancement of White People, National White American party, and Citizens' Council.[17]

Leander totaled up his enemies and decided that, since they all seemed to be working through the federal government, the whole cabal undoubtedly met regularly on the Potomac to coordinate their next baleful power grab. The concept of black equality was so foreign to him that he assumed that it must quite literally be the product of a foreign ideology—namely, communism. For one thing, he thought, black people were not imaginative enough to devise such a nefarious scheme themselves. His reasoning went this way: since Jewish leaders were prominent in the movement for racial equality, which was clearly a Communist conspiracy, the Jews and the Kremlin were therefore in it together; the Jews bankrolled the integration movement and dominated the NAACP; the NAACP had been founded by a Jew and had always had a Jewish rather than a Negro president; it was difficult to get his message across because the Jews dominated the mass media.[18] Some Jews, however, were staunch segregationists, even Citizens' Council members; like Negroes, there were "good" and "bad" ones.

The Judge insisted that this infamous trio of conspirators had masterminded the failure of the Bay of Pigs invasion, the racial strife in America, the trouble in the Congo, the war in Vietnam, and the turmoil in Latin America.[19] The only way to deal with such fanatics, he concluded, was the same way he dealt with local opponents—superior force. Thus he became an advocate of massive expenditures for national defense, perhaps never pausing to consider what use a Communist-dominated Pentagon might make of such weaponry. Foreign aid was a wasteful, dim-witted, "soft-headed" scheme of the American fifth column. Perez favored "big stick" diplomacy, the kind he had successfully employed against Governor Sam Jones in 1943.

Leander was convinced that, if there was any single organization more sinister than the NAACP, it was the United Nations. He industriously compiled a file of material designed to prove that the UN was but the first step toward evolution of a world government to be ruled from Moscow. He linked the "conspiracy" of Reds, blacks, and Jews to sponsorship of the Convention on the Prevention and Punishment of Genocide, adopted by the United Nations in 1948. The convention defined the act of causing "serious bodily or mental harm" to members of an ethnic, national, or religious group as an international crime. Perez exploded at the very idea, terming the proposal a "monstrosity" and "a dishonest subterfuge" intended to undermine states' rights.[20] He feared that ratification by the U.S. Senate would authorize the federal government to prosecute the perpetrator of a racial murder or maiming because, as a national treaty, the convention would supersede state law. He bitterly complained that the genocide convention was "nothing less than an anti-lynching bill and worse in disguise."[21]

As district attorney, Perez "knew" from personal experience that such offenders could best be rendered justice in local courts. Rushing to Washington to testify before a Senate subcommittee that had opened hearings on ratification of the convention, he passionately asserted that local officials charged with causing mere "mental harm" to Negroes could be extradited for trial before an international tribunal comprised of Communists. After hearing Perez, the subcommittee chairman J. Howard McGrath of New Jersey commented, "I simply want the record to show that I do not regard your testimony up to this point as being pertinent to the bill at all."[22]

One of the multitude of reasons that Leander detested Hubert Humphrey was that the senator advocated repeal of the Connally Reservation, which provided that the United States would not accept compulsory World Court jurisdiction in "matters which are essentially within the domestic jurisdiction of the United States as determined by the United States." The Judge also championed a proposed amendment to the U.S. Constitution submitted by Senator John W. Bricker of Ohio in 1953. The Bricker amendment, enthusiastically supported by most southern conservatives, would have nullified any international agreement that conflicted with the Constitution and would have kept treaties from becoming domestic law in the absence of enabling legislation. Although many senators considered the proposal too broad and Secretary of State John Foster Dulles termed it "dangerous to our peace and security," Perez thought that it was far too weak. Again and again he urged Bricker to reword the bill to also prohibit international agreements that abridged states' rights. The Bricker amendment stirred intense and prolonged debate; Perez appeared before the Senate Judiciary Committee to urge its immediate adoption. Finally, on February 26, 1954, the Senate rejected the amendment thirty-one to sixty, one vote short of the two-thirds majority required to pass it.[23]

Through the years Leander developed personal ties with a coterie of conservative senators, congressmen, governors, judges, and state legislators—principally fellow southerners who shared his views on race, communism, and opposition to federal power. His closest associates in the nation's capital were Senator Eastland of Mississippi, whom he referred to as "my Senator," and for whom he sometimes wrote speeches,[24] and Louisiana Congressman F. Edward Hebert, who represented Perez's own First Congressional District. As chairman of the Senate Judiciary Committee, Eastland often invited the Judge to testify against pending civil rights bills, and Hebert (for whom Perez named a boulevard in Belle Chasse) routinely consulted him about local patronage. Both men enjoyed

Leander's hospitality—fishing cruises aboard the *Manta,* congenial conversations over drinks and fine cigars, leisurely card games— and respected his knowledge of constitutional law and his unyielding stand against federal power. The Judge was a friend, but not really an intimate associate, of Senators Allen Ellender of Louisiana and Strom Thurmond of South Carolina. Ellender was a little too moderate and Thurmond was a bit too intellectual to succumb completely to Perez's charm, but both senators were occasional correspondents and steadfast political confidants. Leander's entree into the inner circle of rightist ideologues was his bulging pocketbook and his generosity with his wealth. From his overflowing campaign chest in New Orleans went unsolicited and sizable contributions to such office seekers as Jimmie Davis and John Rarick of Louisiana, Jim Johnson of Arkansas, Ross Barnett of Mississippi, George Wallace of Alabama, and Lester Maddox of Georgia and to scores of lesser-known politicans. The Judge was intuitively endowed with both a measure of political realism and a dash of the quixotic. If his choice lay between aiding a right-wing militant with no chance of winning or an outright liberal, he invariably backed the former. But, if the option lay between two conservatives, Perez supported the probable winner, not necessarily the more conservative. For example, he energetically promoted Jimmie Davis rather than the uncompromising segregationist Willie Rainach for governor in 1959.[25]

President Franklin D. Roosevelt, who had a war and a depression to worry about, happily escaped the Judge's wrath; Plaquemines voted overwhelmingly Democratic in every election in which Roosevelt ran.[26] It was not until after the Great Depression had ended and the oil royalties had made the parish an economically independent sheikdom that Perez became a vociferous critic of deficit spending; in 1936 he attended FDR's inauguration in order to solicit WPA projects for Plaquemines and St. Bernard.[27]

By 1944 Perez, suspicious of Roosevelt's tax-the-rich policies and sympathy for organized labor, disliked the prospect of a fourth term. Having outlasted Governor Sam Jones's attempts to destroy his power base and having made peace with his successor Jimmie Davis, Perez made his initial foray into national politics by attempting to secure the Democratic presidential nomination for a southern conservative, Senator Harry Byrd of Virginia. Before the Democratic National Convention he helped to organize a Byrd-for-president committee in Louisiana. At the convention the Louisiana, Mississippi, and Virginia delegations voted en bloc for Byrd's nomination. Following Roosevelt's renomination, electors pledged to vote against the Roosevelt-Truman ticket appeared on the ballot in three southern states. After heated debate, Louisiana's Democratic State Central Committee pledged its electors to the president; three electors who refused to pledge were dropped from the slate. Perez confined his fight entirely within the Democratic party; in the November election FDR carried Plaquemines and St. Bernard by the customary huge margins.[28]

Shortly into his fourth term Roosevelt died suddenly of a stroke while vacationing in Warm Springs, Georgia. The Judge had kind words for the fallen leader, but was wary of his successor, Harry Truman. The Missouri-born president, a man almost as stubborn and as blunt as Perez himself, eventually vied with Lyndon Johnson for the top spot on the Judge's list of most hated national leaders. Years later the Plaquemines boss would point back to the Truman administration as the time it had all begun: "uppity" Negroes, collusion with the Communists, federal giveaway programs, and deliberate destruction of states' rights. Leander took immediate offense at the new president's civil rights program, minimum wage bill, farm policy, and advocacy of federal ownership of offshore oil resources. Never at a loss for colorful, if somewhat rambling, oratory, the Judge exclaimed, "Now a Trumancrat is a political hydrat [sic], a cross between a Jeffersonian Democrat and a Socialist or Communist or a homo, of whom there have been thousands exposed in Washington lately, which can only produce an illegitimate offspring called a Bastocrat."[29]

Maintaining the South's radical status quo became a major concern after President Truman delivered a special message to Congress in February, 1948, calling for federal protection against lynching, legislation to secure the right to vote for minority Americans, and the creation of a fair employment practices committee. Conservative white reaction throughout the South was immediate and hostile. Anti-Truman sentiment was conspicuous when Louisiana's

Democratic State Central Committee met on March 6 to select delegates to the national convention. Perez was among the forty delegates originally chosen, but his name was deleted when the number was later reduced.[30]

By that time Leander was wholeheartedly engaged in a crusade to derail Truman's campaign. Along with a group of prominent conservative southern Democrats, he traveled to Jackson, Mississippi, for a strategy conference on May 10, 1948, now accepted as the birth date of the States' Rights Democratic party. The bitter but determined southerners were virtually certain that Truman would be nominated by the Democratic National Convention in July; if that occurred they intended to shatter the hitherto solid South by deserting the Democratic party. As yet they had neither candidate nor program, but only a burning resentment of President Truman and his liberal policies and advisers. But plans quickly materialized; a caucus of southern delegates was planned for July 11, before the convention opened. Before the nominating began, the delegates would inform the appropriate convention committee that they would refuse to support Truman or any other candidate who endorsed his civil rights program. If Truman or another liberal candidate were nominated, a special States' Rights party convention would assemble at Birmingham, Alabama, on July 17. The States' Rights Democratic Campaign Committee was created, with Governor Ben Laney of Arkansas as chairman.[31]

The movement was born of outrage and enthusiasm, fueled by southern pride and conservative ideology. Perez was among the fire-eaters—those who urged immediate and remorseless secession from the Democratic party. He was prepared to back the crusade with his unstinting energy, enormous financial resources, and considerable organizational competence. He began the campaign with little consideration of the mechanics of the electoral college or the mathematical probability of victory in the nationwide contest, but he bubbled with schemes to place Louisiana in the Dixiecrat column. The essence of the struggle within the Pelican State would not involve public speeches or open debates but power politics behind closed doors; in this Perez excelled.

On June 8 the Judge met with the campaign committee at the

Heidelberg Hotel in Jackson. This time the emphasis was on serious, hardheaded planning, not oratory. The committee resolved to limit its efforts, at least until after the Birmingham convention, to the eleven southern states. One five-member committee was appointed to arrange for the delegate caucus and another to organize the Birmingham convention. The group decided to create a supervisory three-member executive committee and to hire a full-time campaign director with headquarters at Little Rock. This director was authorized to employ a "November ballot investigator" to learn the steps necessary to get States' Rights candidates on the ballot in each southern state. The campaign committee also approved the organization of a citizens' committee of at least twenty-five persons in each southern state and provided for the employment of three full-time liaison men to work among the eleven states. Newspaper releases, radio addresses, campaign buttons, and the publication of a special edition of a States' Rights newspaper were planned, and an estimated budget of $169,000 was approved for June–July, 1948. Mississippi, the state that had pioneered the movement, contributed $10,000 to get the campaign under way, and Governor Laney pledged an additional $10,000 from Arkansas.[32]

From the standpoint of manpower, funds, and the time allotted for the campaign, the States' Rights drive could in no way compare with the effort of either major party; it could not even equal the resources mobilized by individual candidates seeking the nomination of a national party. But the planning was intense, earnest, and solemn. The campaign differed from the George Wallace crusade twenty years later in that it was organized around an ideology, not a man; there was a Dixiecrat party before there was a Dixiecrat candidate. And the Dixiecrats, unlike the Wallace partisans, undertook their work not with the air of vacationers on a holiday caper but with the attitude of desperate men combating a deadly virus.

As the July 12 Democratic National Convention approached, defiant southern Democrats braced themselves for what they were certain would occur—Truman's nomination. Mississippi once again led the way; at a state democratic convention in June, the Mississippi party instructed its delegation to decline to support the national ticket if Truman were nominated or if a civil rights plank were included in the platform. After both contingencies transpired at Philadelphia, this delegation and half the Alabama delegation theatrically withdrew from both the convention and the Truman-led party. The unhappy and disillusioned Louisiana delegates expressed their displeasure but did not censure the president or walk out of the convention. They resolved to back Governor Earl Long as a favorite son candidate for president, but when the roll call was taken Louisiana's votes were cast for Senator Richard Russell of Georgia.[33]

More than six thousand aroused States' Righters, Judge Perez among them, streamed into Birmingham for their convention on July 17. Armed with Confederate flags and statements denouncing Truman, they left no doubt about their sentiments. The platform made clear the central issue: "We stand for the segregation of the races and the racial integrity of each race."[34] The convention unanimously recommended the nomination of Governor J. Strom Thurmond of South Carolina for president and Governor Fielding L. Wright of Mississippi for vice-president.

Thurmond, who had a higher boiling point than most of the Dixiecrats, was not yet convinced of the wisdom of bolting. The non-smoking, teetotaling Baptist had earned a reputation as a progressive governor by supporting improved education, better rural health facilities, wage-and-hour laws, soil conservation, and reorganization of the executive branch. But above all he was a proud southerner, a firm believer in states' rights, and an unyielding segregationist. H. L. Mencken, the iconoclastic journalist, termed Thurmond "the best of all the candidates," but complained that "all the worst morons in the South are for him." Wright waited for his cue from Thurmond. Also a nondrinker, the Mississippi governor had called a special session of the legislature in 1947 to block racially mixed Democratic primaries and had advised blacks to leave Mississippi if they wanted to end segregation.[35]

Thurmond had supported Russell's nomination at Philadelphia, hoping that he could remain a loyal Democrat. Now, deciding there was no alternative to leaving the party, he let it be known that he would accept the Dixiecrat nomination. Heartened by the news, Perez began energetic preparations for the official States' Rights nominating convention to be held at Houston.[36]

On August 11, ten thousand supercharged Dixiecrats swarmed into Sam Houston Coliseum where they cheered, yelled, demonstrated, and perspired for an hour and a half while their nominees blasted away at the rival tickets. Thurmond, lumping his opponents together in a manner that must have delighted Perez, warned, "The proposed federal police state, directed from Washington, will force life in each hamlet in America to conform to a Washintgton pattern. Russia is ruled from Moscow." The fiery acceptance speeches of the two southern governors touched off a clamorous and exuberant political demonstration. With a band blaring, rebel yells thundering throughout the big convention hall, and scores of banners of all kinds waving—including Confederate flags—the delegates performed snake dances, churned, and paraded through the aisles for more than twenty-five minutes after the conclusion of Thurmond's address. Perez, who was in the midst of the action, was photographed conferring earnestly with Thurmond and fellow Louisiana Dixiecrat, W. H. Talbot.[37]

A few days after the Dixiecrat convention, Louisiana's States' Rights leaders held mass meetings in several sections of the state to lay plans for placing Thurmond-Wright electors on the ballot as a third-party slate. On August 4, zealous Dixiecrats from throughout the state flocked to Baton Rouge for an open strategy meeting. They formally endorsed the Thurmond-Wright ticket, created a statewide organization, and selected the Statue of Liberty as the emblem of the States' Rights Democratic party within Louisiana.[38]

The Dixiecrats never admitted that they had left the Democratic party. The States' Righters were the "true" Democrats, Perez insisted; the liberals had deserted the party. The Dixiecrats backed up their claims by withholding funds intended for the Democratic campaign chest and turning them over to the new party.[39] In Louisiana the debate over who represented the real Democrats had more than theoretical significance. Since the bitter days of Reconstruction, the gamecock or rooster had served as the symbol of the Democratic party in Louisiana, the party that championed white supremacy. Illiterate whites, certain that all Republicans were carpetbaggers, scoundrels, or Negroes, voted for whoever appeared under the column headed by the rooster, unaware of the merits, and often even of the identities, of the candidates. The Judge, who had little faith in the ability of the Louisiana voter to make subtle distinctions, claimed that at least 100,000 Louisianians, primarily elderly people, automatically voted for the candidates listed under the hallowed rooster. He felt that Thurmond would be severely handicapped by running under an unfamiliar emblem such as the Statue of Liberty. Perez rarely missed a potential or actual advantage; certainly he would never concede a 100,000-vote edge to such a detested foe as Harry Truman. According to Leander's legal interpretations, the state and national Democratic parties were separate entities, the former symbolized by the rooster, the latter by the donkey. Therefore, if the state Democratic party rejected the national Democratic presidential nominee, it might name its own candidate who would, of course, run under the rooster emblem. More simply, he was out to capture the rooster for Strom Thurmond.[40]

Quietly, he spread the word among his followers on the Democratic State Central Committee. On August 27, the committee chairman, Perez ally Henry Sevier, called for a meeting to be held September 10 "for the purpose of promulgating the election returns and for transacting any business that might come before it." It all seemed so routine that many of the more liberal committee members did not bother to attend, giving their proxies to conservative friends who, it seemed, all had time to travel to Baton Rouge. Governor Long, who learned from informants that an attempt would be made at the meeting to award the rooster emblem to Thurmond, held a secret strategy conference on September 9 with his forces; the session lasted late into the night. Long initially opposed the rooster grab, feeling that it might antagonize the national administration and hurt the chances of his nephew Russell, who was running for the U.S. Senate. One rumor held that Earl also feared a federal investigation of his income tax returns. Finally he relented, but not before a tacit agreement was arranged with the Judge. The governor gave Leander his proxy, apparently in exchange for a promise from Perez not to oppose a plan to place President Truman on the ballot by petition later.[41]

Although the news media expressed astonishment at the results of the September 10 central committee meeting, the Dixiecrats had carefully rehearsed the proceedings. Perez not only wrote the script, he also directed the action and played the starring role. Following the routine certification of primary election returns, Leander rose and read aloud to the hushed assembly a motion pledging Louisiana's ten Democratic presidential electors to the Dixiecrat ticket. The resolution provided that Thurmond and Wright, as well as all other Democratic nominees for national, state, district, and local offices, would appear beneath the venerable rooster and designated the ten electors, among whom was Perez himself. The committee unanimously adopted the Judge's motion. He then rushed through a motion requesting the slate of Thurmond electors who had qualified by petition under the States' Rights label to withdraw. Finally, the committee approved another Perez resolution providing that no one could be a candidate for the Democratic nomination to any office who was "associated with or an adherent of any organization, association or party inimical to the Constitution of the State of Louisiana or of the United States of America, nor shall he have advocated any such doctrines or matters of government contrary thereto." Presumably, the committee would determine which doctrines were inimical to the Constitution. The Judge had emphatically stated earlier that he considered the Fair Employment Practices Committee and any federal civil rights legislation among such proscribed creeds.[42]

Two Lake Charles AFL officials, who were committee members and who felt they had been hoodwinked into signing away their proxies, immediately filed suit against the central committee and the secretary of state, requesting an injunction to prohibit anyone other than Harry Truman and Alben W. Barkley from appearing on the Louisiana ballot as the Democratic nominees. They complained that they would never have given their proxies if they had been aware that such an extraordinary move had been contemplated. Furthermore, they argued, the Democratic State Central Committee had merely a "ministerial duty" to certify to the secretary of state the nominees of the Democratic National Convention; it had no right by law or tradition to serve as a miniature nominating convention. Perez, one of the defense attorneys in the suit, outmaneuvered his adversaries. A Baton Rouge district court issued the temporary restraining order requested by the plaintiffs but then granted a suspensive appeal that permitted the secretary of state to print the ballots. Had Perez carried the adverse ruling to a state court of appeals, he would have been entitled to a second suspensive appeal, prolonging the case beyond the last practical date for printing ballots. After the state supreme court refused to hear the case immediately, the hapless Trumanites withdrew their suit, saying that there would not be enough time to print any ballots by the time the case was decided. The slate of Thurmond electors who had qualified by petition under the Statue of Liberty emblem withdrew when it was certain that their candidate would appear under the rooster.[43]

It appeared that Truman's name would not even be on the Louisiana ballot, because the central committee resolutions of September 10 had come after the deadline for including electors by petition. The president's only recourse would have been to run as a write-in candidate in Louisiana, an almost insurmountable handicap complicated by the fact that, under Louisiana law, voters desiring to cast ballots for him would have had to write in the names of all ten presidential electors.[44] But Governor Long summoned a special session of the state legislature to enact laws enabling the Truman-Barkley ticket to be placed on the November ballot by petition. His action, coming when Perez was out of the state, made him something of a hero to Louisiana Democratic loyalists, who believed that he was trying to outflank Perez. Actually, the state central committee would never have voted unanimously to make Thurmond the state's Democratic nominee if Long had opposed the move. The governor had disliked Leander's strategy but, realizing that he did not have the committee votes to defeat the measure, had agreed to go along. The Judge, for his part, was quite content for Truman to appear on the ballot under an emblem other than the rooster because he was confident that the president could not carry Louisiana under such circumstances. Long's gesture was merely a sop to appease the national administration; both Perez and Long knew it.[45]

Had the Thurmond (Perez) partisans in the legislature been firmly committed to excluding Truman from the ballot, the governor's bill would not have won approval so easily. Nonetheless, they did insert amendments that specifically denied to the Truman-

Barkley electors the use of the word *Democratic* and the rooster symbol. Democratic National Chairman J. Howard McGrath wanted to hold out for a bill reserving the rooster for President Truman. Such a proposal would have violated the tacit agreement between Long and Perez, and the Dixiecrats in the legislature would never have allowed it to pass. As a result of the juggling of symbols and titles, President Truman appeared beneath a donkey emblem and Thurmond under the rooster.[46]

Apprehensive that the Democratic split might aid Republican opposition to his nephew Russell, the governor included in his bill a provision permitting state and local Democratic candidates to appear in both the column headed by the rooster and that headed by the donkey. These nominees would be listed in both columns automatically unless they filed a formal request with the secretary of state asking to be only in the Thurmond column. Leander, unwilling to concede even a trivial advantage to the detested Truman, feared that the president might receive some ballots from straight-ticket voters who were really interested in voting only for local candidates. Hoping by example to establish a trend, Perez and Congressman F. Edward Hebert announced that they would not allow their names to appear in the national Democratic column. The Judge wrote other state candidates imploring them to do the same. Most Democratic office seekers in Plaquemines and St. Bernard complied, as did a number of local officials from other parishes, but he failed to convince Senator Allen Ellender and senatorial candidate Russell Long, each of whom appeared under both columns.[47]

The Dixiecrats caustically denounced all the rival tickets, but reserved their most acrid comments for the "regular" Democrats. Thurmond contended that Truman's civil rights program had been conceived in response to the "demands of the parlor pinks and the subversives," and a Dixiecrat broadside distributed by Perez insisted that the Truman proposals were designed "in order to win votes from un-American minorities." The *Plaquemines Gazette* later claimed that Democratic vice-presidential candidate Barkley had "shaken down" Chicago liquor dealers for a quarter of a million dollars in campaign contributions. Louisiana's congressmen and senators found themselves in a dilemma not uncommon for southern

Democrats: if they backed the national ticket they would lose support among their constituents, but if they campaigned for Thurmond, who had no chance of winning nationwide, they might provoke disciplinary measures from the national party. Many state politicians were enamored of neither candidate. The most expedient position was neutrality, the course pursued by Earl Long, Russell Long, and deLesseps Morrison.[48]

After the alarmist charges and inflammatory rhetoric that had characterized the birth of the Dixiecrat movement, the actual campaign in Louisiana proved relatively dull. The few true Truman supporters despaired of winning the state and thus felt little incentive to campaign; the Dixiecrats, confident of victory, felt little need to exert themselves. New Orleans was so apathetic to Truman's candidacy that no Democratic campaign headquarters was established there. When Alben Barkley visited the Crescent City, Leander organized an effective boycott; only five hundred persons turned out to meet the Kentuckian, affording him the "coolest reception" of his southern speaking tour. Perez devoted some of his time to directing the Dixiecrat effort in Texas, where Thurmond had no official statewide organization. He energetically solicited campaign contributions and personally donated at least ten thousand dollars to the Thurmond effort. At the outset of the campaign, one States' Rights leader wrote Perez to urge that only strong-willed States' Righters be appointed parish registrars, asserting that "if a Registrar has the guts and intelligence he can cut down the Negro Registration at least 75% from what it is now." Women, he cautioned, should not be made registrars because they would be afraid to deny registration to Negro men.[49]

The presidential campaign generated so little popular enthusiasm in Louisiana that it hardly justified Leander's machinations to obtain every bit of leverage for his candidate. Only 45 percent of the state's electorate turned out, compared with 71 percent of the registered voters who had participated in the previous gubernatorial election. As expected, the Dixiecrat ticket led with 49.1 percent of the total vote, followed by Truman with 32.7 percent, Dewey with 17.5 percent, and all-but-forgotten Progressive party candidate Henry Wallace with .7 percent. In addition to carrying Louisiana, the

States' Rights Democrats won Alabama, Mississippi, and South Carolina and picked up one electoral vote in Tennessee, for a total of thirty-nine votes in the electoral college. The Thurmond-Wright combine amassed more than 93 percent of the vote in Plaquemines and more than 91 percent in St. Bernard. President Truman, however, surprised everyone but himself by winning reelection.[50]

Following the president's victory, the national Democratic party punished its wayward southern members. Perez's intimate, Congressman Hebert, was removed from the House Un-American Activities Committee, an intended chastisement that proved a blessing, for Hebert was spared the embarrassment of association with Senator Joseph McCarthy's witch-hunt for Communists and homosexuals in the federal government. The real showdown, however, came in the Democratic National Committee, which in August, 1949, scheduled a meeting to elect a successor to Chairman McGrath, whom Truman had appointed U.S. attorney general. Louisiana's national committeeman, W. H. Talbot, a wealthy New Orleans attorney who had been active in the Dixiecrat campaign, was not invited to attend but decided to force his way in, accompanied by his lawyer Leander Perez. The Judge heatedly but unsuccessfully argued Talbot's case before the credentials committee. The following day the Democratic National Committee, acting under a fifty-year-old rule, adopted the recommendations of the credentials committee and removed Talbot and four other Dixiecrats from the national committee. Mary Evelyn Dickerson, another committee member from Louisiana, was allowed to remain after she explained that she had voted for Truman although she had been inactive in the presidential campaign. Leander, calling the "entire proceedings a farce," vowed to carry the fight back to Louisiana's Democratic State Central Committee, which was empowered to fill the vacancy created by Talbot's dismissal.

But, by the time he returned to Baton Rouge, the shaky entente between him and Earl Long had crumbled. The governor was ready to make peace with the Truman administration; Perez intended to fight down to the last Dixiecrat. This time it was Long, not Perez, who held the crucial proxies. Unblushingly reversing his field, Leander vehemently objected to the use of proxies on the grounds that it violated parliamentary procedure. Long declined to accept Perez's proposal to use *Robert's Rules of Order* as the operating manual of the committee, commenting, "I'm afraid to go along with anything he's for right now. He's a lot smarter lawyer than I am and has a lot more money." The committee voted to replace Talbot with a new committeeman. The infuriated Perez thundered that President Truman should be "impeached rather than appeased" and threatened to go to court to contest the ouster of Talbot. He told the committee that Truman was operating the most corrupt administration in American history, claiming that only seven billion of the fifty billion dollars Congress had appropriated for national defense had actually been spent for that purpose, with the rest going for graft and corruption. Whatever the sources of his information, Perez was entirely serious in his accusations. He lamentably lacked a sense of humor, though no doubt he would have enjoyed giving a hotfoot to President Truman as he once did to a onetime local political opponent, J. Ben Meyer.[51]

Before the balloting in the 1948 presidential election, Leander had already discussed the possibility of establishing an enduring party structure with other Dixiecrat leaders. On October 24 of that year leading Dixiecrats from throughout the South met at Memphis to create the framework for a permanent organization. Perez, Strom Thurmond, Fielding Wright, and twelve other prominent southerners were appointed members of a "committee on organization" by Governor Laney of Arkansas, the permanent chairman. The Memphis delegates adopted a resolution stating that the objectives that had spawned the States' Rights effort would be pursued "until these objectives have been achieved."[52]

Popular enthusiasm and financial support for the Dixiecrat movement predictably slumped following Truman's victory. A Thurmond elector from Baltimore, Harry F. Klinefelter, proposed a merger of States' Rights Democrats and conservative Republicans to form an "American party." His objective was to get all conservatives into one party and all liberals into another. The present system worked in favor of the liberals, he asserted, because southern conservatives were tied to the Democratic party. Conservatives "should not continue to be separated by the fetish of Party Labels," he insisted. Similar ideas captured the imaginations of other pragmatic Dixiecrats, but most southerners were wedded too devoutly to the Democratic party to make such a scheme possible. On December 31, 1948, the States' Rights Democratic party officially ceased to exist, but in January, 1949, Dixiecrat strategists, meeting in Washington, found sentiment strong to keep the organization functioning. The following month Perez, along with other Dixiecrat chieftains from ten southern states, held a reorganizational meeting in Birmingham, where they made plans to participate in the 1950 congressional elections and in the 1952 presidential election.[53]

On May 10, 1949, the first anniversary of the founding of the Dixiecrat party, organizers from fourteen states returned to the movement's birthplace at Jackson, Mississippi, and created the National States' Rights Committee. It was headed by Ben Laney, with Perez and Wallace M. Wright of Mississippi as vice-chairmen. The delegates framed a constitution providing that an executive committee of two men and two women from each state would be elected annually by the National States' Rights Committee, which was to meet on May 10 of each year. The declaration of principles stated that the committee did not plan to function as a political party; this was probably intended to help secure tax-exempt status. The committee's declared purpose was educational; it would seek to inform the public of the advantages of adopting a states' rights amendment to the Constitution. This amendment would provide that (1) Congress would be forbidden to legislate on such subjects as race relations, labor, and suffrage; (2) nationalization of industry would be prohibited; (3) federal aid to the states would be administered solely by the states; (4) the proceeds from all income, estate, and inheritance taxes would be returned to the states except for funds needed to maintain the armed forces; (5) the national debt would be funded; (6) federal deficit spending would be forbidden; (7) any person violating the amendment would be subject to a maximum penalty of a ten-thousand-dollar fine and ten years in prison.[54]

To help promote its constitutional amendment, the committee opened a national office in Washington to work with senators and congressmen and to keep its newspaper informed of events in the capital. Former Alabama governor Frank Dixon was asked to assume the directorship but declined because of failing health and the pressure of other business. The position was then offered to Perez, who eagerly accepted. Mississippi's Pulitzer Prize-winning journalist, Hodding Carter, asked one Louisiana conservative why the Judge had been selected. The Dixiecrat replied, "I say you've got to fight fire with fire and if you're up against a man who learned what he knows from Pendergast, you can't do better than to get someone who learned from Huey Long." [55]

The Washington office was staffed by two full-time workers and a stenographer. Perez, who served without pay, spent most of his time in Louisiana, directing affairs by correspondence and telephone from his New Orleans law office, although his vital interest in the tidelands issue brought him to Washington occasionally. Much of his energy and that of his small staff was devoted to combating civil rights and antilynching proposals, "world government," the United Nations, disarmament, the genocide convention, high national taxes, federal control of the tidelands, and a strong chief executive in general and President Truman in particular. From the start the Washington bureau was meagerly financed. Though Frank Dixon had insisted that a $125,000 yearly budget would be necessary, under Leander it never exceeded $18,000, of which $10,000 went to pay the salary of the office manager Pope Haley. The Judge purchased the office furniture himself, and before the headquarters finally shut down he had begun to meet monthly deficits out of his own pocket. Several solicitation campaigns were initiated, aimed primarily at industrialists, railroad magnates, and oil companies. The Standard Oil Company of Indiana gave $500, requesting that the contribution be kept secret. Although launched with enthusiasm, the fund-raising drives failed miserably. Justice B. Detwiler, commissioned by Perez to raise funds, complained that there were too many like-minded organizations competing for contributions. [56]

On May 10, 1950, the States' Righters held their second anniversary meeting in Jackson. Georgia sent no representatives, and the other southern states were only nominally represented. In the keynote address, Perez condemned Truman as "the greatest presidential stooge this country has ever seen" and told his fellow Dixiecrats that their slogan should be "fight on through to '52." Despite the

Judge's efforts, both enthusiasm and financial support continued to dwindle. Alabama, Louisiana, Mississippi, and Texas pledged $5,000 each to finance the Washington office for 1950. Mississippi met part of its quota, and Perez personally contributed $5,000 for Louisiana, but Alabama and Texas failed to fulfill even a fraction of their pledges. In August, 1952, the office closed, just about breaking even thanks to a $1,500 personal check from Leander to cover the final month's expenses. The furniture and all of the records were returned to Perez in New Orleans. During its two and a half years of existence, the Washington bureau had made no progress at all in promoting its constitutional amendment, but Pope Haley believed that he and his staff had experienced a little success in preventing some things that they opposed.[57]

As early as January, 1951, Perez made it clear that the Dixiecrats had no intention of running an independent candidate in 1952. He expressed enthusiasm about the possible candidacy of Eisenhower, explaining that the former supreme Allied commander would carry a number of southern states whether he ran as a Republican or a Democrat. Within the Democratic party the white hope of the Dixiecrats was Senator Richard Russell of Georgia, whom they backed for the presidential nomination. Strom Thurmond, utterly unrepentant over his 1948 defection, pointed out that it would be difficult to organize a third-party ticket headed by Russell if he failed to receive the Democratic nomination and accurately predicted that it would be hard to generate opposition to Trumanism if Truman himself were not renominated.[58]

The Judge seemed to sense that the Democrats would nominate an unpalatable candidate. Along with party leaders from five other southern states, he helped plan a postconvention conference to determine whether the national Democratic nominee would be designated as the choice of the state Democratic parties. He also developed a complicated contingency plan to withhold Louisiana's Democratic rooster symbol from the national nominee, possibly intending to try to award the highly valued rooster to General Eisenhower if he were nominated by the Republican party. At a Democratic State Central Committee meeting in October, 1951, Perez proposed that the state's presidential electors be elected by a state-

wide convention rather than appointed by the committee. His grandiose plan called for 428 parish delegates to assemble in the huge
agricultural coliseum at Louisiana State University on June 4, 1952,
to elect the Democratic presidential electors as well as a slate of
delegates for a proposed interstate convention at which the southern states would jointly determine to whom their electors would be
pledged. This imaginative scheme, unlike many of Perez's fanciful
proposals, fell flat. Governor Long, in opposing the measure, complained, "Mr. Perez sometimes puts up things that no one under-
stands but himself." Leander retorted, "It's the same old issue
again—Trumanism and socialism." The central committee, siding
with Long, defeated the plan 52 to 21.[59]

The Judge, however, still possessed enough influence in the committee to merit selection as a delegate to the Democratic National
Convention to be held in Chicago July 21–26. The committee, like
Leander apprehensive of a liberal nominee, instructed its representatives not to feel bound to support the Democratic ticket if the convention selected a candidate or platform opposed to states' rights.[60]

Newly inaugurated Governor Robert Kennon, a resolute conservative and firm ally of Perez, was elected chairman of the delegation, which was riven by several internal feuds. Perez was a bitter
foe of fellow delegate Sam Jones, who was also a personal enemy of
Kennon, although all three held essentially the same views on national issues. The Louisiana delegation anticipated discord at
Chicago; before the convention both Perez and Kennon hinted that
they might support the Republican nominee, Dwight D.
Eisenhower. Kennon, a member of the platform committee, quickly
became angered and alarmed at the planks on civil rights, fair employment practices, filibuster, and tidelands that the committee
prepared. On July 22, the second day of the convention, an obscure
U.S. senator from Michigan, Blair Moody, precipitated an alterca-
tion among the already tense delegates by introducing a loyalty oath
resolution that was easily adopted by a thundering voice vote. The
controversial resolution provided that no delegate would be seated
unless he gave assurances that he would strive to ensure the convention's nominees a place on his state's ballot under the Democratic label. Because he was aware of the pending platform, Gover-

nor Kennon advised the Louisiana delegates not to take the pledge. A caucus of the delegation concurred, citing the resolution of the state central committee that freed its representatives from supporting the national nominees if a platform objectionable to Louisiana's Democratic party were adopted. After receiving a statement from the Louisianians explaining their reasons for resolving to vote against taking the loyalty oath, the credentials committee amended the Moody resolution to provide that the assurances required should not be contrary to state law or to the instructions of the governing body of the state party. The unanimously uncompromising delegation now began to divide. Senator Russell Long voted to take the watered-down pledge, but the majority of the caucus supported Governor Kennon in his stand against accepting the revised oath. The representatives also resolved not to walk out of the convention; if the delegation left, it would be because the national party ejected it. The most adamant opponent of the loyalty pledge was Judge Perez, who boasted, "Personally, I would consider it an honor to be thrown out of this convention."[61]

The credentials committee offered another concession: a "simple statement" of Louisiana's position could replace the objectionable oath. While Governor Kennon was absent the Louisiana group held a floor caucus to consider the latest proposal. With only Perez opposed, they agreed upon a compromise letter in which the Louisianians did not expressly promise to support the national nominee. Kennon, returning just in time to prevent the announcement of Louisiana's acceptance, led the exasperated delegates off the floor to another caucus, where he convinced them not to compromise. It looked as if Perez would receive the honor he sought—being booted out of the convention. As the roll call on presidential nominations began, it appeared that Louisiana, Virginia, and South Carolina would not be permitted to vote. Then Governor John S. Battle of Virginia informed the assembly that state law prohibited the denial of the Democratic designation to Democratic nominees on the Virginia ballot and that his delegation did not intend to contravene the law. It was a slender concession, but a motion followed to accept the admission as satisfactory to the spirit of the loyalty oath. Russell Long then stated that he had no intention of leaving the convention because he personally supported the revised loyalty oath. He was followed by Kennon, who in an impassioned plea declared that the oath was contrary to the instructions of the state central committee. Chairman Sam Rayburn announced that Senator Long could cast all 20 of Louisiana's votes under a rule providing that if part of a state's delegation were absent the remaining members could cast the entire vote. Virginia was seated by a vote of 648 to 512. Battle promptly moved that Louisiana and South Carolina be seated. Spokesmen from the two states assured the convention that under their laws the Democratic nominees would appear under their proper label on the state ballot. Battle's motion was declared adopted by a voice vote. Angry opponents demanded a roll call, but the temporary chairman John W. McCormack decided the issue with a standing vote. In the balloting for presidential nominees, Louisiana gave all 20 of its votes to Richard Russell of Georgia, refusing even to join in making the nomination of Governor Adlai Stevenson of Illinois unanimous as requested by the convention chairman. When the platform had been adopted, Louisiana had been barred from participation, but Governor Kennon addressed a letter to the national chairman stating that, if Louisiana had voted, it would have voted against the platform, which endorsed civil rights legislation, called for large federal expenditures, and failed to mention the tidelands issue.[62] The Judge condemned the economic planks in the platform as just another step toward government take-over of private industry, maintained that the foreign policy statement proposed American financial support for "practically all the world," and insisted that there was "no doubt" that the "Stalinist all races law" was the basis of the party's civil rights plank.[63]

The loyalty oath issue sparked an acrimonious verbal brawl between Leander and Russell Long that erupted on the convention floor and blazed long after the Chicago conclave had ended. In the presence of eight or ten Louisiana delegates, Long accused Perez of plotting to deny the rooster emblem to the Democratic nominee as he had done four years earlier. Harking back to the 1948 election in which he had received the Judge's support in his initial race for the Senate, Long raged, "Yes, it's true that he gave me stolen votes in that election and kept President Truman's name from going under the symbol on the ballot." Ironically, the man Perez had allegedly cheated in order to help Long was Robert Kennon, now governor and Leander's firm ally against Senator Long. The enraged senator continued, "I don't believe that I needed stolen votes in the first election because I would have beaten Kennon anyway. I will never again approve of anything like rigged ballots and stolen votes." The Judge himself was not present during Long's tirade, but his older son, Leander Perez, Jr., who was at the convention as an alternate, violently objected to this denunciation of his father. When the elder Perez was informed of Senator Long's charge, he promptly denied it, terming it "the result of too much liquor."[64]

Afterwards, realizing that if votes had been stolen it reflected on him as well as on Perez, Russell Long told reporters that he had no firsthand knowledge of any irregularities. He said he would be happy to appear before a federal grand jury that was investigating alleged vote fraud in Plaquemines Parish in the 1950 congressional elections, but added, "I know practically nothing about Plaquemines except how election returns come in and the parish's political reputation. Anything I could say would be about 100 per cent hearsay." He continued, "If it is a crime to even have been the beneficiary of his [Perez's] support, then of course I am guilty. I do not propose to be a second offender."[65]

The feud continued to simmer. In a radio address Senator Long defended his refusal to walk out of the Democratic convention on the grounds that he had helped to secure the nomination of Senator John Sparkman of Alabama as Stevenson's running mate and to make the platform more moderate. Perez, retorting that the platform could hardly be more damnable, quoted a North Carolina senator who had witnessed Long's action at the convention as saying, "'And to think I put that little punk on my committee.'"[66]

Between the conclusion of the Democratic National Convention and the convocation of the Democratic State Central Committee to certify Democratic candidates, a wide range of potential actions by the committee was rumored: (1) endorsement of Stevenson and the Democratic platform; (2) endorsement of Stevenson but repudiation of the platform; (3) certification of Stevenson with no mention of the platform; (4) nomination of a slate of unpledged electors; and (5) a

declaration of support for Eisenhower. The state, the national nominees, and the news media awaited some tactical surprise by Perez.
When the committee convened on August 20, its first action was
to adopt a resolution condemning portions of the Democratic platform and praising Louisiana's delegation for its adamant stand
at the national convention. Next, it was moved that Stevenson and
Sparkman appear on the Louisiana ballot under the Democratic
column headed by the rooster. The motion was amended to specify
that this was not to be construed as an endorsement of the Democratic ticket. The Perez faction quickly offered a substitute resolution providing that state and national Democratic nominees appear
under separate columns on the Louisiana ballot, the national candidates under the donkey and the designation National Democrat and
the state nominees under the rooster and the heading Democrat.
Leander argued strenuously for the substitute resolution, but it was
tabled by a vote of fifty-eight to thirty-two. The committee then
adopted by a seventy-seven to nine vote (Perez in the minority)
the original resolution placing all Democratic nominees under the
rooster. Two of the Democratic electors then resigned, announcing
their intention to vote for Eisenhower; two more resigned within a
week.[67]

After failing to cripple the Stevenson-Sparkman ticket by denying
it the rooster, Perez became an enthusiastic supporter of Republican
presidential nominee Dwight D. Eisenhower. He was heartened by
Ike's commitment to state control of offshore oil resources; Stevenson had stated that he supported Truman's veto of bills that would
have vested control of the tidelands in the states. The Judge, accusing Democratic vice-presidential nominee Sparkman of being "a
Fair Dealer first and a Southerner and an American second," described the Democratic platform as a "Russian-style platform advocating government by treaty—a Communist system of government."[68] He accepted appointment as Democratic head of the
Eisenhower campaign organization in Plaquemines and St. Bernard
and played a prominent role in a bipartisan statewide organization
known as Americans for Eisenhower. John Minor Wisdom, a leading
Republican who later became a federal judge, headed the overall
Eisenhower campaign in Louisiana, which concentrated on the

state's most populous parishes. Many influential Democrats endorsed Eisenhower, including Governor Kennon, former governor Sam Jones, and C. C. ("Taddy") Aycock, speaker of the Louisiana House of Representatives and later lieutenant governor. An imaginative Democratic supporter of Eisenhower coined the slogan "J'aime Ike," and more than twenty thousand such buttons were distributed in French-speaking south Louisiana. Senators Long and Ellender and former governor Earl Long stuck with the Democratic nominee, and New Orleans Mayor deLesseps Morrison voted for Stevenson but did not campaign. The poorly financed Democrats endeavored to avoid the issue of Trumanism and stressed the "new conservative" look of Stevenson and the presence of Sparkman on the ticket.[69]

The Democratic ticket carried every state in the Deep South, but Eisenhower succeeded in driving a wedge into the traditionally solid South. The largest GOP vote in Louisiana in the previous twenty years had been 19.4 percent; Eisenhower increased this to 47.1 percent, scoring heavily in the parishes that had been Dixiecrat strongholds four years earlier. He polled 93 percent of the vote in Plaquemines, his highest percentage in any county in the nation. In neighboring St. Bernard it was much closer but Ike won by 150 votes—the first time St. Bernard had gone Republican since Reconstruction. Leander was pleased with the results in Plaquemines, but he was comforted even more by Eisenhower's nationwide victory. "Oh my God," he exclaimed, "anybody who heard Adlai Stevenson make that speech in the Mormon Tabernacle, great scott alive. I went all out against him, of course, and all of our people went along with us." He explained his strategy: "We just tell our voters, wherever you see Dave Dubinsky and his liberal party go, wherever you see Walter Reuther go, go on the other side and you are safe."[70]

The Democratic organization and tradition, the backing of the Long faction, and the strong support among black voters accounted for Stevenson's narrow victory in Louisiana. But the custom of automatically supporting the Democratic nominee was weakening; the national party could no longer take Louisiana for granted.[71]

Leander quickly became disillusioned with Eisenhower, believing that every president since Herbert Hoover (whom he had opposed) had pushed America toward socialism and moral decay. But what most upset him about the administration was the president's stand on the tidelands issue. With Eisenhower's blessing Congress passed the Submerged Lands Act of 1953 quitclaiming undersea land within three miles of the shore to the states. Although the president felt that he had fulfilled his obligation to the coastal states, the Judge demanded state jurisdiction up to ten and a half miles seaward, extending from a base line drawn to include Louisiana's many coastal indentations. In addition, Leander bitterly resented the president's refusal to publicly condemn the Supreme Court's 1954 school desegregation decision. In fact, Perez went so far as to announce the resuscitation of the Dixiecrat party in order "to preserve the vestiges of our inherent freedom." But not enough enthusiasm and financing could be mustered in other states, since any third-party crusade needed the stimulus of a controversial president on which to focus its attack. The renomination of Adlai Stevenson by the Democrats convinced Perez that the only feasible alternative was to support Eisenhower again in 1956. He explained, "We were quite disappointed in him, but there was no choice."[72]

The loyalist Democrats appeared more solidly united behind Stevenson in 1956 than in 1952 despite the disadvantage of facing an incumbent president. Most of the major Democratic factions in the state endorsed Stevenson, including Earl and Russell Long, Mayor Morrison, and Senator Ellender, although Governor Long expediently remained silent during the campaign. But by this time the luster of the Democratic label had dimmed in the eyes of the voters and Republicans had ceased to be regarded as curiosities. Whites no longer viewed the GOP as a Negro party, and black leaders predicted that 30 percent of the state's more than 160,000 Negro voters would support Eisenhower. Most Louisiana voters felt much like Perez about the two candidates: Eisenhower was a safe moderate, and Stevenson was a dangerous liberal. The president won an 85,000-vote plurality, the first Republican victory in Louisiana since 1876. Plaquemines, where Eisenhower polled 81.2 percent of the votes, once again led the state, but the percentage was somewhat down from 1952, reflecting the Judge's diminished ardor. The president polled 50.5 percent of the votes in more populous but less regimented St. Bernard.[73]

In two of his first three serious efforts at presidential campaigning, Leander had been instrumental in carrying Louisiana for a conservative candidate opposed to the nominee of the national Democratic party. Although a lifelong Democrat, he, more than any other state leader, had been responsible for ending that party's monopoly in the Pelican State. In the future no party or candidate could automatically count on the state's electoral votes, and Perez and his right-wing allies would often wield the balance of power. The Judge had established himself as a potent force in national politics whose influence could not be ignored by any presidential aspirant who hoped to win Louisiana.

ELEVEN

Earl Long and the Third Party

In 1956 Perez unhappily found himself with a contentious sheriff in St. Bernard and a bellicose governor in Baton Rouge. The governor was Earl Long, who had been elected in a sweeping first primary victory—the first in Louisiana since 1936. He and Perez had been at odds since about 1950, when Leander had sabotaged Earl's plans for a constitutional convention. The Judge, who had broken with Long over state patronage, insisted that the break stemmed from Earl's refusal to submit his proposed new charter to a statewide referendum. Long claimed that he feared a "Plaquemines count." Judge Perez retorted, "Don't worry about Plaquemines. We have the purest in the state. We match the mountain lily."[1]

Earl Long was a formidable opponent, described by veteran politician A. S. Cain as "the greatest conniver we ever had in public office." Earl was a poor scholar who hated to study, but he knew human nature and mastered the needs and weaknesses of both his allies and opponents. According to Cain, before every session of the legislature he toured the state, "renting" legislators for the coming session. By the time the legislature convened, Long's pet measures were assured of passage. Leander had once been a wholehearted Longite, but that, said Earl, was before he had become "richer than rich."[2] According to Long, Perez had tried to jump back on the bandwagon before the 1956 primary: "Mr. Perez came to me in the last gubernatorial campaign and I told him I didn't want his support. I said it would do me more harm than good. He's never been told that before." Leander, for his part, called Earl a "heartless maniac."[3] One of Perez's close friends claims that, after his break with

197

Long, the Judge rushed over to the Governor's Mansion, shook his finger at Earl, and sputtered, "I'll break you."[4]

The New Orleans *Times-Picayune,* which had been against both Perez and Long, now sided with Perez. Earl sneered, "They (the *Picayune*) don't think any more of Perez than you or I do, but sometimes they think they can use Perez in their main objective that every Long in the state ought to be hung by his toes."[5]

Both Earl and Leander, in their younger days, had frequently engaged political opponents in fistfights. Earl was famed for biting; Perez, for blackening eyes. During an acrimonious dispute, the two once became so vehement that, in addition to the usual shouts and shoves, they almost came to blows in the legislative chambers.[6]

The contentious sheriff was Dr. Nicholas P. Trist of St. Bernard. Since his climb to power in the early 1920s, he had been both a natural foe and an ultimate ally of the energetic district attorney. Perez's amibitions spilled over into St. Bernard; he wanted to dominate both his own parish and its swampy neighbor. Naturally, each sheriff of St. Bernard aspired to be the unquestioned boss of his own bailiwick. But, just as inevitably as Perez fell out with a St. Bernard sheriff, the two would eventually make peace. It had happened with Dr. L. A. Meraux and Dutch Rowley, and now it happened with Dr. Trist. The interests of the two parishes were intertwined; the judicial district, congressional district, and several levee districts overlapped parish lines. Trist, a country doctor in the tradition of Meraux, had become acting sheriff upon the death of Rowley and had subsequently been elected to the post with Perez's blessing. Then, the inevitable break had occurred, and Perez had fought Trist tooth and nail.

The occasion for the reconciliation was Perez's need for an ally to fight Governor Earl Long, who had been appointing Trist partisans to all St. Bernard posts. Leander hoped to keep the truce secret; that way he and Trist could work together without the sheriff losing state patronage. The arrangement was certainly advantageous for Trist; he would gain a potent new ally without losing his old one. But word of Leander's duplicity leaked out, and his supporters on the police jury, led by thirty-year incumbent Celestine Melerine and his friend James Licciardi, erupted with righteous indignation and resolved to fight both Trist and Perez. Melerine thundered, "We had no idea what was going on. Perez should not of acted that way. He kept us in the dark and didn't say a word about the meeting with Trist. We don't like it that way since we went all out against Trist for Perez."[7] He added, "The people of St. Bernard are tired of Perez's dictatorship and have thrown their yoke."[8]

The New Orleans *States* described the confrontation as a "bare-knuckled, knockdown, drag-out political fight" to destroy Perez's power in St. Bernard.[9] The rebellious jurors styled themselves the Third party, although they actually composed a Democratic faction independent of both Perez and Trist. The sheriff himself refused to admit publicly that he had made peace with Perez, but a Third party leader labeled Trist "nothing more than a front man for District Attorney L. H. Perez."[10] The incensed jurors gained a four-to-three majority on the St. Bernard police jury and, at a turbulent meeting that produced two conflicting sets of minutes, voted out Perez's still-loyal henchmen and elected Melerine president and Licciardi vice-president. Ousted police jury president Henry Schindler, taking a page from Henry Clay, solemnly declared, "I would rather be right than be president."[11] The jurors also discharged Perez as legal adviser on the grounds that he had advised the jury against the best interests of the parish.[12]

Outside the police jury, the Third party was led by trapper, merchant, and oil mogul Manuel Molero, who had fought Perez in the trappers' war of 1925 but had later reconciled and run for St. Bernard sheriff on the Perez ticket. Now Molero decided to run for sheriff under the auspices of the Third party. Bankrolling the anti-Perez insurgents, he was able to match the Judge almost dollar for dollar.[13]

Opportunistically, the governor leaped into the fray. Long sustained the rebellious faction with control of the parish registrar of voters, board of election supervisors, and levee districts while rushing through the legislature a series of special measures designed to deprive Perez of his local power. The State Board of Registration, comprised of the governor, lieutenant governor, and speaker of the House, fired the St. Bernard registrar Carmella LeClerc because, according to Long, she was "putting on a one-man Perez show."[14] Before the rift had occurred between Perez and the St. Bernard police jurors, Long had rejected the appointment by the police jury of Adam Melerine, brother of Perez stalwart Celestine Melerine, to replace Mrs. LeClerc.[15] However, once Celestine Melerine had become leader of the anti-Perez faction, Governor Long saw Adam Melerine in a different light and confirmed his appointment as registrar of voters. Adam Melerine had little to recommend him for a public office other than his opposition to Perez and the recommendation of his employer Manual Molero, president of the Delacroix Corporation.[16] Melerine, a tough, hard-drinking former deputy sheriff, had been indicted for murder in 1923 and for manslaughter in 1933, but had been acquitted on both counts.[17]

Perez and Long met head on in a bitterly fought power struggle for control of the Plaquemines–St. Bernard levee boards. When Trist and Perez were political enemies, Long had appointed Trist supporters to the two St. Bernard levee boards. Leander had contested the appointments in court, but the governor had prevailed and the Trist men were seated. After Perez and the sheriff sealed their truce, the Trist men became Perez men. Governor Long then fired his own appointees, replacing them with Third party adherents. Reversing field, Judge Perez went to court a second time to keep in office the men he had previously challenged. The ensuing confusion brought the work of the levee boards to a halt. Levees deteriorated, and employees went unpaid. Perez announced that the parish was threatened with inundation by the swirling brown waters of the Mississippi. Actually there was little danger because the U.S. Corps of Engineers then as now handled major levee repairs along the Mississippi; the levee boards have been reduced to superfluous political plums.[18]

The old members barred the new ones from the board offices and locked away the board records in office vaults, whereupon the new members called in locksmiths. The safes were opened, but the current records remained missing. Parish employees busied themselves painting over the name of the old president with that of the new on the office door; backers of the old board sneaked back in and scraped off the lettering. Perez partisans began removing furniture and fixtures from the first floor office to a less convenient office on the third floor, aided by an order from District Judge Bruce Nunez prohibiting the new board from interfering with the moving of fixtures. Perez stalwarts claimed that the board office was being removed to a larger office on the third floor to make room for the registrar of voters, but the president of the new board complained that the third floor office was the worst place in the entire building.[19]

While the furniture movers worked, Perez's cooperative judge, Bruce Nunez, froze all funds and enjoined Long's new board from interfering with the operation of the old. A compromise was finally reached in theory but collapsed beneath a torrent of charges and countercharges. The state auditor and treasurer agreed to provide emergency funds on warrants signed by both the old and new boards, but the two sets of officials could never agree. Board employees were finally paid with money collected by the Trist political organization.[20]

In Plaquemines, Perez held an iron grip upon the Buras and Grand Prairie levee districts because the police jury had obtained the right to make levee board appointments independently of the governor in 1948, during the friendly administration of Jimmie Davis. The police jury's appointive power, however, was contingent upon the two levee boards remaining in debt. When the debt got down to $82,000, the local governing authority floated a $2,000,000 bond issue, even though the levee boards had on hand a treasury surplus of nearly $4,000,000.[21] Perez purposely perpetuated the indebtedness in order to use the levee board income for parish improvements that had nothing to do with flood control.

Earl Long, determined to end Judge Perez's stranglehold on the levee boards and thus destroy the financial base of his political power, introduced an eleven-bill package empowering the governor to appoint the Plaquemines boards, redraw the levee districts, and change the authority of the levee boards. The vanguard of Long's arsenal was an amended version of a bill introduced by Plaquemines representative E. W. Gravolet, Jr., on behalf of Perez. Put into the hopper as pro-Perez legislation, Gravolet's bill emerged as a patently anti-Perez measure. The original one-page bill gave the Plaquemines levee districts authority over submerged lands in the Gulf of Mexico. After Long's floor leaders had finished amending the measure, it was eleven and a half pages long and entirely different in intent; the expanded bill authorized the governor to appoint twelve additional members to the Plaquemines police jury who would sit with the jury whenever it considered levee board affairs. The consent of seven of these "piggyback" jurors would be necessary for approval of any matter concerning the local levee boards. Gravolet now became the bill's most vociferous opponent. He complained that almost every matter brought up in the watery little parish concerned the levee boards in some way. Representative Sam Cashio, Long's floor leader, chortled, "This bill places Plaquemines Parish back in the Union, back in the state of Louisiana."[22] The Judge turned purple with rage, vowing that he would fight "to hell and back" to prevent Governor Long from gaining control of the Plaquemines police jury. He defiantly warned that "neither Earl Long.nor all of his bodyguards will seat twelve of his appointed thugs to take over our police jury." Perez pledged that he would take the issue to the U.S. Supreme Court, a forum at which he had not enjoyed conspicuous success,[23] and claimed that Earl would have a difficult time finding twelve supporters to appoint in Plaquemines. "There are very few double-crossers in Plaquemines Parish of the stripe who would follow Earl Long against the parish," he bragged.[24]

One of Earl's twelve appointees was Salvador Chiapetta, the man Perez had prevented from voting for so long. Another appointee, Ernest Hingle, voiced the opinion that Leander opposed the governor's interference in levee board matters because of his personal interest in mineral leases. Another of the newly appointed piggyback jurors, sixty-four-year-old barroom owner Gus Fitzgerald of Venice, said, "Ninety per cent of the people in Plaquemines would be against Perez if they weren't afraid. My time is short and I ain't afraid to fight him."[25]

Despite the vehement opposition of Perez's friends, Governor Long rammed all eleven bills through the legislature and signed them into law. Leander was particularly angry at the support the piggyback juror bill received from the New Orleans Old Regulars, headed by James E. Comiskey, an Orleans Parish assessor and whiskey wholesaler. To drive home his chagrin, the Judge announced that Plaquemines barkeepers would henceforth refuse to sell Old Comiskey whiskey in the parish.[26]

Leander, dipping once more into his legal bag of tricks, tied up the piggyback juror law in court by challenging its constitutionality. By the time the Louisiana Supreme Court had finally ruled in favor of the governor's appointees and they were able to take their seats, Long's term was nearly over and he had suffered a nervous breakdown.[27]

During the previous twenty years Perez had written into the state constitution a bevy of special privileges for Plaquemines Parish. Earl now set a state lawyer to work researching these advantages, had the Judge superseded as legal adviser for the Plaquemines boards, and filed suits aimed at transferring to the state the funds that had been diverted to Leander's marshy fiefdom. The legislature created an investigative committee reminiscent of Sam Jones's Crime Commission and appropriated $100,000 for its operation. Governor Long set aside $10,000 for use in his suits against the Plaquemines police jury and hired Richard Dowling, a New Orleans attorney and long-standing enemy of Perez, to represent the levee boards. Dowling was to receive 10 percent of any amount he recovered from the police jury for the levee boards. To remove the litigation from the jurisdiction of Perez's crony, District Judge Bruce Nunez, Earl had his attorney general include the companies paying royalties to the Plaquemines police jury as defendants. Since these companies were domiciled in New Orleans, he hoped that the suits would be tried in Orleans Parish. However, Judge René Viosca in Orleans Parish ruled that the principal dispute was in Plaquemines Parish and should be tried there. The state supreme court sustained his decision.[28]

Meanwhile, Earl tried to increase taxes on gas, timber, and sulphur in order to raise teachers' salaries, redeeming his campaign promises and once again implementing the classic Long program of tax and spend. As a supporter of Huey and Earl, Leander had never before objected to such pork barrel legislation. But this time, as Earl's most adamant opponent, he battled the governor to a virtual standstill in the legislature. The Judge, as the protector of Freeport Sulphur, most vociferously opposed a bill to triple the sulphur tax. Earl claimed that Plaquemines was receiving an override of $100,000 on the sulphur severance tax, which would be ended if the administration proposal were adopted. He singled out Perez as the chief opponent of his tax program, charging that the Plaquemines leader put the welfare of his parish above that of the state. Perez was no less acrimonious; at a House committee hearing he elbowed his way to Earl and denounced the governor as a "damned liar" to his face. Because the Louisiana constitution requires approval of two-thirds of the legislature to levy tax increases, Perez was able to muster enough support to block Long's entire program. Long charged that Perez had stymied his tax package by bribing legislators and exerting pressure on them.[29]

The governor fought back by supporting Perez's Third party adversaries in St. Bernard and Plaquemines. After the Melerine-Licciardi faction gained a one-vote majority on the St. Bernard police jury, it began to purge the Perez partisans from the payroll, cutting off the salaries of Leander's assistant district attorney and investigator for St. Bernard, his secretary, and Bruce Nunez, Jr., the son of District Judge Bruce Nunez, who had been working as an inspector for the parish board of health. The faction also sliced the salary of Perez's elder son, who was second assistant district attorney, from $200 to $62.50 per month. "We got to cut Judge Perez's wings somewhere, you know," the police jury president Celestine Melerine declared. He estimated that the dismissals and salary cuts would save the parish between $15,000 and $18,000 annually.[30]

The opening skirmish in a spectacular court battle between Perez and the Third party–Long forces occurred as the result of an audit of the St. Bernard police jury by the state supervisor of public funds. Perez charged that Governor Long had sent the officer to his parish with instructions to find something amiss. Whether part of a conspiracy or not, the examination of parish accounts did raise some intriguing questions. The supervisor noted that the police jury had been billed for thirty-three cotton mattresses, only thirty of which had been delivered. The other three, he learned, had gone to juror Henry Schindler, the deposed police jury president and a Perez partisan. The audit also uncovered irregularities in deliveries of oyster shells used to suface parish roads. The supervisor claimed to be unable to find the offices of the Lower Coast Construction Company, which had secured a large contract to supply the parish with shells, nor could he learn the source from which the mysterious company had procured the shells allegedly sold to the parish. The identity of the company's officers was secret. Still more interesting, the audit reported that the parish was Lower Coast's only customer.[31]

The Chalmette Civic Improvement Association and the Metropolitan Crime Commission of New Orleans demanded an open hearing into the police jury finances, but District Attorney Perez refused, explaining that an open hearing might expose innocent persons to unfavorable publicity and ridicule. Besides, he said, he didn't think that there was much to the Lower Coast matter but had a much more important investigation pending. When Don Thompson, the president of the Chalmette group, continued to press for an open hearing, Perez angrily warned, "You address me with respect or I'll slap your damn face." He also threatened Thompson with prosecution under the Hatch Act, which prohibits federal civil servants from engaging in political activity. Instead of backing down, Thompson and three other St. Bernard residents filed suit demanding access to the financial records of the St. Bernard police jury and levee boards, but the suit was dismissed by Judge Bruce Nunez.[32]

After rejecting the call for an open hearing, Perez summoned the St. Bernard grand jury into secret session. He quickly disposed of the mattress mystery. According to the Judge's version, Schindler had ordered thirty mattresses for the parish jail from a local dealer. Surprised at the very reasonable price the dealer offered, Schindler instructed the police jury secretary to order three more for his personal account. By the time the delivery had been made, both Schindler and the secretary had been deposed and replaced by Third party partisans. The clerk who had filled the original order had left on vacation, and his replacement had billed all thirty-three mattresses to the parish. Schindler had tried to pay for his three, but the dealer had not yet cashed his check. When the clerk who had filled the original order returned, he informed the new police jury secretary that the jury should have been billed for only thirty mattresses. The treasurer, refusing to change the bill, paid for all thirty-three. It was, Leander implied, a deliberate frame by the Long faction to discredit Schindler, and he insisted that "any fault for overpayment lies with the parish treasurer," who was Philip Rowley, a political opponent of Judge Perez.[33]

The shell deal with the Lower Coast Construction Company was explained with equal ease. Dan Sentilles, a Perez partisan who identified himself as the president of the company, testified that his offices were easy to find. The trouble was, he said, that the state auditor had not come to him for the facts and he himself had not been eager to volunteer information that might involve him in a political squabble. Sentilles expressed surprise at the police jury claim that it had lost the records of the transactions with his firm after the state audit had been made. He did not deny that the parish was the only customer of Lower Coast, which was a new corporation, and explained that his main work was the steamship business, which was handled by another company. When he had decided to sell shells as a sideline, he had incorporated Lower Coast to protect himself from liability. The shells were procured through his steamship company. Sentilles, though declaring that the whole investigation smelled of political persecution, took advantage of the opportunity to complain that the parish still owed him money for some repairs he had made earlier on a police jury drinking fountain. Nothing more was said about the almost five thousand dollars in bills that the state auditor's office recommended not be paid because of the ephemeral nature of Lower Coast's officials and records, and no one seemed to reflect on the incongruity of a steamship corporation president hauling shells and repairing drinking fountains.[34]

The grand jury returned no indictments on the irregularities cited in the state audit. Having turned back the assault against his friends, Perez now took the initiative by convening an open hearing before a St. Bernard justice of the peace to investigate the activities of two leaders of the Third party, newly elected police jury president Celestine Melerine and vice-president James Licciardi. Perez apparently no longer feared that an open hearing might expose innocent men to ridicule.[35]

By the end of Perez's offensive, the report of the state supervisor of public funds had been pushed into the background and Melerine and Licciardi were completely occupied in defending themselves. The two Third party stalwarts, eventually convicted on several counts of malfeasance in office, were sentenced to pay a $1,500 fine each and serve six months each in the parish jail. Although the sentences were confirmed by the Louisiana Supreme Court, Licciardi protested that he had been framed by two witnesses, one of whom was a crook and the other a "booze hound."[36]

Although some of Perez's accusations have all the trappings of a frame-up, there is little doubt that Melerine and Licciardi were guilty of at least a few of the charges against them. However, it is difficult to believe that Melerine, who had been a Perez follower and officeholder for thirty years, and Licciardi, also a veteran Perez politico, had decided to recklessly violate the law only after breaking with Leander. It appears that practically every officeholder in the venal lower delta was guilty of a criminal offense at some time or other, of which Perez was well informed. In fact, he probably encouraged a certain amount of graft among his subordinates; this provided him with ready-made charges to prosecute if they ever deserted his faction.

Governor Long kept the two Third party leaders out of jail by issuing a series of reprieves, commenting that Leander had considered Melerine and Licciardi honest men while they were his political allies but had decided that they were crooks after they had abandoned his faction. He also charged that Perez completely dominated District Judge Bruce Nunez, asserting, "If he (Nunez), ever tried a case down there averse to what Perez wanted, nobody knows about it."[37]

Perez had also filed civil proceedings to remove Melerine and Licciardi from office while the numerous indictments were being tried. The suits were stayed pending the outcome of the criminal charges, but once the two were convicted the cases were resumed and the two officials were removed from office. Governor Long appointed a pair of political novices to replace the Third party leaders, and the newly constituted police jury voted unanimously to also remove the convicted men as members of Sewerage Board No. 2. The new jury furthermore restored some of the salary reductions that had been made against Perez supporters in the parish employ.[38]

Just as things seemed under control in St. Bernard, trouble erupted in Plaquemines. Sixty-three-year-old Emile Martin, Jr., the president of the police jury and a longtime Perez ally, suddenly resigned, announcing that he was joining a new anti-Perez faction led by his son. His term had more than a year to run, but Governor Long hoped to wait until less than a year remained so that he could legally appoint a successor as Eighth Ward police juror. He never got the chance. Leander, secretly summoning the police jury into a special night session, had it unanimously vote to abolish the Eighth Ward, which became Precinct 3 of Ward 7. The anti-Perez faction fought the abolition of the ward all the way to the state supreme court, but the court dismissed the suit. Plaquemines remained without an Eighth Ward until 1961, shortly before the police jury was replaced by a commission form of government.[39] Soon after Martin broke with Perez, one of his sons, Bernard ("Frog") Martin, was fired from his job as operator of a parish pumping station. The elder Martin then severed his last tie with the parish government by resigning as a board member of the City Price Drainage District.[40]

In the broiling delta summer of 1959, the opposing Plaquemines factions squared off to face each other in the local elections to be held the following winter. The anti-Perez faction was counting on the help of Governor Long, who at this time was busy with plans for the gubernatorial election, which would be held simultaneously. Long planned to evade the state law prohibiting a governor from succeeding himself by resigning just before the Democratic primary, a scheme that provoked a torrent of protest. The white-haired, sixty-three-year-old governor was already under a severe physical strain. His voice hoarse and skin pallid, he suffered from a weak heart, hardening of the arteries, cerebral complications, and difficulty in clearing his throat. At his doctor's request he had trimmed from 203 to 179 pounds in a few months, which made his clothes baggy and his jowls sag.[41]

After Long decided to run, he resolved to push through the legislature bills making it easier for his staunchest supporters, uneducated blacks and whites, to vote. His proposals elicited a furious confrontation with Louisiana's most militant segregationist, state senator Willie Rainach of Claiborne Parish. Up to now, Earl had passively cooperated with the segregationists out of political expediency, signing into law the numerous segregation bills voted by the legislature and rationalizing his collusion by explaining that the bills he was signing were useless because they would be nullified by the federal courts. Rainach, however, conceived a plan that forced the governor's hand on the broader question of Negro civil rights. Under

Louisiana law, any two voters could challenge another's registration and have him removed from the rolls for inaccuracies on his registration forms. Voters could be scratched for such minor errors as failing to dot an *i* or cross a *t*. In order to remain on the rolls, challenged voters were required to appear before the registrar in person to correct the inaccuracies or provide affidavits from three registered voters indicating that they were properly registered. Rainach began a systematic, parish by parish purge to remove blacks. In Washington Parish, near the Mississippi line, the segregationists scratched the names of 1,377 black voters out of a total of 1,510. There was, of course, no need for a purge in Plaquemines Parish because few blacks were registered there.[42]

The segregation and voting issues trapped the governor, who was not ideologically racist but was politically ambitious for another term. If he refused to support the segregationists, he would lose much of his following among poor whites and race-minded legislators; if he sided with the segregationists, he would alienate his Negro and liberal supporters. Long's plan to liberalize the state voting laws directly challenged Rainach's voter purge. One of the bills would have prevented challenges of voters who had been registered for more than twelve months, and another was devised to stop the challenging of voters who had made only minor errors on their applications.[43]

The legislature uncharacteristically balked at Long's leadership; both bills were defeated nineteen to thirteen by the Senate. The governor then attempted to sneak the bills through by tacking them onto a House bill authorizing employment of assistant registrars of voters. On May 27, the House Judiciary B Committee, packed with proadministration representatives, met to consider the amendments. The hearing was held in the large House chamber, and Governor Long was present to participate in the debate. Television cameras were pointed at the microphone around which the debate raged; every available seat in the House was occupied, and many persons were standing behind the rails. Rainach, sporting a necktie emblazoned with a Confederate flag, argued that the state's registration laws were based on intelligence, which automatically disqualified most blacks. The governor admonished the senator, "You got to recognize that niggers is human beings,"[44] and insisted that blacks be treated decently, adding, "That goes for the people that sleep with them at night and kick them in the street in the daytime."[45] As the debate wore on, Long strode around drinking grape juice spiked with whiskey, disguised in a Coke bottle, and once interrupted with a profane outburst. The governor's fight was unavailing; the committee rejected his amendments. The following day, Long summoned the legislature into joint session, ostensibly to apologize for his profanity. Instead, he burst into a ninety-five-minute profane discourse before he was finally stopped by the sergeant-at-arms.[46]

Earl began to show signs of strain from his struggle with the legislature. He found himself unable to sleep, began to drink heavily, and take pep pills, and resumed smoking. The governor's wife Blanche became convinced that he could not survive the strenuous statewide speaking tour he was planning. Along with a group of relatives, including Senator Russell Long, she secretly had Earl forcibly committed to a Galveston hospital for psychiatric treatment and rest. On June 17, acceding to her husband's repeated pleading, she allowed him to return to Louisiana on the condition that he would enter the Ochsner Foundation Hospital in New Orleans for a prolonged rest. A rebellious Long flew into New Orleans, signed in at Ochsner, then headed for Baton Rouge to claim the governor's seat. As he raced toward the capital, Mrs. Long had papers drawn up to commit him to a state mental hospital. When he arrived in Baton Rouge, he was met by deputies, who dragged the screaming, cursing governor from his car and drove him to Southeast Louisiana Hospital at Mandeville. Earl ingeniously engineered his own release. First, he filed a suit of separation against his wife, which deprived her of the power to recommit him. Then, he arranged for the firing of the acting superintendent of the hospital and his replacement by a seventy-four-year-old general practitioner and close friend, who declared the governor sane and released him.[47]

Long's breakdown came at the worst possible time for his supporters in Plaquemines, but even had the governor been healthy, his backers would have stood very little chance of upsetting Perez on his home grounds. The opposition, which organized the Plaquemines

Parish Independent Democratic Organization, filed a full slate of candidates. As usual, some of them had trouble qualifying. Walter Blaize, the man Sam Jones had appointed sheriff of Plaquemines in 1943, attempted to run for the Louisiana House of Representatives against a Perez candidate. Blaize and two other opposition candidates found they could not find Leander, who was chairman of the parish Democratic executive committee, to file their applications. Finally they mailed in their forms, but the letters were returned marked "not accepted." [48]

The opposition continued to fight. Emile Martin III filed an affidavit with the parish registrar challenging the registrations of 278 Perez stalwarts on the grounds that they did not reside in the parish. Many of them, 6 of whom were relatives of the Judge, had applied for homestead exemptions in other parishes. Perez correctly pointed out that state law allowed a person to have more than one residence and to choose to register to vote in any parish where he maintained a home. The anti-Perez faction also charged that the Judge had deliberately kept industry out of the parish, which deprived local people of jobs. [49]

The Plaquemines opposition failed to derail Perez's machine, and its slate was swamped at the polls in the Democratic primary election of December 5, 1959. Perez candidates swept every parish and district position except for two offices in Ward 5: police juror and parish democratic committeeman. But this marked the first time in twenty-four years that the Perez administration had failed to elect every Plaquemines police juror. In its account of the inauguration of parish officials, the *Plaquemines Gazette* omitted any mention of the anti-Perez juror. Perez himself was reelected without opposition for another term as district attorney. [50]

The challenge in St. Bernard was more serious; the election was one of the most hotly contested in the history of the parish. With 139 candidates qualifying, not a single parish official was unopposed. Dutch Rowley's son John F. Rowley made a determined effort to unseat Perez's sheriff, Dr. Nicholas P. Trist, and organized a complete ticket to run against the Perez-Trist slate. A third, independent, group also fielded a ticket. The Rowley ticket enjoyed strong labor backing. Victor Bussie, the state AFL-CIO president, speaking in behalf of Rowley, called Leander "the worst enemy labor has in Louisiana."[51]

The Trist-Perez ticket attempted to link Rowley with local gamblers, but Rowley claimed that Trist and Perez only enforced the laws against gambling when it suited their political purposes. Rowley reprinted and distributed New Orleans newspaper articles stating that professional gamblers were immune from prosecution in St. Bernard. One *States-Item* editorial told of professional hoodlums demolishing a jukebox, cigarette machine, and fixtures with gunfire and a blackjack because the proprietor of a St. Bernard restaurant had installed a jukebox belonging to a rival organization. They had not been arrested although five deputies had entered the restaurant while the destruction was underway.[52]

Meanwhile, Perez devised a cunning strategy for recapturing control of the St. Bernard police jury from the Third party. He arranged to have a census taken in Wards 2 and 3, where he was strongest. Acting on the basis of this count, the state attorney general declared that, because of population growth, each of these wards was entitled to two additional jurors. This opinion was implemented by the parish Democratic executive committee, headed by Dr. Nicholas P. Trist. This meant that the two Perez wards would have six of the thirteen seats on the police jury. A census was also taken in the other wards, but conveniently the results were not available until after the election.[53]

Rowley led Trist in the Democratic first primary but lost in a runoff. The Perez-Trist faction also won eleven of the thirteen police jury seats, beating Third party stalwart Charles Leon, who had succeeded Celestine Melerine as president, by one vote in the Sixth Ward. Although Leon led the regular voting, his opponent garnered twenty of twenty-four absentee ballots. He claimed that the absentee ballots should be disallowed because the voting had not been secret, the state had not furnished ballot boxes or commissioners to supervise voting, and the absentee votes had been cast by persons who were not registered voters of the Sixth Ward, but his election suit was dismissed summarily by Judge Bruce Nunez. The two non-Trist seats were won by Celestine Melerine and Blanche Molero, both Third party adherents.[54]

Hardly had the Perez faction returned to power before heads began to roll. The new St. Bernard police jury immediately reorganized. Supporters of the Judge were elected president and vice-president, and the jury dismissed all parish employees who had supported the Third party. Adam Melerine was fired as parish registrar and replaced by Louis C. Riess, the brother of the new president, Valentine Riess.[55]

Before the local elections, Celestine Melerine and James Licciardi had applied to the Louisiana Pardon Board. Although Governor Long continued to issue reprieves to keep them out of jail, the board voted two to one to reject their applications. After Melerine had been reelected to the police jury and Licciardi had been narrowly defeated, both reapplied for pardons, which this time were granted. Attorney General Jack Gremillion, who changed his vote to make the pardons possible, said that he had reconsidered his position because the people had expressed confidence in the two at the polls.[56]

While defending his own Plaquemines–St. Bernard territory, Perez campaigned feverishly on the state level. He could not suffer the election of a candidate handpicked by Earl Long or any candidate who would vigorously execute the legislation passed by Long to divest him of his local power. The gubernatorial campaign, featuring eleven candidates, proved the most tumultuous in twenty years. It was fought out on Perez's favorite issue, race, and was the first time this issue had monopolized a Louisiana governor's election since Reconstruction.

On the final day for qualifying candidates, Earl Long announced that he had given up his plans to seek an unprecedented fourth term as governor. Instead, he would run for lieutenant governor on a ticket headed by James Noe, the man who had turned informer on the Long machine in 1939 and had provided the information that had launched the Louisiana scandals. Noe, now sixty-eight, had been out of active politics for twenty years and had never won a statewide election. In announcing his candidacy as Noe's running mate, Earl piously said, "Honestly and truly, I'd rather be lieutenant governor with the right man than be governor."[57]

Perez could take no chances on backing a little-known puppet candidate in such a crucial election. This time he picked his man early and stuck with him. The Judge's candidate was former governor Jimmie Davis, erstwhile ally of Sam Jones but now an intimate associate of Perez. Davis had been out of politics entirely since he had left the Governor's Mansion eleven years earlier, spending his time writing and recording country music and raising livestock and timber. Davis waged a "peace-and-harmony" campaign, garnished with nostalgic references to his humble origins and the accomplishments of his first term as governor. As he toured the state with his hillbilly band, he talked about bream fishing, squirrel hunting, and home cooking—everything but politics. The Davis campaign was lavishly financed by generous contributions from oilman Buddy Billups and, no doubt, from Perez. Louisiana law did not require the disclosure of campaign contributors, and Davis, when asked the source of his election funds, told me, "I don't know nothing about nothing and especially about that." [58]

Davis' principal challenger was Chep Morrison, four-time mayor of New Orleans, pragmatic reformer, moderate liberal, and unrelenting foe of Leander Perez. Although both Perez and Morrison were against Earl Long, they were also against each other. To the Judge, Morrison's election might mean not only passive acceptance of racial integration, but also the end of Leander's influence in state government and possibly the dismantling of his delta empire. Perez's Plaquemines opponents, led by Emile Martin III, shifted their support from Long to Morrison after Earl's breakdown. [59] Because of Morrison's hometown popularity in vote-rich New Orleans, he was favored to survive the first primary. But he was burdened with insuperable handicaps for a Louisiana gubernatorial candidate: he was a Roman Catholic with an urban image and a reputation as a racial moderate.

The man who injected race into the campaign and made it his principal issue was Willie Rainach, who had served as chairman of Louisiana's Joint Legislative Committee on Segregation, president of the Louisiana Association of Citizens' Councils, and chairman of the Citizens' Councils of America. Normally Perez could have been expected to back Rainach, but Davis was also a segregationist, had a better chance to defeat Morrison, and was more apt to listen to Perez's advice than was the self-reliant Rainach. [60]

The final major candidate was the state comptroller Bill Dodd, a veteran Longite who was often at odds with Earl. Coining the campaign slogan In Dodd We Trust, he promised increased teachers' salaries and old-age pensions and guaranteed a college education for every child in the state—all without raising taxes. Dodd expended much of his energy lambasting Jimmie Davis, because he believed Davis was the contender to beat in order to enter a runoff with Morrison. Dodd explains that he believed that he, or any of the other candidates, could have beaten Morrison in a second primary because Morrison had the largest negative vote of any aspirant. He recounts his strategy using a football analogy: "I didn't have anything particularly against Governor Davis; I was just trying to get into the second primary and win. It was sort of like a football game. I thought an end run would get me in rather than bucking the line, and that was the strategy I used, but I got thrown for a loss every time I got the ball—which wasn't very often." Davis, when asked why he thought Dodd had devoted so much time to attacking him, commented, "I guess he thought I was in the lead. You know, people throw rocks up, not down." [61]

The final tabulations from the first primary showed that, for the first time since Huey Long had been elected governor in 1928, a Long candidate had neither won election nor reached the second primary. Morrison led the voting with 278,956 votes (33.1 percent) to 213,551 (25.3 percent) for Davis and 143,095 for Rainach (17.0 percent). Not surprisingly, Davis gained his highest percentage in Plaquemines, with 66.5 percent of the vote against his ten opponents. He also carried St. Bernard, but polled only 37.3 percent of the votes there. [62]

Both Morrison and Davis eagerly sought an endorsement from Rainach, who after some hesitation backed Davis. Jimmie Noe and Bill Dodd both supported Morrison, but five days before the election Earl Long announced for Jimmie Davis. Judge Perez and Governor Long, who detested each other, thus found themselves supporting the same man for governor. [63]

Perez convinced Davis to abandon his first-primary peace-and-harmony theme in favor of an all-out racist campaign in the second primary. An analysis of Morrison's first-primary strength revealed that most blacks had voted for Morrison. Davis insisted that this constituted a bloc vote controlled by the NAACP, which he described as "a communist Negro organization founded in New York," despite the fact that the state president of the NAACP had endorsed him. Davis partisans, among whom Perez was prominent, also attempted to link Morrison with teamster racketeer Jimmy Hoffa (whom Morrison had never met) because Chep had received the endorsement of the New Orleans teamsters' local. Leander had the *Plaquemines Gazette* print Davis signs, cards, badges, sample ballots, and anti-Morrison letters. He distributed broadsides with photographs showing Morrison presiding at the dedication of a Negro swimming pool in New Orleans and organized the Friends of Rainach for Davis headquarters in the Crescent City managed by his assistant, George Singelmann. Morrison spent much of his time denying Davis' charges and attempting to lure the former governor into a face-to-face debate, a confrontation that Davis declined on the grounds that "he couldn't persuade me to vote for him and so there was no reason for me to waste my time."[64]

Spurred by the emotional racial issue, more than 80 percent of the state's registered Democratic voters turned out for the second primary, a higher percentage than had participated in a Louisiana gubernatorial primary in the past twenty years. Davis easily topped Morrison with 487,618 votes (54.1 percent) to 414,110. The vote was so one-sided in Davis' north Louisiana strongholds that these parishes prevailed over the more densely populated but less politically homogeneous Morrison parishes of south Louisiana. Plaquemines and St. Bernard, of course, stood out as Davis enclaves in the heart of Morrison's home territory. Davis received 71.6 percent of the vote in Plaquemines and 56.5 percent in more populous St. Bernard. Perez's chief contribution to Davis was not, however, his delivery of the customary lopsided majorities in the deep delta, but was his statewide role in financing and distributing campaign propaganda that convinced many white voters that Morrison was a tool of the NAACP.[65]

Under the friendly Davis administration most of the legislation that Earl Long had designed to dismantle Perez's empire was repealed. The new governor replaced the Long appointees on the local levee boards with Perez followers. Although he appointed twelve Perez supporters as piggyback Plaquemines police jurors, he vetoed an outright appeal of the measure authorizing the governor to appoint piggyback jurors, because this would be a formidable weapon should he and Perez ever have a disagreement. The piggyback jurors were permanently eliminated when Plaquemines switched to a commission form of government in 1961.[66]

Earl Long had come closer to destroying Perez's power than any other governor, and, if he had not suffered a nervous breakdown in 1959, he might well have succeeded. The opposition factions in both Plaquemines and St. Bernard were handily defeated. All local sympathizers with the Long organization were removed from the parish payroll, and the ax fell on the last remnants of the Third party when Governor Davis replaced the Long appointees on the Lake Borgne and Chalmette levee boards. Perez's power was never again seriously threatened.

TWELVE

Segregation Forever

At the peak of his power in the mid-1950s, Judge Perez had the prosperous appearance of a successful business executive. He had wavy, iron gray hair and appraising blue eyes, set off by bushy brows and rimless spectacles. In 1956, at the age of sixty-five, he was five feet, nine inches tall and weighed 188 pounds. His strongly set jaw and quick reflexes hinted that beneath his dignified demeanor bubbled volcanic energy.[1]

The Judge, in these later years, dressed like a character in a Tennessee Williams play. As a youth he had always dressed neatly and immaculately. But his idea of fashion never changed. He wore broad-lapelled suits long after they had gone out of style, and the shoes he preferred were so old-fashioned that they were available at only one store in New Orleans. He often wore a panama hat and was seldom photographed without a cigar. He once told CBS newsman Dan Rather that he smoked only a "given" number of cigars a day—as many as were given him. Leander, who disliked seeing young men wearing their shirttails out, thought it great fun to dash about at family gatherings with a pair of scissors snipping them off.[2]

The Perezes of Plaquemines Parish enjoyed a warm and happy home life. The Judge did not enjoy sight-seeing and seldom took a long trip unless he had something important to do at his destination. On the many trips he made to Washington, D.C., to testify before committees of Congress or to argue before the Supreme Court, he was often accompanied by his devoted wife. One summer, as a youth, he had shipped as a crewman aboard a steamer operating in the Caribbean, but after that he never left the country except to make hunting trips to Canada. His younger sister once tried to persuade him to vacation in Europe, but he was not interested. "There's no more there than in the good old United States," he said. In his later years, Perez did do some traveling with his grandchildren. Once, he hired two railroad coaches and took them on a two-week visit to Disneyland.[3]

At the height of his career, the Judge was widely known for his magnificent, rich speaking voice. Though his first language was French, his speech seldom betrayed this heritage; instead he spoke with a deep and mellow southern accent. Perez was at his best speaking extemporaneously or from an outline, preferring not to have his speeches written out. Before friendly audiences, he was usually calm and dignified, but he sometimes lost his temper in debate, drowning his opponent in a torrent of words. Many of his local arguments were carried not by the clarity of his logic, but by the force of his presentation. The boss of Plaquemines, never awed by high officials, once told a United States Supreme Court justice who interrupted him to keep quiet until he had finished his argument.[4]

Although gaining a reputation as a learned constitutional lawyer, Judge Perez lost most of the federal cases he argued. It was his imaginative manipulation and intricate knowledge of the law that made him successful in state courts. Perez's speeches, letters, and legal briefs were usually written rapidly, without polishing. His writing style was nail hard but sometimes needlessly verbose. Although a competent writer, he had little flair for literary style.

Perez was so well known in Louisiana that he received letters addressed "Capitol Building, Baton Rouge," "New Orleans," "Plaquemines Parish," "St. Bernard," or simply "South Louisiana."[5] He was eagerly sought after as a speaker for Citizens' Council rallies, banquets, and fund-raising dinners for conservative candidates, and he appeared on television with such diverse personalities as David Brinkley, William F. Buckley, Jr., David Susskind, and Dan Rather.

Journalists writing in the mid-1950s frequently predicted the Judge's downfall. New people with no ties to the Perez machine were moving into St. Bernard, and Perez himself had made an implacable enemy of Governor Earl Long. But Leander not only survived Earl Long's attempt to destroy him, but he actually extended his influence. He was much better known when he died in 1969 than he had been in 1950. The reason for his increased national stature was his leadership in the fight to maintain southern racial segregation. Perez viewed the Supreme Court's 1954 *Brown* decision ordering an end to racial separation in schools as a challenge. That very year, at a testimonial dinner commemorating his thirty-fifth anniversary as an elected official, the Judge threw down the gauntlet. He announced that he was dedicating the rest of his life to the principle of segregation of the races.[6]

Perez threw himself into the struggle against Negro rights with characteristic vigor. In addition to his fear that integration and racial equality would disrupt the established delta social order and dilute his own political base, Perez certainly was also deeply concerned about the specter of outside control that federal civil rights interventions threatened. He prepared for the battle by doing his homework. He scanned great stacks of right-wing publications, researched the "suspect" backgrounds of liberal leaders, and pored over integration cases from throughout the South. He assembled a voluminous file of legal arguments to meet cases that he expected to arise in Louisiana. Most of the research legwork was done by Perez's loyal assistant George Singelmann, a former newsman. Information and materials were culled from the files of Louisiana's Joint Legislative Committee on Segregation, State Sovereignty Commission, and similar committees in other southern states. The Judge kept in close touch with such other vocal leaders of the southern resistance as George Wallace of Alabama, W. J. Simmons and Tom P. Brady of Mississippi, Jim Johnson and Orval Faubus of Arkansas, and Lester Maddox and Roy Harris of Georgia. Harris, the proud founder of GUTS (Georgians Unwilling to Surrender), once commented that he and Perez did not have to correspond often because they thought so much alike that they each knew exactly what was on the other's mind. Leander's readings, his reflections, and his intimate association with other segregationists served to buttress his ideas, not to broaden them. He assumed that any intelligent man would reach the same conclusions he had and that anyone who did not was either evil or duped.[7]

Judge Perez was not one to mince words about race or anything else. Unlike many segregationists, he never left any doubt as to the real issue; he never softened his statements with such qualifying clichés as, "We love our colored people, but . . ." or "I'm not anti-Negro, mind you, but. . . ."[8] He firmly believed that the black race was intellectually and morally inferior to the white, and he did not mind saying so in emphatic terms to anyone who would listen. Northerners, liberals, and even prominent conservatives were often rudely taken aback by the directness of this powerful man from the delta. "By comparison [with him]," Mary McGrory wrote in the Washington *Post,* "Governor George C. Wallace, of Alabama, seems an angel of reason and moderation, and ex-Governor Ross W. Barnett, of Mississippi, a towering intellect." Congressman John V. Tunney of California thought this description of Perez so apt that he repeated it before the U.S. House of Representatives.[9] Simply speaking, Perez explained, there were only two types of Negroes: "Bad ones are niggers and good ones are darkies."[10]

Perez devoted a great deal of study to the question of Negro intelligence. His library overflowed with material on the subject. In his "research," the Judge was not seeking to verify whether or not the black man was congenitally stupid; he had made that assumption a priori. Instead, he was gathering ammunition for debate. He drew supporting evidence from outdated government publications, turn-of-the-century anthropological and sociological studies, and fringe-group tabloids, such as one that featured an article on the Negro brain illustrated with comparative cranial diagrams of whites, blacks, and gorillas.[11] Perez was undisturbed by the fact that, outside of a few relatively obscure academics, mostly aged men of southern origin, no contemporary scientific investigator could offer his cause any objective support. He simply referred to older sources; after all, he felt that he was dealing with an immutable truth. He was fond of telling people about an article he had seen as a youngster in a shopworn edition of the *Encyclopedia Britannica.* The author, a British anthropologist who had worked among North American blacks, had concluded that the Negro's brain capacity was so limited that the average black child's brain ceased development at age eleven. It never occurred to him or, more likely, it did not matter to him, that other studies had been made since then and contradictory conclusions drawn. He had reasons of his own for believing that Negroes were possessed of a juvenile mentality: "I do know from experience with Negroes— and I've worked with a number of Negroes, employ them on my farm here—I find that in spite of the fact that they may have operated a hay baler for six years, the same hay baler, they make the same mistakes day after day. They have to be told what to do."[12] Any suggestion that differences in white and Negro intelligence might be due to cultural rather than genetic factors the Judge dismissed as an "alibi," an attempt by "propagandists" to instill unwarranted guilt feelings in American whites.[13]

Perez believed that blacks were inherent profligates as well as inherent dullards. He explained: "Yes, they are inherently immoral! You know the Negroes. Why, I have a Negro man comes here with a woman and says this is my wife. But they ain't married. It's the way it has been as long as I've known Negroes, yes. Most of the Negroes, generally, are illegitimates. Most of them."[14] The Judge condemned state welfare expenditures as outright subsidization of black immorality. "At a cost of more than two hundred million dollars annually we're supporting the bastards," he declared. "And what is their [the Negroes'] contribution? They contribute more illegitimates."[15]

The image many whites had of the Negro as a hypersexual beast who indiscriminately spread his seed about, impregnating every female in sight and filling slums, housing projects, and tenant cabins with thousands of naked, government-supported illegitimates, lay at the root of the very real horror with which Perez and his southern comrades contemplated racial integration; to them the crux was the threat of rape and miscegenation. "God save America from a mongrelized race," the Judge once declared before a committee of Congress.[16] He feared that if white and black children were not kept separate during their formative years they would lose their natural scruples against breeding outside of their own kind and America would soon be swamped by a mentally and morally crippled race of "mongrel" mulattoes. In fact, as Perez testified before another Washington committee, this was the deliberate plan of the race mixers. Beginning in grade school, white and Negro children would study together, eat together, play together, and dance together. Eventually, they would sleep together. Leander envisioned leering,

degenerate, oversexed black males literally beating down the bedroom doors of chaste southern belles. He theorized, "You make a
Negro believe he is equal to the white people and the first thing he
wants is a white woman." [17]

Many southerners, of course, hastened to explain that their own
sons and daughters were much too well brought up to copulate with
colored people. The great tragedy, wrote one of the Judge's out-of-
state supporters, would come in a couple of generations when it
would no longer be easy to distinguish the pure white from the racially tainted. The well-bred children of perfectly respectable white
couples might then accidentally marry into families with Negro
blood and thus unwittingly contribute to the downfall of their own
race.[18]

Perez identified and exposed what he saw as a nefarious scheme by
the integrationists to undermine the racial purity of the whites with
infusions of Negro blood. The object of such a design, as far as the
Judge was concerned, could only be to destroy America's moral fiber
by weakening the hereditary stock of its ruling race. He could
hardly attribute such an elaborate plot to the Negro himself—a
dull-witted, shuffle-footed man-ape, incapable of operating even a
hay baler properly, much less of mapping a comprehensive program
of genetic sabotage. The poor, ignorant blacks, Perez declared, were
"just the pawns of Communists . . . part of the overall Communist
ideology to divide and conquer." [19] According to this theory, every
white man preaching integration either took orders directly from
the Kremlin or worked for someone who did.

The Judge was fond of describing the fate Moscow was planning
for America. It would all begin when white American Christians
were finally forced to accept Negroes as equals. Blacks would be
given the vote in areas of the South where they constituted the
majority and then would be told how to vote by their Communist
masters. The plan was already in effect in the "bossed" cities of the
Northeast. Meanwhile, previously all-white schools would be inundated by ignorant black children who would be unable to maintain
the rigorous academic pace set by the white students; educational
standards would be lowered for the newcomers. As a result of the
deterioration of public schools, the supply of engineers, doctors,

lawyers, and technicians would begin to dry up, leading to a corresponding decline in American industry, technology, and economic and social vitality. Once the color line had been abolished in politics, education, and industry, to the detriment of all except the Communists, it would be attacked in that most sinister of battlegrounds—the boudoir. Intermarriage would then bring forth a mongrelized version of the once-superior white race, a flabby, dull strain of Africanized Americans, robbed of their vigor, lacking the ability and the will to resist international bolshevism. Then, Perez liked to conclude with a simile he attributed variously to both Lenin and Stalin, who were interchangeable in his mind: "Then the last bastion of capitalism, the United States, shall fall into their hands like an overripe fruit, without firing a shot."[20]

The energy of the masters of the Comintern, sustained over several generations, must truly have been phenomenal. To hear Perez describe it, nothing went wrong in America without direct authorization from the Kremlin. The international Communist conspiracy was behind the failure of the Bay of Pigs invasion of 1961, all the racial strife in America, and even the war in Vietnam; and, on the world scene, trench-coated agents from Moscow tirelessly fomented trouble in the Congo and turmoil in Latin America. Leander claimed to have unmasked hundreds of undercover operatives cleverly masquerading as patriotic Americans, but, because he relied on reactionary fringe groups for much of his information, he sometimes found it difficult to sort out the handful of genuine Red agents from the multitude of red herrings. The reason the American people did not know more about this furtive network, the Judge charged, was that the press lacked the "guts" to print the truth. In an effort to make his truth known, Perez testified in 1959 before a committee of the United States Senate that the entire civil rights movement had its origin in a plot hatched by Stalin back in the 1930s. "There is a hidden hand that moves in this whole matter of race relations in the United States,"[21] he announced. He went on to describe a far-reaching conspiracy that had originally sought—under the guise of extending civil rights to Negroes—to create an autonomous, Communist-dominated black republic in the heart of the South. When it became apparent that this scheme was doomed to failure, the Judge continued, the Russians had subtly shifted their emphasis to a policy of "infiltration and penetration." On orders from Moscow, Red subversives moved into key positions in Washington and began to contaminate the federal policy-making machinery. Soviet operatives and fellow travelers on the Supreme Court and elsewhere in government were responsible for treasonous designs ranging from efforts to organize collective farms in America through federal agricultural programs to the attempt to aggravate racial tension through civil rights legislation. The greatest problem facing Negroes, Perez told an astonished interviewer, was not poverty or lack of education or opportunity: "You know damn well it's nothing more than the Communist conspiracy to stir up racist hate!"[22] It was Joseph Stalin himself, the Judge claimed, who wrote the world's first modern civil rights law, Article 123 of the Soviet constitution, which guarantees equality of rights to citizens of all races. "This is the law," he charged, "which Joe Stalin used to make himself the supreme dictator of Russia, because it gave him absolute power over all Russians." This insidious "all races" measure, Perez suggested, was probably inspired by similar laws imposed upon the South during Reconstruction and almost assuredly was the progenitor of the various civil rights proposals that periodically came before Congress. "Can there be any doubt," he asked, "that those of the Russian faith who infiltrated in our Federal Government skillfully sponsored the idea of reviving the so-called civil rights Federal legislation in this country—the Joe Stalin way?"[23]

If black people were but the unsuspecting dupes in a larger struggle, then who were the true agents of the Communist conspiracy? Perez had a ready answer: "the most dangerous people in this country today—the Zionist Jews." He charged that the Zionists were the "main driving force behind forced racial integration" and that they were willing to go "beyond the scope of religion" to accomplish their sinister ends. When these anti-Semitic outbursts brought angry protests from Jewish organizations who denounced them as "un-American" and dismissed the integration question as "out of the scope of the Zionist movement," Perez answered them bluntly. Denying that he was personally anti-Semitic, he maintained that the facts spoke for themselves.[24] "The Jews are leading the Negroes," he declared some years later. "They'll resent it and they'll say Perez is anti-Semitic. And when they say that, I say that they are unadulterated damn liars, because I do resent any goddamn Jew trying to destroy our country ... and they are using the Negroes for it!"[25] Leander had plenty of "evidence" that the Jewish effort to destroy "our white Christian civilization" went back a long time. One ninety-year-old Arkansan even wrote to advise him that the Rothschilds had started the American Civil War in order to stimulate race hatred.[26]

Among the tools that the Zionists were using to subvert American society, the Judge listed the churches and the NAACP. He explained, for instance, how the Jews controlled blacks through their pastors: "The Negroes, of course, are largely emotional! ... And unthinking! And they are led and misled, handled through the churches, and the Negro preachers are paid off and bought!"[27] As for the Catholic church, it too was "being used as a front for clever Jews" and was "even putting out literature instructing people how to be brainwashed into accepting integration, and for additional reading on the subject it lists Jewish literature—imagine that."[28] The NAACP itself, according to Perez, was a "Communist-front infested hybrid organization," whose leaders were subversives and "Zionist Jews" and whose racial aims were identical with those of the Communist party. The national political parties, he declared, had sold out to this institutionalized hotbed of traitors and enemy agents, because of its proven ability to deliver the Kremlin-controlled Negro bloc vote. None of this was surprising, the boss of Plaquemines maintained, since the NAACP had been founded by a Jew, was bankrolled by Jews, and had always had a Jewish rather than a Negro president. Perez complained that it was difficult to convey his message to the American people because the Jews dominated the media, but his attacks on the Zionists actually won him a great deal of publicity in the local and even national press. His views were condemned by many, but he was lauded as a hero by a neo-Fascist organization known as the National States' Rights party, whose blatantly anti-Semitic newspaper, the *Thunderbolt,*[29] devoted a special issue to Perez with a front-page picture and article entitled "Perez Turns Spotlight on the Enemy." A Georgia businessman who saw the write-up fired off a heated letter in which he expressed his contempt for the Judge and his opinions and concluded, "Brother, you need prayer, and need it badly."[30]

As much time as he spent attacking them, however, Negroes and Jews were not the only targets of Perez's outspoken racial abuse. He also found time to oppose the admission of Hawaii to statehood. Through both his police jury and the Citizens' Council of Greater New Orleans, he issued strong statements firmly condemning the very idea of such a racially diverse territory being allowed to join the Union and send its nonwhite, left-leaning representatives to Congress. Perez's contempt for Orientals was deep-seated. During World War II Japanese-Americans from California had been brought to Louisiana to work on delta farms, but Perez had barred the nisei from entering his parish, warning federal officials that he would tie them up in the local courts if they persisted. "No matter where a yellow Jap is born," he had said, "he's still a yellow s.o.b."[31]

The race mixers' first major victory was the U.S. Supreme Court decision in the *Brown* v. *Board of Education* case in 1954. Perez never stopped condemning the Court and its ruling until the day he died. In deciding the *Brown* case, the justices—Perez called them "nine dishonest stoogies"—made a dramatic departure from the hitherto revered principle of separate but equal, which had been established by the court in *Plessy* v. *Ferguson* in 1896. In its opinion, written by Chief Justice Earl Warren, the Court overturned a ruling by a three-judge federal panel, which had held that it was constitutional for the city of Topeka, Kansas, to maintain separate schools for white and black children as long as the facilities "were substantially equal" in such tangible areas as physical plants, transportation, curricula, and teacher pay and qualifications. The lower court held to the *Plessy* doctrine even though it admitted in its opinion that it had found that the mere fact of racial separation, independent of any question of physical parity, had a "detrimental effect" on the Negro students. In deciding in favor of the black plaintiffs in the Topeka matter and a group of similar companion cases, the Supreme Court stated in effect that segregation in public education constituted a denial of the equal protection of the laws guaranteed under the Fourteenth Amendment. In its decision, the Court attempted to deal a death blow to the long-held doctrine of separate but equal. Although such a concept may have been admissable in earlier times, the findings of social science had since rendered it unacceptable, the justices concluded. They could not "turn the clock back" to the nineteenth century. Instead they cited a considerable body of scientific evidence on the nature and consequences of racial discrimination and on the role of public education in contemporary American society. Drawing on such sources, including Gunnar Myrdal's classic *An American Dilemma,* the Court determined that segregation itself was inherently incompatible with equality and therefore unconstitutional.[32]

Perez, dismissing as "Communist trash" the scientific writings that the Court had used in arriving at its decision, charged that the ruling itself "marked the pro-Communist penetration of the highest court in the land."[33] Every time a case involving Communists came before them, he declared, the justices would kowtow to the Kremlin. The Judge became quite practiced at reciting the Red connections of the men to whose sociological and psychological works the Court had referred; he could reel them off by heart: "First, there was K. B. Clark, two-time Commy fronter, and employed as Social Science consultant for the legal staff of the NAACP, the real plaintiff in the Black Monday cases; and then Kotinsky and Chein, and then Theodore Brameld, a ten-time Commy-front member, and E. Franklin Frazier, an eighteen-time Commy-front member." He would then ask, "Isn't it more than passing strange that there the court did not cite one white American Christian as its authority on psychology and sociology?"[34]

Leander denied that the *Brown* decision had any basis in established legal precedent. Rather, he charged, it was founded upon "will-o-the-wisp foreign sociological ideas."[35] The Supreme Court "could not," he maintained, honestly hold the time-honored separate but equal doctrine to be unconstitutional, so it had merely declared it "un-sociological, un-anthropological, and un-psychological." He complained that, because the "so-called modern authorities" had not been called as witnesses and their writings had not been submitted in evidence, no opportunity had been afforded the defense to submit authorities of its own. The Court had lifted these sources from an appendix to a brief filed by the NAACP and used them as a basis for a decision in which "constitutional principles were thrown out the window," and, he concluded, "that was that. No law, no 14th amendment. Only psychology and sociology."[36] The result, of course, was that the justices had "junked the Anglo-Saxon concept of equality"[37] and presented "a fellow traveller blank check to the pro-Communist dominated NAACP to go into . . . the Federal courts of the land and secure bogus Communistic decrees for forced racial amalgamation of the American people, to our certain destruction and the surrender in the end to the world wide Communist conspiarcy."[38]

Of all the sources used by the Court in the *Brown* case, Perez was perhaps most critical of *An American Dilemma*. This hefty two-volume study was actually a group effort by a number of reputable American social scientists under the general direction of Myrdal and is still highly respected as a classic in its field. Perez, however, denounced the Swedish scholar as a "Socialist" who knew nothing about Negroes or southern traditions and who had merely pasted together "what other Socialists and Communists and haters of the South had written."[39] Myrdal's corps of assistants, he charged, comprised "between 75 and 100 anti-southern writers, many of them Negroes,"[40] who were bankrolled by the "Carnegie Foundation of Alger Hiss fame." Once, when he referred to the philanthropic Carnegie Corporation in this manner before a Senate committee, he was asked by committee counsel whether Alger Hiss had actually been an employee of the foundation in 1944 when Myrdal's book was written. Perez admitted that he had not, but declared, "I said the Carnegie Foundation of Alger Hiss fame, because it shows the type of management the Carnegie Corporation has . . . the Carnegie Corporation is forever branded, the same as Alger Hiss is branded, because of his traitorous conduct to this country and he was supported by the Carnegie Corporation. Yes sir."[41]

In one of his more quixotic sorties against the integrationists, Judge Perez sought to undermine the *Brown* decision and all subsequent rulings based upon it by demonstrating that the Fourteenth Amendment itself had never been legally adopted and was therefore unconstitutional. He devoted almost four years to researching the history of the amendment and its ratification and composed a treatise documenting his premise that it had been carried illegally. The Plaquemines Parish Police Jury appropriated fifteen thousand dollars to publish the little pamphlet, which quickly became a hot item among ardent segregationists and southern legalists. Requests were received from throughout the country, and hundreds of copies were mailed out.[42]

In Louisiana, the legislature was in session in Baton Rouge in May, 1954, when the Black Monday decision was announced. The solons lost no time in passing a joint resolution censuring the Supreme Court for its "unwarranted and unprecedented abuse of power."[43] But, beyond expressing their indignation, state officials knew little to do. The justices had scheduled the arguments concerning implementation in the fall, and no one knew what shape court-ordered racial integration would ultimately take. Governor Robert Kennon was of the opinion that the state would not be immediately affected, and most of the legislators were content to adopt a go-slow attitude until the extent of the threat became better known. Perez, on the other hand, favored immediate and decisive action. Believing in the deterrent of overkill—applied quickly and somewhat indiscriminately—he hastily drafted and submitted to the legislature a bill that in effect would have abolished the state's public school system. Under the Judge's audacious proposal, local school boards would be empowered to dispose of public school property to private school "trustees" who would be selected by them and would serve under their aegis. Public schooling would be phased out and replaced by private institutions financed by the pupil's families, who would be aided by state tuition grants.[44]

Perez was so proud of his bill that he mailed a copy to his old friend in Alabama, Charles Wallace Collins, an elderly corporation lawyer who in his retirement had become an amateur historian and author of segregationist tracts.[45] A week earlier the Judge had written Collins to inform him, in case he did not already know, that the *Brown* decision was "a result of Communist infiltration and influence through the Carnegie Foundation, headed by the notorious Communist traitor Alger Hiss, which sponsored the Gunnar Myrdal 'DILEMMA,' the Fellow Travellers in Harvard University, the C.I.O., and New York's political N.A.A.C.P."[46]

Collins, after studiously reviewing the proposal, pointed out several weaknesses, the most obvious being that, in placing the private school trustees under the control of the public school boards, the state would be vulnerable to the charge that, whatever its pretensions, it was in fact still operating a segregated school system. His solution was to liquidate the public boards entirely and hand school property over to parents' organizations. He also recommended dropping the bill's "whereas" clauses, since they too obviously linked the measure to the *Brown* decision; even without them, he assured the Judge, the people would know the purpose of the bill. Collins concluded by suggesting that Perez defer action until the court had issued its implementation decree; then he would know what he was fighting. The Louisiana lawmakers appeared to agree; they took no action on Leander's quaint proposal.[47]

Though shying away from headlong or precipitous action, the legislature did move cautiously in the 1954 session to erect a framework for resistance. Many of the lawmakers were unconcerned, but there were enough staunch segregationists to carry a number of measures that appear relatively moderate considering the legislative avalanche that followed in later years. The nerve center of the legislature's antiintegration effort was the Joint Legislative Committee on Segregation, which was created after the Black Monday decision; its chairman until 1959 was Willie Rainach, senator from Claiborne Parish. The committee's mission was to find ways to circumvent the Supreme Court's ruling. Since Rainach was not a lawyer, he looked to Perez for assistance in drafting legislation and, in fact, Perez actually did the bulk of the committee's legal work. Warming to his task, the Judge assembled a large volume of desegregation suits and obstructive legislation from other states that he hoped to use in plotting Louisiana's strategy of resistance.[48]

The first fruits of the joint committee were segregation measures enacted by the 1954 legislature. Included in the package was a constitutional amendment that, directly in the face of the Supreme Court, required the state to maintain a segregated school system and authorized it to use its police power to do so in order to preserve public order, health, and morals. A companion measure defined the operating of a racially mixed public school as a crime punishable by a thousand-dollar fine and a maximum of six months in jail. The package also contained Louisiana's first pupil placement law, under which students entering public school were to be assigned to a particular school by the parish superintendent. The only appeal from his decision was through a cumbersome maze of channels in which the plaintiff would be required to pay court costs after exhausting all administrative remedies; it was hoped the complainants would exhaust themselves before the remedies. Obviously, the superintendent could be expected to assign whites to white schools and blacks to black schools, because he certainly would not wish to be charged with operating an integrated school and thereby risk a fine or jail sentence. The constitutional amendment was ratified overwhelmingly by the public in November. The greatest margins were polled in north Louisiana, especially in parishes bordering Arkansas and Mississippi. It did not fare quite as well in the southern part of the state, where proportionately more Negroes were registered to vote. However, the amendment was immensely popular in Plaquemines Parish.[49]

That the Rainach committee actually expected the *Brown* decision to be circumvented is shown by the fact that, in the wake of the ruling, it made a special study of the state's schools and, finding that Louisiana's separate but equal system was anything but equal, concluded that a crash capital outlay program would be required to bring the black schools up to the standards of the white ones. Such a project, involving perhaps fifty million dollars in expenditures on a school-building program and the construction of an adequate home-to-school highway system during the fiscal year 1954–1955, would be much too expensive for the individual parishes (except perhaps for Plaquemines) to undertake and would have to be financed by the state—an immense burden on the year's budget. A constitutional amendment was voted to permit local school districts to increase their bonded indebtedness in order to underwrite the program. But, whether Governor Kennon thought such a grandiose enterprise, along with the committee's recommendation to immediately construct a new Negro college in southwest Louisiana, too much too soon or too little too late, he vetoed appropriations for it in 1955.[50]

Shortly afterwards, the Supreme Court announced its implementation decree.

The Court assigned the task of overseeing the progress of desegregation to the federal district courts. For the first few years they had little to oversee. Recognizing the tremendous social disruption likely to be occasioned in most communities by such a drastic change, the courts were authorized to proceed under principles of equity, weighing public against private needs. But the justices, cautioning that "the vitality of these constitutional principles cannot be allowed to yield simply because of disagreement with them," directed that integration be accomplished with all due attention to the problems of public administration, but also "with all deliberate speed." [51] There was considerable uncertainty on both sides over the meaning of that last phrase. Grizzled veterans of the civil rights struggle hoped that it meant immediately or sooner, and white and comfortable gradualists inclined more toward an unspecified date in the twenty-first or twenty-second century. Among militant whites of the Deep South, however, the prevailing attitude was indicated by the oft-heard shouts of "Never!" No one shouted louder than Leander Perez.

Though there was over the state a general feeling of relief that the court had ordered gradual rather than abrupt implementation, lines had now at last been clearly drawn. The state's lawmakers descended on Baton Rouge for the 1956 legislative session in a mood to do business. Included in the tough seventeen-bill package enacted during the session was a measure extending the life of the Rainach committee and providing it with ample operating funds. The legislature also adopted a Perez-authorized "interposition" resolution, resurrecting a dusty doctrine from the days of John Calhoun, by which the state purported to place its own sovereignty between its officials and those of the federal government. Closely connected with this was a constitutional amendment providing that only the state, rather than individual officials, could be sued in school desegregation cases. The state, of course, could not be sued without its own consent. Other acts provided for the racial segregation of parks, waiting rooms, sanitary facilities, and athletic and social events.

Public schools in New Orleans were to be classified according to race. Compulsory school attendance laws were to be suspended in any district operating integrated schools. In a cleverly designed move to choke off the steadily increasing court-ordered admission of blacks to white state colleges and universities, a new law required each new applicant for admission to an institution of higher learning to submit a certificate from his local school superintendent attesting to his moral character. When linked with another recently passed provision subjecting school officials who advocated integration to dismissal, this effectively assured that no Negro would qualify to enter a white college. Addressing the Optimist Club in New Orleans, Perez proudly announced, "With these laws it won't be long before we purify our colleges."[52] In another move, excavating a thirty-two-year-old anti-Klan law requiring that organizations file their membership lists, state officials were able to obtain a court order enjoining the NAACP from functioning in Louisiana. Senator Rainach rejoiced at the victory and hoped to win a permanent ban.[53]

The torrent of anti-Negro measures, most of them written by Perez, continued when the legislature convened again in 1958. The Judge kept busy studying measures enacted in other states and preparing final drafts for the Rainach committee. His projects for 1958 included several bills designed to encourage a statewide private school system—an early idea that had finally come of age. The governor was now authorized to close public schools ordered to desegregate and dispose of the school property to private school groups. Provisions were made for the payment of schoolteachers and voter registrars who were unable to function because of federal injunctions, and the state attorney general was authorized to defend local registrars. Another pupil placement law was approved. A final act provided for the labeling by race of all blood used in medical transfusions.[54]

Desiring not to antagonize the legislative militants, whom he stigmatized as "grass-eaters," Governor Earl Long, no integrationist himself, certainly, but a crusty old welfarist with a large black constituency, reluctantly but consistently signed into law the segregation measures. He rationalized his action by asserting that it made no difference, since none of them would stand up in court anyway.[55]

Under Perez's guidance, the legislature erected a set of ponderous and constitutionally untenable legal bulwarks against integration. By 1964 Louisiana had enacted 131 antimixing measures—far more than any other state. When Jimmie Davis succeeded Long as governor in 1960 after a blatantly racist campaign largely managed by Perez, the old Joint Legislative Committee on Segregation was dissolved and the new State Sovereignty Commission was created to take its place. Perez personally drafted the bill that created the commission, basing it on a similar act passed by the Mississippi legislature. He included the governor, lieutenant governor, and attorney general as members because he wanted high-ranking persons on the commission who could work with the officials of other southern states. As part of the Judge's overall strategy for resistance, each southern state would enter briefs on every desegregation case filed against a sister state, and all states would make a concerted effort to defeat civil rights legislation in Congress. Governor Davis offered the directorship of the commission to Senator Rainach, who had resigned from the joint committee to run for governor in 1959. Although the idea for a sovereignty commission had come from his own campaign committee, Rainach refused the position on the grounds that the new body had not been given enough power.[56]

An unofficial resistance movement soon developed to complement the official one. The first Citizens' Council in Louisiana was founded by Senator Rainach in his home parish of Claiborne in 1955. Other councils quickly sprang up, and in January, 1956, the statewide Association of Citizens' Councils was established, with Rainach as president. By 1959, he could claim local organizations in 34 out of 64 parishes with a total membership of 100,000. The councils did much better in the northern sector of the state than in the largely French, Catholic south whose people, though still basically segregationists, were much more relaxed in their general racial attitudes. Annual dues for membership in the state association were $250, well beyond the means of the everyday segregationist. Perez was a paid-up charter member, however, and regularly kicked in extra contributions whenever the organization found itself in financial trouble. It was largely his patronage that kept the movement going long after interest began to dwindle in the early sixties. Many of the local organizations fell into inactivity soon after having been founded with much fanfare and enthusiasm. Council militants were always a little disturbed by the general public apathy toward their efforts and at times even hoped for new crises to spark interest and bring in dues so bills could be paid. To inform the people of its aims, the state council organized a nonprofit educational fund to which Perez contributed $1,000 and his children $250 each. The fund was a tax-exempt operation like the NAACP and the "Carnegie Foundation of Alger Hiss fame," and Perez even suggested changing its slogan from Racial Integrity to Constitutional Government so as not to antagonize federal officials and jeopardize that status.[57]

By far the largest local council was the Citizens' Council of Greater New Orleans, which boasted fifty thousand members at its peak. No doubt one of the reasons for this group's vitality was Leander Perez, who, though he never held office in it, maintained close contact with it, served as its attorney, bankrolled it, and has been credited with personally founding it. He organized affiliate councils in the adjoining parishes of Jefferson, St. Bernard, and Plaquemines and was a frequent and popular speaker at rallies. To increase membership, the Judge contributed trophies and savings bonds to be given as prizes to those persons who rounded up the most recruits. Interest in the movement was high for several reasons. New Orleans' Roman Catholic archbishop, Joseph Francis Rummel, declared in 1956 that segregation was "morally wrong and sinful," and that the Catholic schools, attended by half the city's children, would be integrated. Soon afterwards the Orleans Parish School Board was ordered by U.S. District Judge J. Skelly Wright to submit a plan for desegregation. With the racial apocalypse apparently so near, it is easy to imagine how the Citizens' Council of Greater New Orleans, at the height of its glory, could draw crowds of as many as sixty-five thousand Confederate flag-waving whites to hear Leander Perez and other prominent southern crusaders attack the Supreme Court.[58]

In addition to all the support he gave the New Orleans council, Perez was also responsible for a leadership crisis that eventually led to a split. His open and outspoken anti-Semitism often made his fellow segregationists nervous. Eventually a faction led by the exec-

utive secretary Jackson Ricau, determined to keep the movement
"respectable," abandoned the greater New Orleans council and organized a splinter group, the South Louisiana Citizens' Council,
which by 1960 claimed two thousand members. Undaunted by
Ricau's desertion, the Judge continued his anti-Jewish diatribes
even though he began to receive numerous letters from friends and
allies, both gentile and Jewish, asking him to desist. A leader of the
Shreveport, Louisiana, council advised him that his attacks were
likely to alienate several Jews on the Shreveport council's board of
directors from the movement. Pointing out that there were integrationists in every church, he said that it was unfair to single out
the Jews.[59] One Jewish conservative, a follower of the Judge's,
begged him to stop attacking "Zionists," before his charges of a Jewish conspiracy against the south became a self-fulfilling prophecy or,
worse, before Perez set off a wave of general anti-Semitism. He even
offered to attack individual "pink" Jews himself on the theory that,
as long as the charges came from another Jew, there could be no
question of anti-Jewish prejudice.[60]

Under the Judge's tutelage, the Citizens' Council of Greater New
Orleans engaged in several skirmishes with officialdom over what it
considered racial abuses. Council members once circulated a petition demanding that illegitimate children be denied state support.
Perez, who kept current statistics on such things, doubtless felt that
such a policy would remove thousands of black children from the
welfare rolls. The matter eventually reached the legislature, which,
under the glare of publicity and the threat of federal reprisals, chose
not to act.[61]

On another front, the Judge and his followers tried to force the
resegregation of New Orleans public transportation, which had been
integrated by court order in 1957. In February, 1960, the Citizen's
Council approached city officials about asking the courts to drop the
three-year-old injunction on the grounds that the Louisiana law
against which it had been issued had since been repealed. Once the
court order was lifted, council leaders argued, the city could then
enact its own segregation ordinance under the guise of something
else. When a fare increase was proposed, Perez announced his opposition, stating that the reason public transportation was losing

money was because white people were afraid to ride the integrated buses and streetcars. He claimed that the same thing would happen to the schools if they were mixed—that whites would be run out just as they had been in Washington, D.C., where twelve formerly all-white schools were now 95 percent black. A petition signed by fifty thousand whites demanded "that this black cloud be removed from the transit system." Later in the spring, speaking before a mass meeting commemorating the sixth anniversary of Black Monday, Leander warned that the integration of schools and buses was only the beginning; the end would come with the fall of civilization and the rape of their daughters.[62]

The most ambitious and most widely publicized campaign under-taken by the New Orleans council was a project known as Freedom Rides North. The idea originated with Perez's assistant George Singelmann, who reasoned that he could remove some blacks from Louisiana's welfare rolls by giving them one-way tickets to northern cities. He also hoped to show that living conditions in the North were no better for blacks than in the South. Negro leaders in New Orleans, of course, knew this and urged their people not to go unless they had friends, families, or solid job promises at their destination, but many naïvely accepted the offer anyway. The project got under way in April, 1962, with top priority given to welfare recipients and blacks with criminal records, individuals with maximum publicity potential. Notices of the council's offer were posted in the Orleans Parish prison and in the state penitentiary at Angola. Singelmann would meet his grateful charges at the bus station, give them their tickets and a five-dollar bill for expenses, and make sure that they got away safely. Asked what would become of them at journey's end, he replied, "After I get them on that bus and have that ticket in their hands, I don't care." The destinations selected were those cities that had been prominent in promoting racial integration. "This is a crude way of putting it," Singelmann said, "But we are telling the North to put up or shut up."[63]

The first black man to arrive in New York City on a council-provided ticket was an unemployed father of eight named Louis Boyd. Boyd and his family, immediate celebrities, were featured on the front page of the New York *Times*. He had nothing but praise for the Citizens' Council. "They're wonderful," he said. "They treated us fine." The only reason he had left the South at all, he insisted, was that he could not find work. Out of three job offers waiting for him in New York, Boyd chose a $100-a-week job as a handyman at a Jersey City medical equipment concern. Within two weeks, however, everything went sour. His paycheck proved worthless; the company he worked for partially suspended operations; and his employer, a mad scientist with a scheme to save the world, was hustled off to a hospital for mental observation.[64]

The movement accelerated as the Freedom Rides North received wide publicity. Councils in Macon, Montgomery, Shreveport, and Little Rock soon joined in sending unemployed Negroes north. Over sixty penniless blacks were shipped to Hyannis, Massachusetts, where President John F. Kennedy maintained a resplendent summer home. Others were put on buses for Minneapolis for the stated purpose of having Christmas dinner with Senator Hubert Humphrey. When New Hampshire's governor, Wesley Powell, announced that his state had one of the lowest unemployment rates in the country, Singelmann began exporting out-of-work blacks there. Powell urged residents to make them welcome, and a large crowd, including a number of clergymen, did turn out to greet the first arrivals. The goodwill was far from unanimous, however. During the night a large wooden cross was burned on the highway outside Nashua.[65]

In Hyannis, a resort community with high off-season unemployment, local officials, admitting the existence of "a real, although invisible color line," scrambled to find adequate housing, food, and clothing for newly arrived blacks; in Minnesota, students at Northfield's Carleton College made plans to feed a group due there for Christmas. Not surprising, the reverse freedom rides attracted much more attention in the North than they did in New Orleans. Northern reaction was about what Singelmann had anticipated. Many blacks complained that they were unwelcome in the cities to which they had immigrated. Most were unskilled and could not find jobs. An indignant New York *Times* condemned the council project as "a cheap trafficking in human misery," and Senator Humphrey characterized it as a "cruel hoax." President Kennedy referred to the

rides as "a rather cheap exercise," but at least one Hyannis merchant conceded, "The Southerners have as much right to send Negroes up here as Northerners had to go down there last year on Freedom Rides"—a reference to civil rights activists who had gone south
to test government bans on segregated transportation facilities, a
campaign that had created a great deal of animosity throughout the
region and had inspired Singelmann's idea. Some northern leaders,
including Governor John Volpe of Massachusetts, called for federal
legislation to halt the rides before the North was engulfed by a tidal
wave of hungry blacks. Singelmann had conceived the project as a
means to embarrass comfortably self-righteous northerners by demonstrating their hypocrisy and exploding the myth that beyond the
Mason-Dixon Line the black man enjoyed perfect equality and prosperity. A request for state funds for the project—an idea that
frightened liberal columnist James Reston, who envisioned a massive, publicly financed black horde descending upon New York from
all over the South—met no enthusiasm from legislators grappling
with an immense budgetary deficit. The propaganda value
exhausted, interest in the rides began to decline and money ran low.
The leaders of the movement were also subjected to intense federal
pressure. George Singelmann claims that he was the object of an
exhaustive income tax audit and other forms of harassment by federal officials. Finally, the project was abandoned.[66]

The Citizens' Councils were organized into regional as well as state
and local combines. In 1956 an assembly of the South's most prominent white supremacists, including Judge Perez, voted to create the
Association of Citizens' Councils of America, in order to provide a
strategic and administrative nexus for the numerous councils and
other states' rights and segregationist organizations throughout the
South. Willie Rainach was chosen the association's first president.
The council movement grew rapidly at first, but crested in 1957 and
thereafter began a steady decline, which became precipitous following its failure to prevent the integration of schools in Little Rock
and New Orleans. By 1964 a regional council movement barely
existed.[67]

The Citizens' Council of Greater New Orleans experienced a similar decline. Crowds at meetings grew small, contributions dried up,

and it proved difficult to get publicity. Local newspapers either did not print council press releases at all or whittled them down to practically nothing. The papers insisted upon screening, and often rejected, council advertisements.[68]

While fighting to preserve local segregation, Leander also worked to prevent the passage of national civil rights legislation. He frequently went to Washington to testify before the Senate Judiciary Committee, headed by his close friend and ideological twin, Mississippi's James O. Eastland. Eastland credited Perez with personally having defeated President Truman's omnibus civil rights bill in 1949 by exposing the fact that it "was based on Dictator Tito's all-racial laws." In fact, the Judge's central strategy in such cases was usually to compare the pending measure to some vaguely similar provision in the laws of one Communist country or another and to charge that federal enforcement of civil rights laws within the states would, somehow, lead to a Soviet America. No offer, however, was ever made to undertake the protection of Negroes' constitutional rights within the states and, thereby, to destroy the attractions of the offending "Red" legislation. Perez's testimony did not prevent passage of President Eisenhower's Civil Rights Act of 1957. The first such measure passed since Reconstruction, the law threatened Leander's electoral stronghold because it authorized the government to bring suits in federal court to prevent voter discrimination.[69]

The Judge also tried vigorously to defeat the legislation that eventually became the Civil Rights Act of 1960. He testified before several committees on Capitol Hill and introduced into the record almost two hundred pages of testimony and documents, including portions of the Russian, Yugoslavian, and Latvian constitutions. Much of his information on the "pro-Communist records" of various integrationists was gleaned from a Louisiana legislative committee's investigation of "subversion in racial unrest." Much of this committee's material had, in turn, been obtained from the bulging files of Senator Eastland. Perez was particularly critical of an administration proposal that would have made it a felony to advocate racial discrimination, but he also focused attention on the "Red" background of the Supreme Court's *Brown* decision and on the deterioration of the District of Columbia school system as an example of how integration would destroy American education. Though Perez's testimony pleased Eastland, it ruffled the feathers of another segregationist, Senator Sam Ervin, acting chairman of the Constitutional Rights Subcommittee. When Perez listed Ervin's fellow North Carolinian, former United States senator Frank P. Graham, as one of the "pro-Communists" promoting "integration, mongrelization, amalgamation and regimentation of the American people," Ervin interrupted to assert that he admired Dr. Graham, a former president of the University of North Carolina, who was certainly no Communist, just a "very fine fellow" with an "unfortunate propensity" for joining liberal organizations. Perez replied stiffly that he had merely sought to file Graham's background "from the record, for the record." Not content with simply testifying, the Judge also wired President Eisenhower to warn him that there were Communist fronters in Congress pushing integration and that civil rights demonstrations in America "plainly follow the same pattern as in Africa, and evidently are a part of the international Communist conspiracy." He recommended that the administration's bill be amended to prevent "continued Communist and pro-Communist agitations in this country." When he was informed that his telegram had been forwarded to the Justice Department, Perez sent another copy to Ike's special counsel, David Kendal, angrily demanding that it be shown personally to the president.[70]

Perez's testimony and telegram had no significant effect; the bill passed easily. In 1964 a new and stronger civil rights bill, outlawing segregation in public accommodations and facilities, was pending. Again the Judge trekked to Washington to testify. The parish commission council appropriated five thousand dollars to fight the bill, and Perez circulated a rather superfluous petition in Plaquemines urging Louisiana's senators to vote against the measure. Even after the bill passed Congress, Leander refused to surrender. He had printed petitions mailed to each member of the Citizens' Council of Greater New Orleans, asking the governor to conduct a statewide referendum at which the voters could express their approval or disapproval of the civil rights measure. Such a vote was never held.[71]

The Judge fought painfully and arduously against the voting rights bill in 1965. If passed, it would directly affect Plaquemines because it authorized the president to send federal referees to register voters in areas where discrimination existed. Leander complained that the proposal was so loosely worded that it would allow Communist-controlled aliens to be led down the gangplanks and right into the voting booths. In addition to foreigners, it would also grant suffrage to felons, morons, and maniacs, he charged. The bill removed all moral qualifications for voting. This was not surprising, he sneered, in view of "all the queers and everything in government positions, thousand [sic] and thousands of them."[72]

Perez's appearance before the Senate Judiciary Committee to oppose the measure developed into a minor spectacle. This time he inserted more than 249 pages of testimony and documents, including the entire Soviet constitution, into the record. He charged that if Negroes were granted the vote in the South, the next step would be a "Communist-directed governmental authority in the entire territory of the Black Belt." He asserted that the low percentage of Negro registration in Plaquemines was due, not to discrimination, but to the blacks' own lack of civic responsibility.[73] A large Negro registration was a nuisance anyway, he said, because they had to be paid to vote: "You have got to bribe them." At this point, Republican Senator Everett Dirksen of Illinois, an old-school orator who liked his prose and roadsides flowery, asked meaningfully, "Who tries to bribe them?" Perez replied, "The nigger preachers." As for himself, he swore that he had never bought a black vote. Of course, in Plaquemines there were precious few on the market. Dirksen, though he became restless during Perez's testimony, managed to control his temper until the Judge charged that the bill itself was the direct result of a Communist plot.[74] At this point, Dirksen exploded, calling the assertion "about as stupid a statement as has been uttered in this hearing." Republican Senator Hugh Scott of Pennsylvania commented, "I did not think anybody could outdo the Birch Society, but I am afraid Mr. Perez does it." Senator Eastland, for his part, congratulated Perez on a "very fine statement."[75]

Many of the threats to American democracy that Perez saw arose from the fact that too many of the wrong people were allowed to vote. He often charged that, where Negro registration was high, officials lost their nerve and abandoned their sense of racial integrity.

He reasoned, therefore, that if Negroes were denied the vote, then the wishy-washy politicians would no longer be afraid to repress them; the nation could then return to the "American way of life." He did not believe that a vote against what he believed in could be freely and intelligently cast. Every wrong-minded vote was a controlled one. The Negro vote was controlled by the NAACP and through it, presumably, by the Kremlin. The eastern, liberal voters took their orders from the dangerous Communist traitor David Dubinsky, and the strings to organized labor were pulled by the Russian agent Walter Reuther. In his own marshy kingdom, the Judge kept democracy safe by limiting the suffrage to those who agreed with him—a principle he no doubt would have liked to extend to the whole country.

Perez obviously feared that the 1965 bill would open the voting rolls of his parishes to a flood of benighted "Congolese" who might fail to appreciate the benevolent "democracy" meted out by the parish administration. Registered blacks in Plaquemines were so rare as to be considered curiosities; between 1936 and 1953 not a single Negro citizen had been enrolled by the parish registrar of voters.[76] The registrar indeed proved as elusive to blacks as the *feu follets* [77] of the swamps—and about as helpful. To Negroes who asked where he might be found, the registrar was fishing or diligently enrolling voters in some unspecified but always inaccessible section of the parish. The Plaquemines registrar from 1945 to 1958 was Frank Giordano, Leander's nephew. Until 1954 he kept no regular office hours but instead registered applicants at his home in Buras or at substations throughout the parish. He spent several months each year traveling about the parish to the homes of persons whose names had appeared on the preceding roll of registered voters. His schedule, if he had one, was a closely guarded secret. Speculation had it that he sometimes slipped out through a back or side entrance to the courthouse when potential black voters, or unfriendly white applicants, approached. Blacks who waited around the old building at Pointe a la Hache were warned that the parish did not tolerate vagrancy and were prodded to move on. If a Negro applicant chanced to meet the phantom registrar making his rounds, he was told that the busy man did not have his registration books along. The inquisitive black would have to meet him later at his home or office—if he could catch him in.[78] A group of frustrated blacks described the following incident to the Civil Rights Commission. On their way to register one morning they rode the Pointe a la Hache ferry with Registrar Giordano, who was on his way to work. The ferry landing is only a short distance from the registrar's office in the courthouse. But when the blacks, who had practically followed Giordano to work, arrived at his office, they were told that he was not in.[79]

In something of an understatement, Perez admitted to the Senate Judiciary Committee, "We do not go out and beat the bushes to register the Negroes." In fact, as legal adviser to the registrar, Leander had conducted a ward-by-ward canvass to enroll whites but not blacks. He was not about to commit the mistake made in neighboring St. Bernard, he insisted. In that parish, the registrar had foolishly signed up 800 black voters, and now they had to be paid to vote! Nonetheless, Plaquemines Negroes were well provided for. He explained, "They are being well treated. They are being well taken care of."[80] As of March, 1962, the registered voters in Plaquemines totaled 6,906 whites and 43 blacks—in a population totaling 22,545, of which 28.8 percent was nonwhite. Perez did not find it unusual that so few blacks voted. When asked if the black registration seemed unduly small to him, he snapped, "Not at all. Most Negroes are just not equipped to vote,"[81] and elaborated, "If the Negroes took over the government we would have a repetition here of what's going on in the Congo."[82]

Actually, there was little chance of a revolution in Perez's domain. Few Plaquemines Negroes were either financially or psychologically secure enough to take the risk. Disenfranchisement was such a long-standing convention that blacks did not even expect to vote. Their parents and friends did not vote; no candidates representing their interests appeared on the ballot; and many blacks depended upon parish employment. They knew the hazards of manifesting a desire to vote—possible job loss, increased tax assessments, social isolation, cancellation of the lease on one's house, loss of credit for purchasing at local stores—and they realized that their votes would probably be counted out anyway. Most had been given the runaround for so long that they did not bother to try to register.

That fact did not disturb Perez, who commented, "If they are afraid to come and try to register, they're just afraid."[83]

But even in Plaquemines a few persistent blacks had occasionally demanded their rights. On May 25, 1953, several determined blacks appeared at Giordano's home and asked to be registered. Giordano told them that he did not have his registration books with him and could not register them. On June 30, the same Negroes saw a mimeographed circular in the post office at the small community of Potash, stating that registration would be held at the personnel office in Port Sulphur July 1–3. The blacks made several trips to the personnel office, but each time they were told that Giordano was absent. Finally, they were informed that he had transferred his registration facilities to some other place in the ward. The game of hide-and-seek continued until the exasperated blacks finally sued in federal court requesting an injunction against parish discrimination in voter registration. Suddenly, the hitherto spectral Giordano materialized and welcomed the plaintiffs with open poll books. They were registered on November 4, which Giordano said was the first opportunity he had had to depart from his appointed rounds. Giordano considered the event so important that he invited Robert J. Ourso to witness the registration. Ourso took shorthand notes of the conversations between the registrar and the plaintiffs and had transcripts typed. He then submitted the transcripts to the federal judge as evidence that the suit against Giordano should be dismissed because the issue in question had become academic—the plaintiffs had been registered. His plan failed.[84]

As the case dragged on in court, many Negroes began showing up to register. The Reverend Percy Murphy Griffin, a self-educated Negro who had served as an army officer during World War II, attempted to organize a black registration drive. In March, 1953, he had founded the Plaquemines Parish Civic and Political Organization to encourage timorous blacks to register. On May 1, 1954, Griffin and another Negro caught the registrar at home and asked to be enrolled as voters. Giordano told them that he would be unable to register them that day because the books were "across the river in the courthouse" at Pointe a la Hache. The fabrication was transparent because on that very day Giordano had enrolled two whites. The registrar did, however, offer to sign up Griffin if he would meet him at the courthouse at 4 P.M. on May 3. Griffin showed up at the appointed time, accompanied by about seventy-five other blacks of voting age. The sight of so many Negro applicants startled Giordano. Complaining that the Reverend Griffin had "tricked" him, the flustered registrar retreated to the sanctity of his office—a virtual prisoner besieged by black applicants. Giordano kept most of the Negroes standing in line until closing time; only four were actually registered that day. He explained that the blacks, being poorly educated and rather dull-witted, took longer than most whites to fill out their forms. Giordano exerted little effort to help them, although he testified that previously he had sometimes filled out registration forms himself in order to "hurry up the deal." The following day, the registrar bustled about the parish with demonic energy; he signed up seven whites even though he had to travel more than thirty miles to do so.[85]

With several federal lawsuits pending and Justice Department investigators microscopically scrutinizing his activities, Giordano was compelled to establish regular office hours. But he devised new tactics to discourage potential black registrants. His office door remained shut, and only a few blacks at a time were admitted. The others were kept standing in line for hours until finally they were forced to give up and return home. Some stood in line from 10 A.M. until 4 P.M. when the office closed without ever stepping inside. One black man testified that he had made six or seven trips to the courthouse in vain, waiting in line all day each time, before he was finally permitted to enter.[86]

Once into the office, a Negro applicant still faced a mountain of obstacles. State law provided that the registration forms could be used to determine the literacy of applicants. Before the advent of the black voter drive this provision had rarely been used. A handwriting expert testified that during Giordano's tenure a number of applications had been written in the hand of one person, indicating that the forms had been filled out by someone other than the applicants. Following the first attempts at large-scale black registration, the parish police jury directed the registrar to enforce "strictly" the literacy requirements for all applicants. At the same time, permanent registration was adopted, freezing on the rolls the thousands of white voters who had qualified under the old lenient system.[87] New applicants were compelled to run a gauntlet of technicalities that might have boggled the mind of a Harvard professor—had he been black. Under Giordano's successor, Mary Ethel Fox, blacks were summarily disqualified for minute technical errors on their registration forms, although the deputy registrar who graded many of the applications had only a seventh grade education himself. A black schoolteacher, Norma Johnson Cosse, was rejected five times, once for stating her name on the top of her application form as Norma J. Cosse and then signing it as Norma Johnson Cosse. A Negro preacher who failed to enter the date on his form was disqualified for the omission, although two whites who made identical mistakes were registered. Blacks who listed their color as "tan" and "brown" were rejected, but whites who entered their color as "blond" and "auburn" were accepted. Negroes were frequently turned down for incorrectly stating their age in years, months, and days, a complicated computation. Registrar Fox failed to calculate her own age correctly when asked to do so in court, erring by nearly a month.[88]

Perez was intent on remaining one step ahead of his restless black constituents. While they struggled with spelling, punctuation, and mathematical calculations, he personally devised a "constitutional interpretation" examination to disqualify any Negroes who might manage to fill out the forms perfectly. The Judge selected twenty-five passages, some from the U.S. Constitution, others from the ponderous constitution of Louisiana. Each applicant, handed a test card containing three of the passages, was required to interpret two of the three correctly. Leander wrote sample answers to assist the registrar and assistant registrar in grading the tests. Some of the constitutional excerpts called for a lengthy explanation; others could be answered by short, familiar phrases such as "freedom of religion" or "freedom of speech." Theoretically, a potential voter selected one of the twenty-five cards at random, but a Justice Department statistical sample revealed that 86 percent of the qualified white voters had received Cards 2 or 8, those with simple answers.[89] Most of the responses listed by white registrants were identical to the sample answers prepared by Perez, leading federal officials to suspect that whites had been shown the sample answers before taking the test. In fact, one white applicant mistakenly signed the answer card rather than the test. On another occasion the deputy registrar wrote out the answers on a separate sheet of paper so that a white registrant could copy them. When asked to do so in court, some white voters could not even read the questions they claimed to have answered. Registrar Fox admitted that she had helped some people with the constitutional interpretation test, but claimed that she had done so only after they had already answered two questions successfully. There was nothing irregular about this, she contended, because only two correct answers were necessary. Justice Department investigators characterized Fox's explanation as nothing more than a rationalization for discrimination. If two questions had already been correctly answered and that was all that was required, then there would have been no point in answering the third question at all, they argued. Besides, one white registrant had testified that she had been given aid in "interpreting" all three questions. The registrar's contention that she helped those who requested it in filling out the registration card but volunteered no information was likewise sophistical, the Justice Department asserted. It was absurd to say that an applicant had passed a test to which he had been given the answers but had failed because he had not requested the answers. This made the application form a test of temerity rather than literacy, United States attorneys maintained.[90]

In the first five years that the constitutional interpretation test was utilized in Plaquemines, only five blacks managed to register. None of the registered Negroes had received Cards 2 or 8. Whites responding with doubtful answers were sometimes registered, but black applicants whose responses were not letter-perfect were disqualified without explanation. One white was registered who simply answered "I agree" to a statement on the test card. Numerous instances of such blatant discrimination were brought out in hearings held by the Civil Rights Commission in New Orleans in 1960–1961. Before the commission hearings began, the Louisiana legislature hastily moved to forestall potentially incriminating testimony by making it a crime for anyone to complain to federal officials without justification.[91] These efforts were entirely unavailing; a procession

of Plaquemines blacks trooped to the witness stand to tell of en-
demic intimidation and discrimination in the lower delta, coupled
with social and economic ostracization of any black who manifested
a desire to vote. After evaluating the testimony, the Justice Department filed suit against the Plaquemines registrar of voters,
Mary Ethel Fox.[92]

Leander Perez, charging that the litigation was strictly a "propaganda suit" designed to discredit his parish, promised personally to
assist in the registrar's legal defense. He insisted that the only reason blacks did not vote in Plaquemines was because they did not
want to. As he later told a Senate committee, "They [Negroes] do not
have the ambition, they do not have the urge, they do not know
enough about government, they do not care." He claimed that only
thirty-three blacks had attempted to register in Plaquemines since
1956. Of that number, Leander admitted that "there may be four
doubtful cases of those who have applied to register." He said that
one of the doubtful cases was a Negro teacher and another a
preacher.[93]

Justice Department attorneys pored over old parish records,
documenting scores of misdeeds that had occurred during Giordano's tenure. It was not enough to enjoin the parish from future
discrimination, they argued; the courts must rectify past injustices.
Fox, strongly seconded by Perez, firmly disagreed. She admitted
that some irregularities had occurred under her predecessor. But
the past was past; the inequities had been corrected. What counted
was how she ran her office now. Evidence of discrimination during
her own term was less abundant, but it did exist. Outright fraud was
rarely necessary any more because exclusion from the rolls had become ingrained in most blacks, who had given up all hope until the
Justice Department had moved in. Fox stated that most of the
documented discrepancies during her incumbency were due to the
actions of a former deputy registrar, whom she had fired after only
two months on the job. Her record was one of improvement, she asserted. Considering the conditions in Plaquemines when she took
office, her statement was true enough.[94]

The Louisiana legislature, eager to defuse charges that the constitutional interpretation test was discriminatory, enacted during

the Fox trial legislation replacing the controversial test with an "objective," multiple-choice "citizenship" examination. This was intended to silence critics who claimed that registrars had discriminated in grading the old tests. The protracted tension induced by the proceedings worked Fox into a state of nervous exhaustion; she had to be replaced as registrar.[95]

The decision of U.S. District Judge Robert A. Ainsworth, Jr., furnished half a loaf to both plaintiffs and defendants. The Justice Department had proved that some discrimination had indeed occurred, but it had failed to substantiate a *pattern* of discrimination in Plaquemines, Ainsworth stated. And, the chief barrier to Negro registration, the constitutional interpretation test, had now been abolished. The judge explained that he could not issue a blanket order directing the Plaquemines registrar to enroll all blacks of voting age as requested by the Justice Department, because this would in effect abolish state registration requirements. Registration was a state function and the literacy test, if administered equitably, was not unreasonable, he said. But, to prevent a recurrence of attempts to exclude Negroes from the voting rolls, he enjoined the defendants "against discrimination because of race or color in the registration processes in Plaquemines Parish." To ensure compliance he directed the registrar to file with the court monthly reports "reflecting the name, address and race of each applicant for registration, the disposition of his application and, if rejected, the reason therefor."[96]

The decision was considerably less than total vindication for Plaquemines, but the Justice Department appealed because Ainsworth's order failed to rectify the racial imbalance created by the freeze of illiterate whites on the voting rolls. The Fifth Circuit Court of Appeals disputed Judge Ainsworth's contention that no discernable pattern of discrimination existed, but rather than overturn his preliminary injunction it remanded the case, ordering that the permanent injunction be tried on additional evidence.[97]

The litigation bogged down and was eventually superseded by the Voting Rights Act of 1965. Black registration in the deep delta increased only haltingly until passage of this law. At the time of the 1964 gubernatorial election the Plaquemines books showed 7,675 whites and only 95 blacks registered. Meanwhile, Perez frenetically combatted black voting on the same level. His most imaginative proposal was a 1964 bill that would have charged each voter a per capita share of the total cost involved in conducting a statewide election—a sort of poll tax. This measure never cleared the legislature.[98]

When federal registrars entered Plaquemines to enroll Negroes pursuant to the Voting Rights Act, Perez countered with a white registration drive, vowing that more whites than blacks would register with the federal examiners. He appeared on television statewide to urge that the rest of Louisiana follow the example of Plaquemines in beating the federals at their own game. The Plaquemines Parish Commission Council joined the fray by offering a five-hundred-dollar reward for the arrest and conviction of any person who threatened a Negro for failing to register with the federal examiners. The number of Negro voters in Plaquemines increased dramatically, but the Judge made good his promise; more whites than blacks signed up with the federal officials.[99]

Even without Leander's recruitment of new white voters, there were far too few Negroes enrolled to threaten his political domination. In fact, if every black in the parish had registered, it would not have mattered; the Negro population was simply too small. The warfare between Perez and the federal government was a contest of pride and willpower; the spoils of office were not at stake. Far more significant, from a practical standpoint, were federal efforts to end racial segregation in public schools. In this all-out struggle Judge Perez employed tactics that might have made General William Tecumseh Sherman blanch. But it was a fight he was doomed to lose.

THIRTEEN

The Second Battle of New Orleans

The prolonged court battle to desegregate the New Orleans public schools began in 1952 when a Negro plaintiff filed the case of *Bush* v. *Orleans Parish School Board*. The school board fought a tedious and costly court battle to maintain a separate system of schools, advised by some of the leading segregationists in the state, including Leander Perez. The battery of attorneys, who developed ingenious arguments, at one point claimed that the plaintiffs had not proved that they were in fact Negroes. In 1956 the federal district judge, J. Skelly Wright, enjoined the school board from operating a segregated school system and ordered implementation of desegregation "with all deliberate speed," but he set no deadline. Although admitting that the process of desegregation would be difficult, he concluded that "the magnitude of the problem may not nullify the principle." [1]

In the summer of 1959 the plaintiffs asked Wright to clarify his injunction, and the New Orleans-born judge then ordered the school board to submit a desegregation plan by May, 1960. In April the school board polled the parents of public school children to determine whether they preferred closed schools to integrated schools. The parents voted for open schools by a small majority; but, counting only the votes of white parents, the result was overwhelmingly for closed schools. The board announced that it would consider only the opinions of the white parents. [2]

When the board failed to submit a desegregation time-table by May, Wright drew up his own plan. He outlined a grade-a-year schedule, beginning with the first grade, and ordered it to be put into effect in September, 1960. [3]

253

The Orleans Parish Schools were administered by a five-member board, all white and all of whom had been elected to office as segregationists. But four of them, convinced that their legal remedies had been exhausted, felt that they had no alternative but to obey the court mandate. They were determined to keep the schools open, even if this meant accepting token integration. The fifth member, Emile Wagner, was a die-hard segregationist who preferred closed schools to desegregated ones.[4]

Many observers predicted that school desegregation would come to New Orleans without incident. The Crescent City was known for its cosmopolitan, permissive atmosphere, and on racial matters south Louisiana was considered the most liberal section of the Deep South. Most of the members of the Orleans Parish School Board had agreed to accept the court order, and the mayor, deLesseps Morrison, was a racial moderate. Had the problem been left entirely in the hands of city officials, desegregation might well have proceeded smoothly.[5]

But the New Orleans area was also the home of Leander Perez and the largest Citizens' Council in the state. The Judge prepared legal briefs, wrote legislation, delivered back-stiffening speeches at council rallies, encouraged prosegregation demonstrations, and helped organize boycotts. Perez had recently masterminded the election of Governor Jimmie Davis in a blatantly racist campaign, and Davis had made Perez stalwart E. W. ("Kelly") Gravolet, Jr., of Plaquemines his Senate floor leader. The legislature was dominated by unyielding segregationists from north Louisiana who believed that token integration in 1960 would soon lead to full-scale integration. Segregationists throughout the South watched New Orleans carefully because it was the first Deep South city to face school desegregation. Mississippi Supreme Court justice Tom Brady telegraphed Mississippi governor Ross Barnett that if they lost the "battle of New Orleans" they would be fighting on their own soil within a year. Southern segregationists resolved to make a determined stand in Orleans Parish.[6]

Perez drafted legislation creating the thirteen-member State Sovereignty Commission to lead the battle. The commission, vested with broad powers of investigation and subpoena, served as a clearinghouse for segregation legislation. Many of its bills sprang from the fertile mind of Perez or were copied from other states. Almost all of them were actually drawn up by the Judge, who even researched the Reconstruction era for ideas with which to thwart integration. The sheer bulk of the state's legal defense meant that it would take some time for the federal courts to review it and declare it unconstitutional. By that time new measures could be developed. The federal courts eventually resorted to wholesale declarations of unconstitutionality against groups of laws at one time.[7]

Louisiana's attorney general, Jack P. F. Gremillion, secured an injunction from a state court to prevent the Orleans Parish School Board from assigning black pupils to white schools. The legislature authorized the governor to close all public schools in the state if any were integrated, and on August 17 Governor Davis issued an executive order by which he superseded the Orleans board and seized control of the city's public school system. That same day, thirty-one white parents filed suit, in the *Williams* v. *Davis* case, to prevent the closing of New Orleans public schools. The white parents first requested that the court revoke its integration order because it put the local school board in a position of having to defy either state or federal law. Alternatively, they asked Judge Wright to prevent the state from enforcing its segregation laws, which would permit the school board to carry out the federal court mandate. Wright issued an order fulfilling the latter request. The state court was enjoined from enforcing its injunction, and Attorney General Gremillion was prohibited from attempting to procure additional injunctions interfering with desegregation.[8]

The school board was finally free to devise a desegregation plan, but little time remained before the September deadline. A week before the scheduled opening of the schools, the vexed board requested that the deadline be extended. Impressed by the policy makers' sincerity, Judge Wright extended the deadline until November 14. The schools opened in September on a segregated basis, but attendance was down by about 3,000 because of the uncertainty of the situation. The Citizens' Council of Greater New Orleans responded to the school officials' cooperation by circulating petitions for removal of those board members who preferred integration to closing the schools.[9]

The school board used Louisiana's pupil placement law to screen out most of the 135 blacks who applied for transfers to white schools by subjecting the applicants to a battery of mental and psychological tests. Finally, 5 little Negro girls were selected as the first of their race to enter white schools. Their identities, as well as which schools they were to enter, remained secret.[10]

Meanwhile, New Orleans held what amounted to a referendum on open or closed schools. Matthew Sutherland, one of the four moderates on the school board, faced reelection opposed by three other candidates. His chief rival was John Singreen, whose platform was to close the schools rather than integrate. Singreen, whose campaign was partly planned in Perez's office, had strong Citizens' Council backing, but on November 8, Sutherland defeated all three of his opponents by a convincing margin, seemingly an endorsement of moderation.[11]

On that same day, Louisianians also voted in the Nixon-Kennedy presidential election. Before this election the federal government had not been a party to the *Bush* suit because Eisenhower feared that intervention in behalf of the plaintiffs by a Republican administration would hurt Nixon's chances of winning Louisiana. Nixon, however, lost the state despite the caution. Two days after the election the United States attorney in New Orleans requested and received an injunction from Judge Wright restraining all Louisiana sheriffs, police chiefs, and mayors from interfering with federal officers in their duties arising from school desegregation. Just as the federal government stepped up efforts to compel the state to desegregate, Perez and his fellow segregationists endeavored to persuade Louisiana's electors to break their pledge to vote for Kennedy unless he agreed to forestall integration in New Orleans. A group of state political leaders, headed by Governor Davis' executive secretary Chris Fraser, approached Kennedy for his reaction to the court restraining order against state leaders. Kennedy, wary of alienating southern supporters before the electoral votes were cast, declined to comment on the order and instructed his liaison man, Clark Clifford, to attempt to appease the angry southerners. This temporizing angered Kennedy's northern supporters; the Chicago *Daily Tribune* admonished him for demonstrating a lack of courage.[12]

Three days after the presidential election both New Orleans daily newspapers editorialized in favor of open schools, even if this meant accepting limited integration. An organization called Save Our Schools worked to keep the New Orleans public school system open, but moderates still had little voice in the state government. On October 28, Governor Davis called for a special session of the legislature to assemble November 4, ten days before the New Orleans schools were scheduled to desegregate. Judge Perez was present at a secret strategy session held several days before the legislature met. Davis, refusing to reveal his plans so as not to tip off opponents or the federal courts, unveiled his segregation package only twenty minutes before the lawmakers convened at noon on November 4. Davis leaders rushed a package of twenty-nine segregation bills to the administration-dominated House Judiciary B Committee, whose chairman was E. W. Gravolet of Point a la Hache. The first bill appropriated $168,000 to cover expenses of the special session. Other bills provided for the closing of all state schools if a single school were integrated, emasculated the Orleans Parish School Board of all of its authority, and denied diplomas and credits to children who attended integrated public schools. The state's compulsory attendance law was repealed, and provisions were made to revoke the certificates of teachers instructing classes in violation of the state's segregation laws.[13]

The package, a combination of laws borrowed from other southern states and old Louisiana statutes, was compiled by Perez and other militant segregationists. The theoretical basis of the package was a bill that purported to interpose the state's sovereignty between the Orleans Parish School Board and the federal government and provided for the arrest of any federal officials who attempted to enforce a national decree that the state had nullified. Perez—who had been studying the old doctrine of interposition ever since the *Brown* decision and in 1956 had addressed the American Bar Association on the topic "Interposition: What Is It?"—personally drafted the measure.[14] Davis' whole segregation package cleared both houses with only token opposition.[15]

Before the obstructive acts could be put into effect, Judge Wright issued a temporary restraining order against enforcement of the entire collection of laws. Governor Davis promptly summoned the legislature back into session on November 13, twenty-four hours before desegregation was to begin. The lawmakers proclaimed November 14 a state school holiday, but Wright enjoined enforcement of the vacation. At the request of the Orleans Parish School Board he also ordered more than seven hundred state and local officials not to interfere with the orderly desegregation of New Orleans schools. The legislature responded by removing the four moderate school board members; it also fired Orleans Parish school superintendent Dr. James Redmond and school board attorney Samuel Rosenberg.[16]

On November 14 schools throughout the state observed the legislature's school holiday, but New Orleans schools remained open under court order. One small Negro girl attended William Frantz Public School and three other black first graders attended McDonogh No. 19. Both schools were in the Ninth Ward, a low-income section of the city that was probably the least ready to accept racial mixing, and McDonogh No. 19 was only a few blocks from the Orleans–St. Bernard border, where Perez's domain began. No violence occurred at either school, but crowds of shouting, resentful whites milled around outside. White parents arrived all day to remove their children from the two schools, but by the end of the day it appeared that desegregation had been accomplished without incident. The staid *Times-Picayune* featured an editorial entitled "Dreadful Day Comes at Last," but called for only legal resistance and cautioned against violence.[17]

The following day dispelled any hopes that mixing might be brought about smoothly. Large crowds of protesting adults and teenagers, many of them from Plaquemines and St. Bernard, gathered outside the two desegregated schools. Twelve persons were arrested for rowdy conduct, but no violence occurred. Among these was a St. Bernard deputy sheriff, who was paroled by District Judge J. Bernard Cocke at the request of District Attorney Perez.[18]

That night more than five thousand embittered whites packed a Citizens' Council protest rally at the Municipal Auditorium and began signing a petition to impeach J. Skelly Wright. The rally featured a play on "mongrelization," in which half of the cast of white children appeared with blackened faces. They held hands with and kissed their unblackened schoolmates while the moderator told the audience, "This is what will happen when niggers get in your school."[19] Speaking at the rally, former state senator Willie Rainach advocated a "scorched earth" policy for integrated schools, meaning a total abandonment by whites. Rainach and Perez both called for a march on the school board building, mayor's office, and Judge Wright's office, and Perez pilloried Mayor Morrison, the Communists, and "Zionist Jews." He called Morrison "the real culprit, malefactor, and double crosser—the weasel, snake-headed mayor of yours." Perez concluded, "Don't wait for your daughter to be raped by these Congolese. Don't wait until the burrheads are forced into your schools. Do something about it now."[20]

The next morning the protest march materialized with belligerent whites chanting, "Two, four, six, eight; we don't want to integrate."[21] A crowd estimated at 1,000 to 3,000 whites, mostly truant teenagers, stormed the school board building and city hall, but were contained by policemen using clubs and fire hoses. The frustrated mob then broke into smaller groups and roamed the city. White teenagers threw rocks at Negroes in cars and buses. That night a Negro porter was knifed, two white men were shot by a Negro, and another was shot by a roving band of Negroes. The police made 250 arrests, mostly of blacks.[22] Both Mayor Morrison and Governor Davis made statements deploring the violence, but Perez was incensed because police had been used against white demonstrators. Morrison attributed the outburst of sporadic rioting to racial animosity aroused by the Citizens' Council rally.[23]

The state legislature began its second special session with both houses adopting a resolution commending the resisting parents for their "brave fight." Governor Davis' second parcel of antimixing measures was sped through with even less opposition than the first. One administration strategy was to deprive the Orleans Parish School Board of all financial support. Businesses were asked not to deal with the "defunct" board, and banks were ordered not to honor school board checks. Perez outlined a bill providing for education grants for children attending nonsectarian, nonprofit, private schools, which was quickly approved by the lawmakers.[24]

Leander also concocted a scheme to avoid a federal ruling on a new law replacing the Orleans Parish School Board with an appointive one. Ordinarily, federal courts will not review decisions of state courts unless one of the litigants appeals. If both parties in a suit testing a segregation statute were segregationists, the decision was not likely to be appealed, so Perez's assistant, George Singelmann, filed suit to nullify the act authorizing the governor to appoint a new school board. The state supreme court upheld the law and dismissed the suit. Singelmann, of course, did not appeal, but the ploy failed because the Justice Department challenged the ruling in federal court. A three-judge federal panel nullified the law, pointing out that it was part of a larger proceeding in which a federal question was involved. The statutes enacted by Davis' second special session, like those of the first, were soon invalidated by the federal courts.[25]

While Perez busied himself framing legislation for Governor Davis he also helped organize boycotts of the integrated schools. By the end of the first week of desegregation every white child had been withdrawn from McDonogh No. 19. Less than two months later, when John Thompson, a white, decided to defy the boycott by sending his son there, he promptly lost his job at Walgreen's drugstore. The company's national office intervened to reinstate Thompson, but within a few days he had succumbed to local pressure and left town.[26] At Frantz, where only one little Negro girl attended, the boycott was never total. The child's father, a gas station attendant, was fired because his white employer feared his business would be hurt, but was then hired by a black gas station owner. The pressure on the white parents who continued to send their children to Frantz was even greater; they were subjected to an organized telephone campaign of threats and abuse. One home was smeared with red paint. Rocks were hurled through the windows of one family's home every night; the whole family moved into one bedroom that was relatively sheltered from the rock throwing. Vandals slashed the tires, cracked the windows, and twisted the radio aerial on another family's car. Volunteers who drove the white children to school were threatened with death, arson, and disfigurement.[27]

The boycott at the two schools would not have been nearly so effective if Perez had not arranged for most of the white children enrolled there to attend school in neighboring St. Bernard Parish. Some of the children entered the regular St. Bernard school system, but the parish's public schools could not accommodate all of the displaced students. Perez, Citizens' Council leader C. E. Vetter, and others leased an old Ford Motor Company warehouse in Arabi. Vetter made available paint, lumber, and other materials, and a horde of volunteers converted it into a school in little more than a weekend. The St. Bernard school board furnished most of the operating funds for the school for the remainder of the school year. Before it opened for the fall session of 1961, the Justice Department filed suit to stop the school board from funding the private, white school. While the case was pending, Leander arranged to build a permanent school in New Orleans, the Ninth Ward Private School, to serve the same purpose. The school was completed while the litigation to close the St. Bernard school was in progress, and most of the students transferred there.[28]

Perez had been active in an effort to create private white schools even before the public schools had opened in 1960. He urged the parents of each New Orleans public school to organize a cooperative to create a private school if the public one were closed. Perez drafted charters for the schools and explained to interested parents the procedure for forming co-ops. He not only helped raise money among his wealthy friends and made generous contributions himself, but he also made property available, arranged for buildings, and enlisted volunteer workers. In New Orleans 24 private school cooperatives were chartered, but this was far from enough; New Orleans had 118 public schools. The school board at first allowed the parents organizing the co-ops to use the public school buildings for meetings, but permission was withdrawn after the board officials decided that the meetings had become political in nature.[29]

Governor Davis called the legislature to five consecutive special sessions, a new Louisiana record, and expended more than half a million dollars of state money in his futile fight to prevent the desegregation of New Orleans schools. In his own phrase, the legislature had taken the "last step before secession." [30] On the eve of the fifth special session, administration leaders and leading segregationists, including Judge Perez, held a secret strategy conference in the governor's office. Davis, who was under federal court orders not to interfere with desegregation, claimed that he did not attend, but reporters saw him, with his coat collar turned up to conceal the lower part of his face, slip from the meeting room through a side door. [31]

Support for the Davis segregation measures dwindled as it became apparent that the federal courts would continue to declare the legislature's works unconstitutional. The first real legislative opposition to Davis occurred when he proposed a one-cent sales tax increase to finance a program of tuition grants. Although the bill was labeled a segregation measure, it would have provided seventy times more revenue than would be needed for the grants. The sales tax was defeated by a coalition that included former senator Rainach, labor leaders, and New Orleans legislators. Rainach's influence had declined after his defeat in the 1959 gubernatorial campaign, and Perez had become the governor's chief adviser on segregation. Davis would probably not have gone as far as he did in trying to preserve racial separation had he not been influenced by Perez. By the fifth special session, the Davis administration had shifted from a policy of defiance to one of minimizing actual integration. [32]

Governor Davis, wary of the federal injunction against interfering with desegregation, made himself unavailable to federal officials who sought to determine his role in the obstruction of orderly integration. When federal marshals attempted to serve him with a summons, the governor could not be found. The marshals then tried to serve Davis' aides, who refused to reach out their hands when the summonses were offered. The papers fell to the floor, where they were laminated under sheets of plexiglass, except for one, which was plastered over. Davis never did appear in court, but the issue soon became academic. [33]

In December, 1960, Perez, who had been serving as assistant district attorney to his son Lea, retired in order to devote full time to the segregation crusade. Later that month he appeared on David Susskind's nationally televised "Open End" program along with four other guests. The Judge monopolized the conversation, informing his host that the 1954 Supreme Court desegregation decision was no more the law of the land than "any other Communist doctrine." Following his appearance, Perez received a spate of congratulatory letters and telegrams, but was pilloried by liberal newspapers.[34]

In 1961, four additional Orleans public schools admitted eight more blacks. The Citizens' Council sustained a boycott briefly but soon abandoned the effort. Most whites seemed ready to adjust to the accomplished fact. Segregationists turned to the creation of a private school system financed by state tuition grants. The following year desegregation proceeded more rapidly as Judge Wright ordered all New Orleans public schools to desegregate the first through sixth grades and enjoined the parish school board from utilizing the pupil placement law. Wright's desegregation plan was subsequently modified, but the prohibition of the pupil placement law was retained. Under the new plan, twenty New Orleans public schools accepted about one hundred Negroes for the 1962–1963 session.[35]

Judge Perez remained unmoved, refusing to hold out any hope for a peaceful solution to the desegregation problem. "The integration movement," he said, "is a Communist conspiracy backed by misguided Federal politicians. But the schemes of the Communists and fellow travelers are proceeding slowly in comparison with public resistance." After the school board announced the integration of four additional schools in 1961, Leander predicted it would be followed by the "usual avalanche of brain-washing propaganda." Some of the propaganda, he said, would emanate from "press releases by rabbis and other 'brotherhood' church people."[36]

Before the 1962–1963 school year white children assigned to integrated schools had sometimes found a haven in segregated Catholic schools. By 1962, fully half the city's white students were enrolled in Catholic schools; before the integration crisis, Catholic school enrollment had been significantly smaller. On March 27, 1962, Archbishop Joseph Francis Rummel ordered all parochial schools in the New Orleans archdiocese to desegregate all twelve grades. He had been a foe of segregation for many years; as far back as 1949, Rummel had branded racial segregation un-Christian. The next year he had ordered White and Colored signs removed from churches under his jurisdiction. In 1953 he had issued an order stating that blacks should no longer be required to take communion last, and in 1956 he had again labeled segregation sinful and announced plans to desegregate Catholic schools. The boss of Plaquemines vehemently objected to the archbishop's school integration proposal; he ceased contributing to the Catholic church and urged other segregationists to follow his example. The Citizens' Council denounced Rummel, and a cross was burned on the prelate's lawn. A group of prominent Louisiana Catholics led by Emile Wagner formed the Association of Catholic Laymen to oppose parochial school integration but was disbanded after Rummel threatened its members with excommunication. However, the strong opposition to his plan forced him to rework his timetable for desegregation. He realized that integration of Catholic schools before public schools were mixed would cause a flight of Catholic children to public schools. When the public schools were integrated in 1960, Rummel had a pastoral letter read in churches throughout the archdiocese urging the people to pray for integration. Perez denounced the letter through the newspapers and over television, and in Plaquemines the church was denied use of the Belle Chasse auditorium for a fund-raising fair.[37]

Despite Rummel's pronouncements, Catholic schools remained segregated when the public schools were integrated. The archbishop's declaration that desegregation would begin in 1962 brought a torrent of protest from Perez and other segregationists. Leander urged "every decent white parent" to take his child out of the parochial schools and to cease contributing to the church. "Cut off their water," he said. "Quit giving them money to feed their fat bellies, and you'll see an about-face."[38]

Senator Gravolet of Plaquemines warned that Catholic schools would face a boycott if integration were carried out. Jackson Ricau, executive director of the New Orleans Citizens' Council, issued a statement condemning the Catholic hierarchy for "imposing integration on an unwilling people." Mrs. B. J. Gaillot, Catholic leader of a small but militantly segregationist group known as Save Our Nation, rounded up eight sign carriers to picket the archdiocese. The total soon dwindled to one or two. Although Save Our Nation never gained more than a handful of followers, Gaillot became the most vocal of all New Orleans segregationists. Author of a pamphlet entitled *God Gave the Law of Segregation to Moses on Mount Sinai,* she insisted that God had written the covenant of segregation on a tablet of stone and given it to Moses. She told an interviewer that she had a bank vault filled with notes from which she planned to write a two-volume book about race. Gaillot had disliked Perez for many years, but their mutual fight against the integration of Catholic schools had finally made them allies.[39]

On March 31, 1962, Archbishop Rummel addressed letters of admonition to Perez, Gaillot, and Ricau: "In the spirit of fatherly solicitude we deem it our duty to admonish you that any further attempt by you through word or deed to hinder our orders or provoke our devoted people to disobedience or rebellion against the Church will subject you to excommunication."[40] Ricau and Gaillot acknowledged receiving the letters, but Perez claimed that he had not received one. The New Orleans chancery said that a letter had been delivered to the Judge's home on Newcomb Boulevard in New Orleans marked "special delivery, registered mail, return receipt requested, deliver to addressee only." The letter was returned to the chancery with notations showing that the post office had tried to deliver it on March 31, April 2, and April 6. Notices were left at the address informing Perez that a special delivery letter awaited him at the post office.[41]

Gaillot demanded an audience with Rummel, threatening to sit on his doorstep until he saw her. After being denied an audience, she published the warning letter. Gaillot blamed Archbishop John Cody rather than Rummel for the planned desegregation. Cody, who had been elevated from bishop of Kansas City to coadjutor archbishop the previous year, was scheduled to succeed the eighty-five-year-old Rummel in the New Orleans archdiocese.[42]

Perez, Ricau, and Gaillot did not curtail their segregation activities. The day after Gaillot published the archbishop's letter, Leander denounced integration in a speech to the Citizens' Council of Greater New Orleans. Ricau published a reply to Rummel claiming that the archbishop had exceeded his authority by threatening excommunication. The prelate proved as unyielding as the segregationists. On April 16, 1962, Monsignor Charles J. Plauche, chancellor of the archdiocese, told a news conference that Perez, Ricau, and Gaillot had been excommunicated for defying the archbishop's warning. The three would be denied the church sacraments and church burial. They also lost their right to attend mass, but would not be physically ejected if they chose to attend.[43]

The day following her excommunication, Gaillot hurled herself at the feet of Archbishop Rummel while he was leading a group that had come on a pilgrimage. She pleaded for mercy but declared that she would not change her views on segregation. The archbishop, surprised at this emotional outburst, managed to ignore her, and she was dragged away by some of the pilgrims.[44]

Perez, on the other hand, was utterly unrepentant. Claiming that his excommunication was merely an attempt to intimidate others, he continued to attend mass and also to speak to segregation groups. He helped organize a new group called the Parents and Friends of Catholic Children and told the members, "Excommunication cannot send you to hell, but integration can send your children to a hell on earth."[45] As he entered the hall for one speech, the Judge handed out slips of paper reading, Better Excommunication Than Integration.[46] Perez claimed that a three-million-dollar federal grant for a low-cost housing project sponsored by the New Orleans archdiocese was a bribe to encourage the church to integrate. He solemnly compared his excommunication to the burning at the stake of Joan of Arc, who was later canonized. In a more jovial mood, he told a reporter that he and a group of friends had organized their own church. "We call it the Perez-byterians," he chuckled.[47]

Both Ricau and Gaillot took their excommunications more seriously. Gaillot quit picketing and stopped attending church with her family. She demanded an audience with the pope, warning that if she did not obtain one she would publish a book revealing the sinfulness of integration. The embattled housewife scheduled a debate with a New York social worker but canceled it upon discovering that her opponent was a Negro. Gaillot also experienced financial difficulties as a result of her stand for segregation. Her husband lost his job, so Perez helped put one of her sons through college. Ricau toned down his opposition to integration but continued his work with the South Louisiana Citizens' Council. Sixteen months after his excommunication he had risen from executive director to president of the organization. Ricau was prohibited from escorting his own daughter down the aisle at her church wedding.[48]

Archbishop Rummel persisted in his plans to desegregate parochial schools. Ironically, the first one in the archdiocese to be integrated was Our Lady of Good Harbor, a small elementary school at Buras, in the heart of Perez's delta bailiwick. No effort had yet been made to desegregate the public schools in Plaquemines. Our Lady of Good Harbor was scheduled to open in late August, 1962, several days before schools in New Orleans. Leander promised that schools in his parish would not be desegregated without a fight. The night before the school was to open, the Judge held a mass rally in the Buras auditorium, where he told Catholics that they should withdraw their children if the school were desegregated and that parents who did not participate in the boycott should be ostracized. Perez even suggested that protesters form a human ring around the school to prevent blacks from entering. He arranged to cut off all local aid to the parochial school, thus denying it the use of parish school buses, new state textbooks, school lunch funds, and federal milk funds distributed by the parish.[49]

On the same night as the rally, Father Christopher Schneider, the parish priest of Buras, prepared to gas up the parochial school buses that would be used the following day. As he started out of the driveway, he discovered that the vehicles had no brakes. The master cylinders on both buses had been drained of all brake fluid.[50]

Before the school opened, word leaked out that Marcus Prout, a Negro, planned to send his children to Our Lady of Good Harbor. His employer called and asked him to come by for a talk. When Prout arrived, his employer told him, "Marcus, I don't know what you did, but Judge Perez told me that I have to get rid of you or he will get rid of me. I have to stick with the people with the money."[51]

Despite losing his job, Prout sent his children to Our Lady of

Good Harbor on the first day of school. Five black children attended class along with thirty-eight whites. A large crowd of angry white parents gathered in front of the school. Parish officials unloaded folding chairs for the white protesters and arranged them in neat rows, and umbrellas were set up to shield them from the blistering August sun. The parish government also supplied ice water for the demonstrators. Perez appeared to address the crowd, telling them that the present crisis was a greater challenge than the many hurricanes the parish had endured. Father Schneider, deciding to hold only a half day of school, dismissed the children at noon. As he left the school, one of the whites shouted, "You haven't seen the end of this."[52]

That night Marcus Prout received a phone call from Sheriff Chester Wooten, who asked him to take his children out of school until he could get the situation under control. Something dreadful might happen, he warned. Prout then called a New Orleans businessman and arranged for a job in the city. The next morning he and his family moved out of Plaquemines.[53]

During the same tempestuous night, an anonymous caller warned Father Schneider that a bomb had been planted in the school, but nothing was found. When school opened the following morning, about a hundred white parents and twelve pickets were present. Twenty-six white children showed up for class, but none of the blacks returned. At noon an automobile equipped with two loudspeakers parked on the highway across from the school, and a record of "Dixie" was played as the children marched back from church services.[54]

Strong pressure was also exerted on the few white parents who had kept their children in school. Squads of segregationists, assigned to the families with children in school, made harassing phone calls to the families and threateningly drove by their homes at night in a lengthy parade. One of the parents who had not observed the boycott was Harold Mitchell, a mechanic for a large company located in Plaquemines. At 2 A.M. Mitchell received a call from a representative of his company, followed a little later by a visit. The representative said that he had been told by top company officials to ask Mitchell to withdraw his children from school. The whole company had been threatened with closure if he refused to comply, an occurrence that would put five hundred men out of work. Mitchell took his family out of the parish that very night.[55]

One of the Catholic sisters at Our Lady of Good Harbor also received a call that night, which warned that the sisters and priests would be tarred and feathered the next morning. When morning came, Father Schneider found the sidewalk in front of the school littered with feathers, as if someone had split open a mattress. He then called the press over and announced that the school would be closed because of numerous threats of physical violence and insufficient police protection. The Catholic school for mulattoes at Buras was also shut down because the mulatto parents had protested when several blacks had been admitted.[56]

Our Lady of Good Harbor remained closed over the Labor Day weekend. When it reopened on Tuesday the crowds were again present, and Perez made another speech. None of the blacks and only thirteen white children reported for class. Attendance rose to eighteen by Thursday, but then dropped to zero by Friday, September 7. Father Schneider thereupon shut down the school again. It reopened after the weekend, but no students showed up. Months after all students had ceased attending classes, pickets continued to keep a morning watch at the school. One day the teachers found the door padlocked and chained shut. The janitor had to cut through the chain with a hacksaw so that the priests and nuns could get into their own school. In mid-November, two gun barrels of bird shot were fired into the rectory of Our Lady of Good Harbor Church by someone passing in an automobile.[57]

For 249 days the doors of the empty schoolhouse remained open as a symbolic gesture. The teachers reported to work daily and awaited students, but none came. Finally, Our Lady of Good Harbor closed for the summer, and Father Schneider planned to reopen on a desegregated basis for the 1963–1964 session. Shortly before classes were scheduled to begin, however, one of the nuns received a sinister phone call from an unidentified person who warned, "If you take those Negroes into our new white school it will be blown to pieces with you in it." That night the roof of the school was soaked with gasoline from three five-gallon cans, a fuse was made from forty feet of string, and just before midnight the fuse was lit. One classroom was demolished and the remainder of the school was damaged.[58] The following day Archbishop John Cody announced that the school would be closed to protect the lives of the sisters, priests, and children. Our Lady of Good Harbor has never reopened. The damage to the school was repaired, but, because Plaquemines officials refused to grant a repair permit, electrical service was withheld.[59]

In September, 1963, CBS television aired an hour-long national program entitled "The Priest and the Politician," which was narrated by Dan Rather and detailed the struggle between Perez and Father Schneider over Our Lady of Good Harbor School. The telecast elicited mail from all over the country, much of it from people who had never heard of Perez before. Most of the correspondents urged the Judge to keep up the fight.[60]

Although Leander managed to prevent desegregation in his native parish, integration of parochial schools in New Orleans proceeded on schedule. The impact of racial mixing in all twelve grades of the Catholic institutions was lessened by the fact that the public school system moved from token to full-scale integration at the same time. On the first day of Catholic school desegregation, 104 blacks attended 20 previously all-white schools. The changeover was peaceful, although white crowds gathered at most of the schools and white mothers picketed two schools and the archbishop's residence. Among the pickets at one of the schools was Mrs. B. J. Gaillot, who carried a sign reading, "Cody Scared to Talk Bible with Me." Attendance at the desegregated parochial schools gradually rose to almost normal levels after an initial decline. During the next two years, parochial schools were not inundated with blacks as the segregationists had feared. By October, 1964, there were 19,917 white children and only 661 black children attending integrated Catholic schools in New Orleans. In none of the integrated schools did the blacks constitute as much as one-half of the enrollment.[61]

Most white New Orleanians gradually came to accept integration as inevitable, but resistance remained militant in Plaquemines, where the effort to integrate parochial schools had failed. There were no organized civil rights groups in the parish, and the federal government was slow to move. Plaquemines remained one of the final redoubts of segregation.

FOURTEEN

Leander's Last Stand

In 1959 Leander Perez boasted to the New Orleans Citizens' Council, "I'll be damned if they ever integrate Plaquemines Parish. If they come to Plaquemines, we will deputize every able body [sic] person in the Parish if necessary." But the federals pressed on. Three years later, after New Orleans had ungracefully yielded to court-ordered integration of its public schools, the Judge was no less adamant in defense of his segregated fiefdom. He threw down the challenge: "They won't have as easy a time integrating Plaquemines Parish as they have had in other places."[1] It was a rare Perez understatement.

For several years after the New Orleans schools had been integrated, the Plaquemines commission council[2] voted yearly appropriations of five thousand dollars for "expenses in defense of parish interest in segregation." The resolution authorizing the 1964 expenditure directed that the money be used to fight the civil rights bill then pending before the Senate, which if enacted "would impose a federal gestapo to supervise and enforce communistic regimentation of our people and our way of life." The council used the money to employ John C. Satterfield's right-wing Coordinating Committee for Fundamental American Freedoms, Inc., to research the bill and submit proof to the Senate that it was designed by the Communists to stir up racial strife. Satterfield's proof must have been unconvincing; the landmark legislation passed.[3]

Racism permeated every aspect of life in the deep delta. A white girl who traveled down from New Orleans to watch a Negro religious celebration was accused of being a Communist by sheriff's deputies and thrown in jail for "disturbing the peace." Blacks considered "uppity" were tried before local courts on trumped-up charges and invariably received stiff sentences.[4] A parish appropriation of two thousand dollars to the local Girl Scout troop was made contingent upon a guarantee that the troop would never be integrated. The Plaquemines Parish Health Unit dramatically withdrew from the Louisiana Department of Health because the state agency accepted federal funds that might be used as a "bribe" to compel integration. Perez ordered local authorities to "crack down" on persons who contracted venereal disease (99 percent of the VD cases treated by the parish health unit were blacks). Persons suspected of having VD were subject to a compulsory examination and could be shipped off to an "isolation center" at dark and gloomy Fort St. Philip, which Perez had refurbished as a stockade for civil rights demonstrators. "We are not going to operate a Health Unit for VD'ers and repeaters," the Judge declared. The parish even withdrew from a Red Cross Hurricane shelter program because there was no guarantee that the shelters would be segregated.[5]

The Judge was inordinately proud of the rigid segregation practiced in Plaquemines and never failed to point out the advantages of racial separatism to northern visitors. In 1964 he took time out from his hectic schedule to genially conduct a tour of Plaquemines for a group of female sociology students from Sarah Lawrence College in New York. The girls were making a field trip to study changing patterns of life in the South and were evidently curious to see if anything had changed in Plaquemines. Leander read to them from the new Plaquemines charter, proudly commenting, "Doesn't that bring you back to the days of Thomas Jefferson?" The Sage of Monticello had never been privileged to administer so marvelous a public facility as the solidly constructed $250,000 parish jail that Perez next showed the students. Feeling that perhaps the girls could use a course in personal hygiene, the Judge remarked, "Do you know why this water fountain is for whites only? Because almost all Negroes have communicable diseases. You can look up the statistics when you get back to New York." Then he handed everyone a cigarette lighter that played "Dixie" when lit. "We ordered a gross of them," he said. "They were made in Japan."[6]

Most Plaquemines whites wholeheartedly supported their pugnacious leader in his determined stand against federally forced integration. The only moderating influences within the Judge's territory were the handful of courageous Roman Catholic priests who served there. In 1963, following the first futile attempts to desegregate the small parochial school at Buras, Father Frank Ecimovich, pastor of the church serving Belle Chasse, incurred the enmity of some of Leander's more hotheaded followers by inviting white and black children to attend a biracial retreat at Our Lady of Perpetual Help Church to receive their final instructions before their first communion. Three of the white children were kept away by indignant segregationist parents. Father Ecimovich initially decided that the three would not be permitted to receive their first communion but later changed his mind, saying that small children should not be penalized for the prejudices of their parents. Four of the parents, including Leonard Mackenroth and his wife, called upon the priest in his rectory to discuss the situation. Angry words were exchanged, and Mackenroth became violent. According to Father Ecimovich, the enraged man set upon him, fists flying, and blackened both of his eyes before being pulled away by the other parents, but threatened that he "would come back and maul me so that I wouldn't be able to preach the next day."[7]

Mackenroth was automatically excommunicated for striking a priest. Father Ecimovich also filed simple battery charges against his hot-tempered parishioner with a local justice of the peace but later dropped the charges. Perez boasted that the "integrationist" priest had decided not to prosecute because his accusations would not have stood up in court; this was perhaps true since the case would have been tried before the Plaquemines–St. Bernard district court. The other parents who had been present backed Mackenroth, and the local judge was a segregationist as well as a crony of Perez. The beleaguered priest retreated from the escalating controversy, but one of Perez's fellow deltans took up the gauntlet. George Hero III, a Plaquemines electrician, condemned Leander's public statement and began circulating a petition in defense of the abused clergyman. After obtaining the signatures of 100 of the priest's parishioners, Hero read his petition over WDSU-TV in New Orleans and had it published in the *Times-Picayune*. Shortly afterward the parish commission council, headed by President Leander Perez, dismissed Hero from the Board of Electrical Examiners "considering his services are no longer required." The *Plaquemines Gazette,* which conspicuously refrained from printing Hero's petition, did publish a letter denouncing the document and questioning the validity of the 100 signatures.[8]

Having repulsed the efforts of the Catholic church to break the color line in Plaquemines, Perez next took on the United States Navy. It might seem an uneven match, but Leander eventually prevailed. The flamboyant, widely publicized dispute involved Alvin Callender Naval Air Station, a small training facility near Belle Chasse used chiefly by weekend reservists. The base employed no more than 650 military personnel and fewer than 500 civilians; nonetheless it stood as an island of federal authority within Perez's kingdom. Since World War II all branches of the armed services had been under executive orders to work toward eliminating racial discrimination. Black morale was low; Negro servicemen complained that they were infrequently promoted, were assigned menial labor more often than whites of the same rank, and lacked social and recreational facilities, both on and off base. Shortly after assuming office, President John F. Kennedy appointed a committee comprised of seven prominent attorneys, civil rights leaders, and social scientists to investigate the effects of racism in the armed forces and submit recommendations. They produced a study popularly known as the Gesell report, named for the committee chairman Gerhard A. Gesell, but principally written by Nathaniel S. Colley, a black attorney for the NAACP. The report concluded that off-base discrimination was the most irritating problem for black soldiers and sailors and suggested that military posts be shut down in communities where extreme bias existed. Secretary of Defense Robert McNamara considered the proposed solution impractical; closing down bases throughout the country would cripple the military without helping anyone. He decided instead to employ the tactical weapon of economic reprisal and outlined his plan in a directive issued on July 26, 1963: base commanders who made progress in ending bias would be given special consideration for promotion; the commanders were to work with local officials to eliminate discrimination in establishments patronized by military personnel; as a last resort—and only after having obtained the prior approval of the secretary of the military department concerned—base commanders might declare off limits any areas where "relentless discrimination persists."[9]

The McNamara directive infuriated Perez, who claimed that it had been written by Adam Yarmolinsky, "a Russian Jew with Communist connections." He charged that the insidious directive was part of a crafty Communist conspiracy to undermine American military morale by encouraging black fighting men to go over the heads of their superiors and "make secret anonymous complaints." With military discipline broken, the Communists could simply wade ashore and take over, the Judge explained. He contended that under the directive base commanders would be required to invite more black women to social functions "and fewer girls, or ladies, who believe in segregation." McNamara's Negro servicemen would be encouraged to "push themselves on white girls," Leander grumbled. "We don't want our people to go to social functions where post commanders are expected to have at least half of those there Negro girls. Do you want to hasten the day of mongrelization?"[10]

The *Plaquemines Gazette* reported that an "unprecedented" number of blacks had been observed using the swimming pool at Callender during the past few days and that some of these had been "spotted" as northern Negroes. The editor surmised that white servicemen would be shipped away from the base and replaced by imported blacks. Perez himself noted with alarm that the military had canceled agreements with white undertakers in the area and had given the contract to bury all military dead to a Negro funeral home. "They would even rob the graves of our people to destroy our military," he wailed. He resolved to beat the navy to the punch: "We say the hell with you. We'll take the initiative and declare you off limits." Even before official action had been taken by the parish governing body, the *Plaquemines Gazette* announced in front-page headlines: "JUDGE PEREZ MOVES TO KEEP TROUBLE OUT OF PARISH THRU DEFENSE DEPARTMENT ORDERS."[11]

First, Leander summoned his sycophantic advisers—the members of the Plaquemines Parish Administration Advisory Council—into a special session in which as president he delivered a forty-five minute diatribe, lashing out at the Gesell report (the "Gesell-Yarmolinsky conspiracy"), the civil rights march on Washington, D.C., which had occurred two days earlier ("not so much black as it was red"), and the loathsome, meddlesome Kennedy administration. The members recommended that the parish commission council do whatever Perez thought necessary, whereupon the Judge closed the meeting and immediately convened the commission council. As advisory council president, he then informed the president of the commission council (none other than himself) of the urgent need for a preventive strike to scuttle the surreptitious black-Communist-navy conspiracy. The commissioners were no doubt flattered by the grinding away of local and national network television cameras, but no one other than Leander got much of a chance to show his forensic talents. The council, demonstrating to its national television audience the "100% cooperation" of which the Judge had often boasted, unanimously adopted an ordinance prohibiting parish bars and restaurants from serving uniformed military personnel—white or black. Violators could be fined twenty-five dollars or sentenced to thirty days in the parish jail or both. Leander claimed that the ordinance was not intended to be a form of social ostracism; it was merely meant to avoid the "provocation to violence" that would occur if mixed groups were allowed to drink locally.[12] He later told the Citizens' Council of Greater New Orleans, "They're [Negroes] practically told to go out and chase white girls. Now you know what would happen if a Negro man came chasing a white girl in Belle Chasse." The Judge explained that the restrictions against accommodating uniformed military personnel applied only to restaurants and lounges, not business establishments. "We do not intend to interfere with free enterprise," he said.[13]

The parish lawmakers also declared Callender off limits to civilian residents of Plaquemines, but this resolution was only advisory and carried no legal sanction. Leander indicated that it would not apply to civilian workers on the base. More ominously, he warned that the local school board might bar all children of navy personnel from parish schools. The board complained that overcrowding caused by a massive influx of navy children had compelled it to construct a $250,000 annex without "one dollar of federal aid." Yet just one week earlier the board had refused to accept any federal funds after the parish commission council had voiced objections to federal money. The Judge, later backing down, allowed navy children to be admitted for the 1963–1964 school term on a "conditional" basis because of the hardship that excluding them would have imposed upon many of the "right thinking" people in the Belle Chasse area.[14]

From New Orleans, Rear Admiral Charles H. Lyman III, commandant of the Eighth Naval District, responded to the Perez-inspired commission council resolutions and other assorted threats with a sprightly official release of his own: "In Navy parlance, we were sitting peaceably on our sea bags gazing out the porthole when we were whacked over the head by this reported threat. . . . I stand ready to go to General Quarters [battle stations], while hoping that sensible people both in Plaquemines Parish and elsewhere will stand up on their hind legs and prevent such foolishness." The admiral insisted that Leander's declaration of war was utterly unprovoked; the navy had never attempted to integrate Plaquemines schools or interfere in local affairs in any way. He said that he would go to court if the Judge tried to bar navy children from school, pointing out that such a vindictive act would only harm the children and their parents, not McNamara, Gesell, or Kennedy. After receiving Lyman's spirited reply to Perez, the Pentagon ordered that all of his future remarks on the subject be cleared through Washington.[15]

Although most Plaquemines whites wholeheartedly backed the Judge in his fight with the navy, some bar and restaurant owners feared that it would hurt their business; a few had not even heard about the new ordinance a week after its adoption, despite its being reported on national television. The first to feel the effects of Perez's handiwork were two navy men who tried to buy cups of coffee at the Hummingbird Restaurant on the New Orleans side of Belle Chasse. The operator of the restaurant said she pointed to a large sign reading, "Parish Law Forbids Me to Serve Military Personnel in Uniform," and that the two had then left without comment. She added that the ordinance "is bound to hurt my business." One bartender, although obeying the letter of the law, showed that his sympathies lay with the ostracized military men. After refusing to let a uniformed sailor buy a drink, he said, "Listen, buddy, I can't sell you a drink or I'll get in trouble. So come on, I'll buy you one instead."[16]

Undaunted by unfavorable publicity, Perez demonstrated military zeal himself by addressing the issue to various Plaquemines and New Orleans audiences in his characteristically uninhibited style. He maintained that "this Gesell Report, backed up by Yarmolinsky's military order . . . would absolutely turn over the military to the NAACP."[17] Resolutions and angry letters poured from New Orleans area civic groups, public officials, and concerned parents. Perez received sackfuls of letters praising him for his adamant stand. An ecstatic Kansas City, Missouri, man suggested that Leander undertake a coast-to-coast speaking tour, and an ardent but somewhat incoherent supporter from Slidell, Louisiana, urged him to run for governor, commenting, "Lets hope that Louisiana will elect a governor that can stand with the other Southern states as well as South Africa which seems to be handling their Negroes very fine, except the Kennedys have tried having nose trouble in their affairs also."[18]

Meanwhile, southern congressional leaders began attacking the Gesell report; among the most outspoken critics was Leander's own congressman, F. Edward Hebert, an influential member of the House Armed Services Committee. A Mississippi congressman wrote Perez that he and Hebert had joined in an effort to "alarm the country." Congressman Armistead Selden of Alabama authored a resolution calling for a congressional investigation of the Gesell report, and Congressman Carl Vinson of Georgia introduced a bill to nullify the McNamara directive.[19] To top it off, the navy itself objected to McNamara's order. The frustrated secretary of defense insisted that some form of sanctions be retained, but took the boycott initiative away from local commanders and put it in the hands of the secretary of the navy. There it remained, virtually a dead letter. The Judge had torpedoed the navy.[20]

To Perez, it might have seemed that his hodgepodge of adversaries had decided upon a deliberate strategy of encirclement. No sooner had he vanquished the navy than the Congress of Racial Equality reared its ugly head. In October, 1963, the hitherto sleepy town of Plaquemine, in Iberville Parish, suddenly became the scene of a series of nationally directed, potentially explosive racial demonstrations. The Judge claimed that he had word on good authority that CORE leader James Farmer had intended the marches for

Plaquemines Parish, but due to a faulty knowledge of spelling and geography his hirelings had descended upon the upriver community. Perhaps the Judge was right; there is no reason for CORE to have singled out the town named Plaquemine. But the decision may have been based less on geographical ignorance than upon an appreciation of the kind of treatment that awaited civil rights activists who dared enter Perez's Plaquemines. Leander refused to rest so long as rumors of marches and sit-ins flitted about his satrapy. In early October he disclosed that he had learned that a "national race agitator" had been in Plaquemines "stirring dissension among the Negro population of the parish." He said that he and his "special investigator" had personally sought out the anonymous conspirator, who luckily was nowhere to be found. The Judge's theory was that Attorney General Robert Kennedy had masterminded a scheme to dispatch James Farmer to Plaquemines in order to capture the Negro bloc vote in the northern states. Another possibility Perez considered was that the phantom agitator was actually Martin Luther King. Leander requested and promptly received authority from the commission council to personally take King into custody "should he see fit to visit the parish in case of trouble."[21]

Judge Perez had definite ideas about where such potential troublemakers belonged, but the parish jail was far too small to accommodate the horde he expected. Pondering the problem, he hit upon a bizarre solution. Deep in the tidal swamps, sixty miles below New Orleans, lay a grim and crumbling Fort St. Philip, constructed by the French in 1724 and later rebuilt by the Spanish. This abandoned, inhospitable garrison, surrounded by expanses of marsh prairie, could be reached only by boat or helicopter. Rattlesnakes, water moccasins, and coral snakes, along with swarms of mosquitoes that sometimes choked cattle to death by clogging their nostrils, rendered the hot, humid site unfit for human habitation. Leander thought that it would make a perfect stockade for civil rights demonstrators.[22] "A few days here and anarchists would surely come to understand our way of life," he said. "This is a peaceful spot, a perfect place to meditate."[23]

Predictably, the Plaquemines Parish Commission Council approved the plan to renovate Fort St. Philip and authorized Leander to negotiate a lease with the heirs of the late owner. The Judge quickly executed a contract in which the parish leased the forbidding place for five years. It was not to be used for common criminals but exclusively for "outside agitators" and any newsmen who might accompany them. The Plaquemines boss promised to integrate fully this public facility: white and black "anarchists" would be housed together.[24]

As soon as the rental agreement had been signed, Perez and his parish engineer inspected the stronghold to plan the transformation of the historic site into an imposing albeit uncomfortable prison. Parish work crews cut weeds, cleared out muck and cattle manure, and strung an electrically charged barbed wire fence around the entire four-acre enclosure. The intimidating fence, rising eight feet above the foot-thick, five-foot-high brick walls, encompassed the underground casements, compound and storage area, raised gun emplacements, an orange grove, and four wooden buildings constructed during the Spanish-American War. The sweltering, damp, underground accommodations for the prisoners, which would afford them some shelter from the elements but not from insects and snakes, consisted of several rooms and a corridor, all with bare concrete floors and six-foot ceilings.[25]

Perez's ambition was to construct an escape-proof enclosure that could contain a maximum number of prisoners at a minimum cost to the parish. He was particularly proud of the barbed, electrified fence, which he explained would save money on guards. He estimated that he would need only six guards, three on duty and three off. Any attempt to escape would be foolhardy if not suicidal: the entire fortress was encircled by a moat twenty-five feet wide; beyond that the mile-wide Mississippi served as a barrier on one side; on the other, swampland stretched as far as the eye could see.[26]

The Judge provided access to his Bastille-in-the-swamps by creating Plaquemines' first mass transit system. Boat docks were constructed along the banks of the Mississippi. Two boats, a gleaming, white forty-nine-foot converted trawler and a forty-foot craft appropriately christened the *Respect,* were equipped with cattle pens. Into these, Leander told a newsman, "we can pack a hundred demonstrators . . . if necessary, and haul them across the river."[27]

Although transportation would be free, a parish ordinance provided that prisoners incarcerated at Fort St. Philip would be required to pay for their own food and lodging while in jail. The culinary fee was set at three dollars per day. Furthermore, the inmates would be assessed a prorated share of payment for any property damage occurring during an illegal demonstration, which was defined as an activity that "may have a clear and present threat of disturbance of public peace." Penalties were fixed at thirty days in jail and a fine of twenty-five dollars in addition to the charges for room, board, and property damage.[28]

Finally, Fort St. Philip was ready for the barbarian invasion Perez expected. No demonstrators appeared, but rumors continued to pass from ear to ear among the Judge's partisans. Leander's personal assistant, George Singelmann, announced that black militant Malcolm X had told a news conference that he had been invited to speak in Plaquemines Parish. Judge Perez promptly fired off a telegram to the black leader demanding to know "when and where and for what purpose" he planned to speak. Malcolm X remained mysteriously silent. Singelmann suggested that the commission council offer a ten-thousand-dollar reward for the capture of the black activist if he entered Plaquemines Parish.[29] Several months passed and still the "anarchists" did not descend upon the parish. Then, early in July, 1964, the Judge was handed a letter addressed to the "Mayor of Pointe a la Hache." It was from Ronnie Moore, the CORE field secretary who had been directing the civil rights activities in the town of Plaquemine, asking that Plaquemines Parish voluntarily desegregate its public accommodations in compliance with federal legislation and threatening nonviolent demonstrations if the parish did not act. Leander, who wrote back that Pointe a la Hache had no mayor and that as president of the parish governing body he was responsible, warned that if CORE came into his parish it "would meet with a reception befitting its Communistic role to stir up racial strife, turmoil and violence and disunity." In closing, he asked Moore to furnish the names of Plaquemines Parish Negroes "who would integrate parish facilities."[30]

With Fort St. Philip ready, Perez industriously shored up his parish's legal defenses. He persuaded the commission council to adopt unanimously an ordinance outlawing use of any public facility—buildings, parks, playgrounds, boat docks, ferries, fishing and recreation areas, and public dumps—without a special, written permit. Perez, as council president, was authorized to designate and appoint supervisors, chairmen of appropriate committees, and other persons in charge of public accommodations to grant permits to "residents of Plaquemines Parish" for use of the facilities. Violators faced fines of up to $250 or imprisonment not to exceed sixty days or both. The Judge explained that the ordinance had been passed because certain persons were improperly utilizing a garbage dump and otherwise misusing public property, a situation that suddenly seemed to demand emergency action.[31]

After an Associated Press article describing the fort made national headlines, Leander began receiving letters from around the country commending him for his brave stand. An Iowa man applied for a job as a "gord," specifically "Captain of the Yards." He suggested that the Judge import Gila monsters from the West to station around his stockade. As to his qualifications, the writer explained, "I have a special certificat [sic] as a sniper for being an expert shot slow or rapid fire." He also inquired about the salary Perez would be willing to pay and hinted that he might be able to bring some of his friends along to help. An eighteen-year-old Texan, who wrote to assure Leander "that the older generation is not the only one that is for racial segregation," urged the Plaquemines boss to run for governor of Louisiana, commenting, "Sir, it is my feeling that next to George Wallace and Ross R. Barnett, you are the greatest thing that ever happened to the South." A Washington, D.C., lady, who apparently thought that Perez lived in his new creation, addressed her letter simply as "Mr. Leander Perez, Fort Saint Philip, Plaquemine Parish, South Louisiana." She appealed to Leander to come to the nation's capital: "But please Mr. Perez, can't you come to Washington, D.C. with all your snakes, mosquoties, 32 revolver, dungeons, electrified wire and everything else you can bring which might be a warning to these Negroes."[32]

Righteously indignant newspapers and television stations throughout the nation lambasted the creation of the Nazi-style compound and its legal accouterments. WDSU-TV, New Orleans, editorially denounced Perez's project. In an equal-time reply to the tele-cast, Perez defended his action by explaining, "We do not intend to let communist directed outside troublemakers destroy the ideal situation existing in our Parish."[33]

The entire scheme to remodel Fort St. Philip was of course a crafty publicity ploy by Perez. Although not known for his humanitarian impulses toward civil rights demonstrators, he correctly assumed that he would never have to utilize this abominable chamber of hor-rors. Leander told newsmen that he doubted that he would have to use the fort because James Farmer had said that CORE would leave any initiative in Plaquemines up to local blacks, who were already thoroughly cowed. It cost the parish only five hundred dollars to re-furbish the old fort; thanks to the efforts of network television and credulous journalists, Perez received several million dollars' worth of publicity that effectively intimidated civil rights organizers.[34]

Although independent civil rights groups might be overawed by Leander's theatrics, it was only a matter of time before the federal government moved in to desegregate the parish's public schools. Twelve years after the United States Supreme Court had ordered desegregation of all public schools in the nation "with all deliberate speed," segregated education remained an incontrovertible way of life in Plaquemines; neither speed nor deliberation was much in evidence. In 1966 enrollment in the parish public school system was 5,342 whites and 1,732 blacks. There were three combination elementary and high schools for blacks and five for whites, plus a tiny one-room school at remote Pilottown. The schools, both white and black, boasted the finest physical facilities of any rural school system in the state. All of the buildings were gleaming modern structures sprawled upon expansive, meticulously manicured grounds, featuring efficient cafeteria services and impressive ath-letic plants. A fleet of forty-nine buses shuttled children to and from school daily. The spacious buildings alone represented a capital in-vestment of more than $11,000,000. Of the cornucopia of public im-provements that Leander had bestowed upon his parish, he cherished the school system the most. He shielded the local institu-tions from federal supervision with patriarchal jealousy. Year by year the paranoia wrought by the specter of federally forced integration increasingly preyed upon the Judge's mind. In 1961 the parish school board began to require health certificates of all children; in 1963 birth certificates, indicating race, were added; both were devices to screen potential Negro applicants. Local blacks for the most part seemed satisfied; if not, they dared not complain. But the shadow of federal authority lengthened. In 1963 Perez directed the parish school board to spurn all federal aid to education; the board complied without a dissenting vote. He attempted to rationalize the new policy by arguing that it was immoral for the national government to contribute money to local school programs when the federal treasury was billions of dollars in debt. Such extravagance represented a mortgage upon many generations of the unborn, he explained, adding, "Our children are not for sale for any filthy, tainted, federal bribes."[35]

Nonetheless, federal efforts to break down pockets of segregationist resistance relentlessly, if slowly, made headway. In 1965 Governor John McKeithen, who had been elected as a segregationist, was informed that he must sign forms pledging compliance with the Civil Rights Act of 1964 for all departments of Louisiana's state and local government as a condition for receiving federal aid. Judge Perez boiled over at the new requirement and demanded that the state reject all federal aid, because "the vast majority of the people of Louisiana do not want to surrender their state and local governments to federal bureaucracy." He suggested that the state cut back on its multimillion-dollar school lunch program by making parents pay more. When asked what would happen if Louisiana refused the aid and then the federal courts moved in to order school desegregation anyway, Perez said that this would require a suit in every school district, involving tedious litigation. He boasted that "no federal court would dare order social integration."[36]

Less than six months after condemning Washington for trying to deplete an already impoverished federal treasury by aiding local schools, Leander became involved in a vituperative dispute with the Department of the Interior, which threatened to withhold $654,000 in federal funds from Plaquemines. The money represented the parish's share of oil royalties on federal leases in the Delta National Wildlife Refuge, located in Plaquemines. Counties normally receive

25 percent of federal royalties obtained from "products of the land" extracted within their boundaries, but Plaquemines had refused to sign forms agreeing to comply with the Civil Rights Act of 1964, causing the money to be withheld. Instead of signing the forms, Perez had attached a commission council resolution indicating that the oil royalties would be used to construct a four-lane highway. All persons in the parish, regardless of race, would be allowed to use the highway on equal terms, he explained. Interior Department lawyers refused to accept this as a full compliance. The Judge threatened to sue to recover the land, which, he explained, Plaquemines had generously sold to the United States government for only one dollar per acre.[37]

In June, 1966, the federal government suddenly escalated its war against Plaquemines. On June 14, School Superintendent S. A. Moncla received a letter from John Doar, the assistant attorney general for the Civil Rights Division of the Department of Justice. He indicated that he had received a written complaint from black parents alleging that their children were being denied equal protection of the law in Plaquemines by being compelled to attend racially segregated schools. Doar directed the parish school board to devise a desegregation plan, enclosing guidelines from the Department of Health, Education, and Welfare. Three days later Moncla replied, arguing that the local school system already operated under a freedom of choice plan and that he was under no obligation to observe the HEW guidelines because the parish did not receive federal funds for its schools. Other correspondence followed, but by the middle of July the school board still had not submitted a timetable for desegregation. On July 14, one of Doar's assistants telephoned Moncla. Time had run out; the Justice Department would take the issue to court. One week later the suit was filed. It called for the desegregation of the first, seventh, tenth, and twelfth and two other grades to be selected by Plaquemines school officials, during the first year. All school services and programs, including athletics, were to be integrated, and the hiring of teachers was to be done without regard to race, except to compensate for past discrimination. Formerly black schools were to be upgraded to a level equal with formerly all-white schools in the parish. Perez vowed to fight "to the last ditch, come hell or high water," against the suit, which he termed "just another part of the communist conspiracy."[38]

On July 15, the day after Moncla received final notice from the Justice Department, he notified the school board of the pending litigation. The board resolved to conduct a "census" to record each parent's preference for enrolling his children. Two types of forms were drawn up. One, known as the "white" form, was circulated by white persons to white parents, who were instructed to sign one of the two statements: (1) "I will not send my children to an integrated school with negro children"; or (2) "I will send my children to an integrated school with negro children." A second kind of census sheet was distributed to black parents by blacks employed by parish officials. This version simply requested: "Please state below the school of your choice for your child (children) to attend during the 1966–67 school year." Nowhere on this form were any schools named; nor were Negro parents advised that they could choose formerly all-white schools; nor were the persons who circulated the forms instructed to so advise them. However, Plaquemines school officials insisted that local blacks were "extremely well informed" of their freedom to choose any school. When queried as to why he did not send forms to black parents asking them if they wanted to send their children to integrated schools, Superintendent Moncla replied, "I didn't think that it made that much difference."[39]

School principals, faculty members, bus drivers, and janitors distributed the questionnaires. None of the papers were left with white or black parents for consideration; they had to be filled out in the presence of the person who delivered them. If a parent wished to discuss the census with the husband or wife, the distributor would take the form and leave, instructing the parents to call him when they were ready to sign. Families were advised that their children must be registered by August 1 in order to attend school during the 1966–1967 school year. Those who refused to sign a form were told to appear at the school in person to register their children. White parents who signed the form on the bottom line, indicating that they would send their children to an integrated school, were repeatedly contacted by school board agents who tried to persuade them to change their minds. Personal friendship, loyalty to the parish, and vague threats were used to cajole recalcitrant parents. After Mrs. David Smith of Buras signed the "wrong" statement on the white form, she and her husband were subjected to a series of anonymous phone calls in which the caller would hang up as soon as one of the Smiths would answer the phone. The census distributor returned to the Smiths' home twice, and the Buras principal telephoned. The Smiths were not going along; parish leaders wanted all whites to sign on the top line to demonstrate that they were 100 percent behind the local administration, the officials explained. The Smiths reluctantly gave in. Mr. and Mrs. Harold L. Smith, another white couple, also signed the "wrong" line but were persuaded to change their minds. Harold Smith later testified about the atmosphere of intimidation in which the census had been conducted. When assured in court by school board attorney Sidney W. Provensal, Jr., that he was in no danger of losing his job because of the way he had signed the form, Smith said, "Well, I don't fear anything anyway. In fact, if my signing this paper the other way means that I would lose my job, that is not what I fear. What I fear is losing my rights. If I am going to give up my rights, then we may as well move out of the parish." Provensal replied, "I agree with that, Mr. Smith. If you want to move out of the parish, you have a perfect right to do."[40]

The few bold black parents who indicated that they would prefer to send their children to previously all-white schools were subjected to even more intimidation, no less effective because of being implicit rather than explicit. Alberta Anderson, a mother of ten, signed the form showing that she would prefer to enroll her children at Woodlawn rather than Phoenix, the black school they had previously attended. About two weeks later, she was sought out at work by Alba Guidroz, a representative of the school board. When Guidroz asked why she had selected Woodlawn, she explained that her children passed the school on the way to Phoenix, which was ten to fifteen miles farther on. He then tried to persuade her to sign a second form specifying Phoenix as her choice. After Guidroz's visit and two telephone conversations with School Superintendent Moncla, Mrs. Anderson gave in and signed up her children for Phoenix because, she said, "I was afraid of being either fired from my job or run out of the parish." The distraught mother emphasized that Guidroz had been polite, never threatening her, but said that she would not have changed her mind without his visit or the telephone conversations with Moncla. She explained, "Well, I have heard that if you don't do what they want you to do, they will do something about it."[41]

White parents representing more than five thousand children signed the census statement indicating that they would refuse to send their children to an integrated school; parents representing only fifty-seven children signed to the effect that they would permit their children to attend racially mixed classes. Not a single black parent designated an all-white school as the preference for his children. Leander boasted, "There are no Negroes in Plaquemines Parish asking for integrated schools. Not one."[42]

The Plaquemines commission council leaped into action when informed that a complaint had been filed with the Justice Department. Its strategy had all of the traits of a Perez-inspired legal subterfuge: audacity, pugnacity, and transparent charlatanry. On June 30, contracts were executed transferring title on the land, buildings, supplies, and equipment used by the parish's eight major schools from the school board to the commission council, which paid nothing in return for receiving the property. The action, Leander explained, had been taken "for convenience." The council had originally paid for the land and improvements, he said, and the parish was just now getting around to returning the holdings to their proper owner. The school board also "sold" forty-six school buses to the commission council for the balance that the board owed the council for the vehicles. If the public schools were to utilize the buildings, property, and buses, they would have to lease them from the commission council, an arrangement that the council apparently considered "convenient." Time dragged on. By mid-August no effort had been made to execute such a lease. Luke Petrovitch, the parish public safety commissioner, told a federal court that he had been working full time on the litigation with the federal government involving school desegregation and had had no time to talk about leases with the school board. The board, if indeed it really made an effort, found it difficult to procure money for such a lease because the commission council had cut off all funds except those that the board derived independently. Previously, the council had chipped in $900,000 per

year to help the public schools. Justice Department officials suspected that the parish was planning to lease its educational
facilities to individuals who would operate them as private schools,
thus abolishing the public school system entirely. As the school term
approached, another peculiar piece of legal sorcery turned up. The
school board and commission council dusted off the contracts under
which the school property had originally been purchased and brought
them into court. The deeds specified that the schools to be constructed
on the property were to be for whites only; if blacks were ever allowed to attend, the land would revert to the original owners without
further litigation. The court ruled this unique clause in the contracts
unconstitutional.[43]

When the Justice Department discovered the sleight-of-hand
transfer of school property from the board to the council, it amended
its desegregation suit to make the council a codefendant. Leander
claimed that the commission council was not prepared to go to
court, that it would need additional time, but Judge Herbert W.
Christenberry ordered the hearings to begin on schedule. He quickly
enjoined the parish governing body from transferring the newly acquired property to a third party, overruling strenuous council objec-
tions that such an order violated its rights to dispose of its property
as it saw fit. Stuck with a multitude of empty school buildings that it
could rent to no one but the school board, the commission council
finally got around to drawing up a lease. The board agreed to pay the
council $40,000 per month to use the buildings that it had munifi-
cently deeded away several months earlier.[44]

Perez did not limit himself to legal maneuvers; he set about
mobilizing the white parents. On July 31, informal meetings of disgruntled, resentful whites were held at all four of the large parish
schools on the west bank of the Mississippi River. Notice of the
meetings was spread by word of mouth, and large crowds showed up.
Leander was introduced at each gathering by the local principal as
the main speaker. He delivered identical back-stiffening but nonviolent speeches, designed to fortify his people in their resistance. The
Judge began by renewing his vow to dedicate the remainder of his
life solely to maintaining racial segregation. He devoted the first
half of his talk to the familiar premise that integration was a Com-

munist conspiracy. Then he struck closer to home. The desegregation crisis was more menacing than the brutal hurricanes that had
ravaged the parish, he said, but the people had bravely fought back
and had overcome storm after dreadful storm; surely they would not
surrender in the face of this man-made tragedy. The going might get
rough, but if the white people stuck together they would weather the
storm and emerge stronger than before. He held up as an example
the brave white parents of Prince Edward County, Virginia.
Threatened with a federal takeover of their painfully erected public
school system, they had created private schools as a haven for their
children. Perhaps Plaquemines could do the same. The people went
away heartened and united, convinced that the Judge would somehow pull them through.[45]

Privately, the Judge was pessimistic as he prepared to go to court
to defend the parish. He admitted that he was not hopeful about the
outcome "because I don't know how ruthless the federal courts,
backed up by the armed forces of the United States, will be."[46]

The case was heard by Judge Christenberry, a gray-haired, be-
spectacled former prosecuting attorney who had known Perez personally for many years. From past experience, Perez knew that
Christenberry would be unsympathetic to his point of view. He
therefore requested that the suit be heard by a three-judge panel
rather than by Christenberry alone. Motion denied. He asked that
the trial be postponed to allow more time for the commission council
to prepare its defense. Motion denied. He demanded a jury trial on
the grounds that the portion of the preliminary injunction prohibiting the commission council from selling or leasing school property
involved a money question in excess of twenty dollars. Motion denied. He called upon the court to inform him of the names and addresses of the Negro complainants so that he could cross-examine
them. Motion denied.[47]

At all of the hearings relative to making the commission council
party to the injunction, Perez appeared as the defense attorney as
well as president of the council. He was assisted by the public safety
commissioner, Luke Petrovitch. The school board defense was handled by Sidney W. Provensal, Jr., a fortyish, chain-smoking New Orleans attorney who had attended law school with the Judge's

younger son.[48] At one point in the hearing, Leander put Petrovitch on the stand as a character witness. Perez's questioning was mainly a monologue about himself with Petrovitch occasionally answering "Yes, sir" and "Yes, Judge." Perez asked, "Do they [the people of Plaquemines] know me as a man of integrity and veracity?" Petrovitch replied, "Yes, Judge." Perez continued, "And as a man who knows something about the law?" Petrovitch answered, "Yes, Judge, and let me give you an example of that. I heard people say that they had heard a certain minister, a certain preacher, say that Judge Perez was dishonest and was immoral, and that the members of that church resented an untrue statement of that type." At this point Christenbery interrupted, "Well, this is all hearsay. I don't think that has anything to do with the case." Perez continued, "Would you please tell the court if Judge Perez isn't regarded as a leader and a personal friend of the people in the Parish, and if he hasn't given his life to provide good educational standards for the people in the Parish." Christenberry again broke in to say that he had known Perez longer than the witness.[49]

Leander attempted to show that the black schools were equal if not superior to the white ones in physical facilities. He warned that chaos would erupt if the schools were integrated. White teachers, bus drivers, and administrators would resign, and white students would boycott classes. A school board member testified that every board member would resign if the court ordered desegregation. School officials testified that the government's freedom of choice plan might necessitate costly long-distance busing to transport students to the school of their choice. Federal attorneys pointed out that under the existing system Negroes were already bused an average of 42.4 miles per day and whites were bused an average of 25.8 miles. Some blacks within walking distance of the Boothville-Venice School were bused more than 20 miles to the Sunrise School. Frank Patti, an administrative assistant to the school superintendent, testified that freedom of choice as requested by the federal government would disrupt the entire school system; he was unable to explain why the locally devised freedom of choice plan under which the school board claimed to be operating was not disruptive. The hearing progressed from the curious to the bizarre. During the questioning of Superintendent Moncla, the United States attorney Hugh Fleischer asked Moncla to state his telephone number. Perez leaped to the protection of the witness by demanding to know if the information would be used by the Department of Justice for wiretapping. Incredulous, Judge Christenberry asked Perez if he was serious. Perez replied that he was. Fleischer assured the court that the information (which was available in the phone book) would not be used for wiretapping.[50]

Leander scraped the bottom of his legal barrel for his next device: he solemnly claimed that Plaquemines was already operating an integrated school system. This must have surprised even the school board, not to mention local blacks. To support this argument he introduced photographs of students attending the Grand Bayou School, a remote, two-room facility located on an island accessible only by boat or helicopter. No one seemed to know much about the place except for the Reverend Malcolm Davis, Jr., who identified himself as a "teacher missionary" who had taught there for thirteen years. Fleischer said that he understood that the school had been closed since 1962, but school board attorney Provensal replied that it was still operating. In fact, Davis had distributed freedom of choice forms there.[51] The Judge's photographs purportedly showed "that there were black negroes, light-colored persons and extremely white persons attending the same school." Later, the defense introduced birth certificates for some of the children enrolled there, which listed their race as Negro. Davis testified that the children who attended school there had darker skin than most whites, but lighter than Negroes, and did not appear to have Negro blood. A federal witness who claimed to be familiar with Grand Bayou School said that the residents of the area considered themselves to have French-Indian ancestry.[52]

Having failed to make Grand Bayou a pivotal point, Judge Perez based his concluding arguments on a far broader issue: he claimed that the Fourteenth Amendment had never been legally adopted. Leander, who had spent several years researching the curious genealogy of the amendment, had used the same argument in other cases. And, he knew what kind of reaction to expect from Judge Christenberry, who likewise could anticipate Perez's tactics. During the hearing Leander confessed to Senator Eastland of Mississippi,

"I'm sure that the court will ignore the 14th Amendment." He explained, however, that he planned to distribute hundreds of copies of his brief on the Fourteenth Amendment and asked Eastland if it would be possible to have this one, as well as his brief on the *Brown* decision, published in the *Congressional Record*. Leander argued that, since the Fourteenth Amendment had never been legally ratified, there was no constitutional sanction for the civil rights laws that the Justice Department was attempting to enforce. Christenberry brushed aside this attack upon the Fourteenth Amendment with the comment, "That's all right for some meeting of laymen, but not for lawyers."[53]

Judge Christenberry's summary dismissal of Perez's carefully prepared arguments frustrated and incensed the Plaquemines boss. He declared that he wanted a complete record of the evidence introduced to be made available to the appeals court in case the presiding judge ruled against Plaquemines without considering the evidence. This brought an angry outburst from Christenberry, whose patience was almost exhausted: "Just a minute. Once before this Court warned you, counsel. I have respect for your years. I have known you a long time, but you are suggesting again, as you did once before, that this court might decide this case without considering the facts or the law. Now, you are close to contempt. I wouldn't like to put a man of your years in jail."[54]

After hearing testimony for three days, Judge Christenberry issued the sweeping preliminary injunction requested by the Justice Department. The order prohibited Plaquemines from operating a segregated school system and enjoined parish officials from interfering with desegregation in any way, including participation in creating a private school system. Christenberry warned that, if he heard of any Plaquemines officials trying to persuade business firms in the parish to pressure their employees into avoiding desegregated schools, he would have the FBI investigate and consider charges of obstructing justice. The federal judge revealed that he had been told of reprisals against one witness who had testified in the case. Perez left the court with his eyes red and watery. His voice quavering, he told newsmen, "No case was presented more methodically, thoroughly, or convincingly—to no purpose." Judge Christenberry had a different opinion of the Plaquemines defense; he called it "the most disorderly case I've ever seen presented."[55]

Perez managed to contain himself while in court, but once outside he unleashed a barrage of pent-up invective, terming Christenberry's injunction "a worse disaster than Hurricane Betsy."[56] He fumed: "Christenberry takes orders from Washington. Christenberry don't know what the hell's back of it. When I explained to him the background of the Black Monday decision, the Supreme Court decision, I doubt if he knew that the court based its decision on the adoption of communist writings." The more he raged, the more angry he became. Turning from the judge to the Democratic party, he thundered: "They're not Democrats, they're mobocrats—mobocrats. Politics has degenerated below the gutter level. Now our children are the pawns. That's enough. Why in the hell talk any more about a God damned disgrace that's imposed upon us!"[57]

Following the court decision, telephone lines in Plaquemines buzzed late into the night. Enraged white parents demanded a total boycott of parish schools. Classes opened on August 31, but it was just another day of summer vacation for most students. School buses ran, but there were few riders; less than 25 percent of the white children showed up for class. School cafeterias were empty, and no lunches were served. Not a single white student attended classes at Woodlawn, where five Negro boys became the first of their race to enroll at a formerly all-white public school in Plaquemines. Some fifty white children and their parents walked through an equal group of pickets at the previously all-white school at Belle Chasse. None of the children were molested. Each picketing white parent carried a sign lettered with the single word *Don't*. Across the road, an FBI agent slouched in his car, watching.[58]

Attendance at the public schools gradually climbed, although it remained far below normal. Governor McKeithen, admitting at a news conference that Plaquemines people were not obeying the state's compulsory attendance law, declined to take action, remarking that the law was also being disobeyed in Harlem. District Attorney Leander Perez, Jr., said that no white child would be penalized for not going to public school until private schools could be opened. By mid-September only seventy-two white children were attending school at Belle Chasse along with eighteen blacks. One morning, without warning, the teachers there simply failed to show up. The pupils were returned to their homes with the explanation that all fifty-three teachers had resigned and that the school was closed. Archbishop Philip A. Hannan offered to assign Catholic nuns to relieve the critical teacher shortage at Belle Chasse, but the Plaquemines school superintendent rejected the offer, saying that "a large percentage" of the parish population was non-Catholic and might object and that it was against his policy "to mix church and state affairs." Judge Christenberry speedily stepped in and ordered the school reopened under threat of contempt of court. New Orleans housewives were brought in to teach.[59]

At Woodlawn High School, the only formerly all-white school on the east bank, there was a total withdrawal of white students, teachers, bus drivers, and maintenance personnel. Only the principal and thirty-one black students remained until Woodlawn too was shut down. On September 1, Moncla resigned as school superintendent. Six days later his successor, Frank Patti, resigned along with his lone assistant, Alba Guidroz. L. M. Tinsley was made acting superintendent. The white public school teachers who doggedly stuck it out were not signed to yearly contracts as had been the custom in the past. Luke Petrovitch said that no contracts had been issued by the school board "because we didn't have time to do it."[60]

Actually, the absence of contracts was intended to free the teachers from any legal obligation to the parish so that they could resign at any time to join the segregated private school system that was being hastily organized. One teacher, a veteran of twenty years in the Plaquemines public school system, testified that she had been intimidated when she had refused to switch to a private school. She said that she had been given an application form for private school-teachers and told to fill it out "for my own protection" by the former principal of the public school at which she taught.[61]

The school board attorney, Sidney Provensal, met with the faculty of the Boothville-Venice School and forecast a bleak future for the parish's public schools. He told the apprehensive teachers that faculties would probably be integrated the following year and that they would have to teach with black teachers or at a black school.

The new superintendent of schools, L. M. Tinsley, was no more encouraging. He told several teachers that he could not get them pay increases because he was finding it hard enough to obtain the money to pay their present salaries.[62] Teachers who inquired when the school lunch program would be reinstated at Boothville-Venice were asked by Provensal whether they wanted to feed the children or get paid themselves. After hearing voluminous testimony on the matter, Judge Christenberry concluded, "It is my belief that the officials of Plaquemines Parish, including the school board, have made pawns of the school children of the parish and dupes of the teachers, who have been led into abandoning the public school system."[63]

Despite continued complaints of a lack of funds, the public schools still refused to accept federal aid. When asked why by government attorney Hugh Fleischer, Superintendent Tinsley replied, "Mr. Fleischer, we can operate without the Federal funds that are available. We are in a rich Parish, and there's no point in our being a burden on the Federal Government." Little effort was made to hire teachers to replace those who resigned. In response to a question by Judge Christenberry concerning what efforts were being made to hire new teachers, Provensal said that the school board was planning to run a want ad in the *Plaquemines Gazette*. Christenberry commented, "Well, that's amusing really."[64]

Problems piled upon problems. Students found themselves in classes without teachers, and many teachers found themselves with no students or with only a handful. Although technically operating under a freedom-of-choice plan, the schools remained segregated de facto, because few white students attended those schools at which large numbers of blacks were enrolled. There was almost a total breakdown in communications among the commission council, school board, superintendent, and teachers and principals—a stark contrast to the close cooperation that had existed in the past. Superintendent Tinsley said that he rarely talked with the school board.[65] He complained that he had to spend many hours each day traveling from one end of the elongated parish to another just to ensure that the schools kept functioning. Services were reduced to a bare minimum; cafeteria personnel were laid off; bus drivers resigned; buildings deteriorated. The acting principal of the

Boothville-Venice School testified to such maintenance problems as painting, broken screens, and rats in the buildings. Textbooks were removed from public schools for use in the new private schools. A fourteen-year-old black student testified that he had only one textbook for seven courses and that none of the students in his class had a complete set of books.[66] He said that the entire athletic program at his school consisted of a teacher bringing a baseball and the youngsters bringing bats. The coach at Belle Chasse, who later became the principal of a private school, locked the gymnasium and refused to allow the children to use it. The football coach at Boothville complained that practically all of his school's athletic equipment had been removed following the desegregation order. The school board used an unusual method to comply with the injunction ordering the equalization of all parish schools: it downgraded the white schools rather than upgrading the black ones. Industrial arts, band, and French were dropped from the curriculum at Boothville-Venice, as well as kindergarten and all outside clubs.[67]

A small group of concerned parents organized the Plaquemines Parish Committee for the Preservation of Public Education, but the puny movement was discouraged by parish authorities. The principal at Belle Chasse refused to allow the parents to use school facilities to hold a meeting; the committee eventually met in the Belle Chasse Catholic school. Perez kept close tabs on all such groups. Confidential informants provided him with a list of the members of the Save Our Public Schools organization, including notations indicating where each person was employed. The parents who banded together to preserve the public school system represented only an infinitesimal percentage of the parish population; most whites solidly supported the defiant attitude of the parish administration. Local property owners overwhelmingly voted down a proposal to increase parish property taxes to provide revenue for the public schools. Leander boasted that the referendum proved that his people had "repudiated" the federal court order that had "confiscated" the parish schools.[68]

WDSU-TV editorially accused Plaquemines authorities of deliberately destroying their own school system, a policy that the station termed "planned chaos." Stung by the criticism, Judge Perez an-

swered with an equal-time telecast in which he attributed the chaos
to the federals. He asserted that the FBI and attorney general were
under secret orders from President Johnson to integrate every public school in the nation before the next presidential election. Other
Plaquemines officials jumped to the attack. Provensal claimed that
disorderly blacks frequently interrupted classes but that teachers
and principals hesitated to discipline them, fearing citation for contempt by the federal courts. He said also that a twenty-one-year-old
bearded black man was attending school with fifteen- and sixteen-
year-old white girls at Port Sulphur and that a little white girl had
been kissed by a Negro boy in another school. Petrovitch complained
that the Justice Department had subpoenaed so many teachers from
the Boothville-Venice School that it had had to be temporarily shut
down, depriving pupils of a day's education. He charged that the
United States attorney general "is destroying the public school system quicker than the officials of Plaquemines Parish are." The
mutual recriminations multiplied. Superintendent Tinsley grumbled that he found it difficult to work with federal officials snooping
about his office, peering over his shoulder, demanding records, and
calling at all hours of the night.[69]

Tinsley was caught between the parish administration, which
employed him, and the federal courts, which threatened to prosecute
him for contempt of the desegregation order. To obey the federal
injunction, he had to keep the public schools functioning; to appease
the parish administration, he had to operate the public schools so
that they remained an unpalatable alternative to the private white
schools. The conflict ran even deeper. By temperament, upbringing,
and personal philosophy he wholeheartedly opposed racial mixing or
any federal interference with local government, yet he had dedicated his life to improving the Plaquemines public school system.
Much the same was true of many other men caught in the power
struggle between parish and federal authority. Segregationists and
Perez partisans all, they had nonetheless devoted years of painstak-
ing effort to building up the parish's public schools. Now they not
only had to watch the results of their labor crumbling before their
very eyes, but they were also expected to participate in its destruction. Most of them relinquished their jobs rather than walk the

quivering tightrope. After Moncla and Patti had resigned as school superintendent in rapid succession, the job was offered to the next man in line, Alba Guidroz. Guidroz had wanted to become superintendent all of his life, but now he turned down the job "because I couldn't do what had to be done." He quit his position and moved out of the parish.[70]

As confusion multiplied in the Plaquemines school system, Leander slipped quietly into the background. Enjoined from engaging in any speech or action that might retard desegregation, he purposely maintained a low public profile. Although he still attended parish meetings and dedications, he was more often a spectator than a speaker, and he appeared less frequently in the *Plaquemines Gazette*. But outside of Plaquemines he was far from silent on issues not directly circumscribed by the injunction. Embarking upon a Save Our Children speaking crusade before the 1968 presidential election, the Judge urged his audiences to bombard Governor McKeithen with letters, telegrams, and telephone calls because "he has gone too far to the left."[71]

Despite the smoldering resentment that accompanied forced desegregation in Plaquemines, no violence erupted. Leander told his people that violent acts would only provide an excuse for the Justice Department to send more "secret gestapo" into Plaquemines. The Reverend Aubrey V. Veuleman testified in federal court, "It is my understanding that the word has come down through channels that there is to be no trouble in connection with this thing, and there hasn't been any."[72]

Throughout the 1966–1967 term, the public schools in Plaquemines sputtered along, characterized by a total absence of clear-cut policies and a lack of mutual understanding, wholehearted cooperation, and trust among the school board, administration, teachers, and federal officials. Time and again the Justice Department was compelled to go to court to force the parish to maintain its public schools. In late October, Judge Christenberry concluded, "I am satisfied from all that I have heard here that a determined effort is being made to wreck the public school system of Plaquemines Parish, and one mistake that this Court made was in crediting some people with good faith which they just do not possess."[73]

While the public schools languished, a system of segregated white private schools arose almost instantaneously. Only sixteen days after Plaquemines public schools were desegregated by court order, the first private school opened at Promised Land, the former plantation home of Judge Perez, which he had handed down to his daughter. Within a few days after Christenberry's injunction, local people appeared with saws, lumber, cement, and plumbing and electrical equipment to begin working on the stately old mansion. No Trespassing signs were posted to keep reporters out. The main building was renovated, and an extension added. A small building was moved onto the grounds to provide two additional classrooms. The teaching staff from Woodlawn School deserted en masse to become the faculty of the East Bank Promised Land Academy. Regular attendance reached 250 for the twelve grades—exactly the number of white students who had previously attended Woodlawn. Perez, wary of the court order not to interfere with desegregation, claimed to know nothing of the conversion of his old home into a private school, but congratulated his daughter for her wise and generous utilization of family property.[74]

Leander had advocated private academies as an ultimate retreat from the inevitable desegregation of public schools ever since the Black Monday decision of 1954. He had collected information on independent school systems in other states, researched the legal problems, and helped found such institutions throughout Louisiana. Now all of his contingency plans were put into effect, although, publicly at least, not by the judge himself. Since all parish officials, including Leander, were enjoined from interfering with desegregation, the main burden of organizing the new school system fell upon his younger son, Chalin. Even so, many parish leaders concede that the elder Perez masterminded the movement, and at least one believes that he financed the private school system "in toto."[75]

It appears, however, that at least some of the money came from other sources. The School Investment Corporation, capitalized at $2,000,000, was hastily formed. Serving as a sort of holding company, the corporation became the owner of all private school properties, which it then leased to independent, nonprofit corporations formed in each school district. Shares in the parent corporation were sold for $100 each, with the shareholder free to designate the school area in which he desired his investment to be used. Frank Patti, who had resigned as Plaquemines school superintendent, was hired to coordinate the parishwide system of independent schools. In early October more than a thousand anxious whites crammed into an auditorium at the small settlement of Empire to hear Patti outline the nascent project. He promised that the parish would provide free textbooks and transportation for the children attending the private academies and that teachers would be paid the state minimum salary by the corporation. After the meeting, $15,000 worth of stock was purchased. Several weeks later Patti announced that tuition had been set at $450 per year but that no white child would be turned away because of inability to pay. Money dribbled in from other sources. The Belle Chasse Fire Department raised $1,500 for scholarships at a benefit dance. Patti undertook a drive to enroll members in a "$500 club"; each member was to pay a full year's tuition for one child. The Association of Citizens' Councils of Louisiana began a statewide drive to collect books for the all-white Plaquemines schools, labeling the effort Project Perez. In April, 1967, the council trucked eight thousand miscellaneous books from Shreveport to Plaquemines. Sinister rumors circulated to the effect that not all monetary contributions were voluntary. Judge Christenberry indicated that he believed that some of the large companies operating in Plaquemines had been shaken down for contributions to the private schools in lieu of paying taxes for public education.

The funding of the schools is even more inscrutable considering that construction of the academies had already begun before Patti began publicly soliciting contributions and selling stock. Indeed, work had begun even before Christenberry had handed down his decision in the desegregation suit. Prefabricated buildings had been set up on concrete foundations poured by volunteer workers. By the time the preliminary injunction was issued, the independent system was almost ready. The new buildings were hardly as plush as the old. All were single-story, blue gray, warehouse-type structures constructed of sheets of lightweight metal. They lacked gymnasiums, football and baseball fields, and libraries, but these were to be added later.[76] Textbooks were pirated from the public schools. Superintendent Tinsley admitted that he had transferred state books from public to private schools in a school board truck without bothering to ask the board, but said that he had been assured by the Louisiana Department of Education that the reassignment was legal. Teachers, principals, coaches, and administrators were persuaded to abandon the public schools in favor of the private ones. The coach at Belle Chasse actively recruited teachers for the private system while still a public school employee. The former principal of the Boothville-Venice School became an undercover recruiter for the private schools, using a parish driver education car for his recruiting trips. Sometimes he went to the school grounds to enlist prospects; at other times he visited public schoolteachers in their homes. He advised one teacher not to tell anyone that he had come to her home and to destroy her private school application form if she did not mail it in.[77]

In mid-October River Oaks Academy was opened at Belle Chasse with 1,400 white students preregistered. Congressman F. Edward Hebert, the principal speaker at the dedication, told his audience that, although the courts had enjoined parish officials from speaking out, they could not silence him. He urged the people to vote out of office all officials who supported federal "seizure" of public schools. In early November three more private schools were dedicated. Lieutenant Governor C. C. ("Taddy") Aycock was the featured speaker at the three-way dedication held at Buras. Judge Perez was not on the speakers' stand, but was given a thunderous standing ovation when introduced as a spectator.[78]

Outside observers had predicted that it would take two years to create a parishwide network of independent schools, but within two months it was operating. The completed co-op system comprised five schools, one to correspond to each major desegregated white school. By late January of 1967 there were 2,700 white students enrolled. Within six months, all of the new schools were accredited by the Louisiana Department of Education. It was a day of beaming salutations and back-patting when in June, 1967, 90 seniors became the first graduates of Plaquemines' three high school co-ops. Leander's son Chalin was the featured speaker at each of the three commencement ceremonies.[79]

The private schools in Plaquemines and in other parishes expected to receive a large portion of their operating funds from the state. Between 1954 and 1967 Louisiana enacted four grant-in-aid laws. Perez, instrumental in drafting the bills and shepherding them through the legislature, also served as attorney for the state when they were attacked in federal court. The initial laws were rather transparent attempts to preserve state-supported segregated schools disguised as private institutions, but the measures grew progressively more sophisticated. However, the courts concluded that the Constitution "nullifies sophisticated as well as simple-minded modes of discrimination."[80]

The first grant-in-aid acts were rubber-stamped by the legislature as part of the comprehensive segregation package nominally sponsored by the Kennon administration (1953–1957) but largely drafted by Perez. Acts were passed legalizing the incorporation of nonprofit educational cooperatives by concerned white parents and providing for state grants to children who attended private, nonsectarian schools. Although the organization of co-ops was not found to be unconstitutional, the direct grants were disallowed by the federal courts. The Judge's search for a panacea to the problem posed by forced integration again turned in 1960 to state tuition grants during the hysteria of the New Orleans school desegregation crisis. Grant-in-aid acts were among the plethora of antimixing measures pushed through during Governor Davis' quixotic series of special sessions in 1960, but were summarily nullified by the federal courts later that year along with all other obstructionist contrivances. Outraged by the blanket nullification of scores of assembly-line segregationist laws, a state representative, Wellborn Jack, protested, "Since when does the supreme court have the right to go around giving constitutional rights like they were Christmas presents?"[81]

The next legislative effort to fund private schools was written into the state constitution. In 1962 Louisiana voters approved an amendment creating the Louisiana Financial Assistance Commission. Headed by E. W. Gravolet, Jr., state senator from Plaquemines Parish, the commission was authorized to allocate grants of up to $360 per year for each child attending an independent, nonsectarian school. After the Plaquemines private school system had been organized in 1966, application forms for more than five thousand such stipends were distributed in the parish. Before the harvest of state funds could be reaped, however, a group of Negroes filed a class action suit challenging the constitutionality of the commission, and the Justice Department intervened on their side. A group of white parents whose children were attending Plaquemines private schools intervened in behalf of the commission, contending that their civil right of freedom of choice would be violated if the commission were enjoined from operating. Meanwhile, the administrators of the Plaquemines co-ops began to worry. Before the suit could be heard, they announced that the independent schools would refuse to accept state assistance because it might jeopardize the private nature of the institutions.[82]

Anticipating that the commission would be declared unconstitutional, Perez masterminded the creation of a surrogate agency while the suit languished in court. He had Senator Gravolet introduce a bill seeking legislative authorization for a bureau to be called the Louisiana Education Commission for Needy Children. Perez's concoction, however, encountered substantial opposition from labor leaders and New Orleans legislators. But the Judge rallied his troops. He personally appeared before a House committee to passionately exhort approval of the bill while stalwarts armed with placards reading Save Our Children packed the galleries of the huge House chamber. The committee deadlocked nine to nine, but the chairman's vote broke the tie in favor of Leander. The legislative struggle was a new experience for him; it appeared that segregation bills no longer shared a pedestal with the Ten Commandments. Faced with an onerous floor fight, the Judge summoned his multitudes. Thousands of fervent segregationists thronged the steps of the capitol demanding passage. After two weeks of intense debate the legislation cleared both houses and was signed by the governor. The newborn addition to Louisiana's bureaucracy inherited the offices, director, personnel, and clientele of its beleaguered progenitor. Governor McKeithen somewhat indiscreetly described it as a "standby" agency to be activated if its precursor were found to be unconstitutional. Sure enough, in August, 1967, the U.S. district court enjoined operation of the Louisiana Financial Assistance

Commission, ruling that "tuition grants damage Negroes by draining students, teachers, and funds from the desegregated public school system into a competitive, segregated 'quasi-public' school system."[83]

When the Justice Department discovered the Louisiana Education Commission for Needy Children lurking in reserve, it filed an amended complaint asking the court to include the new agency in its original injunction. But the case had already gone to the United States Supreme Court on appeal, a certain master of constitutional law slyly pointed out. Nonetheless, the federal court inserted in its original injunction an added prohibition to dispatch to martyrdom Judge Perez's latest legislative brainchild.[84]

About this time Attorney General Jack Gremillion, nominally the chief defense attorney, dropped out of the litigation, leaving the task to Perez, who summoned his illimitable powers of imagination and legal wizardry in preparing a defense. The crux of the problem lay in verbally transmuting the Louisiana Education Commission for Needy Children from an instrument of segregation into something more acceptable to federal judges. Leander knew he was in trouble when the three-judge panel assigned to hear the case was announced: it included his perpetual nemesis, Herbert W. Christenberry.[85] Perez audaciously called upon all three judges to disqualify themselves on the grounds that they had demonstrated personal animosity toward him and had ignored the law. The motion was denied.

Finally, the trial got under way. The courtroom was jammed with curious and concerned spectators, many of them white parents wearing SOC (Save Our Children) badges. The central issue was the purpose of the law that had created the new commission. Was it just another segregationist ruse, or was it a genuinely humanitarian measure? The Justice Department introduced newspaper clippings and sworn statements from reporters asserting that the intent was to encourage white students to abandon desegregated public schools. Enraged, Leander jumped to his feet to object to the introduction of the clippings as evidence. The news stories were blatantly biased and inaccurate, he declared. Quoting from one that identified him as the "boss" of Plaquemines Parish, he denied that he was a boss. This brought a smile to the face of Judge Christenberry. Perez also objected to the smile. Failing to have the clippings thrown out of court, Leander decided to attack the credibility of the offending papers, the New Orleans *Times-Picayune* and *States-Item*. He hauled in a stack of miscellaneous clippings, replete with factual errors, to demonstrate their inaccuracy. The judges were unimpressed. Next, Perez set about to prove that the purpose of the Louisiana Education Commission for Needy Children was to combat juvenile delinquency by preventing school dropouts. He charged that "helpless white children" were being sadistically driven from the public schools into the streets by "intolerable situations" fomented by "a hoodlum element" and would doubtless turn to crime unless given aid to attend private schools. The intolerable conditions included the beating of white children by Negroes, who pursued them on the way home from school and cornered them in public buses. The Judge submitted affidavits from public school principals alleging that white children were subjected to harassment, including sexual advances, by blacks. These arguments failed to sway the judges.[86]

Leander entered as intervenors for the defense the principals of eight predominantly black private schools serving more than a thousand retarded children in New Orleans. When the earlier commission had been declared unconstitutional, these schools for retarded blacks had been forced to close, he explained. It would be naïve to think that the state would provide only for needy Negro children, so the new act had also extended aid to needy white children. Assistance to black children alone could not be given, he said, because that would be unconstitutional class legislation. The court, brushing aside this sophistry, enjoined the operation of the new agency on the grounds that it was a subterfuge designed "to give state aid to private discrimination." The decision was upheld by the U.S. Supreme Court.[87]

State tuition grants, once the white hope of segregationists, had proved only another empty promise; the last redoubt of segregation had been overrun. A few diehards suggested that Governor McKeithen once again invoke the paper tiger of state interposition, but he replied that it had been declared unconstitutional twelve years earlier "in about one and a half lines." Asked if he would call a special session of the legislature to erect additional barriers to segregation, the governor indicated that he had run out of ideas. "I don't know what to do with a special session if I get it," he said.[88]

In his last-ditch effort to preserve segregated schools, Perez had finally been driven from the field in both his own domain and statewide. St. Bernard schools were desegregated in 1966. The Judge defended the St. Bernard school board against a Justice Department suit, but the result was a foregone conclusion. Sporadic incidents occurred in Plaquemines' sister parish: protesting white parents hoisted signs defiantly proclaiming Never; a school bus transporting blacks was halted and pelted with stones; a private car belonging to Negro parents was rocked nearly to the point of overturning; rebellious teenagers set fire to the curtains in the St. Bernard auditorium. Leander was handcuffed by the federal court order that prohibited him from interfering, and St. Bernard lacked the financial resources needed to establish a parishwide system of private schools.[89]

In April, 1967, the Justice Department went before Judge Christenberry to request that Plaquemines be permanently enjoined from operating a segregated public school system. This order was to include safeguards to prevent deterioration of the public schools such as had occurred during the 1966–1967 academic year. The defense immediately filed a motion demanding that Judge Christenberry disqualify himself because of personal prejudice against Perez. In hearing testimony before issuing his temporary injunction eight months earlier, the federal judge had stated that his door was always open for citizens who wished to be heard. Plaquemines officials complained that this meant that he "welcomed outside gossip and propaganda inimical to the defendants." Furthermore, the petition continued, he had threatened Perez with contempt of court three times during the hearing "for the sole purpose of trying to intimidate said Perez, and to hold him up to ridicule and scorn to the Courtroom audience, including some of Judge Christenberry's visitors and guests who were anti-Perez partisans." Luke Petrovitch, attorney for the commission council, admitted that Perez had helped him with the motion requesting the judge's recusation. Christenberry ruled that the charges were unfounded and ordered the hearing to continue. A parade of witnesses testified that, during the eight months since the preliminary injunction, the Plaquemines public school system had descended into utter chaos. On June 27, Judge Christenberry signed a permanent injunction that tolerated no insubordination. All grades would be desegregated for the 1967–1968 academic year. Students would be permitted to enroll at any school in the parish and would be provided with free transportation if the school they wished to attend was more than a mile from home. Faculties would be integrated. The school board and commission council were required to maintain and repair the school buildings, provide library services for every student, and supply athletic equipment at all schools. If local resources were insufficient to furnish such services, the school board was to make proper application for the federal funds available.[90]

When Plaquemines schools opened in the fall of 1967, blacks outnumbered whites in the public school system for the first time in the twentieth century. Because the teacher shortage remained critical, the school board decided to eliminate the tenth, eleventh, and twelfth grades at Boothville-Venice and transfer the 110 pupils to Buras High School ten miles away. The students, both black and white, refused to leave. Some 70 of them, carrying placards, milled about outside their school as children in the first nine grades attended classes. The protesters shouted to passing cars, "We want to get rid of the great white father Perez and then maybe we'll get the school system we should have." Other pupils said that they would attempt to teach themselves and make up their own homework. Leander responded, "I have washed my hands of the schools since the Federal Government has taken over their operations."[91]

The situation gradually improved. Teachers returned to work, and white children came back to the public schools. By October, 1971, 5,856 children were enrolled in public schools in Plaquemines and only 2,230 in private and parochial schools.[92] Circumstances are still far from ideal but, ironically, desegregation seems to have worked better in Plaquemines than in nearby New Orleans. The Judge continued to speak at state and regional Citizens' Council rallies and other meetings but remained discreetly quiet in his little delta empire, muffled by the federal court injunction that remained in effect until he died. The judicial fight had failed, and guerrilla warfare in Plaquemines had finally been stamped out, but Leander was still unwilling to surrender. His only remaining hope was to win the political fight by electing a president who sympathized with the South.

FIFTEEN

Saving the Country Again

In recent times Louisiana has had difficulty finding a niche in presidential elections. In the seven elections between 1948 and 1972, its electoral votes went to the Republicans three times (1956, 1964, 1972), the Democrats twice (1952, 1960), and to third parties twice (States' Rights, 1948; American Independent, 1968). Perez avidly supported Eisenhower in 1952 but quickly became disenchanted with him after he took office. The Judge had assumed that Ike was a doctrinaire conservative, when in fact the general had no clearly formed political philosophy at all; he had even had trouble deciding which party to join. When Eisenhower failed to act as Perez thought a "responsible" conservative should—that is, to denounce the Supreme Court's 1954 desegregation decision and order Congress to turn over all tidelands oil resources to the coastal states—Leander felt betrayed. The only explanation was that the president had been duped by Communist advisers, which only proved the extent to which Kremlin agents had infiltrated the federal bureaucracy. After the Democrats nominated former Illinois governor Adlai Stevenson for a second run at the presidency in 1956, Leander found himself in an embarrassing dilemma: should he support an incumbent president who was surrounded by Communist advisers or a "far-left" candidate who might well be a Marxist himself? Reluctantly, he decided to back the Republican—a basically good man who could perhaps still be alerted to the Kremlin threat. During Eisenhower's second term, Perez fired off a telegram to the chief executive, warning him that Marxists were plotting the direction of the American civil rights movement. The president's "far-left" advisers, of course, never let him see the telegram. With both the Democrats and Republicans

310

gasping beneath a Red tidal wave, the Judge resolved to reeducate the public in civics, at the same time teaching both major parties that continued flirtations with fifth columners would lose them the votes of millions of patriotic Americans like himself.[1]

Perez had little hope that the Democrats would nominate a man he could support for president in 1960. Of the leading candidates, John Kennedy of Massachusetts was a liberal who had attended Harvard, a hotbed of sedition, and Lyndon Johnson was a "renegade Texan" who openly preached racial integration. Nonetheless, despite his well-publicized antipathy to the national leadership of the party of which he was nominally a member, Leander was selected by the state central committee to be a delegate to the Democratic National Convention in Los Angeles. His ally from neighboring St. Bernard Parish, Sheriff Nicholas P. Trist, was also named to the delegation, which was to be headed by Governor Jimmie Davis. Willie Rainach, Davis' rival in the recent gubernatorial campaign and an acrimonious critic of the national Democratic party, was chosen as the delegate to represent his parish. To Camille Gravel— Louisiana's national committeeman and cochairman of the national party's credentials committee—inviting Perez and Rainach to the Democratic National Convention was like inviting Benedict Arnold to a DAR picnic. Gravel announced that he would attempt to have the credentials committee bar the two from the convention on the grounds that they had deserted the party in 1948, 1952, and 1956. But, under pressure from backers of Senator Kennedy, who either didn't know Perez or thought that he could be persuaded to change his mind, Gravel abandoned the challenges. His own status as Louisiana's national committeeman was curiously ambiguous. A liberal, Gravel had sanctioned the Democratic platform on civil rights in 1956, after which militant segregationists on Louisiana's state central committee had passed a resolution removing Gravel and replacing him with Harry Booth, a conservative. The Democratic National Committee, however, claiming that it alone could remove one of its committee members before his term had expired, continued to recognize Gravel.[2]

The national convention, confirming Perez's suspicions that it was acting on secret orders from Moscow, nominated Kennedy for president and Johnson as his running mate. These nominations, coupled with the adoption of a liberal platform including a strong civil rights plank, provoked Perez to announce that he was "1001 per cent" against the Kennedy-Johnson ticket: "I have sized up Kennedy and his platform and he's no better than Henry Wallace in 1948. Kennedy is the Henry Wallace of 1960."[3] Wallace, Perez explained, was the man who had run for president in 1948 "on an out and out Communist platform, under the name of the Progressive Party."[4] Continuing his history lesson, he pointed out that Lyndon Johnson was "the renegade who is credited with passing the first civil rights bill—and he admits it."[5] The Plaquemines boss insisted that Senator Kennedy was a "stooge of Walter Reuther, a student of Moscow." (Perez pronounced *Reuther* as if it were the last word in *Roto Rooter.*) Leander's hatred for Johnson was even greater because Johnson was a southerner who, by encouraging racial integration, had betrayed his own section. An anecdote about Johnson printed in the *Plaquemines Gazette* read: "A scalawag said: 'Johnson is Texas' greatest son.' A loyal Texan said: 'You did not complete your sentence.'"[6]

The candidates were bad enough, but the Democratic platform was downright criminal, Perez charged. He pointed out that his hated foe, Attorney General Jack Gremillion, was a Democratic elector. How could the state's chief legal officer, responsible for upholding law and order, endorse a platform that would clearly be criminal in application, he demanded. Describing the platform as a "Congolese Constitution," Perez likened it to Marx's Communist Manifesto and insisted that it was largely the handiwork of Congressman Emanuel Celler, whom the Judge described as "the multiple pro-Communist member of Congress from Brooklyn." Not only were the leading Democrats pseudo-Communists, Perez raged, but they were also plagiarists. The civil rights plank of the nefarious platform had been cribbed from Article 123 of the Russian constitution ("Equality of rights of citizens of the U.S.S.R., irrespective of their nationality or race, in all spheres of economics, government, cultural, political and other public activity, is an indefeasible law") and Article 21 of the Yugoslavian constitution ("All citizens of the Federal People's Republic of Yugoslavia are equal before the law and enjoy equal rights regardless of nationality, race and creed"). Perez insisted that the Democrats had sketched a step-by-step blueprint for Communist takeover: the pledge to guarantee full employment meant surreptitious government takeover of all industry and agriculture in the guise of providing employment; support of the United Nations would lead to a world government run by foreign Communists; the promise to eliminate discrimination in the administration of justice would result in the imprisonment of local law officials who jailed Negro culprits and would encourage blacks to defy the law, because "we know what the U.S. Supreme Court does invariably in freeing Negro degenerates who rape white women." Perez warned that the Democratic platform would lead to a complete breakdown of law and order: "The law of the jungle would prevail. Every man would be on his own. His only protection would be his shot gun."[7]

It was a bleak forecast indeed, but according to Perez it was lamentably not limited to the Democrats. Richard Nixon, after all, had been surrounded by the same left-wing advisers who had convinced President Eisenhower that school desegregation was a constitutional doctrine and that Louisiana was not entitled to tidelands oil beyond its three-mile limit. Sometime during Nixon's variegated political career, which had included the hunting down of Reds of many shades, the Republican standard bearer had become, in Perez's mind, "an exponent of anti-Americanism." According to Leander, there was "not a dime's worth of difference" between the Democratic and Republican candidates because both had "sold our birthright for a mess of communists, pro-communists, and Negro bloc votes." He predicted that Louisiana Democrats would refuse to vote for Kennedy, then added, "And they are not in love with Republicans and don't feel that Nixon is any white hope, and I do mean white."[8]

Convinced that both major candidates were influenced if not entirely controlled by the Kremlin, lesser men might have despaired. Not Leander Perez. He quickly became Louisiana's most prominent evangelist for the unpledged or "free" elector movement, an idea that had been promoted by Louisiana's States' Rights party and conservative pressure groups in other parts of the South even before the national nominating conventions. The concept of voting for electors who were uncommitted to any specific candidate was not new; that was what the Founding Fathers had originally intended. But it had never, in recent times, been employed on a large scale to achieve the results desired by Perez. Normally, the electors were figureheads; they pledged to vote for a particular candidate and traditionally they did so without much fanfare. The number of electoral votes equals the sum of the members of Congress, which in 1960 was 537. In order to gain election a candidate had to poll an absolute majority of the electoral votes (269 in 1960). If no candidate gained this majority, the president would be chosen by the House of Representatives from the three top candidates, with each state having one vote in the process. The aim of Perez and his fellow southern conservatives was, by choosing electors unpledged to Kennedy or Nixon, to prevent either from obtaining an electoral majority, thus deadlocking the election. At this point, theoretically, several scenarios could ensue—each featuring the unpledged southern electors as power brokers wielding the balance of power. The uncommitted electors, during the interval between popular balloting and the meeting of the electors to cast their votes, could await concessions from the frustrated candidates: promises to slow down implementation of racial integration, appointment of southern conservatives to the Supreme Court and cabinet, and support for legislation restricting the federal government to an inactive role in such fields as voting rights and education. Should Kennedy and Nixon both prove unyielding, the uncommitted electors could cast their votes for a southerner such as Virginia's Senator Harry Byrd or South Carolina's Senator Strom Thurmond. When the election reverted to the House of Representatives, in Perez's words, "each Southern state's vote will count as much as New York's Harlem and pro-communist dominated 45 electoral votes."[9] It was the scheme of desperate but determined men, contingent upon a succession of improbable events. Perez, however, instinctively liked the idea: it was bold and aggressive; it involved legal technicalities; it would serve as a rallying cause for the persecuted South and scornfully defy the liberal Northeast.

Even many who sympathized with the objectives of the free-elector movement considered the strategem impractical. It would require a crash course in civics for millions of southerners who only vaguely understood the electoral college, if indeed they were aware of its existence. The absence of a flesh-and-blood candidate confused many voters, who felt that they were being asked to vote for "nobody." The militant southern conservatives badly needed a vigorous, articulate young candidate to replace the shopworn faces of Strom Thurmond and Harry Byrd as a symbol for their neo-Dixiecrat movement. They accidentally discovered such a person in George Corley Wallace, an obscure but glib and personable state judge from the red clay hills of rural Alabama. This diminutive former amateur boxer blended states' rights conservatism, agrarian populism, and southern racism with a dynamic, charismatic speaking style that made him, suddenly, a highly sought speaker at free-elector rallies. Wallace was in such demand that once, when he was unable to journey personally to Louisiana for an unpledged-elector fund-raising banquet, four hundred persons listened intently as he addressed them by long-distance telephone.[10]

Public speaking exhilarated Wallace; the more he spoke, the more he yearned to lead an all-out southern crusade. He entered no Democratic primaries in 1960, nor did he extend his speaking efforts beyond the South; but he gradually began to recognize his own potential as a presidential candidate.

Unpledged-elector spokesmen countered the claim that their plan was unworkable by arguing that it had succeeded once already—in the presidential election of 1876. In that hard-fought campaign, Democrat Samuel Tilden had challenged Republican Rutherford B. Hayes. Tilden received a clear majority of the popular vote and was only one electoral vote short of victory, but the electoral votes from three southern states still under carpetbag rule—Louisiana, South Carolina, and Florida—were disputed. The free-elector advocates of 1960, anxious to read into the 1876 election anything that would help their own campaign, claimed that these southern states, through the use of unpledged electors, had forced concessions from Hayes, namely the removal of the remaining federal troops from the South and the abandonment of the Republican carpetbag governments there, in return for their electoral votes. Unpledged-elector newspaper advertisements, repeatedly appealing to the purported

success of the 1876 strategy, boasted, "Louisiana did it before. . . .
Louisiana must do it again."[11] One states' rights enthusiast, who
evidently had trouble remembering the first names of the presidents,
asserted in a letter to the New Orleans *States-Item* that in 1876
the southern states had "blocked together with unpledged electors
who finally elected Rufus B. Hayes on their terms."[12]

Actually, the Hayes-Tilden election had little relevance to the
1960 situation. In 1876 there were no slates of unpledged electors on
the ballot in any state, and it was not bargaining by southern electors that determined the result of the election. Dual sets of returns,
certified by rival governments in each state, were sent in from
Louisiana, Florida, and South Carolina; and an electoral commission with a Republican majority ruled early in 1877 that all three
states should be counted Republican. It was only after Hayes had
been declared the winner that any kind of "deal" took place; southern Democratic congressional leaders agreed to abandon a Democratic filibuster designed to prevent the formal proclamation of the
electoral votes in return for certain commitments from Hayes. Although the deal to end carpetbag rule in exchange for "unpledged"
electoral votes never actually took place, the story persists in the
political mythology of Louisiana and other states in the Deep
South.[13]

The first meeting of southern rightist political leaders after the
1960 Democratic convention was held near Biloxi, Mississippi, to
organize segregation groups to oppose Negro use of Gulf Coast
beaches. Perez, the principal speaker, urged Mississippians to follow
the lead of their governor, Ross Barnett, in overcoming the bloc vote
of northern blacks with a southern bloc of unpledged electors. The
Judge also warned Gulf Coast citizens that, if they did not resist the
efforts of blacks to use the beaches, "you may as well close your
shops and hotels, barricade your homes and keep your wives and
daughters off the front porches."[14]

Perez launched the Louisiana free-elector campaign by inviting
conservatives from throughout the state to attend a strategy conference in New Orleans on August 4. About fifty members of the Democratic State Central Committee, state legislators, district attorneys,
sheriffs, and mayors, including several leaders of Louisiana's States'

Rights party, attended. Fervid segregationists from rural north Louisiana parishes packed the meeting, and most of the delegates from south Louisiana were close associates of Perez. Willie Rainach was among the prominent state Democrats in attendance; others who came included former governor Sam Jones and Secretary of State Wade O. Martin, Jr. Rainach, who had broken with Governor Davis earlier over a dispute about segregation legislation, said that he would prefer to run a southern candidate for president, but that a free-elector ticket would be the best alternative if the South could not agree on a nominee. Although invited by Perez, Davis himself did not attend; but he was represented by his trusted ally Arthur Watson, vice-chairman of the Democratic State Central Committee. The free-elector partisans made plans to attempt to have the committee certify a slate of unpledged electors to be placed on the ballot under the traditional rooster emblem. Heading the unpledged slate with the rooster, Perez told the delegates, "will assure us of victory." A committee was appointed to circulate a petition providing for the placement of a slate of unpledged electors on the ballot as a third party in case the central committee voted to pledge Louisiana's Democratic electors to John Kennedy. A Shreveport representative at the meeting suggested that if all else failed the state central committee could select Camille Gravel, A. P. Tureaud, and "eight other niggers" as electors for the Democrats.[15]

Although the Democratic ruling body was not scheduled to meet before September, Leander suggested that Governor Davis be persuaded to summon a special meeting before August 27, the deadline for filing petitions for electoral slates with the secretary of state. Prompted by this suggestion, a five-man committee of free-elector partisans tried to phone Davis at the Governor's Mansion. After receiving only a busy signal, they went to the mansion in a mood to "barge in" if necessary. The governor welcomed the delegates, met with them for over an hour, and expressed sympathy for the movement, but avoided a public commitment. He did agree to summon a special session of the Democratic State Central Committee for August 11 to resolve the unpledged-elector issue. Perez and his allies were anxious to have the question settled because Kennedy supporters in Louisiana were already actively campaigning. Both the Reg-

ular Democratic Organization of New Orleans, which had backed
Davis for governor, and the Crescent City Democratic Association,
which had supported deLesseps Morrison, were already canvassing
for Kennedy.[16]

Senator Kennedy, aware of the importance of the central committee showdown and of Perez's influence in that body, wired the Judge
just before the meeting to request his support, promising to deal
with Louisiana's problems "with justice and understanding." Kennedy concluded his message, "Your support in the November election may make a major difference in the future of our country." The
telegram failed to sway Perez, who had no intention of supporting
the Massachusetts senator. As it turned out, Kennedy did not need
Perez's help because the central committee voted fifty-one to forty-
nine to pledge Louisiana's ten Democratic electors of Kennedy.[17]

After failing to obtain the Democratic rooster for the slate of unpledged electors, Leander openly merged his faction with the
Louisiana States' Rights party. He became state finance chairman of
the free-elector campaign and a member of the four-man state campaign and policy committee, whose chairman was States' Rights
leader David Treen, a New Orleans attorney who later became a
Republican and was elected Louisiana's first GOP congressman
since Reconstruction. Seven of the ten candidates for elector on the
States' Rights ticket, including Perez himself, were Democrats, and
the other three were members of the States' Rights party. Some
States' Rights leaders, fearing that a ticket of unpledged electors
would only help Kennedy by taking conservative votes from Nixon,
urged a fusion ticket of Republican and States' Rights electors in
return for a commitment from Nixon to appoint strict construc-
tionists to the federal judiciary. Most Louisiana rightists, however,
so detested the Republicans (whom they considered as integrationist
as the Democrats) that they insisted on an independent ticket even
though it might inadvertently help John Kennedy. Convinced that
they represented the only hope of white Louisianians, the States'
Righters adopted a resolution declaring that it was useless for the
Republicans and Democrats to continue campaigning because the
States' Rights party represented the will of "70 to 80 per cent of all
Louisiana voters."[18]

Both the Citizens' Council of Greater New Orleans and the South Louisiana Citizens' Council campaigned for the unpledged-elector ticket, but few prominent Democratic officeholders in the South endorsed the free-elector movement. When Lyndon Johnson flew to New Orleans for a campaign rally, he was joined by Senators Russell Long and Allen Ellender, New Orleans Mayor deLesseps Morrison, and most of the Louisiana congressional delegation. Senators James O. Eastland and John Stennis of Mississippi both remained loyal to the Democratic ticket. Eastland, Perez's closest friend in the Senate, candidly explained, "If I would bolt the Democratic party I would be removed as chairman of the Judiciary Committee." Mississippi's Ross Barnett was the only southern governor to participate wholeheartedly in the free-elector crusade. Leander even had trouble in his own domain; Nicholas Trist, sheriff of St. Bernard, refused to endorse the free-elector ticket, although he also declined to declare for either Nixon or Kennedy. A Trist supporter commented that economics now outweighted integration as an issue and that jobs were more plentiful under a Democratic administration.[19]

There was also dissension among the leaders of the free-elector movement. David Treen wanted to make opposition to high taxes and to paternalistic government the principal issues, but some of the Democratic defectors preferred to base the campaign entirely on race. One such Democrat, explaining that many adherents of Huey Long's political philosophy favored high taxes on the rich and make-work and welfare programs, complained that Treen's campaign strategy was losing votes because it was anti-Long and anti-union; it was much better to run on an issue upon which there was general public accord, such as white supremacy.[20]

The nascent unpledged-elector movement, brimming with enthusiasm but understaffed and meagerly financed, could hardly match the firmly established statewide organization of the regular Democrats. The States' Rights campaign was designed to make best use of the group's limited funds by concentrating on half-hour telecasts and spot commercials, which would reach a maximum audience. States' Rights leaders complained that, except for their paid advertisements, the Louisiana news media were ignoring their campaign. To compensate for this lack of coverage at least in New

Orleans, the States' Righters developed a scheme to dominate the letters-to-the-editor columns. A volunteer group was organized to write four or five letters per day to the Crescent City dailies, taking care to disguise the correspondence so that the editor would not realize that all the letters were from the same group. Seeking further exposure, Perez challenged the state campaign directors for Kennedy and Nixon to a three-way debate, but both declined.[21]

Perez crisscrossed the state delivering fiery speeches and trying to raise money for the free-elector crusade. At a campaign kickoff meeting in Baton Rouge, he explained why he considered Kennedy and Nixon fellow travelers: labor leader Reuther, a Kennedy supporter, had studied in Moscow for two years; Kennedy himself had attended school in England under a Communist teacher; Nixon had stood by while bayonets were used against protesting whites at Little Rock and had promised greater progress for the NAACP in the next few years than in the past 150. The Judge confidently predicted that the southern states would elect 30 to 36 unpledged electors: 10 in Louisiana, 8 in Mississippi, 6 in Alabama, a minimum of 3 in Georgia, and 8 in Alabama. He boasted, "With this balance of power, instead of Kennedy and Nixon advocating sit-ins in lunch counters and kneel-ins in churches, they would come kneeling to us." [22]

When the Democratic vice-presidential candidate, Lyndon Johnson, came to New Orleans, Perez organized a boycott of the rally that slightly reduced the size of the turnout, although many of Louisiana's most influential public officials attended. The Republicans countered Johnson's trip with a Louisiana speaking tour by Senator Barry Goldwater, who was expected to appeal to local conservatives. Goldwater, however, stirred little sympathy among unpledged-elector advocates, who claimed that Nixon was committed to a platform contrary to Goldwater's conservative positions. Leander imported Dan Smoot, a right-wing radio commentator and former FBI agent, as his answer to the more illustrious speakers of the major parties. Addressing almost a thousand States' Righters at a fund-raising banquet in New Orleans, Smoot pilloried the United Nations, the Earl Warren Supreme Court, and foreign aid and told his appreciative audience that in 1956 he had voted for T. Coleman

Andrews for president, a candidate who had advocated, among other things, abolition of the federal income tax.[23]

As election day approached, few political analysts would predict what Louisianians would do. Chep Morrison, a Catholic who had been labeled an integrationist, had been defeated in the governor's race nine months earlier by those very questions of race and religion. Would the same issues cripple Kennedy? Kennedy's biggest asset in Louisiana was the state's traditional loyalty to the Democratic party, but the presidential election of 1948 had proved that white supremacy was a more emotionally potent issue than party fealty. Would the unpledged-elector movement take away more votes from Kennedy, the liberal Democrat, or Nixon, the more conservative Republican? One question that no one asked, because everyone knew the answer, was how Plaquemines Parish would vote.

When the Louisiana voter, after considerable soul-searching, made up his mind about the candidate (or noncandidate in the case of the free-elector ticket), he still faced the task of deciphering a complicated ballot. There were four columns: a Democratic column headed by the rooster; a Republican ticket listed under the elephant; a slate of unpledged electors appearing beneath the old Dixiecrat Statue of Liberty emblem; and a fourth column, also headed by the rooster, listing Democratic candidates for congressional and local offices. Perez declared that the rooster above the Kennedy slate "should be shown with his tail feathers plucked and a scrawny neck to make it truly resemble what the Democratic Party stands for; that is, more like a vulture than a rooster."[24]

Louisiana's voters, it turned out, feared liberalism and Catholicism more in a governor than in a president. The chief effect of Perez's campaign for unpledged electors was to enlarge Kennedy's margin over Nixon. The Democratic nominee, running especially well in Catholic south Louisiana, polled 407,339 votes (50.4 percent); Nixon received 230,980 (28.6 percent); the unpledged slate finished third with 169,572 (21.1 percent). Perez could take some comfort in the returns from Plaquemines Parish, which the unpledged ticket carried with 65.1 percent of the vote; Kennedy finished second and Nixon trailed badly. The vote was much closer in St. Bernard, but the independent slate edged Kennedy there, as well. The free-elector movement fell far short of its goal throughout the South, winning only eight electors in Mississippi and six in Alabama.[25]

Defeated at the polls, the embittered States' Righters still refused to concede the election. Die-hard segregationists, editorially encouraged by the Shreveport *Journal*, tried to persuade Louisiana's ten electors to break their pledge and withhold their votes from Kennedy unless he promised to postpone desegregation. If Louisiana held out, other states might join; the *Journal* pointed out that six southern states had already adopted laws specifically freeing their electors to vote for whomever they wished. Mississippi's eight unpledged electors and Alabama's six agreed to vote for Harry Byrd in an effort to block Kennedy's election. Louisiana's legislators, besieged from all sides, received telegrams from Ross Barnett and the Mississippi and Alabama unpledged electors, asking them to replace Louisiana's ten electors with men who would vote for Byrd; and Howard Jones, a state senator and an intimate of Governor Davis, carried around a resolution providing for such a plan for two weeks before finally giving up.[26]

The unpledged-elector campaign of 1960 had been chimerical from its inception, lacking both an effective regional organization and the endorsement of prominent politicians. Kennedy and Johnson had further undermined the movement by promising patronage and threatening forfeiture of committee assignments for bolters. Perez, who sometimes altered his tactics but never surrendered, now became convinced that the dilemma of southern conservatives could be remedied by restructuring the electoral college. In the Judge's mind, the system of awarding all of a state's electoral votes to the candidate who polled a bare plurality favored the minority ethnic blocs in large states by giving them a balance of power. He reasoned that bloc-voting blacks determined who received the entire electoral vote of such states as New York and California; that the numerous electoral votes of these states in turn decided the election; ergo, that black voters in populous states controlled presidential elections.[27]

Electoral college reform had been a popular project among liberals at least as far back as the New Deal, though for reasons quite different from Perez's. Liberals felt that the electoral college denied ethnic minorities a proper voice in the democratic process. For example, although Negroes constituted a considerable segment of the population of the southern states (though, until recently, not of the *voting* population), they had never been able to ensure that at least some of the electoral votes from their states would be cast for candidates who would represent their interests. Several prominent liberals, therefore, joined such unlikely allies as Perez in demanding that something be done about the electoral college. The liberals, however, usually favored different solutions; one proposal was to abolish the electoral college entirely and award the presidency to the candidate obtaining the greatest number of popular votes; another was to divide electoral votes in proportion to the popular vote within each state.

True to his instinct for manipulating legal details, Perez did not wish to abolish the electoral college entirely, but simply to tinker with its mechanism to the advantage of white conservatives. He proposed to substitute for the statewide winner-take-all system of awarding electoral votes a scheme whereby each congressional district would determine how its one elector would vote. Two additional votes would go to the candidate who carried the entire state. Perez's plan would have prevented metropolitan centers from outvoting rural, traditionally conservative areas; urban influence would be limited to the congressional districts in which large cities were located. Under such a setup Perez could be certain of personally controlling at least one electoral vote, that of Louisiana's First Congressional District. The Judge theorized that, even though slates of unpledged electors might be defeated statewide in the South because of the relatively heavy concentration of liberals and blacks in metropolitan areas, many rural congressional districts would elect uncommitted electors whenever both major parties nominated liberals. A few independent electors from each southern state, added to some in the Midwest and West, might not only constitute a bloc that could determine the election, but might also dissuade the major parties from nominating liberal candidates in the first place. In a close contest the old strategy would prevail: the rival candidates would be forced to bargain with the uncommitted electors, and these electors would be even more militantly conservative than the South as a whole.[28]

Although each state was constitutionally permitted to replace its unit system with a district method of awarding electoral votes, few states could be expected to reduce their influence in the electoral college by splitting their own vote while neighboring states cast their votes in a bloc. Perez decided that the only certain means of preventing states from casting their electoral votes in a bloc was a constitutional amendment making the district scheme mandatory in every state. During the Kennedy administration, a number of constitutional amendments to reform or abolish the electoral college were introduced in Congress, including one by South Dakota's Senator Karl Mundt to implement the district system. There are two methods by which a constitutional amendment may be proposed: by a two-thirds' vote of Congress or at the request of two-thirds of the state legislatures, a method that had never been utilized. When the Mundt amendment stalled in Congress, Perez became convinced that concerted pressure must be applied on both the state and congressional levels as "the only hope of saving this country from all-out socialism and worse, because of the demands made by minority blocs which have the balance of power in key states in the presidential election."[29]

The Judge, together with a small group of like-minded electoral reformers from the midwestern and mountain states, was instrumental in organizing and financing the National Electoral Reform Committee, which operated under the auspices of the American Good Government Society, a nonprofit organization with headquarters in Washington, D.C. Edwin C. Johnson of Denver, former Democratic senator and governor of Colorado, was named chairman. Johnson's strategy was to keep the movement small, aggressive, and unpublicized in order to concentrate on influencing congressmen and state legislators rather than converting masses of voters. Although some efforts were made in Washington, the committee's primary objective was to convince two-thirds of the state legislatures to petition Congress to summon a constitutional convention to enact electoral college reform. In December, 1962, the committee hired Fred Poole, a former public relations representative for the Association of Oil Pipe Lines, to lobby for passage of resolutions calling for a constitutional convention by working among legislators and key public officials in selected states. Although such a resolution was drawn up for presentation to the Louisiana legislature, it was never introduced and Poole did not lobby there, which was included on a list of states "not to approach," possibly because outside efforts might have jeopardized Perez's own labors. Barely four months after hiring the lobbyist, the committee began to fall behind on Poole's salary. Leander personally contributed five thousand dollars to the committee in 1963, but a fellow organizer wrote him, "You are the only patriot that seems to be carrying the financial burdens of our operation." Perez enlisted the backing of Dallas billionaire H. L. Hunt, who contributed far more unneeded advice than money. Hunt feared that, if a constitutional convention assembled, delegates dominated by Communists, the United Nations, or the Supreme Court might try to rewrite the entire Constitution. By the winter of 1964 the movement had lost momentum and could no longer afford to employ Poole. Financial support continued to decline during the following years, and several of the leaders died; as late as 1967 only twelve of the thirty-four states necessary had adopted resolutions requesting Congress to call a constitutional convention.[30]

In the spring of 1963 Perez began making plans for the presidential election to be held in November, 1964. He was certain that the Democrats would renominate Kennedy, whom he blamed for the acceleration of school desegregation in Louisiana, and believed that the Republicans would nominate a "me too" candidate as liberal as the president, such as Governor Nelson Rockefeller of New York. Although he had already decided not to support the Democratic or Republican nominee, whoever they might be, Perez was uncertain exactly whom he would support. Perhaps he would back some prominent southern conservative or, if no outstanding candidate emerged, another slate of unpledged electors. But Perez was sure of one tactic; whoever he supported should run under the rooster, the traditional symbol of white supremacy as well as of Louisiana's Democratic party. Voting for the candidate listed beneath the rooster had been standard procedure for Louisianians for so long, particularly for those who were illiterate, that Perez was convinced that any candidate running under the rooster emblem would have an automatic advantage of 75,000 to 100,000 votes. Most political observers believed that the symbol's importance had declined as literacy had risen, making it worth far fewer votes, but each faction nonetheless wanted the rooster for its candidate. Fearing that the Democratic State Central Committee might again refuse to assign the rooster to a free-elector slate, as it had in 1960, Leander developed a plan to circumvent the committee. Although the state central committee had since Reconstruction always designated Louisiana's presidential electors, Leander now decided that it was undemocratic for the Democratic governing body to "handpick" the electors. No matter that the electors were figureheads, whose offices provided no remuneration and lasted for a few hours of a single day; the people should vote for the electors in a statewide contest. Critics of the idea pointed out that campaigning for a nonpaying office on a statewide basis would prove so expensive that only the wealthy, such as Perez himself, could afford to run. Money was no object, Perez answered, when the issue involved the right of the people to vote. But why, the Judge's critics continued, had he waited until now to change the method of selecting electors if the central committee had been acting improperly for so many years? Could it possibly be that Perez had not previously objected because until now he had controlled a majority of the committee? Such arguments were sophistical, Perez insisted, and were designed to distract attention from the "issue," which was the right of the "dear people" to choose their own electors.[31]

The true issue, of course, was not who would be honored with the office of elector; it was which electors would have the right to use the coveted rooster. According to Leander's scheme, which became known as the "Perez plan," two opposing slates of Democratic electors, both certified by the Democratic State Central Committee, would run in a special primary election held on July 25, 1964, the date of the Democratic congressional primaries. The winning slate would appear on the ballot in the November presidential election as Louisiana's Democratic slate of electors, headed by the rooster emblem. The losing electors, if they felt it worthwhile, could petition their way onto the ballot as a third-party slate.[32]

The whole rather loosely reasoned scheme was made even more bizarre by the fact that Perez had started his crusade so far in advance of the actual presidential election that neither he nor his opponents had yet chosen presidential candidates. Presumably, one ticket of electors on the July 25 ballot would be pledged to the national Democratic nominee, and the other would be unpledged or pledged to a southern conservative. The Judge at first seemed to lean toward an unpledged slate and lent credence to reports that he intended to lead another independent-elector crusade by attending several free-elector fund-raising banquets. But he abruptly reversed himself, branded unpledged electors "impractical," and said that the alternative would be a list of electors pledged to "some fine, upstanding southern or western Democrat."[33]

An additional complication was the fact that the July 25 primary would occur a month before the Democratic National Convention, which meant that the voters could not know who the party's nominee would be. Furthermore, voters in the primary would be free to choose some electors from one slate and others from a second slate, which might result in a split electoral vote. State AFL-CIO President Victor Bussie, a loyalist Democrat and one of the chief opponents of the Perez plan, complained that the scheme would "confuse the people to the point to where they won't know what they're voting on."[34]

Perez's plan was logical to him even if no one else understood it. He assumed that his conservative unpledged electors would have a better chance against the national Democratic candidate in an election in which neither ticket was permitted to use the rooster. If the conservative slate won, it would have the advantage of the rooster in the November general election. If the Perez ticket lost, it could still petition its way onto the ballot as a third party.

When the Louisiana legislature convened in May, 1963, a bill designed to implement the Perez plan was introduced. The legislation easily passed the House, but was defeated in the Senate by two votes, largely through the efforts of Victor Bussie. Undaunted, Leander prepared to carry his fight to the Democratic State Central

Committee, which was purportedly dominated by a majority of loyalists. At the September 7 meeting, Perez and his fellow conservatives engaged in a tedious debate with the loyalists, led by J. D. DeBlieux, a former state senator. Attacking the Perez plan, one loyalist charged, "This is just another effort to convert this committee from the Democratic committee to an anti-Democratic committee." Nonetheless, the Perez forces unexpectedly routed their liberal foes; the Perez plan passed fifty-three to forty-two.[35]

Passage of the Perez plan more than a year before the presidential election was a moral victory for Louisiana's rightists, but hardly more than that. A new Democratic State Central Committee, elected before the scheduled July 25, 1964, primary for electors, was empowered to repeal any action of its predecessor. Loyalist members of the new committee immediately prefiled a motion to rescind the Perez plan; the committee then assembled in the House chamber in Baton Rouge on April 11, 1964, to consider the motion. A number of Citizens' Council delegations from north Louisiana were among more than two hundred placard-waving demonstrators who lined the sides of the crowded chamber and cheered the boss of Plaquemines. No one could predict what the committee would do. The original motion had been adopted when President Kennedy had seemed sure to be the Democratic nominee, but since then he had been assassinated, making President Lyndon Johnson, a Texan with more support among Louisiana liberals, the probable nominee. Perez opened the meeting with a flourish of oratory, offering a substitute resolution to delay consideration of the Perez plan until the Louisiana legislature had considered two prefiled bills to postpone the elector primary until after the Democratic National Convention. His opponents sought to table this resolution. When the latter move failed to carry by a fifty-one to fifty vote, Perez speeded through a motion to adjourn, thus maintaining the status quo.[36]

The loyalists were temporarily stunned by Perez's blitzkrieg tactics, but they regrouped and planned to try again. Governor-elect John McKeithen, who took office in May, had remained neutral in the April 11 showdown, although his spokesman, former state senator C. H. ("Sammy") Downs, who had been elected chairman of the committee, had repeatedly ruled in favor of the Perez group. But McKeithen, who had described the free-elector movement as "trickery" during his campaign for the Democratic nomination, might well reverse his stand, particularly if Perez's tactics threatened to jeopardize a possible tidelands settlement.[37]

While the controversy over his plan raged, Leander himself switched his support from a free-elector ticket to a slate of electors pledged to George Wallace, now governor of Alabama. Wallace had first attracted national attention in 1958, when as a young circuit judge he had refused to turn over the voting records of Barbour and Bullock counties to the U.S. Civil Rights Commission. He had impounded the records for local grand jury use, charging that the federal commission was attempting to interfere with the functioning of state courts. His defense of states' rights and defiance of the federal authority responsible for breaking down racial discrimination instantaneously made Wallace a southern hero. One reward of his newfound status as a demigod was a long-distance telephone call from Judge Perez; the two discussed the legal implications of the case and struck up a friendship. Perez had discovered his candidate; Wallace had found a friend with a fat bankroll and an agreeable political philosophy. Though based on politics, the friendship ran deeper; each enjoyed the other's companionship as well as the prestige of the relationship. It was Perez who, recognizing Wallace as a promising crowd pleaser during the unpledged-elector crusade of 1960, had invited him to Baton Rouge to be the principal speaker at a free-elector fund-raising banquet to be telecast in Louisiana, Arkansas, Mississippi, and Texas. Jittery during his first live speech before TV cameras and somewhat carried away with enthusiasm for the cause, Wallace missed the cutoff signal and continued speaking to a non-existent television audience. Finally, even he tired and paused to ask how much time remained, only to be told by an indulgent companion that the telecast had ended half an hour earlier.[38]

Three years later the Judge proudly sat on the speaker's stand while Wallace took the oath of office as governor of Alabama on the precise spot where Jefferson Davis had been inaugurated as president of the Confederacy 102 years earlier, the governor's hand resting on the same Bible that Davis had used. In his inaugural address, Wallace firmly declared, "And I say segregation today . . . segregation tomorrow . . . segregation forever."[39]

In 1964 Wallace entered Democratic presidential primaries in

Maryland, Indiana, and Wisconsin and proved to the astonishment of regular Democrats and to the delight of Perez that he commanded considerable support outside the Deep South. His most impressive showing was in Wisconsin, where he captured 33 percent of the total Democratic vote. Perez began inserting Wallace-for-president advertisements in Louisiana newspapers as the prelude to a full-scale campaign.[40]

On May 22, 1964, the Democratic State Central Committee met again to consider repeal of the Perez plan. This time the loyal Democrats beat back move after move of the Perez faction: a motion instructing Louisiana's delegates to the Democratic National Convention to vote against any platform including a civil rights plank; a motion instructing the delegates to vote for Governor John McKeithen as a favorite son presidential candidate on every ballot if such a plank were included; a motion instructing the delegates that they were not bound to support the national party's nominee; a motion to reserve the rooster emblem for a slate of unpledged electors; a motion to adjourn intended to head off future confrontations that Perez knew were coming. Then the loyalists moved to abolish the July primary for electors and instead to place two slates of electors on the November ballot—one committed to President Johnson, headed by the rooster; the other unpledged to any candidate, under the heading Unpledged Electors. This motion sparked a clamorous four-hour debate, during which one loyalist delegate facetiously suggested that the unpledged-elector ticket be headed by a picture of Perez. Finally, a curious compromise was arranged. The July primary was eliminated, and two slates of Democratic electors were certified to appear on the general election ballot in November. One was pledged to Lyndon Johnson, who would appear beneath the rooster; a second was pledged to George Wallace, who would appear beneath the donkey, the emblem of the national Democratic party.[41]

Disappointed at failing to secure the rooster for his favorite, the Judge had a group of Wallace backers file suit to compel the state central committee to revert to its original plan to hold a primary to select presidential electors. Alternatively, the plantiffs requested an injunction prohibiting presidential voting at all, on the basis that the Democratic governing body, by certifying two slates of electors, had violated a state law limiting each party to one candidate per office in a general election. A Baton Rouge district court ruled that there was no law requiring a primary and dismissed the pretension that it could issue an injunction against holding a presidential election in Louisiana, but it did enjoin the secretary of state from placing two sets of Democratic electors on the ballot. A court of appeals upheld the decision and the Louisiana Supreme Court refused to review the litigation, the entire cost of which was underwritten by Perez. The legal battle had backfired. The courts had ruled that only one set of Democratic electors could appear on the ballot, without specifying whether it should be the Johnson slate or the Wallace slate; the central committee, with a loyalist majority, was certain to select the Johnson ticket.[42]

Before the Democratic State Central Committee could meet again to choose between the two slates of electors, the results of the Republican National Convention made the outcome of the effort to secure the rooster for Wallace academic. In June, 1964, when it had appeared that the conservative senator, Barry Goldwater of Arizona, would win the Republican nomination, Perez and Justice Jim Johnson of the Arkansas Supreme Court had journeyed to Montgomery to confer privately with Wallace. Both men had asked the governor to withdraw in favor of Goldwater, since the Republicans were at last offering "a choice, not an echo." But Wallace had resisted; he wanted to continue the fight until his own campaign became hopeless. Perez and Johnson, unconvinced of the wisdom of Wallace's course but steadfast in their loyalty, had agreed to stick with him as long as he stayed in the race.[43]

Wallace, however, soon saw that his cause was doomed. Few prominent southern politicians would now support him, and both the enthusiasm and cash contributions of his financial backers declined rapidly. He knew that he would be blamed if Johnson carried the South because of a split in the conservative vote, so a month before the Democratic convention he announced on CBS television's "Face the Nation" that he was withdrawing from the campaign. With Wallace out, the press asked Perez whom he would back. Would he support another unpledged-elector movement? No, said Leander, that would only help the "Texas renegade." What about

Senator Goldwater? Undecided, Perez answered. Well, would he just throw in the towel? "That wouldn't be like Perez, would it?" the Judge quipped.[44]

Although selected as a delegate to the Democratic National Convention in Atlantic City, Perez decided to stay home, feeling that the convention would be thoroughly orchestrated by President Johnson. Leander was stunned by who was appointed to replace him, loyalist Democrat J. D. DeBlieux of Baton Rouge. Back in the Louisiana Senate after a brief absence, DeBlieux, who was Perez's most untiring foe on the central committee, went to Atlantic City and, in the Judge's words, "chilled my seat."[45]

As Perez expected, the convention nominated the president and rubber-stamped Hubert Humphrey, whom Leander equally detested, as his running mate. Perez vented his malice at the meeting of the Democratic State Central Committee summoned to certify a state ticket of electors following the convention. Swarms of Perez sympathizers crowded the House chamber, brandishing pro-Goldwater placards bearing such slogans as Sink the U.S.A. with L.B.J. When the meeting opened, Perez denounced the selection of DeBlieux as his replacement at Atlantic City; when DeBlieux tried to reply, he was booed by the Perez partisans in the packed galleries. Next, trying to embarrass the loyalist Democrats, the Judge attempted to name two black NAACP leaders to the state's slate of Johnson-Humphrey electors; the proposal was summarily rejected. More heated oratory followed, but the committee finally pledged Louisiana's Democratic electors, as well as the rooster emblem, to the Johnson-Humphrey ticket.[46]

Following the Democratic convention, Perez marshaled his forces for an all-out effort to capture Louisiana for Barry Goldwater. Comparing Goldwater with Eisenhower, Perez reflected, "If you saw the picture of Eisenhower in the morning paper, with his meaningless smile, and Goldwater, you will have noticed that Goldwater was gritting his teeth. He showed his strength of character."[47] The Judge maintained that he was not worried about Goldwater's efforts to make peace with the liberal wing of the Republican party, commenting, "When he's talking to s.o.b.'s, I think he's versatile enough to use s.o.b. language."[48]

Leander asserted that, with the labor bosses, the NAACP, CORE, and the Communists and fellow travelers backing LBJ, every conservative vote would be needed for Goldwater to win. He apocalyptically predicted, "If LBJ is reelected, race riots will break out to such an extent that our civilization will be pushed back into the jungle age,"[49] and charged that Johnson had arranged a moratorium on racial demonstrations until after the election. After that, he warned, "all hell will break loose."[50]

Perez bought radio, television, and newspaper ads for the Republican nominee, paid for circulars and envelope stuffing, managed fund-raising drives, and planned banquets and rallies. He helped organize the 50–20–10 Club for Goldwater, comprised of fifty charter members who each in turn pledged to recruit twenty men who would contribute $10 each. The initial luncheon of the club, with Perez as the featured speaker, raised $10,000. In his talk, Perez quoted the perennial Socialist presidential candidate, Norman Thomas, as having said about twelve years earlier that there was no reason for him to continue to run for president because the Democratic party had adopted his platform.[51]

On October 7, simultaneous fund-raising dinners for Goldwater were held in New Orleans, Shreveport, and Baton Rouge, linked together by a statewide television hookup. Later that month the Republican vice-presidential candidate, Congressman William Miller of New York, was the featured speaker at a $25-per-plate banquet in New Orleans. Leander met Miller at the airport and was photographed presenting the somewhat embarrassed candidate with a "three-dollar" bill. The front of the bill featured a picture of President Johnson and was signed by "Treasurer" James Farmer and "Secretary" Martin Luther King. The back of the bill depicted a building resembling the White House, which was labeled "Baker and Jenkins House," referring to Bobby Baker (Johnson's former errand boy turned con man) and Walter Jenkins (a homosexual who had been an adviser to the president).[52] Two weeks before Miller's arrival in New Orleans, Perez had dispatched a $20,000 check to Goldwater as an advance against ticket sales for the banquet. This was the Judge's standard procedure for a favored candidate; he would send a check before a fund-raising event and worry about reimbursing himself later.[53]

The highlight of the Goldwater campaign in Louisiana was a personal appearance by the candidate himself at a mammoth rally in Tulane University's huge Sugar Bowl Stadium. Despite an early evening shower, the stadium was about one-third full; Goldwater enthusiasts estimated 40,000 to 45,000 persons attended; Johnson partisans claimed there were closer to 25,000 or 30,000. Speakers included Lieutenant Governor C. C. Aycock, Secretary of State Wade O. Martin, Jr., former governors Sam Jones and Robert Kennon, and state GOP chairman Charlton Lyons. David Treen, now a Republican congressional candidate opposing Perez's hated foe Hale Boggs, served as master of ceremonies. Perez, who enjoyed the affair immensely, sat beside Senator Strom Thurmond and frequently applauded throughout Goldwater's speech. Afterwards, he mingled with the dignitaries, slapping backs, shaking hands, exchanging anecdotes, and reminiscing. Plaquemines residents turned out in force to glimpse their heroes—with their own Judge right among them. Free chartered buses brought Plaquemines people all the way from Venice and Pointe a la Hache, where the roads ended on the west and east banks, and high school bands from Port Sulphur, Buras, Belle Chasse, and Woodlawn were present to strike up rousing renditions for the Republican nominee.[54]

Goldwater probably would have carried conservative Louisiana even without Perez's financial and organizational efforts, but not by nearly so great a margin. Although he lost enormously nationwide, Goldwater swept Louisiana with 56.8 percent of the ballots, including 86.4 percent of the votes in Plaquemines and 56.8 percent in St. Bernard.[55]

Leander's infatuation with the Arizona senator was only temporary; when Goldwater supported the Voting Rights Act of 1965, Perez decided that he too had succumbed to leftist pressure. The Plaquemines boss wrote a Republican organizer that he had "helped materially" to win Louisiana for Goldwater but could hardly be expected to continue supporting the Republican party "while its recognized leaders make common cause with the communist conspiracy and the Democratic Party leaders represented by Dave Dubinski of New York and Walter Reuther of Detroit."[56]

Perez began planning the 1968 presidential campaign almost as soon as the 1964 contest had ended. This time he was determined to stick with George Wallace to the end. At a routine meeting of the Democratic State Central Committee during the summer of 1966, he presented a resolution providing for a primary to elect presidential electors prior to the general election—a reincarnation of the abortive Perez plan of 1964. The loyalist members of the committee were caught flat-footed; many were absent, and some had given their proxies to conservative friends who cast them in favor of the revived Perez plan. The Judge's surprise parliamentary maneuver succeeded; the plan passed fifty-seven to thirty-nine. But, as in 1964, a new committee would take office before the scheme could be implemented. At this time, too, everyone assumed that the Democrats would renominate President Johnson. Perez expected the primary to pit Wallace electors against Johnson electors. As before, his objective was to gain the prized rooster emblem for Wallace.[57]

Perez's rightist majority on the state central committee, tenuous at best, was threatened to be swept away entirely by that bugaboo of conservatives, reapportionment according to population. For many years representation on the committee had been based upon representation in the lower house of the state legislature; recently the legislature had been forced to reapportion, with the rural parishes losing seats to new population centers. If the usual practice had been followed, the sparsely populated country parishes—the strongholds of conservatism—would have also lost representation on the central committee. While his clique still dominated the committee, Perez had the reapportionment plan amended; the urban parishes were awarded additional seats, but each rural parish retained at least 1 member. The 105-member committee was boosted to 117 by guaranteeing to 12 sparsely populated parishes the seats they would have normally lost; for the first time the committee was larger than the Louisiana House of Representatives. Perez's parliamentary arsenal was not yet exhausted. Knowing that many of his followers on the committee, confused about the issues, simply waited to see how he would vote and voted likewise, Perez arranged to have Plaquemines Parish designated District 1 in the reapportioned committee; this meant that he, as the Plaquemines committeeman, could cast the first vote on each roll call.[58]

Leander knew that preserving the Perez plan depended upon

electing conservatives to the Democratic State Central Committee in the November, 1967, primary and December runoff. Quickly he took the offensive, mailing qualification papers to known conservatives, urging them to run so as to leave no committee seat held by a Democratic loyalist uncontested. He personally financed the campaigns of Wallace partisans who needed aid, placed newspaper ads for them, and compiled information on the number of Negro "bloc" votes received by loyalists in previous elections to use against them. Leander kept up a running correspondence with Wallace partisan Arthur Watson of Natchitoches in a concerted effort to fashion a rightist ticket. Never before had such a heated, yet highly organized campaign been waged for central committee seats, which had often been conceded without opposition in the past. The melee between backers of President Johnson and those of Wallace resulted in more than 350 candidates contesting 75 percent of the committee seats statewide. Perez put up pro-Wallace candidates in the major population centers, as well as in traditionally conservative rural parishes, and arranged for rightist speakers to stump every section of the state. Some pro-Wallace candidates resented Perez's efforts to run their campaigns and rejected his open support, fearing it would hurt their candidacies, but most accepted enthusiastically.[59]

The gubernatorial primary, held at the same time, was not much in doubt, being a battle between the weak right-wing congressman John Rarick and the still-popular incumbent governor John McKeithen, also a conservative. Thus, many Louisiana liberals stayed home, and the pro-Wallace faction was able to eke out what appeared to be a narrow victory in the contest for Democratic committee seats. The conservative victory was apparently confirmed at the first gathering of the newly elected committee when it ousted loyalist chairman Edward Carmouche and replaced him with Henry C. ("Happy") Sevier, a Wallace backer. But the rightist movement was not monolithic; Governor McKeithen, for one, expressed dissatisfaction with the idea of a primary to choose presidential electors, stating that President Johnson should be permitted to run under the rooster emblem. He feared that if the president were denied the rooster he might resort to economic retaliation against Louisiana, such as closing the huge NASA plant at Michaud, deactivating Fort Polk at Leesville, or withholding the more than a billion dollars in the tidelands escrow fund by rejecting a compromise settlement.[60]

While the Perez plan remained in limbo, Leander continued to campaign energetically for Wallace. In April, 1968, he debated conservative journalist William F. Buckley on Buckley's television show "Firing Line." The discussion was supposed to be about the Wallace presidential campaign, but ranged into Communist infiltration of the federal government, voting patterns in Plaquemines, St. Bernard, and New York State, and racially integrated education. The debate soon developed into a roundhouse argument in which Buckley, finding his uninhibited guest much to the right of himself, was unable to squeeze in more than a few words. The host resorted to sarcasm; Perez, missing the subtlety, responded to facetious questions with serious answers. The normally relaxed and eloquent Buckley was so astounded by some of Perez's answers that he was unable to think of suitable replies. After hearing Perez's interpretations of how Gunnar Myrdal's *An American Dilemma* ("a compilation of what other Socialists and Communists and haters of the South had written") had influenced the Supreme Court "in violating their oaths to support and defend the Constitution of the United States" by handing down the *Brown* school desegregation decision, Buckley could only comment: "Judge Perez, your ignorance is *staggering!*" Although the exchange following Buckley's editorial comment was no doubt enlightening, the transcript of the interview simply records, "Both talking at once—can't be understood." At a press conference afterwards, Buckley said, "The best thing Judge Perez could do for the cause of states' rights is to shut up."[61]

On May 11, the state central committee met to lay plans for the Democratic National Convention. The committee unanimously adopted a resolution designed to ensure national party nominees a place on the ballot; in the event that the state central committee failed to certify a slate of electors pledged to the national nominee, the national chairman could certify such a slate, which the Louisiana secretary of state would be required to include on the ballot. Perez supported the resolution; his loyalist foes could no longer argue that his plan for a primary for electors was designed to exclude the national party's nominee from the state ballot. The committee further specified that candidates for presidential electors be listed in separate columns from candidates for state, district, and local offices in the November general election, a device previously employed in 1948 and 1960. This ensured that the national Democratic nominee would not benefit from the votes of Louisianians who cast their ballots for state Democratic officials. Two months later the Louisiana legislature adopted bills that in effect made both resolutions state law. The committee also instructed its delegation to the Democratic convention in Chicago to support Governor McKeithen as a favorite-son nominee on the first ballot. Finally, a motion to repeal the Perez plan was prefiled for consideration at the next meeting.[62]

On June 14 the central committee met to consider repeal of the Perez plan. Parliamentary acrobatics and envenomed speeches were predicted; none occurred. Perez sat calmly silent while a resolution abolishing his plan was unanimously adopted. Encouraged by their easy success, the loyalists promptly moved to pledge the state's Democratic electors to the national party nominee, running on a ticket headed by the rooster. Now the Perez faction sprang to life. The committee chairman, Arthur Watson, ruled that the motion was "premature" because a national nominee had not been chosen. The loyalists appealed the ruling, but Watson was sustained by the Perez stalwarts. Consideration of which candidate would receive the rooster was postponed until after the national convention.[63]

The Judge did not give up his efforts to have George Wallace certified as the state's 1968 Democratic nominee, but, to cover all contingencies, he began circulating a petition at courthouses and shopping centers throughout the state to ensure Wallace a place on the ballot as a third-party candidate. Only 10,000 signatures were required by law, but Leander planned to collect more than 100,000. "It would be a disgrace for small states like Maryland and Massachusetts to have more names on their nomination papers than Louisiana," he explained.[64] Wallace himself made a whirlwind tour of southern cities, appealing to voters to help him petition his way onto the ballot. Perez was on hand to greet him when he landed at New Orleans International Airport. In early August Leander filed a

Wallace petition with 24,000 signatures, claiming to have 100,000 in reserve.[65]

From the White House, a somber, fatigued President Johnson startled the nation by announcing that he was withdrawing from the presidential race and halting the air war against North Vietnam in order to seek peace in Southeast Asia. Perez, who could not believe his ears, claimed that Johnson's statement was a ploy to deny opponents equal time on television during the preconvention campaign. Johnson would later arrange a draft for himself that he would claim he could not turn down, the Judge explained.[66]

Suddenly, the chief national object of Perez's enmity was gone; Hubert Humphrey became the Democratic front-runner. Although Perez found it equally easy to hate Humphrey, Governor John McKeithen did not. He and the vice-president were friends, and Humphrey had received a master's degree from LSU, where McKeithen had taken his law degree. The governor even fantasized that he might be selected Humphrey's running mate. To strengthen his chances for a vice-presidential offer, McKeithen announced that he would support Humphrey at the Democratic convention, withdrew as a favorite-son candidate, and authorized the Louisiana delegation to vote for Humphrey on the first ballot. This prompted an angry telegram from Perez, who tartly told the governor to retain his favorite-son candidacy. After the offer of the vice-presidency failed to materialize, McKeithen left the convention early and announced that he would remain officially neutral in the 1968 presidential campaign. Perez impishly explained, "McKeithen, in effect, said to Humphrey, 'I'll marry you tomorrow for a honeymoon tonight,' but the honeymoon did not work out, so there's no marriage."[67]

Wallace's chances of winning Louisiana received a boost from McKeithen's disenchantment with the Democratic ticket. The Wallace forces now concentrated on selecting a vice-presidential running mate who would lend respectability to the ticket without alienating conservative backers. Perez had been an early and forceful advocate of the former air force chief of staff, Curtis LeMay, whom he physically resembled and whom he termed "an outstanding figure of military history." The Judge confidently predicted that the selection of LeMay ensured Wallace's victory in Louisiana, but

LeMay later embarrassed Wallace by stating that integration was
the solution to the nation's racial problems and that nuclear
weapons should be used only as a last resort to end the conflict in
Vietnam. LeMay was hustled out of the country on a "fact-finding"
mission to Saigon.[68]

As the time for printing the ballots approached, a furious squabble developed over the right of the Humphrey ticket to appear under
the Louisiana rooster. The state central committee, on September
16, had adopted an ambiguously worded resolution that provided
that electors for the national Democratic party appear "under the
National emblem of the Democratic Party" but "in the same form
and manner that the Democratic Party's electors were placed on the
ballot in the 1964 general election." Wallace partisans, stressing the
first part, argued that the donkey was the symbol of the national
party; loyalists emphasized the second, pointing out that the Democratic ticket had appeared under the rooster in 1964. Although lean-
ing toward Wallace himself, Secretary of State Wade Martin announced that he would award the rooster to Humphrey, following an
exchange of letters with the chairman of the Democratic National
Committee, who had advised that the rooster was considered the
official Democratic party emblem in Louisiana. Arthur Watson,
chairman of the state central committee, admitted that it seemed
that Humphrey was entitled to the rooster.

But Judge Perez was unwilling to concede; he had the ten Wallace
electors file suit to prevent the secretary of state from placing Humphrey on the ticket under the rooster. If Perez won, Louisiana's
emblem would be reserved for Democratic nominees in state elections only. The flamboyant court battle that followed produced
another classic confrontation between Leander and his liberal an-
tagonist, J. D. DeBlieux. DeBlieux maintained that Wallace, as a
third-party candidate, had no business trying to decide what
emblem another party should use. Perez quoted from a book in
which the late Sam Rayburn had said that the donkey, originating
in the Thomas Nast cartoons of the 1870s, was the national party's
emblem. But DeBlieux countered by quoting from *The Rooster,*
whose author claimed that the rooster originated in Indiana as the
party emblem in the 1840s. DeBlieux also submitted an affidavit

signed by a national party official stating that there was no such thing as a national emblem for the Democratic party. Debate next ranged over what had actually taken place at the September 16 central committee meeting at which the ambiguous resolution had been adopted. At one point discussion became so confused that attorneys for both sides retired for forty-five minutes to hear a tape recording of what had actually occurred at the meeting. The district court ruled in favor of DeBlieux, but Perez appealed to the Louisiana Supreme Court, which held that the donkey was the emblem of the national Democratic party and that Humphrey must appear under that symbol—notwithstanding the fact that in Louisiana the rooster had headed every Democratic presidential slate in the twentieth century except in 1948. Perez celebrated the decision by wearing a tie tack shaped like a rooster, a gift from his daughter. Thus the long fight for the rooster ended in a stalemate: Humphrey appeared under the donkey; Wallace appeared under the emblem of his American Independent party, an eagle grasping an American flag above a banner saying Stand Up for America. No one had the coveted rooster.[69]

Publicly, the Wallace campaigners exuded confidence, a necessary pose to counter the "reverse-bandwagon" psychology; that is, many conservatives, fearing a Humphrey victory if they voted for Wallace, decided to vote for Richard Nixon. The Shreveport *Times,* for example, supported Nixon on the premise that a vote for Wallace would only help Humphrey because Wallace had no chance to win. Privately, some of the leaders admitted that the best they could hope for was a cabinet position or a slowdown in the federal civil rights and welfare programs as a result of the conservative backlash fueled by Wallace's candidacy. There was a faint chance that they could deadlock the election in the electoral college, diverting it to the House of Representatives—the old unpledged-elector strategy. But, at the very least, the Wallace boosters could gleefully defy both major parties, a prospect that delighted Perez.[70]

Leander was unrelenting, untiring, and a bit unorthodox as Louisiana's state campaign manager for Wallace, terming the 1968 presidential race "our most important election in a lifetime." The alternative to his favorite was the hated Humphrey, whom he variously referred to as "a Marxist" and "a damned socialist." Speaking to a Wallace-for-president rally, Leander complained, "Our own President went before Congress in his state of the union message and sang the international Communist song of hate—'We Shall Overcome.'"[71]

Perez energetically but unsuccessfully tried to convince all three major television networks to give full, live coverage to the American Independent party convention. He bought a full, front-page ad in the New Orleans *Jewish Civic Press* consisting of a picture of Wallace with the caption "Best Wishes For a Happy New Year to the Entire Jewish Community. Support George C. Wallace For President." Debating William Buckley, Perez insisted that Wallace did not oppose desegregation, but simply resented having it forced upon the states by the federal government.[72]

Wallace's central campaign organization scored telling points by emphasizing his record on aid to the needy, which depicted him as a friend of the farmer and the worker. Yet Wallace's neopopulism occasionally disconcerted doctrinaire conservatives such as Perez. When Buckley pointed out to Perez that the per capita debt of Alabama was greater than the national debt per capita, the Judge insisted that the difference was that the bonds floated by Governor Wallace had been used for capital investments rather than "giveaway programs." In mid-October Perez, disturbed when Wallace termed the 27.5 percent oil depletion allowance a "tax loophole," wrote his candidate to explain that the deduction was necessary for the business cost of exploration inherent in oil and gas production. Leander was generous with advice; ten days later he urged Wallace to emphasize in an upcoming speech his opponents' advocacy of "one world government" through the United Nations. During the same month Perez met Wallace in Roanoke, Virginia; afterwards he said that they had conferred about "Richard M. Nixon . . . and other traitors."[73]

Although he was unsuccessful in luring the state campaign managers for Humphrey and Nixon into a direct debate, the Judge did appear with representatives of the rival nominees in a current events program in Baton Rouge held at LSU. In an interview with the campus newspaper before his speech, Perez told student reporters that Wallace's demand for law and order was not a synonym for white supremacy. He insisted that Plaquemines Parish had no disorders because potential troublemakers knew that local people would meet force with force, adding, "My shotgun is loaded." Referring to the fact that one of his rivals, who would speak in behalf of Humphrey, was formerly chairman of the Americans for Democratic Action, Leander said that "the ADA is a prototype of the British Labor Party, which is responsible for the downfall of the British Empire." He asserted that academic freedom was dangerous because it allowed Communists to teach at universities and termed the U.S. Supreme Court a "politburo." [74]

Such statements, predictably, did not endear him to his student audience, which was already congenitally antagonistic. His initial appearance on the stage was greeted by sarcastic cheers, victory signs, and Nazi salutes from an apparently well-organized group of students scattered strategically throughout the auditorium. When Perez, the last speaker on the program, approached the microphone, he was met with hisses, boos, cheers, and an occasional "Here comes de judge." The audience ridiculed him by applauding his every statement; he retaliated by shifting his appeal from "ladies and gentlemen" to "boys and girls." During his talk, strains of "We Shall Overcome" occasionally drifted up from the audience. The crowd, however, was not devoid of Perez-Wallace partisans, and amid the disruptions some shouts of "shut up you punk and let the man speak" were heard. Finally, LSU Union personnel began patrolling the aisles to quell the rowdy students. Just before leaving, Perez said, "I never thought my Alma Mater L.S.U. would descend to such low depths.... I hope the effort made by the state to give you an education is not wasted." [75]

Perez made numerous less provocative and more productive fund-raising appearances for Wallace throughout the state. On September 13, the Judge addressed more than a thousand Wallace enthusiasts at the Evangeline Club in Ville Platte, a small town in southwestern Louisiana. Those who could not fit into the building strained to hear him from their cars. One local reporter who listened to the Judge said that she forgot all about Wallace and went out ready to vote for Perez. [76] Just a few days later, Wallace flew to New

Orleans to address the American Legion's fiftieth anniversary convention. While he was there, a $25-per-plate fund-raising luncheon at the Roosevelt Hotel was arranged by Perez. The affair was a rousing success; two thousand Wallace partisans attended and welcomed both Perez and Wallace with a standing ovation. A month later Leander raised $30,000 for Wallace at a New Orleans testimonial dinner featuring John Bell Williams, governor of Mississippi, as the principal speaker.[77]

Perez organized a house-to-house fund-raising drive in Plaquemines Parish and mailed out letters to each voter in his congressional district soliciting campaign contributions. Leander's son Chalin officially headed the Wallace organization in the First Congressional District and maintained, "This is the first time in my life that I will cast a presidential vote I can be proud of."[78]

The Judge and his intimates also gave generously of their own personal funds to finance the state campaign. Among those donating more than a thousand dollars were a son, a nephew, a son-in-law, the Plaquemines clerk of court, and an associate of the Louisiana Land Exploration Company. In addition, Perez personally financed a nationwide speaking tour by Dr. Alexander Sas-Jaworsky, an Abbeville veterinarian and a Soviet refugee, who had been named "Ukrainian of the Year" in 1958. Sas-Jaworsky had previously attracted nationwide recognition as a highly successful contestant on the "$64,000 Question" television quiz program and statewide attention as the result of an angry and loud confrontation at Louisiana State University with a high-ranking official of the Soviet embassy. The press was unable to report the substance of the argument in any detail because it was conducted entirely in Ukrainian.[79]

Perez's intensive campaign helped produce a more than 220,000-vote plurality for Wallace in Louisiana. In Plaquemines, Wallace overwhelmed his two opponents with 75.3 percent of the vote; in St. Bernard he received 68.6 percent. The only Plaquemines precinct he did not carry by an overwhelming margin was predominantly Negro.[80]

Wallace's smashing 1968 victory in Louisiana was the crowning achievement of the Judge's long involvement in presidential politics. Nationwide, the American party candidate polled 13 percent of the vote; in the South, 36 percent, making him the most formidable third-party candidate since Theodore Roosevelt's Bull Moose crusade in 1912.[81] It was only a moral victory; Wallace did not divert enough electoral votes to deadlock the election and Richard Nixon became president. Yet moral victories meant much to Perez and his clique. Less than a month after the election, the indomitable Judge began making plans for the 1972 campaign. But Leander Perez would not live to see another presidential election.

SIXTEEN

The Judge Retires

Despite his political activities, Leander Perez always found time for his family. The Perezes were closely knit in the Old World tradition. He and his wife Agnes, to whom he was married for half a century, were nearly inseparable. Agnes, who had her own boots and gun, often accompanied her husband on hunting trips, and she always went with him to Baton Rouge when the legislature was in session. The Judge was not a great music lover; he said that classical music was pretty but that he did not understand it. His favorite song was "Asleep in the Deep," by Arthur J. Lamb. Although he watched television only infrequently, he did enjoy westerns. His favorite shows were "Bonanza," "Lancer," and "Perry Mason." He liked to watch the news and an occasional sports program and also enjoyed western movies such as *How the West Was Won*.[1]

Leander often used his wife as a sounding board for his political decisions. While she knitted he would explain the options that seemed open to him, and she would follow the details and give her opinion. Agnes was sometimes embarrassed by her husband's open displays of affection. Never a political activist herself, she usually slipped away when the picture taking began. She was so camera shy that some of the news media were hard pressed to find a suitable picture upon her death.[2]

Although he was always busy, Leander was a devoted father who enjoyed taking his children hunting and fishing. His political authoritarianism apparently did not carry over to his family, for according to one of his sons Perez was not a stern parent, perhaps not strict enough. After his two sons returned from military service in World War II, the Judge took them on a trip to renew their intimacy.

They spent two weeks in Canada hunting moose, deer, and bear. Perez enjoyed having children around the house; after his own children had grown up, his grandchildren were frequent visitors. He impishly told them that Agnes was their grandmother, but that he was too young to be a grandfather.[3]

Perez did not reduce his activities in state and local politics during the last decade of his life, even though he was in his seventies. Instead, he busied himself preparing for the transition of power to his successors. He transferred much of his property to his relatives, so that his succession records would not reveal the true extent of his wealth. He also arranged the smooth transfer of local political power to his sons.

Perez was certain that he could win reelection as district attorney as long as he was healthy, but he was uncertain about his ability to pass on the office to his elder son. Consequently, he devised a plan. After announcing that he would run for reelection in 1960 for his seventh consecutive six-year term, he won the Democratic primary without opposition, which was tantamount to election. He then resigned before the general election, and the Democratic executive committee of the Twenty-fifth Judicial District, of which he was a member, certified Leander Perez, Jr., as the Democratic nominee. Lea was then elected without opposition. The Judge remained in office as an assistant district attorney to his son until September, 1961.[4]

Perez, though believing that Lea's position was secure in Plaquemines, was unsure of his ability to maintain control in St. Bernard, which had outgrown Plaquemines in population. Should a strong St. Bernard rival challenge Lea, the larger parish could outvote Plaquemines and depose him as district attorney of the entire district. To guard against this possibility, Perez had the legislature pass a constitutional amendment dividing Plaquemines and St. Bernard into separate judicial districts, with a district attorney and district judge for each parish. As a constitutional amendment, the proposal had to be voted on statewide. It was defeated in the general election.[5]

Following his retirement as district attorney, nine hundred persons jammed into the Roosevelt Hotel in New Orleans to honor

Perez at a testimonial dinner. Governor Davis, through an emissary, made the Judge an honorary colonel on his staff. The principal speaker was Leander's close friend, Congressman F. Edward Hebert, who likened him to such leaders as Washington, Jefferson, Lincoln, Wilson, the two Roosevelts, and Huey Long. He termed Perez "the noblest Roman of them all" and said that the Judge's family life was a model for every American couple to follow.[6]

Even as he planned his retirement as district attorney, Perez was also devising a new form of government for Plaquemines Parish. He had the regular session of the 1960 legislature pass a constitutional amendment authorizing parishes to draft a charter creating a commission form of government. The legislation was vetoed three times by Governor Earl Long, who suspected some Perez trickery, but it was finally slipped through. The amendment later won approval by state voters, and the Plaquemines police jury appointed an eleven-man commission to draw up a charter. Among the members of the commission were Perez's son Lea and his brother R. A. Perez. Although the Judge was not a member, he was appointed legal adviser and did the actual drafting. It took him only twenty-nine days to write the new charter. The police jury then voted itself out of existence, and the parish voters ratified the new form of government.[7]

The new charter gave Plaquemines the most powerful local government in the state. The nine-member police jury was replaced by a five-member commission council. Although the commissioners are elected parishwide, each comes from a particular district—two from the sparsely populated east bank and three from the populous west bank. The commissioners take office even if they do not receive commissions from the governor, and each receives the same pay as the parish sheriff. The charter abolished Earl Long's twelve piggyback jurors, who sat with the police jury when it considered levee board matters.[8] The commission council is empowered to do anything not prohibited by state law, whereas the police jury had to request permission for powers not specifically designated. The council, rather than the governor, is empowered to fill all vacancies on parish boards, which lost the power to legislate for their districts and became wholly advisory. The charter even makes the presumptuous statement that, in the event of any conflict between parish ordinances and state law, the parish ordinance shall prevail.[9]

Under the Plaquemines charter, the incumbent administration holds all of the cards. The commissioners are elected for overlapping six-year terms; if the parish voters desire a change in government, it has to be achieved piecemeal, over a long time. Candidates running for commissioner must produce petitions demonstrating that they have the support of at least 5 percent of the registered voters. The original charter provided that the district judge must certify the literacy and moral character of each candidate for commissioner, but this was later amended to have the chairman of the parish Democratic committee (Perez) pass upon the qualifications and character. The charter also provided that when two commissioners were to be elected, the candidates must qualify jointly and run as a ticket, but this provision was subsequently abolished.[10]

The first candidates for the five commission council seats were nominated at a mass caucus of the Perez faction. Handpicked Perez candidates won unanimous endorsement for four of the seats, including the Judge himself, who was chosen as the administration candidate for commissioner of public affairs. For the fifth seat, commissioner of public improvements, Perez backed Jim Armstrong, a soft drink distributor, but Sheriff Chester Wooten supported Joseph Hingle, a police juror who had at times shown an inclination to disagree with Perez. Hingle edged Armstrong by twenty-eight votes at the caucus. Leander seems to have been momentarily angered, but finally agreed to support the sheriff's man. All five nominees were unopposed, and the election was called off as unnecessary.[11]

At the council's initial meeting on September 5, 1961, Perez was elected president by acclamation. He seemed surprised when a reporter asked him if there had ever been any doubt as to who would be president of the council. "Well, why should there be?" he asked. He explained that the commission council had been his brainchild and added, "What is the objection to Perez being the leader?"[12]

The Plaquemines Parish Administration Advisory Council was created to work with the commission council. Comprising most of the parish officials and twenty-eight other members from the ten wards of the parish, the advisory council met just prior to the first meeting of the commission council and also elected Perez chairman. The advisory council was to meet quarterly, hear reports from the members from the various wards, and make recommendations to the commission council. There was a great deal of work for both groups to do. The commission council began poring over all legislation passed by the police jury during the previous twenty years and reenacted laws that were deemed worthy. All parish employees who had worked for the police jury were asked to reapply to the new commission council.[13]

Caucuses of the advisory committee met to nominate candidates for all parish offices. Leander said that the committee represented the political thinking "of about 95 percent of the people in Plaquemines." The first set of commissioners drew lots to determine whether their first term of office would be two, four, or six years; following this initial term, each was to last for six years. Perez drew a six-year term. When the first two-year terms ended in 1963, the nominees of the advisory council were elected without opposition.[14]

The Perez machine in St. Bernard suffered a jolt when Sheriff Nicholas P. Trist died of a heart attack in June, 1962. John F. ("Jack") Rowley, Dutch Rowley's son, who had given Trist a close race in 1960, immediately qualified for the special election to choose a successor. The Perez-Trist organization endorsed Valentine Riess, president of the police jury, and several lesser candidates also qualified. The first primary drew 92 percent of the registered voters to the polls. Riess led Rowley by just over three hundred votes, and the two top contenders entered a runoff.[15]

The second primary was even more hotly contested than the first; the registrar found it necessary to open a second office to handle the flood of new applicants. One morning, more than one hundred persons were standing in line when the registrar's office opened at 9 A.M., and three of them had been in line since 7 A. M. During the day, the line increased to several hundred persons. Some began shouting complaints, and sheriff's deputies were finally called in to quell the disturbance. Rowley claimed that the registrar's office was purposely working slowly to hold down the number of newcomers allowed to register and charged that some people had waited in line for four and a half hours. The registrar claimed that he had employed nine additional deputy registrars and had registered more than nine hundred people in two days.[16]

Rowley also charged that several parish employees had been fired for failing to support Riess in the first primary and that Riess was guilty of payroll padding. An investigation by Rowley showed that the number of employees on public payrolls controlled by the St. Bernard police jury had increased by as much as 300 percent between the first and second primaries. The road district, for example, had added forty-nine men in the two-month period. After Rowley's investigation, the police jury adopted a resolution placing its employees under civil service.[17]

The turning point came when Sidney Torres, who had polled over 2,000 votes in the first primary, gave his support to Rowley. Almost 94 percent of the registered voters turned out for the second primary. Rowley defeated Riess by nearly 1,500 votes and was reelected by a landslide in the regular election a year later. Leander soon made peace with Rowley and his machine. In his relationship with the Perez faction, Jack Rowley has proved to be much like his father. He will collaborate when it is expedient but does not like to sacrifice his freedom to maneuver.[18]

Perez and Rowley followed different paths in the 1964 gubernatorial campaign, with Rowley backing Perez's archenemy deLesseps Morrison. As Jimmie Davis' term drew to an end, Perez noted that, though many people had criticized the singing governor, Davis was much better than Chep Morrison would have been. Why, if the liberal Morrison had been elected, the Judge declared, it would have become impossible to distinguish New Orleans from Harlem or even Washington, D.C.[19]

Thanks largely to Perez, Louisiana had escaped such a fate, but the threat reappeared late in 1963 when Chep announced that he would be a candidate for governor for the third time in 1964. The Judge's antipathy to Morrison had, if anything, increased since the last gubernatorial contest. After losing in the second primary, Chep had turned quisling by associating himself with the detested Kennedy administration as ambassador to the Organization of American States. In Perez's mind, this made Morrison almost as bad as the president himself. This time, Perez had a plethora of ten candidates from which to select a favorite, always with the object of defeating Morrison. The strongest were former governor Robert F. Kennon (1952–1956), who had cooperated closely with Perez in the past; the state superintendent of education Shelby Jackson, a champion of anticommunism and white supremacy; Congressman Gillis Long, a fifth cousin of Senator Russell Long and the senator's favorite; Public Service Commissioner John J. McKeithen, whose campaign manager was Blanche Long, Earl's widow; Public Works Director Claude Kirkpatrick; and Louis Michot, a state representative.[20]

The most conservative candidates were Kennon and Jackson, the latter an extreme segregationist. Jackson was farther right ideologically, but Kennon had a better chance to win, so Perez backed him. Almost as important to the Judge was the race for state attorney general, in which his detested enemy, Jack Gremillion, was a candidate for reelection. Perez went all out for Gremillion's sole opponent, Charles A. Riddle, Jr., of Marksville, the chairman of the Democratic State Central Committee.

Perez attempted to unite Louisiana's white supremacist groups behind Kennon, but upstate Citizens' Council leaders Willie Rainach and John S. Garrett lined up behind Shelby Jackson. As state superintendent of education, Jackson had organized anticommunism workshops for high school students and had made the teaching of anti-Communist ideology mandatory in all state schools. Leander insisted that opposition to the national administration of John Kennedy was the critical issue in the campaign because of the president's civil rights program; he claimed that Kennedy had experts watching the Louisiana campaign "like hawks—or vultures." He termed Kennon "the only independent candidate who can be elected over the three Kennedy candidates for governor," whom he identified as Morrison, Long, and McKeithen. Leander explained that the president had not yet picked a single standard-bearer, but controlled Louisiana's 125,000 Negro votes "under push button orders" and would deliver them to the candidate he finally decided upon.[21] Kennedy's assassination just two weeks before the first primary brought him instant martyrdom, including sudden praise from erstwhile vilifiers, including Perez. The largest Kennon rally in the state was held at Belle Chasse, where an estimated 2,500 people packed the high school gymnasium to hear the candidate speak; Judge Perez directed the event as master of ceremonies.[22]

Despite Perez's efforts, Kennon was able to finish no better than fourth statewide in the field of ten candidates. DeLesseps Morrison piled up an impressive first-primary plurality of 142,398 votes (33 percent) by scoring heavily in south Louisiana. The surprise second-place finisher was McKeithen (17 percent), followed by Long (15 percent), Kennon (14 percent), and Jackson (12 percent). Kennon, of course, easily carried Plaquemines with 4,365 votes to only 780 for Morrison and 334 for McKeithen. But in St. Bernard, where Sheriff Rowley had endorsed Morrison, Kennon finished fourth behind Morrison, McKeithen, and Long, respectively. The contest for attorney general was a big disappointment to Perez; incumbent Jack Gremillion trounced Riddle, winning an easy first-primary victory. Although Riddle swamped Gremillion in Plaquemines with 4,702 votes to 713, Gremillion triumphed by a large margin in St. Bernard, as he did in the rest of the state.[23]

In the second primary Perez gave his wholehearted support to John J. McKeithen. Under Perez's advisement, the second-primary strategy was a repeat of the race-issue strategy that had been so successful for Jimmie Davis in 1960. McKeithen accused Morrison of receiving a Negro bloc vote in the first primary. Handbills were distributed showing the large vote that Morrison had received in predominantly Negro wards. Perez, stating that the showdown between Morrison and McKeithen would "decide the fate of the white man's position in our State government," exclaimed, "The challenge which now faces every citizen of Louisiana is unmistakable. It is— Shall we have a Communist controlled NAACP-CORE-MARTIN LUTHER KING dominated State government?"[24] Perez drafted television commercials, collected voting data, and researched Morrison's past for damaging information, in addition to helping McKeithen financially. George Singelmann, who had headed the Friends of Rainach for Davis organization in 1960, now headed the Friends of Jackson-Kennon for McKeithen.[25]

McKeithen's strategy was successful; he overcame Morrison's large first-primary lead and defeated the New Orleans mayor. More

than 75 percent of the Plaquemines voters went to the polls, and
they gave McKeithen a better than four-to-one margin. In St. Bernard the vote was much closer, but McKeithen still edged his rival.
McKeithen still faced a Republican challenger in the general election, Charlton Lyons, who was even more conservative than he was.
Lyons did best in the most conservative rural parishes, with the no-
table exception of Plaquemines, where Perez made the general election a test of his loyalty to McKeithen. The parish responded by
giving the Democratic nominee almost 93 percent of the vote.
Statewide, Lyons received 39 percent of the vote, an impressive total
for a Republican office seeker in Louisiana.[26]

Just a year after the election, Plaquemines suffered the worst
natural disaster of Perez's lifetime, when in September, 1965, Hurricane Betsy ripped across the parish with winds up to 160 miles per
hour. Buildings were torn from their foundations and smashed.
Then winds forced tidal waves over the Mississippi River levees and
over the back levees intended to protect the parish from the Gulf.
Oyster beds and citrus groves were destroyed. The Pointe a la Hache
ferry was torn from its moorings, blown miles up the river, and set
atop the levee. The parish courthouse was flooded, so the commission council held its meetings in Perez's home at Idlewild. Power
lines were destroyed, drainage stations wrecked, and hundreds of
cattle drowned. Water moccasins infested the area. Nine persons in
the parish died.[27] Following the calamity, Perez sealed Plaquemines
off from the outside world. He set up roadblocks at the parish line
and refused to admit all outsiders, including newsmen and insurance agents seeking to assess damage. Hundreds of auxiliary deputies wearing sidearms kept the parish closed. Leander at first opposed even allowing the Louisiana National Guard to enter the
parish, but finally relented, explaining that he had closed off the
parish to prevent looting and the spread of epidemics. The parish
hospital immunized local people and rescue workers against
typhoid.[28]

The parish found itself short of laborers, so the local ordinance
requiring the fingerprinting and photographing of itinerant workers
was suspended, but the hours of liquor sales were limited where
itinerants were at work. Several Negroes complained that they had
been compelled with clubs and guns to work in parish clean-up

operations. The New Orleans branch of the NAACP asked President Johnson to investigate. Two Negro schoolteachers who had reported their forced labor resigned their jobs because they feared reprisals. When asked about the reports of enforced service, the Judge commented that "it's too bad that the damn Niggers had to do a little cleanup work." [29]

Leander personally organized the parish for the massive job of recovery. He induced local industries to lend heavy equipment; he organized a pool of attorneys to provide free legal aid in settling claims with insurance companies; he established a clearinghouse to help people obtain building materials, house movers, electricians, and plumbers. Homeowners were given a $200.00 parish subsidy to return their homes to their foundations; welfare recipients were offered $12.50 to $13.50 per day to help in hurricane clean-up work; local carpenters were encouraged to expand their operations, and agreements were negotiated with outside contractors to bring in several hundred carpenters. To restock orange groves, the parish offered free trees, on a matching basis, to citrus farmers. [30]

Despite his antipathy toward the United States government, after Hurricane Betsy Perez was happy to receive federal aid for disaster relief. The U.S. Corps of Engineers did most of the heavy work in the parish. Loans were arranged through local banks or the federal Small Business Administration. Once the immediate cleanup had been completed, Perez embarked upon a multimillion-dollar rebuilding program, which included constructing hundreds of miles of back levees, raising the river levees, building an all-weather highway, extending water and sewer systems throughout the parish, and installing drainage pumping stations. [31]

The parish tragedy was soon followed by a personal one for Leander. On February 10, 1967, Agnes Perez died of a heart attack while visiting a duahgter in New Orleans. She died at age seventy-one, just three months before she and Perez would have celebrated their fiftieth anniversary. Those who knew Leander well say that her death affected him deeply. For a time he seemed to lose his usual vigor. He confessed that he had a hard time forcing himself to go on, but he would find some escape by plunging into the 1968 Wallace campaign. [32]

Perez's grief did not cause him to soften his stand against political opponents. In 1967 and early 1968, he engineered a stratagem to cripple civil rights work in Louisiana by disqualifying out-of-state lawyers from practicing in the state. Because Negroes involved in civil rights activity had found it hard to get local attorneys to represent them, volunteer lawyers associated with the Lawyer's Constitutional Defense Committee had sometimes aided them. One such attorney, Richard Sobol, who appeared in the Pointe a la Hache district court to defend a Negro charged with striking a white child, was arrested for practicing law in Louisiana without a license. Sobol had graduated from law school in Arizona and had associated himself with a Louisiana firm handling civil rights cases, but he had not been admitted to the Louisiana bar. The case was crucial because it would set a precedent for civil rights attorneys practicing in other states. Perez tried to keep the case in state courts, but Sobol was successful in appealing to a federal court, which dismissed the Judge's charges.[33]

Before the 1967 parish primaries, Leander announced that he would not be a candidate for reelection as commission council president. Instead, his younger son Chalin qualified for the post. Perez briefly considered running for state representative from Plaquemines, but changed his mind because he felt the legislative position would tie him down too much. He finally endorsed Frank Patti, the superintendent of the Plaquemines private school system, for representative. Thomas McBride, a Perez opponent, also decided to run. McBride expected trouble qualifying, so he took two friends to Perez's home to witness the filing of his qualification papers. Candidates were required to file their papers at the residence of Perez, who was the chairman of the parish Democratic committee. The Judge, incensed because McBride had brought witnesses, had his bodyguard eject them from his property. Later in the day Perez also became angry at a New Orleans newspaper reporter and ordered him out of the parish courthouse in order to teach his employers "the meaning of respect."[34]

Other opponents had trouble even locating Perez to qualify. Finally, they mailed in their forms and qualifying fees. Leander, saying that the forms and checks had arrived after the deadline, disqualified the entire ticket. The disqualified candidates brought their case to district court, where it was dismissed by Judge Eugene E. Leon, a Perez ally. Perez also assured himself of an overwhelming majority of election commissioners by entering dummy candidates. His own bodyguard qualified as a candidate for sheriff against the true Perez candidate, incumbent Chester Wooten.[35]

The most bizarre incident of the local elections in 1967 involved Lawrence J. Rousselle, an adamant enemy of Perez. On July 10, Rousselle accompanied a group of Perez opponents to witness the qualifying of Ernest Hingle as a candidate against Perez's son Chalin for public affairs commissioner. Rousselle tells a story of intimidation and harassment from the moment he arrived with Hingle. A Perez employee brandished a gun while the Judge leveled threats at members of the rival delegation. Leander said that he had heard that Rousselle had been slandering him and using his name in vain and that the next time he saw him in public he would "slap his face." Three days later Rousselle, awakened at his home at 12:30 A.M. by two employees of the district attorney's office, was told that he was under arrest for conspiring to murder Perez. He was then driven to the parish jail and incarcerated. The next day Judge Leon set bond at $75,000. Rousselle was returned to jail, where he was fingerprinted and photographed. He was kept in prison for nineteen days. For the first three he was confined in a blackened room with no washing facilities. Then he spent nearly two weeks in an isolation cell where the light burned around the clock. Finally, after the state supreme court reduced the bond to $10,000, Rousselle was able to post bond and was released.[36]

Perez claimed that a group of outside gamblers had conspired to hire local people to murder him. In return for these services, the locals would then be given gambling concessions. He exclaimed, "A group of sonofabitches raised $25,000 to murder me!"[37]

Rousselle was not allowed to see the charges against him and was never subsequently indicted. On August 4, he was subpoenaed to appear in court on the following day. This time he was charged with "conspiracy to do bodily harm" to Perez. Witnesses testified that Rousselle had said that he wanted to "get rid of Perez" at political meetings. The beleaguered Rousselle explained that he had meant to vote Perez out of office.[38] When Perez's witness was asked if he would take a lie detector test, he replied that that was up to District Attorney Leander Perez, Jr. "Whatever he wants me to do, I'll do. Whatever he wants me to say, I'll say." The district attorney said that no lie detector test would be necessary because he had no reason to doubt his witness.[39]

Rousselle, who operated a self-service laundry, told of continued harassment. He said that the gas to his building had been periodically turned off and that Out of Order signs had been mysteriously placed on working machines in the laundry. He complained that he could not get a permit from the parish to operate a more modern laundry behind the old one.[40]

Despite these melodramatic moments, the local elections went precisely as Perez had planned. In the election for commissioner of public affairs, the Judge urged voters to "cast a record vote for my son Chalin, as a vote of appreciation to me, for my work for the Parish over the years." He characterized his son's opponent as "strictly a troublemaker" and "part of the flotsam and jetsam that comes to the surface at times like these."[41] Chalin defeated Hingle by more than a four-to-one margin. In the Democratic primaries, Perez-backed candidates swept to victory in all the parish and district offices in Plaquemines and St. Bernard.[42]

The gubernatorial election also went according to Perez's plan. In his first term (1964–1968) John McKeithen had pushed through a number of long-needed reforms and had become one of the most popular governors in Louisiana's history. He was so popular, in fact, that he convinced the legislature and the voters to repeal the constitutional prohibition against a governor succeeding himself and then ran for a second term. This time McKeithen's opponent was John Rarick, the state's most conservative congressman, whom Perez had originally urged to run for Congress. Rarick was definitely to the right of McKeithen ideologically, especially on the race issue, but everyone knew that he had little chance to win. Some conservatives who felt that McKeithen was straying too far to the left urged Perez himself to run, but the Judge never seriously considered the idea. He stuck with McKeithen, who coasted to an easy first-primary victory over his rival.

Perez was quite influential in both McKeithen administrations.

Persons seeking jobs or political appointments frequently asked him to intercede with the governor. In 1968, the governor appointed Perez to the Board of Highways. Despite this fellowship, however, Perez vigorously fought the governor's tax increase proposals, calling them "a shameful waste of good public money." When McKeithen called a special session to raise taxes, Perez spent much of his time lobbying against the increases and appearing before legislative committees to testify against them. The governor's tax program provoked opposition from many erstwhile supporters, and was the beginning of a sharp decline in McKeithen's popularity, which reached an ebb near the end of his second term.[43]

On November 30, 1967, Perez officially retired as president of the Plaquemines commission council. At the age of seventy-six he severed his last official connection with the parish, after forty-eight years as judge, district attorney, and council president. At the final meeting at which he presided, the commission council adopted a budget of $3,796,802.50. All other business was set aside except for the swearing in of Chalin Perez to his father's position as commissioner. Leander watched with moist eyes and, before stepping down from his seat, said, "I have no other remark, except to say, I have no regrets for my career. If I had it to do over again I would do it willingly."[44]

After he was sworn in, Chalin nominated Clarence T. Kimble, commissioner of public finance, for council president. Kimble declined, and a vote on his nomination was never taken. Instead, Public Safety Commissioner Luke Petrovitch nominated Chalin Perez, who was unanimously elected. Petrovitch explained that, although it might seem unusual to have a new member become president, Chalin had worked with the parish government for twenty years in an unofficial capacity. Chalin presided only a few minutes before adjourning to a reception at the community center, where he and his father joined in cutting a huge cake inscribed "L. H. Perez, Sr., 1919–1967 / Chalin O. Perez, 1967–?"[45]

A series of testimonial dinners for the senior Perez followed. The annual Fourth of July celebration at Fort Jackson was made an occasion to honor him. He was awarded a lifetime honorary membership in the Louisiana Senate and House of Representatives, signed by Governor McKeithen, which carried all of the privileges of the floor. Among the dignitaries present were Congressman F. Edward Hebert, Senator James O. Eastland of Mississippi, and Tom P. Brady, associate justice of the Mississippi Supreme Court. The climactic tribute of the day was a fireworks display featuring Perez's face with his characteristic cigar and his hat on his head.[46]

After retirement, the Judge kept as busy as ever; his correspondence seemed to proliferate rather than diminish. There was still the Wallace campaign, his position on the Board of Highways, and his continued fight to maintain the remnants of segregation. He did, however, now find a little more time for his two favorite outdoor diversions, hunting and fishing. He frequently combined business with pleasure by taking senators, congressmen, and company presidents aboard the *Manta* for parties and fishing. Leander loved to cook for his guests; among his specialties was something called red bean taco soup. Although he made yearly hunting trips to the Far West and had killed a huge bear in Wyoming, most of the Judge's hunting was carried on from his camps at the southern tip of Plaquemines Parish. For many years he had kept a camp at Baptiste Collette, at the end of Main Pass, but of late he had given it up and built a new one at Tiger Pass, below Venice.[47]

On January 10, 1969, Perez took some time off to entertain some friends on a hunting trip at his camp at Tiger Pass. He rose early, had his coffee, and dressed for hunting. Half an hour later, he told his guides to go ahead without him, that he did not feel like hunting. His cook, Clarence Gartoucies, stayed in the camp with him. Soon after the party left, the Judge began to have trouble breathing. He tried several homemade indigestion remedies, but soon realized that he was seriously ill and asked for oxygen. Gartoucies sat him in a chair and bundled him with blankets to keep him warm. He called to a companion to warm up the motor of the cabin skiff *At Last* and radioed the Port Sulphur police to meet him at the Venice boat dock with a police car and an ambulance with oxygen. He also asked that the parish hospital be alerted. Gartoucies then raced Perez to Venice. Normally the trip from Tiger Pass to Venice took about twenty minutes, but the little boat made it in half that. By the time they arrived, Perez was gasping for breath. Gartoucies, borrowing oxygen from a nearby asthmatic who kept a reserve supply, administered it to the Judge. Within a few minutes the police car arrived, equipped with oxygen, and Perez was transferred to the car in his chair, still covered with blankets. Then he was rushed to the hospital while oxygen was administered. A heart specialist was flown in from New Orleans to meet him at the Port Sulphur hospital. Perez's sons were notified and also flew to the hospital, where they were waiting when he arrived. Leander was kept there for several days and then, after it was determined that he had had a heart attack, was transferred by a Freeport Sulphur Company helicopter to Baptist Hospital in New Orleans. His family and friends stayed by his bedside around the clock. Perez recovered steadily from the severe heart attack and was soon transferred from intensive care to a private room. He remained in the hospital for about a month and then was taken to his daughter's house in New Orleans before finally returning to his home at Idlewild.[48]

By mid-March the Judge seemed to have recovered sufficiently to resume an almost normal routine. On March 19 he was taken to New Orleans for his final checkup. His doctor said that he was in good shape and could start returning to Baton Rouge in a day or two as long as he avoided excitement and took his medicine. Perez returned home from New Orleans, ate a hearty supper, and went into his study. He played with his little dog Tinkerbell for a few minutes, then said that he had some work to do. His sister-in-law, who was staying with him, went outside for a few minutes, and when she returned Tinkerbell was barking. Thinking that strange, she called out for Perez, but he did not answer. She called again, because the old man had grown slightly deaf. Finally, she decided that the dog was trying to tell her something. She walked into the study and found the Judge slumped in the chair by his desk. He had died instantly from his second heart attack.[49]

The following evening, thousands lined up outside the Bultman Funeral Home in New Orleans to file past the Judge's silver casket. During the early part of the night, two lines stretched from the front door onto oak-lined St. Charles Avenue and around the corner onto Louisiana Avenue. A spokesman for Bultman remarked, "This is the largest wake I have seen in my 33 years here."[50] Most of the

Louisiana judges from all court levels attended the wake, as did Victor H. Schiro, mayor of New Orleans. George Wallace arrived in tears and embraced Leander's personal secretary. At one point a group of children from the Prytania Private School arrived in procession carrying a heart-shaped spray of red and white carnations, which they placed near the casket. The Perez family afterwards requested that contributions be sent to the Plaquemines private school system in lieu of flowers.[51]

Then, amid the somber pomp, came a surprising announcement. Perez had been secretly reconciled with the Catholic church and would be allowed to have a church funeral. A short set of prayers was recited at the mortuary before the casket was closed and a blanket of red roses placed over it. St. Bernard parish deputies on motorcycles, followed by city and state police, then led a two-hundred-car motorcade to the stately, red-brick Holy Name of Jesus Church on the campus of Loyola University, where a requiem mass was held. More than a thousand persons packed the church, and several hundred more lined the streets outside. Cars were double-parked for ten blocks. The funeral attracted the governors of Louisiana and Mississippi and Senators Eastland and Ellender. Governor Wallace of Alabama, attired in a blue suit and sunglasses, followed the coffin into the church along with a contingent of Alabamians. Eight of Leander's grandsons served as pallbearers. Immediately behind the casket proceeded his two sons, Chalin and Lea, and his two daughters, Mrs. J. Douglas Eustis and Mrs. Richard Carrere.[52]

The Reverend Peter Boerding of St. Thomas Church in Pointe a la Hache began the service with a prayer: "We humbly pray, You . . . do not hand him over to the powers of evil but command his soul to be taken up by the Holy Angels." After the funeral, a long line of cars wound its way to the family mausoleum at Idlewild, where the Judge's wife had been interred. As the procession of thousands drove down the Belle Chasse highway, people closed their businesses and stood along the highway to watch their leader make his final trip.[53]

A close friend of Leander's said that a day had seldom passed during the previous two years that Perez had not visited the resting place of his wife and upon leaving showed visible signs of his bereavement. The mausoleum is situated in a grove of giant live oak trees draped with Spanish moss. The architectural style complements the rambling red-brick home called Idlewild that Perez had built about a decade before his death. Near the mausoleum is the small, white frame house in which Leander and Agnes spent their weekends for several years before Idlewild had been constructed.[54] Father Boerding, sprinkling the casket with holy water, prayed that God would not punish the deceased for his sins but would "make him a companion of your saints" and "grant to him everlasting rest and happiness." After the simple ceremony, Judge Perez's casket was moved into the mausoleum and placed in an open crypt alongside that of his wife.[55]

Eulogies poured in. George Wallace termed Perez's death "a loss to his state, the Southland, and the entire nation."[56] Former governor Jimmie Davis said, "There are many who might have disagreed with the causes he championed, but there are few who would disagree with the personal sincerity and integrity of Judge Perez himself. He did what he felt and believed was right."[57] Former governor Robert Kennon, who had first known Perez in the 1920s, commented, "I found him really Louisiana's most interesting political figure. Over the years he has been much loved by those who knew him well."[58] Senator Russell Long telegraphed Perez's children, "It has been said that some people never stand for anything. That cannot be said of your father, who was an indefatigable fighter for his convictions."[59] Former governor Sam Jones, once an obdurate foe of Perez, said, "Perez stood for what he considered was right and he advocated a philosophy which an element of Louisiana people believed in."[60] The Louisiana legislature adopted a joint resolution eulogizing Perez. The Plaquemines Parish Commission Council unanimously decreed that, in honor of "the dear departed Father of Plaquemines Parish . . . brilliant statesman, noble leader, and truly Great American, Judge L. H. Perez," and because of his "love, devotion, and untiring efforts," all flags in the parish should fly at half staff for two weeks and "the birthdate of Plaquemines' Great Father," July 16, should be an official parish holiday each year.[61]

Not everyone mourned. Upon hearing the news of the Judge's death, five young blacks entered a Plaquemines bar and announced their intention to celebrate. They were soon arrested on charges of drunkenness and "disturbing the peace" and sentenced to six months in the parish prison. The sentence was later reduced to three months.[62]

Perez's Catholic funeral also stirred protest. On the day that he was buried, six priests, five of them theology professors at Catholic universities in New Orleans, addressed a letter of protest to Archbishop Philip Hannan, in which they called Perez's reconciliation "token" and "a mere legalism." They complained that Perez had made anti-Negro statements on television and should have been required to recant before cameras. The priests wrote, "In all candor we consider the event a disgrace to all right-thinking persons, Catholic and non-Catholic alike. The leading racist of the South was buried with full and solemn honors in a Christian church, on the premises of an important Catholic educational institution, with the leading figures of the racist world assembled there under one roof during the Mass, sacrament of unity and brotherhood."[63]

Archbishop Hannan explained that Perez had been reconciled with the church eighteen months earlier and had been receiving the sacraments since. A highly placed church source said that the initiative for the reconciliation had come from the New Orleans archdiocese shortly after the death of Perez's wife in February, 1967. The old archbishop who had excommunicated the Judge was dead, and a new archbishop, Philip A. Hannan, sat in New Orleans. The church had discreetly let Perez know that anything he said that could be construed as support for church authority would be enough to lift the censure. The opportunity came in March, 1968, at a groundbreaking ceremony for a new incinerator at Fort Jackson. This was a minor civic event, attended by a few townspeople and workmen and not reported by the press. Two priests were also in the audience. In his speech Perez made unusually kind remarks about parochial schools and the new archbishop, and the priests relayed the news to the archbishop. Some time later Perez was notified by a priest privately that he was absolved from the six-year excommunication. According to the church source, it had been arranged in advance that Perez would make his retraction at the incinerator ceremony. Neither the *Plaquemines Gazette* nor the Catholic archdiocese newspaper reported the ceremony. Archbishop Hannan said, "The fact that it was not reported by the press does not affect the case and is a matter of freedom of judgment of the press." Church officials said that it was up to the person to announce his reinstatement or to remain silent.[64]

Many of Leander Perez's opponents believed that his political empire would collapse immediately following his death. This has not happened, because his sons have stepped into the breach and provided leadership. Five years after his death, every appointed or elected public official in Plaquemines was a member of the Perez faction. In 1972 his son Lea was reelected to another six-year term as district attorney. Facing stiffer competition than his father had confronted since the 1920s, Lea easily carried Plaquemines but won only narrowly in St. Bernard. St. Bernard Parish, which has far outgrown Plaquemines in population, constitutes the greatest threat to the Perez dynasty. Plaquemines is still safely Perez country, but St. Bernard, with almost twice as many voters as its sister parish, is drawing away.

Lea Perez, the Judge's older son, had been groomed by his father as his successor, but Lea has been reluctant to assume the mantle. While Perez was still alive and Lea was district attorney, he was wholly dependent on his father for advice and direction. Lea was parish prosecutor in name only; his father was still the power in the district attorney's office. Both sons grew up in the shadow of their famous father, but this affected them in different ways. Lea seems relaxed, self-indulgent, and hedonistic, and Chalin appears industrious, reserved, and contemplative. Lea is taller, slimmer, and less forceful than Judge Perez; neither son has the drive or intensity of the father. Lea's forte seems to be the cocktail circuit, the hunting lodge, and the racetrack rather than the smoke-filled room of the veteran politico. One gets the impression that politics to him is a necessary nuisance, a family business that occasionally interrupts the more pleasurable aspects of life. He has a television set in his office and can more often be found conferring about racehorses than about political affairs. Lean, graying around the temples, with a kindly face, he does not seem a typical Perez.

The real power in Plaquemines today is the younger son Chalin, the commission council president. He has the short, stocky frame of his father, and his complexion is dark, perhaps harking back to the French-Spanish origins of the family. Chalin is the worker of the family. He savors the exercise of power after operating so long on the fringes of authority. The *Plaquemines Gazette* has made it clear that Chalin is the new boss of the lower delta. It praises him in the same manner in which it formerly extolled his father and has called upon the people of the parish to transfer their "respect, loyalty, and affection" to Leander's younger son. Of his accession to the office of parish president, Chalin said, "I had no thoughts or aspirations for public office. But when asked by my father to accept the position, I readily accepted."[65]

Unlike his father, Chalin's participation in politics as an officeholder did not come until late in life. After growing up in New Orleans, he received a degree in business administration from Tulane University in 1943. Upon graduation, he also received an officer's commission from the naval ROTC. He served in the Pacific Fleet for two years, accumulating five battle stars, then returned to Tulane and received his law degree. He immediately went into a law partnership with his father and also became a behind-the-scenes man in the government of Plaquemines. Because he was not a parish official and therefore not included in the federal injunction prohibiting interference with public school desegregation, Chalin became the central figure in raising funds to build the private school system. He also spearheaded the Plaquemines Recreational and Educational Association, which built swimming pools and playgrounds for the white children of the parish. Despite his behind-the-scenes efforts, Chalin was relatively unknown when he took the reins of leadership. He owned a plantation home called Stella on the east bank of Plaquemines at Braithwaite, which he had sometimes occupied during the summers, but he was primarily a New Orleanian. After becoming recognized as parish leader, Chalin moved to Stella permanently.

Under his leadership, the tempo in Plaquemines is slower and the parish attracts less national attention, but the Perez family remains firmly in control. Chalin has not been front-page news as often as his flamboyant father and he lacks the spectacular rhetoric of the Judge, but he has consistently made the back pages of the larger papers through his work in Louisiana's constitutional convention of 1973–1974, his intention to construct a giant superport under the auspices of Plaquemines, and his public works projects in the parish. Chalin's first year as titular parish leader proved eventful. Just four months after he stepped into his father's shoes as president of the Plaquemines commission council, "Judge" Perez died. Then came Hurricane Camille, the most destructive storm ever to strike the southern coast of the United States. After previous natural disasters, Leander had always taken charge. Following Camille, Chalin assumed command, committing the parish to an ambitious recovery program largely financed by federal funds. The father had always been suspicious of federally funded projects, but the son welcomed the new influx of money. The younger Perez also accelerated the capital improvements program that had been instituted by his father. He seemed less reluctant than Leander to spend both parish and federal money. Between 1948 and 1965, Judge Perez had spent $15,000,000 in parish revenues, but had built up a cash surplus of $26,000,000. In the first two years after the Judge's death, the parish spent an estimated $23,000,000, not counting the highway program that devoured $10,000,000 of the parish royalty road funds. Money was spent on water, sewerage, and drainage improvements, new ferries and landings, fire equipment, and municipal buildings. "We've taken over additional responsibilities we never had before," Chalin commented.[66]

Chalin's most controversial project has been his attempt to locate a superport off the Plaquemines coast. In 1970 a legislative act created the Plaquemines Parish Port Commission and gave it authority to construct the superport for deep-draft tankers that need water depths of a hundred feet or more. After Governor Edwin Edwards (a liberal on the race issue and therefore an enemy of the Perezes) took office, he had the legislature adopt a second act taking control of the proposed port from Plaquemines and giving it to the state. He then appointed Gillis Long, who had supported Edwards in the gubernatorial second primary after being himself defeated in the first, to head the state group. At the meeting to create the task force, Chalin cast the lone dissenting vote against making it a statewide group. In his emotional condemnation of Governor Edwards for taking the superport project out of the hands of Plaquemines, Chalin's rhetoric approached that of his father. Denouncing Edwards for stepping in at the "ninth hour," he complained that at the rate the state was working it would "take 10 to 15 years to get a deepwater port."[67]

Chalin was more successful in drafting a new constitution for Louisiana. Edwin Edwards had made a campaign pledge to rewrite the fifty-one-year-old document and after taking office set about fulfilling his promise. At first Chalin opposed any constitutional revision at all, fearing that it would wipe away many of the special privileges for Plaquemines that his father had written into the 1921 constitution. Soon realizing that he lacked the power to prevent a constitutional convention from meeting, he decided to join the deliberations to try to assure that only a minimal number of changes would be made affecting local government. He was easily elected a delegate by the people of Plaquemines and then was appointed by the convention chairman, E. L. ("Bubba") Henry, to head the committee on local and parochial government. At the outset, Chalin went on record as opposed to a short, concise document modeled on the federal constitution, because it "is impossible for the mind of man to put in a few words all the limitations people want to put on their government."[68] In his determined stand to assure a maximum of freedom for local governing bodies, Chalin found himself aligned with some of his father's old enemies, including deLesseps Morrison, Jr., of New Orleans, the son of the former mayor. A number of delegates who were ideologically opposed to Chalin on most issues agreed with his position on local government because they wanted the municipal governments to have the flexibility to solve their own problems without interference from the state. Chalin had two principal objectives that were different from the motives of many of the delegates who allied with him: to maintain the legality of the leases to state land that had been awarded to his father's dummy corporations and to which he was heir; and to continue the constitutional provisions that enable the Plaquemines commission council (formerly the police jury) to receive the income from the levee districts located in Plaquemines as long as those districts remain in debt. Chalin succeeded beyond his expectations; the new Louisiana constitution grants a greater degree of home rule than the constitution of any other American state. The Plaquemines home rule charter is confirmed, the governing of the levee boards by the commission council is constitutionally authorized, and the state is prohibited from nullifying or altering existing levee board contracts, including those under which the levee boards signed away millions of state dollars to the mysterious shareholders of the Delta Development Company. Under the new document, the amount of funds that the state will share with the parishes is substantially increased. In place of Leander's old road royalty fund, the parishes will receive a larger share of mineral royalties from state lands lying within the parish, with no strings attached. Most of the other parishes, particularly Orleans, were glad to go along, since home rule essentially means more freedom; however the effect in Plaquemines is to perpetuate, and even to augment, the power of the Perezes.

Chalin and Lea have remained active in national politics, with Chalin again taking the lead. In 1972, the presidential campaign of George Wallace received $15,000 in contributions from the Perez family—$5,000 from Chalin, $5,000 from Lea, and $5,000 more from their sister, Mrs. Chester Gelpi. However, Chalin's support of Wallace lacked the crusading zeal of his father. He was realistic enough to admit that Wallace had little chance to gain either the Democratic presidential nomination or the presidency itself. What he hoped for was a cabinet position or a concession in favor of "law and order" in the platform. Chalin has adopted a less extreme stand on race relations than his father, although he is still an ardent segregationist. "Race relations should be local," he says. "Race relations would be better served in Plaquemines if the carpetbaggers and the outsiders will leave us alone to work out our problems."[69]

Chalin seems anxious to establish his own identity. He wants to be known as something more than simply the son of the Judge and asserts that he "is not a chip off the old block." The younger Perez doubts that he will become as politically influential as his father. He explains, "My father spent a lifetime in politics. I wasn't cast in the image of my father. Every man, I believe, must stand on his own feet."[70]

In 1973 Chalin was elected to another term on the commission council without opposition, and in August, 1973, the members of the council elected him to serve another six-year term as president.[71] The Perez family's domination of Plaquemines is thus assured at least until 1979 and will no doubt last as long as Chalin is alive and healthy. Beyond that, it is difficult to predict. The heir apparent is Chalin's son "Cop" (Chalin O. Perez, Jr.), who at this writing is a law student at Tulane University. Short, sandy-haired, freckle-faced, and affable, he emphatically denies that he is interested in perpetuating a dynasty of any type, and he means it, although the role may some-day be thrust upon his reluctant shoulders. But dynasty in terms of the absolute dictatorship operated by his grandfather is gone forever, and perhaps Cop feels that it is a good thing. Occasionally in his law classes he will speak up in favor of the rights of labor or tenant farmers. That is easy to do when one's future and fortune are assured, but he does it with evident sincerity. Cop firmly rebuked a writer who had tried to put words in his mouth in searching for some indication that he was cut from his grandfather's mold.[72]

It may well be that the Judge himself was an atypical Perez rather than a true representative of his family. Discussion is freer in Plaquemines now, and most decisions are made collectively. Asked to explain how the parish differs now that Perez is gone, veteran politician J. Ben Meyer summed it up: "The thing is, you couldn't find very many people that would talk back to Leander."[73]

Epilogue

What of the storm when the night is o'er?
    There is no trace or sign!
Save when the wreckage hath strewn the shore,
    Peaceful the sun doth shine.

        Arthur J. Lamb,
        "Asleep in the Deep"

A former sulphur executive who had worked for many years in the lower delta once commented, "Perez, in his own mind, is the greatest citizen since George Washington, maybe even greater. *He* didn't chop down any cherry tree." [1]

This attitude was not confined to the Judge himself; both his partisans and enemies were equally opinionated. He was loved and hated with equal fervor, and his own feelings were likewise intense. During his long life he demonstrated a profound capacity for tenderness and kindness, especially toward his own family—and an unlimited ability to hate. There is no inherent contradiction between Perez's sentimental affection for his own family and his passionate hatred of Negroes and Jews. Love and hate went hand in hand with Perez; his fear that his affiliative relationship might be interrupted led him to hate the agent thought to be responsible for the interruption. He feared that his blood line, something he prized dearly, would be "contaminated" by Negro blood or that his filial social life would be encroached upon by blacks.

Although prejudice is frequently considered only in the negative sense, it can apply to positive feelings as well. Leander liked some people and places without sufficient warrant just as he disliked others without sufficient warrant. His overestimation of the things he

371

loved led to an underestimation of their contraries. Perez built fences as much to protect what he valued as to wall out what he distrusted and did not understand. The Judge glorified Plaquemines to such an extent that all other places suffered by comparison, and his local and regional pride narrowed into insularity and xenophobia. Perez, not gifted with much insight or empathy, found comfort in the simple and tangible values of his childhood, which were based upon a patriarchal society and the institutions of the church, school, and family. He enjoyed security and even a certain amount of tranquillity in his ordered, rigidly controlled little kingdom, where he understood the people, their rural folkways, and their relatively uncomplicated way of life. Judge Perez was provincial and parochial; he was not well traveled or sophisticated. He summarily rejected the unfamiliar. When his sister tried to persuade him to tour Europe he told her, "There's nothing over there you can't find in the good old U.S.A."[2] The Judge's provincialism extended to international affairs; the farther removed a people or culture, the greater was his suspicion of them. His impatient craving for definitive judgments led him to overcategorize world affairs upon the basis of limited information. A wit has defined prejudice as "being down on something you're not up on."[3]

Psychological studies have shown that extreme bigots are likely to be superpatriots; a prejudice against the foreign is likely to be coupled with a prejudice in favor of the familiar. The Judge viewed the world as a pitched battle between the forces of good and evil, between him and his numerous opponents. Many seemingly unrelated experiences could evoke his Communist phobia: membership in the United Nations, the passage of civil rights legislation, the growth of labor unions, admission of Hawaii to the Union, pacifistic statements by intellectuals, and American adherence to the rulings of the World Court. He had certain catch personalities—David Dubinsky, Walter Reuther, and Joseph Stalin—who were apparently interchangeable and undoubtedly indefatigable since, according to Perez, they had been behind every "subversive" plot for at least twenty years. Without questioning his dubious "evidence," Leander became thoroughly convinced that the world was a place of conspiracies. There were conspiracies of Communists, Jews, and blacks. Not only that, but all three (no matter that they had little or nothing in common) were involved in the same conspiracy. His evidence? Just common sense, the Judge would say. And anyone who doubted that must himself be part of the conspiracy! Leander lived in a world of absolutes; all Jews were Zionists; all blacks were inferior; and all Communists worked day and night to overthrow the "American way of life" as practiced in Plaquemines Parish.

A normal person is capable of casting aside the shell from which he grew, but the development of Perez's personality was arrested; in fact, it seemed to regress. As he reached maturity he became less open-minded; he moved from relative passivity to aggressive belligerence; he hardened and toughened and shut out all ideas he could not immediately grasp. He aimed for the quick and simple; the less time and effort expended in thought, the more that remained for action. He neither learned patience nor mastered the art of weighing contrary evidence. There is not a single recorded instance in which he conceded that he had even momentarily been mistaken. Perez's failure to grow, to expand and develop his early ideas, was not because he lacked flexibility entirely. After all, in politics he might impeach a man one year and then support him at the next election. But the Judge found comfort and security only in the old and familiar. He valued security above freedom, and he expected similar priorities from others.

Perez represents an almost perfect example of what psychologists term the authoritarian personality. Such a person fears change; socialism, communism, racial integration, intellectualism, and liberalism all represent some departure that threatens his ordered life. The Judge possessed most of the characteristics of this personality type: intense aggressiveness, an inability to relax, and a refusal to consider opposing viewpoints. When contradictory evidence was offered, he obstinately twisted it to suit his previous convictions. One method of subverting such unpleasant ideas was to discredit the objectivity of their exponents; thus, those favoring racial integration became Communists, Zionists, atheists, or opponents of the American way of life. He defined American way of life as an acceptance of social Darwinism, the values of nineteenth-century rural America, and unobstructed capitalism; a distrust of intellectualism; and a condemnation of any unorthodoxy. The most characteristic aspect of the authoritarian personality is the lack of a sense of humor. True humor has been defined as the "ability to laugh at the things one loves (including, of course, oneself) and still to love them."[4] Perez enjoyed flattery and was unable to look at himself critically. His idea of a good joke was giving a hotfoot to a former political opponent or snipping off the shirttails of his younger relatives who failed to keep them neatly tucked in.[5]

In his youth, Leander was not a champion of the established order in the delta but was even something of a crusading revolutionary. Had he died at the age of forty, he would have been known as neither an arch-reactionary nor a racist. Yet the seeds of the traits that were to dominate his adult life were present as early as adolescence in his immaculate dress, his penchant for fisticuffs, and his interest in politics. Once he had overturned the established order and had become the dominant authority in the delta, his essential conservatism acclimated to his personal habits quite congenially. He had everything to lose from change: his political power, his immense fortune, and the adulation he received from his fellow deltans. It was this last that Perez could least tolerate losing. He yearned for power; he enjoyed wealth; but he craved respect, praise, and even fear from those beneath him.

Although in public Perez was confident to the point of arrogance, the private man must have lived in a state of constant anxiety. His shady oil deals might be discovered; local political opponents might undermine his power; an unfriendly governor might destroy his base of operations; the federal government might compel the registration of political opponents and blacks. His anxiety sought personification, so he lashed out in all directions, striking first at those who were closest and most identifiable: blacks, "Zionist" Jews, and "Reds." His prejudice fed on inward insecurity; he was vaguely terrified by any sign of ambition or progress in potential competitors. Since he was ashamed of his concealed concerns, the external manifestation took the form of grossly exaggerated confidence. Perez was the middle-class country boy, striving to prove his superiority to the urban intellectuals who seemed increasingly to dominate life in the twentieth century. He could not do so by sophistication, so he did so by aggressiveness and an unrelenting will.

Although he was inveterately self-conscious, the Judge never examined himself critically. He seldom labored over decisions; his ego would not tolerate doubt. As a man of affairs, Perez was able to function efficiently because he did not stop to question what he believed in. Capable of intricacy in planning how to achieve his goals, he never paused to reflect upon them. He never second-guessed himself or his allies and did not for a moment concede that his opponents might be right. He was capable of crushing men who were his intellectual peers but who paused to doubt. Although he claimed to value consistency in thought, what he actually practiced was inflexibility. Perez was so much a creature of habit that the habits remained long after the original reasons for developing them had ceased to exist. In the 1920s he had found it necessary to deny the ballot to political opponents in order to perpetuate himself in office. By the 1950s he had grown so powerful in Plaquemines that his adversaries were pathetically helpless, yet he continued to practice superfluous electoral chicanery.

Leander Perez was both rigidly consistent and uncomplicated and, on the other hand, a bundle of contradictions. He approached all problems from his own narrow, particularistic viewpoint, yet the solutions he worked out were sometimes unorthodox and frequently contradictory. He was charming, engaging, and hospitable, yet intensely vindictive; he was exceptionally intelligent, yet naïvely credulous of highly dubious sources; he was materially progressive, yet clung to outdated and outmoded beliefs and customs; he was considered an astute attorney, yet lost almost every case he argued in federal court. He denounced federal tyranny and posed as a defender of states' rights and home rule, yet no one ever ran a tighter dictatorship than he did in his own bailiwick. He worked hard to build up Plaquemines economically and keep its taxes low, but at the same time drained its resources into his own coffers through his dummy corporations. The Judge could be tough, unyielding, cantankerous, and insulting, bulldozing his way to what he wanted and giving opponents no quarter, but he could also be a gracious, charming host.

He enjoyed entertaining and never tired of leading visitors on tours of the public improvements he had made in Plaquemines. The same man who incarcerated a political opponent in an unheated, unlighted cell for several weeks was perfectly capable of enjoying the carefree pleasures of Disneyland with his grandchildren. He poured all of his passion for invective into his public life so that there was only tenderness left for his family. Because few people knew the complete man, few were able to judge him fairly. Some knew only of his many concrete accomplishments for Plaquemines Parish or of the many families whom he personally and generously helped without asking anything in return. Others saw only the tyrant. They experienced strong-arm tactics and found it difficult to believe that Perez could love. Those close to him experienced only the love and found it impossible to believe that he could resort to trickery and deceit. Those associated with him in his many rightist crusades on the national and regional levels no doubt did so without realizing the crude tactics he sometimes utilized in his home parish.

Simply because Judge Perez despised certain minorities, it does not follow that he was unintelligent; even bigots may be brilliant outside the narrow scope of their disorder. Perhaps a key to his closed-mindedness was his inability to relax and to feel at ease with conflicting view-points or personalities. He disciplined himself to exclude everything that might annoy him; thus he was at once outwardly confident and inwardly neurotic. Judge Tom Brady of Mississippi wrote Leander that he had never seen him truly serene except when sitting in the prow of his beautiful boat, gazing at the blue sky and tranquil water of the Gulf, or after vanquishing all opponents in a hand of poker or blackjack.[6]

Perez was doggedly persistent in his unrelenting quest for power. He knew exactly what he wanted, and he bent every energy to that end. But his desire was to be a leader rather than to lead the people somewhere; power seemed to be an end in itself. Once he attained it, his principal aim was to perpetuate himself in his privileged position rather than to map out a program of social reform. This is not to say that Leander was incapable of generous impulses, but his generosity, except to his family, was inspired by the sense of power it gave him. By doing for others what they could not do for themselves he could dominate them; this was the quintessence of Perez's paternalism. His entire life was directed toward obtaining immediate needs—the construction of a new road, the reduction of a tax, or the annihilation of a political enemy. He seemed to have no conception of what he hoped to achieve overall. If he had any theoretical goal at all, it was to preserve the values of nineteenth-century rural America, which had already become anachronistic even in Plaquemines. In some respects, such as his writing style, which used one hackneyed phrase after another to depict the same cast in a nefarious scheme to enslave the world and give Negroes the vote, Perez was wholly unimaginative, but in his legal and financial manipulations the Judge revealed an inventive, if devious, mind. Like that of George Washington Plunkett, his epitaph might have read: "He seen his opportunities, and he took 'em."[7]

As Perez found inner security through an external display of arrogance, the people of Plaquemines also found protection under the aegis of his leadership. Autocracy and Perez's type of demagoguery, exploiting false rather than actual issues, cannot flourish in a strong, secure population. The people of the lower delta are among the most insecure in the nation; they must cope with hurricanes, insect pests, the destruction of their animal life, and strangers monopolizing their abundant resources. They are acclimated to boss rule because they have a need for the stability it provides. To a lesser extent, this has been true of Louisiana as a whole.

Perez governed his fiefdom according to the Old World patriarchal tradition under which he grew up. As the "father" of Plaquemines Parish he accepted the responsibility for the welfare of his children (not unlike the attitude that Bienville adopted toward the Indians). Obedient and loyal children were well rewarded; the prodigal and rebellious were chastised or disowned. He saw himself as a feudal lord bound to protect his faithful vassals—a knight errant, a crusader against the depredations of the pillaging barbarians from the North, who were laboring under atheistic and alien doctrines, such as world government, collectivization, mongrelization of the races, and federal control of offshore oil. It is not without significance that his favorite comic strip was "Prince Valiant."

The Judge could never be photographed in an undignified pose, even when hunting, playing softball, or cooking for friends, which he especially enjoyed. When he set out to prepare a dinner, Leander drove everyone else out of the kitchen. Then he set about carving meat with gusto, as if he were carving up the carcass of a political opponent.

Although Perez's early career smacks of outright thuggery, by middle age he was venerated as almost a demigod by his devoted followers. In 1954, Perez was awarded an honorary Ph.D. as a "doctor of worldly wisdom" by the Boswell Institute of Chicago. He was one of only a handful of distinguished persons so honored, including General Charles de Gaulle, former president Harry S. Truman, and Winston Churchill. Rousseau Van Voorhies of Lafayette, chancellor of the institute, described Perez as a "Leonardo da Vinci of the 20th century."[8]

By all odds, Leander stood tall compared with his fellow deltans. Plaquemines is no redoubt of the Inquisition, as northern writers have sometimes depicted it, but neither is it an intellectual community. Perez did not have a voracious literary appetite. In his particular environment he was a cultured man but, considered in a broader sphere, he was not a cosmopolitan or urbane one. He might have become an object of amusement if he had tried to peddle his ideas in New York or London. Perez realized that he was king for life in Plaquemines and that he might become only a pawn upon a larger battleground. Although he was so aggressive in his local encounters as to appear fearless, he did not want to personally campaign in a broader theater of operations. He was satisfied with a greater degree of control over a smaller geographic area.

The Judge had a superb talent for mastering legal technicalities but not a broad education. His temperament was best suited to single-minded domination of one specific field, and the field he chose was politics. If one word could fully describe Perez, it would be *indomitable*. He never gave up. Even when he had no chance of winning, he always had another trick up his sleeve—no matter how farfetched, ridiculous, or petty it may have seemed.

Once he had attained wealth and office and was assured of remaining in power, Leander was a conscientious worker for "his people." They comprised only those who supported him and, among blacks, only those who did not attempt to vote or integrate. Perez's concern for his parish was real and deep, not merely hypocritical. His material achievements in Plaquemines were extensive and beneficial, but they were less than might have been accomplished had not great amounts of energy and millions of dollars been siphoned off for personal gain and to keep Perez's machine entrenched in power. The Judge never gave anything to his people without first taking it away from someone else. The money he used to build up his delta fiefdom should have gone to the state rather than the parish because it came from royalties on oil and sulfur found on state land. What he gave to Plaquemines was not his to give; he did it at the expense of the state as a whole. Even for the people of the lower delta, material progress was bought at the price of personal freedom. It should also be kept in mind that Plaquemines was a rich parish with few people; it would have prospered with or without Perez. To concede that his authoritarian methods were necessary to bring material growth to the people is to admit that democracy is not a workable form of government.

Leander Perez possessed many of the attributes of greatness, but he was not a great man. He had a superb mind, resourcefulness, purposefulness, an infinite capacity for hard work, and an unyielding determination. At his best under pressure, he never cracked, never ceased working, and never surrendered, even when common sense and the law of averages were on the opposing side. For all of this, Perez fell short of greatness because he lacked patience, flexibility, curiosity, conceptual capacity, an appreciation for opposing viewpoints, and a firm moral purpose. He was unable to learn from others or from his own mistakes; indeed, he was unable to admit that he ever erred, even to himself. To him, everything was white or black, patriotic or subversive, holy or satanic.

It is as a theoretician for lost causes that Leander appeared at his weakest. Although he claimed that he was not a racist, he certainly fit Webster's definition of a racist, as William F. Buckley pointed out. In a misguided effort to show that Leander did not hate blacks, one of his sisters said, "They say he called them niggers. He never used the word *nigger*; he called them darkies."[9]

It is tempting to search for a single source for Perez's racism—

some person who markedly influenced his life, something he read as a youth, or some striking aspect of his education. Prejudice, however, is rarely that simple; it almost always has multiple causes. The Judge was in no way personally threatened by the Negro—or, for that matter, by the Zionist Jew or Communist—but there was something inside him that, taken with his early training, accounted for the unusual depth of his hatred of minorities. Perez was a rabid racist long before there was any actual threat of desegregation in Plaquemines. In his first twenty years in parish politics, however, he had neither the leisure nor the regional influence to engage in a crusade concerning national issues. Once he became the undisputed leader of Plaquemines, he not only sought to extend his influence but he viewed every change in the established order with distrust, whether the threat was chimerical or legitimate. It was not the existence of the Negro per se but a shifting of his status and an increase in his self-consciousness that aroused the latent prejudice in Perez. Perhaps these reasons account for his passive support of President Roosevelt but his vehement opposition to Presidents Truman, Kennedy, and Johnson.

As a child Leander learned that power and authority dominate human relationships, a lesson he was never to forget. He grew up with a hierarchical view of society. Sociologists have determined that a home where the parents' word is law, such as Leander's, is likely to prepare the groundwork for group prejudice.[10] Despite this tendency, prejudice is only partly environmental; sometimes youths reject the prejudice of their parents. But in a family as closely knit as the Perezes, this would have been treason. Leander never questioned the values he learned in his childhood. School, church, and his social milieu only reinforced his beliefs. His circle of friends was limited and his interests parochial.

Study shows that hostility diminishes as intimate contact increases. Perez's contact with blacks was casual and always limited to superordinate-subordinate relationships. He met Negroes only as underlings, and he met liberal intellectuals only as opponents. He never developed a lasting friendship with an educated black man or a thoroughly rounded intellectual of any race. Being furnished with suitable stereotypes of Negro inferiority, Perez became sensitized to detect examples of the traits that he believed were common to all blacks; the inability to operate a hay baler by the Negroes on his farm was taken as a barometer of intelligence for all Negroes.

The simplicity of race as an answer to all problems appealed to Perez because it had the stamp of finality. The theory of the inherent inferiority of a particular race was attractive because it appealed to latent prejudices and it spared the pains of examining the complex economic, cultural, political, and psychological conditions that enter into group relations. The Judge's life was much simplified by putting large numbers of his fellow humans into categories that he could summarily reject. He could then exclude a maximum number of people with a minimum amount of thought, which was agreeable to him because he preferred action to contemplation. Studies have shown that prejudice is related to certain personality characteristics, most of which can be found in Perez: moralism, dichotomization, a need for definiteness, externalization of conflict, institutionalism, and authoritarianism. To be good and angry at someone is like living on a spree, and Leander enjoyed a constant release of pent-up emotions in his tirades against blacks and Jews.[11]

In downgrading Negroes, Perez was correspondingly elevating himself and feeding his voracious ego. It conferred upon him a sense of personal status and security. Perez yearned to command; a commander needs an army; and an army needs an enemy. The Judge had few competitors of equal wealth, persistence, or oratorical ability in the lower delta. The easiest (and most politically profitable) idea to sell to the downtrodden inhabitants of the area was that they were superior to someone else. Prejudice feeds on doubt of one's own importance and ability; certainly self-doubt permeated the minds of the impoverished, provincial inhabitants of Perez's two-parish stronghold. The Negro provided a layer of social support for the self-enhancement of the lower-class whites in Perez's empire. This explains why Leander's ideas were so readily accepted in the isolated lower delta, and it partly, but not entirely, explains why he became an arch-segregationist in the first place. His racism was sincere, not merely an instrument to maintain political power, although that may have been a contributing motive. But he stuck to his racist rhetoric and beliefs even when they cost him far more than he gained in political influence and personal wealth. As a child, Leander had subconsciously adopted the prejudices of his parents, playmates, teachers, and friends. His preoccupation with his own dignity involved an effort to suppress his emotions that, turned outward, erupted into flights of profane disparagements of minorities and, in his younger days, fistfights.

According to psychologists, people tend to falsely attribute to others traits that are their own. If one can castigate others, he is saved from the pain of critically examining himself. Thus Perez could bitterly denounce President Harry S. Truman for "dictatorship." The fact that such qualities were Perez's own made it that much easier to see them in others. I recall a conversation with a prominent, elderly segregationist from Georgia, who boasted of his own sexual exploits as a collegian and, in the next breath, condemned Negroes for "sexual immorality."[12]

A modified form of this tendency, called *projection,* occurs when a person does not attribute his own frame of mind to others, but rather uses their supposed attitudes to justify his own. In a further expression of projection, many people with suppressed sex drives desire the same freedom attributed to the Negro. The inhibited are sometimes secretly envious of the uninhibited, and indignation against the supposedly superpotent black evades guilt and restores self-respect. In some cases the difference in color is somehow stimulating. Sex is forbidden; the Negro is forbidden and strange; the ideas begin to merge. As Gordon Allport explains, "This illicit fascination may become obsessional in some localities where life is otherwise intolerably dull," a description that certainly applies to Plaquemines.[13]

The central issue of race mixing is allegedly miscegenation. Intermarriage is combated heatedly because it symbolizes the ultimate abolition of prejudice. Sex with blacks is unthinkable because sex is an equalizer; to have intercourse with an inferior is to lower oneself to his level. Racists believe in a sort of sexual domino theory; unless all forms of discrimination are institutionally maintained, intermarriage will result. The same reasoning was used to defend slavery. The argument against interracial sex combines an amalgam of sexual repression, guilt, status superiority, occupational advantage, and anxiety.[14]

Perez had learned to appreciate the simple life; at barbecues he hosted he wore a chef's apron stamped with the motto Keep It Simple. Nothing could be simpler than to categorize all Negroes on the basis of a few individual cases. For a man raised in his environment, with his particular psychological makeup, exposed to the limited intellectual stimuli he received, it is not surprising that he became an arch-segregationist. Ultimately, he could not escape his environment or his own emotions.

Prejudice against the Negro was only one aspect of the Judge's racism; he was also anti-Semitic. Studies show that in the United States the well-to-do are most prone to anti-Semitism. The Jew is seen as a possible economic competitor, and to keep him down is to avoid symbolically all potential threats. Like many racists, Perez attempted to translate his prejudice into objective reality by qualifying his hatred. He did not despise all Jews, only "Zionist" Jews. This qualification permitted him to make exceptions for individual Jews, who might be members of the Citizens' Council or supporters of George Wallace. It was easier to hate the group than the individual because he did not have to test his stereotype of the group against reality.[15]

The Judge expended much time, energy, and money in attempts to elect a man with similar views to the presidency, but he was doomed to be disappointed in any "white knight" he chose to support, even if the unlikely possibility of his election had materialized. These men did not operate on the same assumptions that he did, nor did their souls burn with the same ardent fire that his did. Strom Thurmond did not have Perez's intensity and, unlike the Judge, recognized the politician's art of engineering a sincere compromise. General Eisenhower was certainly no racist, nor could he really be concerned with Leander's interest in offshore oil. Senator Goldwater's conservatism was genuine, but his commitment to states' rights was never made at the expense of basic human rights, especially those, such as the vote, that were guaranteed by the Constitution. Had Perez lived long enough he probably would have become disenchanted with Governor Wallace, whose adventures in racism were more likely a marriage of political convenience than the combination of anthropological theory and religious fanaticism that characterized

Perez's. Wallace is more properly thought of as a populist, whose attacks on bigness in government the Judge could loudly applaud but whose attacks on bigness in industry he found it necessary to counsel against. All of these men found it necessary at times to accommodate themselves to a national base. Personal avoidance of the national arena for the insularity of his delta empire was the price Perez paid for the luxury of his uncompromising and single-minded attitude toward American politics.

Leander Perez was so forceful that he managed to stamp his image permanently in the 1960s even after his type of politics, not to mention his political philosophy, had long passed. By sheer will he prevented those years from becoming a dull sequence of logical events. The particular circumstances that enabled Perez to become the omnipotent political boss he was will probably never recur in America. People are now too educated, and there are simply not many places with the financial potential in an isolated, underdeveloped area that was available to Perez. The rough-and-tumble politics of the Huey Long era, when Perez became a potent force in Louisiana, have largely vanished. Even if such a man as Leander Perez were born today, he could not lead such a career.

Gazing out at the broad, muddy Mississippi from the Plaquemines free ferry at Pointe a la Hache, it is easy to imagine the stumpy, fiery figure of the Judge standing at the helm, dominating all in sight, including the mighty river. Traveling in Plaquemines, the word *Perez* can still be heard frequently on the lips of swarthy fishermen, oystermen, and roughnecks. And even today, as the twentieth century finally overtakes Plaquemines, the older people can sometimes be heard to lament, "If only the Judge were here."

Notes

PROLOGUE

1. Baton Rouge *State-Times,* April 3, 1965.
2. Robert K. Sanford, "In His Corner of the South Few Persons Dare Talk Back to Leander (the King) Perez," Kansas City *Star,* January 26, 1964.
3. In Louisiana, counties are known as parishes.
4. Richard Austin Smith, "Oil, Brimstone, and 'Judge' Perez," *Fortune,* LVII (March, 1958), 151; David Baldwin, "Perez Takes Meraux's Political Scalp," New Orleans *Item,* June 22, 1950.

CHAPTER ONE

1. Harnett T. Kane, *Deep Delta Country* (New York, 1944), ii–xiii.
2. Mrs. W. E. Anderson, taped interview with the author, Baton Rouge, La., February 9, 1972.
3. Lester Velie, "Kingfish of the Dixiecrats," *Collier's,* December 17, 1949, p. 10; Reese Cleghorn, "The Perils of Plaquemines," *New Republic,* September 21, 1963, p. 9; John Berton Gremillion, *Plaquemines Parish* (Baton Rouge, 1963), 1; Lew Dietz, "Trembling Prairie," *Field & Stream,* LXIX (February, 1965), 58; Kane, *Deep Delta Country,* x–xiii.
4. Chalin O. Perez, taped interview with the author, New Orleans, La., June 21, 1972; Anderson, interview with the author.
5. Anderson, interview with the author; *St. Bernard Voice* (Arabi, La.), November 4, 1939.
6. Anderson, interview with the author.
7. *Ibid.; St. Bernard Voice,* November 4, 1939.
8. *Ibid.;* Anderson, interview with the author; Chalin Perez, interview with the author; Mrs. Claude P. Foret, taped interview with the author, New Orleans, La., March 13, 1972; Mrs. Chester Gelpi, taped interview with the author, New Orleans, La., March 13, 1972.
9. Anderson, interview with the author.
10. *Ibid.*
11. *Ibid.*
12. *Ibid.;* Etienne Barrios, "King of the River People?" *Commonweal,* June 6, 1962, pp. 365–66; Gremillion, *Plaquemines Parish,* 7.
13. Anderson, interview with the author; Gelpi, interview with the author; Chalin Perez, interview with the author; Mrs. Richard J. Carrere, taped interview with the author, New Orleans, La., March 13, 1972.
14. Anderson, interview with the author.

15. *Ibid.; Holy Cross College Yearbook, 1904–1905; Holy Cross College Yearbook, 1905–1906;* New Orleans *Times-Picayune,* June 4, 1924.
16. Leander H. Perez transcript, 1906–12, Louisiana State University, Baton Rouge; *Plaquemines Gazette* (Belle Chasse, La.), May 7, 1965.
17. Perez transcript, Louisiana State University; Anderson, interview with the author.
18. Perez transcript, Louisiana State University; *Gumbo, 1912* (Louisiana State University Yearbook).
19. Foret, interview with the author; Dr. J. B. Francioni, taped interview with the author, Baton Rouge, La., February 17, 1972.
20. Anderson, interview with the author.
21. Francioni, interview with the author; *Gumbo, 1912.*
22. Anderson, interview with the author.
23. *Gumbo, 1911* (Louisiana State University Yearbook); *Gumbo, 1912;* Francioni, interview with the author; Lewis Gottlieb, taped interview with the author, Baton Rouge, La., March 1, 1972; Hermann Moyse, taped interview with the author, Baton Rouge, La., March 1, 1972.
24. Anderson, interview with the author.
25. *Ibid.*
26. Perez transcript, Louisiana State University; *Plaquemines Gazette* (special undated issue), November, 1967.
27. Percival H. Stern, taped interview with the author, New Orleans, La., July 28, 1972; Edward Haspel, taped interview with the author, New Orleans, La., July 27, 1972.
28. David Baldwin, "How Perez Got His Start in Politics," New Orleans *Item,* June 16, 1950; *Jambalaya, 1914* (Tulane University yearbook).
29. J. Ben Meyer, "Judge Leander H. Perez: Hi Lites of His Life" (Typescript in possession of the author), 3.
30. Chalin Perez, interview with the author.
31. Kane, *Deep Delta Country,* 205; David Baldwin, "Everybody Votes in the Perez Parishes," New Orleans *Item,* June 13, 1950.
32. Baldwin, "How Perez Got His Start in Politics"; Lester Velie, "'Democracy' in the Deep Delta," *Collier's,* December 24, 1949, p. 42.
33. Foret, interview with the author.
34. *Ibid.;* Anderson, interview with the author.
35. Foret, interview with the author; certificate of marriage, Mater Dolorosa Church, New Orleans, La.; New Orleans *Item,* May 14, 1917.
36. Foret, interview with the author; *Plaquemines Gazette,* November, 1967.
37. Foret, interview with the author; statement of service, Leander H. Perez, United States General Services Administration, Washington, D.C.; Meyer, "Judge Leander H. Perez," 3.
38. *St. Bernard Voice,* July 31, 1920; testimony of John Dymond, in *Philip R. Livaudais* v. *Leander H. Perez,* No. 26,307, Supreme Court of Louisiana, New Orleans, La.
39. Baldwin, "How Perez Got His Start in Politics"; *State ex rel Leander H. Perez* v. *H. C. Cage, Judge,* No. 23,844, Supreme Court of Louisiana, New Orleans, La.
40. Baldwin, "How Perez Got His Start in Politics"; Meyer, "Judge Leander H. Perez," 3.
41. Testimony of John Dymond, *Livaudais* v. *Perez;* New Orleans *Times-Picayune,* December 12, 1919.
42. Testimony of John Dymond, *Livaudais* v. *Perez.*

CHAPTER TWO

1. Kane, *Deep Delta Country,* 201–205; text prepared for testimony of Leander Perez, *Livaudais* v. *Perez;* Haspel, interview with the author; *Plaquemines Protector* (Pointe a la Hache, La.), February 2, 1924; A. S. Cain, Jr., taped interview with the author, New Orleans, La., July 19–20, 1972.
2. Velie, "'Democracy' in the Deep Delta," 42; New Orleans *Times-Picayune,* May 16, July 22, September 9, 1920; *Plaquemines Gazette,* November, 1967.
3. *St. Bernard Voice,* August 14, 1920.
4. David Baldwin, "Parish Foes Sue to Oust Judge Perez," New Orleans *Item,* June 17, 1950; *St. Bernard Voice,* September 18, October 16, 1920.
5. Plaquemines had only 1,304 registered voters in 1920.
6. Testimony of Ernest Alberti and testimony of John Dymond, *Livaudais* v. *Perez; Plaquemines Protector,* October 15, 1921.
7. *State of Louisiana* v. *William Dymond,* Nos. 389, 420, 421, Twenty-ninth Judicial District Court, Plaquemines Parish, La.; *State of Louisiana* v. *John Dymond, Jr.,* No. 386, Twenty-ninth Judicial District Court, Plaquemines Parish, La.; *Plaquemines Protector,* May 20, 1922; New Orleans *Times-Picayune,* November 11, 1922; testimony of John Dymond, *Livaudais* v. *Perez; Lower Coast Gazette* (Pointe a la Hache, La.), July 15, 1922.
8. *Plaquemines Protector,* August 5, 12, 1922; *Lower Coast Gazette,* July 15, 1922.
9. *Livaudais* v. *Perez; State of Louisiana* v. *Emile Martin,* No. 383, Twenty-ninth Judicial District Court, Plaquemines Parish, La.
10. Testimony of John Dymond, *Livaudais* v. *Perez.*
11. *Livaudais* v. *Perez;* Velie, "'Democracy' in the Deep Delta," 42; *St. Bernard Voice,* September 23, 1922.
12. *St. Bernard Voice,* September 23, October 7, 1922.
13. Cain, interview with the author; *ibid.,* October 8, 1938.
14. Kane, *Deep Delta Country,* 180–82; *St. Bernard Voice,* January 6, 1923, March 5, 1927; *Plaquemines Protector,* February 2, 1924.
15. Baldwin, "Parish Foes Sue to Oust Judge Perez"; *St. Bernard Voice,* April 21, 1923.
16. Baldwin, "Parish Foes Sue to Oust Judge Perez"; *St. Bernard Voice,* April 28, May 5, 19, July 28, 1923, July 5, 1924, October 11, 1930; *Plaquemines Protector,* July 28, 1923.
17. *St. Bernard Voice,* August 4, 1923.
18. *State ex rel Philip R. Livaudais, District Attorney,* v. *L. H. Perez, Judge,* No. 26,174, Supreme Court of Louisiana, New Orleans, La.; New Orleans *Times-Picayune,* May 27, 1924; *ibid.,* November 17, 24, December 1, 1923.
19. Baldwin, "Parish Foes Sue to Oust Judge Perez"; *St. Bernard Voice,* July 28, 1923.
20. *Livaudais* v. *Perez;* Baldwin, "Parish Foes Sue to Oust Judge Perez."
21. Velie, "'Democracy' in the Deep Delta," 42.
22. *Livaudais* v. *Perez;* Baldwin, "Parish Foes Sue to Oust Judge Perez"; New Orleans *Times-Picayune,* October 11, 1923.
23. *Ibid.*
24. Velie, "'Democracy' in the Deep Delta," 42; New Orleans *Times-Picayune,* November 1, 1923, May 6, 13, 14, June 4, 1924; David Baldwin, "Suit to Impeach Judge Perez Ends in a Love Feast," New Orleans *Item,* June 18, 1950.
25. "Racist Leader," *Time,* December 12, 1960.
26. Baldwin, "Suit to Impeach Judge Perez Ends in a Love Feast"; New Orleans *Times-Picayune,* June 5, 1924.

27. Baldwin, "Suit to Impeach Judge Perez Ends in a Love Feast."
28. *St. Bernard Voice,* July 26, November 8, 1924.
29. Cleghorn, "The Perils of Plaquemines," 8; Meyer, "Judge Leander H. Perez," 4.
30. *St. Bernard Voice,* October 6, December 29, 1923.
31. New Orleans *Times-Picayune,* July 25, 1924.
32. *St. Bernard Voice,* September 6, 1924.
33. New Orleans *Times-Picayune,* July 30, 1925.
34. *St. Bernard Voice,* January 19, April 26, September 6, 1924, November 21, 1925; *Plaquemines Protector,* February 2, 1924.
35. *St. Bernard Voice,* November 24, 1923, February 23, 1924; *Plaquemines Protector,* February 2, 9, 23, 1924.

CHAPTER THREE

1. Kane, *Deep Delta Country,* 172–77; *St. Bernard Voice,* August 21, 1926.
2. Kane, *Deep Delta Country,* 172–77; *St. Bernard Voice,* August 7, 1926; Carleton Beals and A. Plenn, "Louisiana Skin Game: Independent Fur Trappers Starving," *Nation,* December 25, 1935, pp. 738–40; Carolyn Ramsey, "Louisiana's Fabulous Muskrat Marshland," *Readers' Digest,* XLVI (March, 1945), 77.
3. *Plaquemines Protector,* February 2, 1924; Kane, *Deep Delta Country,* 173–75; *St. Bernard Voice,* August 7, 1926; *St. Bernard Trappers' Association* v. *J. Walter Michel,* No. 28,264, Supreme Court of Louisiana, New Orleans, La.; *Plaquemines Gazette* (Pointe a la Hache, La.), November 10, 1928; Carolyn Ramsey, "Rats to Riches," *Saturday Evening Post,* May 8, 1943, p. 78.
4. Kane, *Deep Delta Country,* 172–77; Beals and Plenn, "Louisiana Skin Game," 739; *St. Bernard Voice,* April 24, 1926.
5. Kane, *Deep Delta Country,* 172–77; Ramsey, "Rats to Riches," 78.
6. The Phillips lands consisted of 99,512 acres, 88,180 in Plaquemines and 11,332 in St. Bernard. Most of the land was owned directly by the Phillips Land Company, but some of it belonged to individual company officers. *St. Bernard Trappers* v. *Michel.* See also Kane, *Deep Delta Country,* 176.
7. *St. Bernard Trappers* v. *Michel; St. Bernard Voice,* November 29, December 6, 13, 1924; *Louisiana Muskrat Ranch* v. *Manuel Molero et al.,* No. 18,560, U.S. District Court, New Orleans, La.
8. The St. Bernard Trappers' Association was organized December 9, 1924, with $20,000 worth of stock subscribed. *St. Bernard Voice,* December 13, 1924; *St. Bernard Trappers* v. *Michel.*
9. *St. Bernard Trappers* v. *Michel.*
10. Affidavit sworn by John R. Perez, August 6, 1926, *ibid.*
11. Foret, interview with the author; act of sale, John R. Perez to J. Walter Michel, *St. Bernard Trappers* v. *Michel.*
12. New Orleans *Times-Picayune,* July 22, 1926; *St. Bernard Trappers* v. *Michel.*
13. *St. Bernard Trappers* v. *Michel;* New Orleans *Times-Picayune,* July 20, 1926. It can be assumed that, in keeping with the factional tradition of delta politics, dodgers announcing the stockholders' meeting were left only at those stores whose patrons were considered politically reliable.
14. *St. Bernard Voice,* April 3, 1926.
15. *St. Bernard Trappers* v. *Michel;* New Orleans *Item,* April 16, 1926.
16. *St. Bernard Trappers* v. *Michel.*
17. *Ibid.*
18. *Ibid.;* New Orleans *Times-Picayune,* July 21, 1926; New Orleans *States,* April 16, 1926.

19. *St. Bernard Voice,* April 17, 1926; *St. Bernard Trappers* v. *Michel;* New Orleans *Times-Picayune,* April 13, 1926.
20. New Orleans *Times-Picayune,* April 13, 1926.
21. New Orleans *Item,* April 11, 1926; *St. Bernard Trappers* v. *Michel.*
22. One must admit that the board was probably correct in charging that a number of the angry trappers at the meeting were not bona fide members of the St. Bernard Trappers' Association. Estimates of attendance ranged as high as 800, and friend and foe alike usually put the membership of the association between 400 and 500. It has been noted previously that the stock ledger showed 467 shareholders. Of course, the corporation itself never knew exactly how many members it had or who they were. Many of the "nonmembers" present were probably men who did not pay dues but did pay the $50 annual rental fee for trapping lands and were now upset about having to pay more. At any rate, the board's own claim to represent "the bulk of trappers in the entire parish" was transparently ridiculous.
23. *St. Bernard Trappers* v. *Michel;* New Orleans *Times-Picayune,* April 13, 1926; *St. Bernard Voice,* April 17, 1926; New Orleans *States,* April 18, 1926.
24. *St. Bernard Trappers* v. *Michel.*
25. To further illustrate the rampant nepotism in the delta is the fact that the head janitor at the courthouse was the president's father, Victor Morales, Sr. *Ibid.*
26. New Orleans *Times-Picayune,* May 10, 25, July 1, 22, 1926; New Orleans *Item,* May 9, 1926; *St. Bernard Voice,* July 31, 1926.
27. New Orleans *Times-Picayune,* May 25, 1926.
28. *Ibid.,* July 19, 1926.
29. *Ibid.,* May 9, July 18, 1926; *St. Bernard Voice,* April 14, May 15, 1926; *St. Bernard Trappers* v. *Michel;* New Orleans *Item,* April 23, May 16, 1926; New Orleans *States,* May 8, 1926.
30. New Orleans *States,* May 9, 1926; *St. Bernard Voice,* May 15, 1926; New Orleans *Times-Picayune,* May 9, 1926.
31. New Orleans *Times-Picayune,* May 9, 1926; New Orleans *States,* May 9, 1926.
32. New Orleans *States,* May 18, 1926; *St. Bernard Trappers* v. *Michel;* New Orleans *Times-Picayune,* May 19, 1926.
33. New Orleans *Times-Picayune,* July 23, 1926; *St. Bernard Trappers* v. *Michel.*
34. New Orleans *States,* July 20, 1926; New Orleans *Times-Picayune,* July 23, 1926.
35. New Orleans *Times-Picayune,* September 21, 1926; *St. Bernard Voice,* September 25, October 9, 1926; *St. Bernard Trappers* v. *Michel.*
36. *St. Bernard Trappers* v. *Michel.*
37. *Ibid.*
38. New Orleans *Times-Picayune,* July 22, 1926; *St. Bernard Voice,* July 24, 1926.
39. *St. Bernard Trappers* v. *Michel.*
40. *Ibid.*
41. *Miguel Perez* v. *Canadian Land and Fur Co., Inc.,* No. 18,457, U.S. District Court for the Eastern District of Louisiana, New Orleans; *St. Bernard Voice,* July 3, 1926.
42. *St. Bernard Voice,* July 31, 1926; New Orleans *Times-Picayune,* July 27, 1926; New Orleans *States,* July 26, 1926.
43. Judge Meraux issued a temporary injunction. He later recused himself from the case. *St. Bernard Trappers' Association* v. *Anthony Alonzo et al.,* No. 163, Twenty-fifth Judicial District Court, St. Bernard Parish, La.; *St. Bernard Voice,* September 25, 1926; New Orleans *Times-Picayune,* September 21, 1926.
44. New Orleans *Times-Picayune,* April 14, August 31, 1926; New Orleans *States,* August 31, 1926; *St. Bernard Voice,* September 4, 1926.
45. *St. Bernard Voice,* October 30, 1926; New Orleans *States,* October 27, 1926; *Louisiana Muskrat Ranch* v. *Molero; St. Bernard Trappers* v. *Michel.*

46. *St. Bernard Trappers* v. *Michel; Trappers* v. *Michel,* 110 So. 617 (1926); New Orleans *States,* November 2, 1926; New Orleans *Times-Picayune,* November 3, 1926; *St. Bernard Voice,* November 6, 1926.

47. *St. Bernard Voice,* September 4, October 23, November 6, 1926; New Orleans *States,* October 8, 1926.

48. New Orleans *States,* October 7, 8, 1926; *St. Bernard Voice,* October 9, 1926.

49. New Orleans *States,* November 16, 1926; New Orleans *Times-Picayune,* November 17, 1926.

50. New Orleans *Times-Picayune,* November 18, 1926.

51. *Ibid.,* November 17, 18, 1926; New Orleans *States,* November 16, 1926.

52. New Orleans *Times-Picayune,* November 17, 1926.

53. *Ibid.,* November 17, 18, 1926; New Orleans *States,* November 16, 1926.

54. New Orleans *States,* November 18, 1926; New Orleans *Times-Picayune,* November 17, 1926.

55. New Orleans *Times-Picayune,* November 18, 1926; New Orleans *States,* November 18, 1926; Smith, "Oil, Brimstone, and 'Judge' Perez," 148.

56. New Orleans *Times-Picayune,* November 17, 18, 1926.

57. *Ibid.,* November 24, December 28, 1926; New Orleans *States,* November 23, 1926; *St. Bernard Voice,* November 27, December 25, 1926, January 1, 1927.

58. *St. Bernard Voice,* October 30, 1937; Kane, *Deep Delta Country,* 178; Beals and Plenn, "Louisiana Skin Game," 740.

59. New Orleans *Times-Picayune,* February 8, 11, 12, 1927; David Baldwin, "How Perez Saved Huey Long from Impeachment," New Orleans *Item,* June 19, 1950.

60. *St. Bernard Voice,* February 19, 1927.

Chapter Four

1. Velie, "Kingfish of the Dixiecrats," 73.

2. Baldwin, "How Perez Saved Huey Long from Impeachment"; T. Harry Williams, *Huey Long* (New York, 1969), 90, 133, 138–47.

3. Williams, *Huey Long,* 192–213; Secretary of State, *Compilation of Primary Election Returns of the Democratic Party, State of Louisiana, Held January 17, 1924* (Baton Rouge, 1924).

4. Williams, *Huey Long,* 244–78; Secretary of State, *Compilation of Primary Election Returns of the Democratic Party of Louisiana Held January 17, 1928* (Baton Rouge, 1928).

5. Harvey Peltier, taped interview with the author, Thibodaux, La., September 18, 1972.

6. *Ibid.*

7. Williams, *Huey Long,* 302–10, 346.

8. Cain, interview with the author; *ibid.,* 368.

9. Cain, interview with the author; Peltier, interview with the author.

10. *Ibid.;* Velie, "'Democracy' in the Deep Delta," 42.

11. Peltier, interview with the author.

12. Williams, *Huey Long,* 382; Baldwin, "How Perez Saved Huey Long from Impeachment."

13. Williams, *Huey Long,* 351.

14. *Ibid.,* 401–403.

15. *Ibid.,* 393–96, 403–407; *Official Journal of the Senate of the State of Louisiana Sitting as a Court of Impeachment for the Trial of Huey P. Long, Governor of the State of Louisiana, May 16, 1929,* Special Sess., March 20–April 6, 1929.

16. Williams, *Huey Long,* 406–407; Cain, interview with the author; *St. Bernard Voice,* May 4, 1929.

17. Smith, "Oil, Brimstone, and 'Judge' Perez," 154; Secretary of State, *Report of the Secretary of State to His Excellency the Governor of Louisiana, January 1, 1921* (Baton Rouge, 1921).

18. David Baldwin, "The Enormous Power of Leander Perez," New Orleans *Item,* June 14, 1950; *Plaquemines Gazette* (Point a la Hache, La.), October 1, 1938; Smith, "Oil, Brimstone, and 'Judge' Perez," 154; J. Ben Meyer, taped interview with the author, Promised Land, La., June 19, 1970; "The Priest and the Politician," CBS television documentary, September 18, 1963.

19. J. Emmett Williams to Leander Perez, October 13, 1949, Act 556 of 1964, Senator E. W. Gravolet to Public Affairs Research Council, August 25, 1964, Perez to Ray W. Burgess, director of Louisiana Department of Highways, October 31, 1962, all in Leander H. Perez Files, New Orleans, La.

20. Harry E. Bovay to Leander Perez, February 13, 1930, Perez to O. K. Allen, February 25, 1930, Tommy Powers, Department of Highways press release, August 9, 1970, all *ibid.*

21. Secretary of State, *Compilation of Primary Election Returns, September 9, 1930, and Second Primary, October 14, 1930* (Baton Rouge, 1930); *Percy Saint v. Harry W. Fisher, Registrar of Voters, and Parish Democratic Executive Committee for the Parish of St. Bernard,* No. 31,656, Supreme Court of Louisiana, New Orleans, La.; New Orleans *Item,* October 6, 1932; David Baldwin, "Perez—Tough, Able Political Boss," New Orleans *Item,* June 12, 1950; Baldwin, "Everybody Votes in the Perez Parishes"; Kane, *Deep Delta Country,* 201.

22. New Orleans *Item,* October 6, 1932; Williams, *Huey Long,* 300; Baldwin, "Everybody Votes in the Perez Parishes."

23. Baldwin, "Everybody Votes in the Perez Parishes."

24. Secretary of State, *Compilation of Primary Election Returns, January 19, 1932* (Baton Rouge, 1932); New Orleans *Item,* October 6, 1932; Kane, *Deep Delta Country,* 201; *ibid.*

25. New Orleans *Item,* October 6, 1932; Baldwin, "Everybody Votes in the Perez Parishes"; Secretary of State, *Compilation of Primary Election Returns, September 13, 1932* (Baton Rouge, 1932); Secretary of State, *Compilation of Primary Election Returns, October 18, 1932* (Baton Rouge, 1932).

26. Secretary of State, *Compilation of Primary Election Returns, January 21, 1936* (Baton Rouge, 1936); Velie, "'Democracy' in the Deep Delta," 21, 42.

27. *St. Bernard Voice,* August 2, 1930, December 7, 1935, January 26, 1936.

28. *Ibid.,* October 15, November 5, 1938; *Plaquemines Gazette,* May 13, 1939.

Chapter Five

1. Robert Sherrill, *Gothic Politics in the Deep South* (New York, 1968), 7; Chalin Perez, interview with the author; George Singelmann, taped interview with the author, New Orleans, La., March 15, 1972.

2. Succession of Roselius E. Perez and Gertrude Solis, No. 1,953, Twenty-fifth Judicial District, Plaquemines Parish, La.; Sherrill, *Gothic Politics in the Deep South,* 29; Smith, "Oil, Brimstone, and 'Judge' Perez," 159.

3. David Baldwin, "How Did Perez Become a Millionaire?" New Orleans *Item,* June 26, 1950; Velie, "Kingfish of the Dixiecrats," 10.

4. New Orleans *Times-Picayune,* April 1, 1959.

5. Sherrill, *Gothic Politics in the Deep South,* 14.

6. Sanford, "In His Corner of the South Few Persons Dare Talk Back to Leander (the King) Perez."
7. *Ibid.;* Smith, "Oil, Brimstone, and 'Judge' Perez," 148.
8. Velie, "Kingfish of the Dixiecrats," 11.
9. *Ibid.*
10. Earl Long, typescript of radio and television address [1959?], in Perez Files.
11. Howard Suttle, "Blast Dixiecrat Leader in National Magazine," unmarked clipping, Edgar Poe to Perez, January 7, 1950, and Salvador Chiapetta to speaker of Mississippi House of Representatives, undated, all *ibid.;* unmarked clipping, in Ben Meyer Scrapbook, Tulane University Archives, New Orleans, La.
12. David Baldwin to the author, April 4, 1972.
13. Baldwin, "How Did Perez Become a Millionaire?"
14. *Ibid.*
15. Extract from the minutes of a meeting of the board of commissioners for the Buras Levee District held at Buras, La., September 8, 1928, in Plaquemines Parish Conveyance Original Book, 66, fol. 266.
16. New Orleans *Times-Picayune,* November 13, 1941; overriding royalty agreement between Gulf Refining Company of Louisiana and Robert J. Lobrano, in Plaquemines Parish Conveyance Original Book, 69, fol. 407.
17. Baldwin, "How Did Perez Become a Millionaire?"
18. *Ibid.*
19. Smith, "Oil, Brimstone, and 'Judge' Perez," 148.
20. Deposition of Robert J. Chauvin, March 15, 1954, Vol. III, *Richardson and Bass* v. *Board of Levee Commissioners of Orleans Levee District,* No. 42,057, Supreme Court of Louisiana, New Orleans, La.
21. Application for second rehearing, *ibid.*
22. Chauvin deposition, *ibid.*
23. Dalcour *Times,* May 4, 1950; Braithwaite *Challenger,* April 11, May 2, 1942.
24. Velie, "Kingfish of the Dixiecrats," 11.
25. Leander Perez to Achille Guibet, May 10, 1939, in Perez Files; lease, board of commissioners for the Buras Levee District to Creole Oil Company, Inc., February 6, 1937, in Plaquemines Parish C.O.B., 83, fol. 510.
26. Smith, "Oil, Brimstone, and 'Judge' Perez," 148.
27. Sherrill, *Gothic Politics in the Deep South,* 30.
28. Smith, "Oil, Brimstone, and 'Judge' Perez," 154.
29. *Ibid.*
30. Thomas Martin, *Dynasty: The Longs of Louisiana* (New York, 1960), 176.

CHAPTER SIX

1. David Baldwin, "Perez Gains Power; Goes After Scalps of Meraux, Rowley," New Orleans *Item,* June 20, 1950.
2. *St. Bernard Voice,* March 16, 1940; Dalcour *Times,* May 4, 1940; Cain, interview with the author.
3. *St. Bernard Voice,* November 25, December 2, 1939, January 6, 1940.
4. David Baldwin, "The Perez Habit of Winning Elections," New Orleans *Item,* June 15, 1950; Baldwin, "Perez Gains Power"; New Orleans *Morning Tribune,* January 12, 1940; New Orleans *Times-Picayune,* January 11, 1940.
5. *St. Bernard Voice,* January 6, 1940; New Orleans *Times-Picayune,* January 11, 1940.
6. New Orleans *Item,* May 20, 1950; New Orleans *Times-Picayune,* March 5, 1940; Meyer, interview with the author; Hodding Carter, "Dixiecrat Boss of the Bayous," *Reporter,* January 17, 1950; Meyer, "Judge Leander H. Perez," 1.

7. New Orleans *Times-Picayune,* January 12, 1940.
8. *Ibid.,* January 20, 1940; New Orleans *Morning Tribune,* January 20, 1940; Baldwin, "Perez Gains Power"; *St. Bernard Voice,* January 20, 1940; *Plaquemines Gazette,* January 20, 1940.
9. New Orleans *Times-Picayune,* February 2, 1940, January 7, July 30, 1941; New Orleans *Morning Tribune,* February 1, 1940; *St. Bernard Voice,* January 20, 1940, January 11, 1941.
10. *St. Bernard Voice,* February 3, 1940; New Orleans *Times-Picayune,* February 1, 1940; New Orleans *Morning Tribune,* February 1, 1940; petition for recusation of Judge Meraux, Re: Leander H. Perez, District Attorney for the Parishes of Plaquemines and St. Bernard, State of Louisiana, No. 1,558, Twenty-fifth Judicial District Court, Plaquemines Parish, La.
11. New Orleans *Item,* February 16, 1941.
12. Brief by Herman L. Midlo, attorney for petitioners to impeach Perez, in response to Perez application for writs, Re: Leander H. Perez, District Attorney for the Parishes of Plaquemines and St. Bernard, No. 35,721, Supreme Court of Louisiana, New Orleans; *St. Bernard Voice,* September 2, 1939.
13. *St. Bernard Voice,* June 15, 1940; brief by Midlo, Re: Leander H. Perez, No. 35,721; St. Bernard Parish Grand Jury, hearing on the shooting of Mrs. Angela Treadaway, October 5, 1939, in Perez Files.
14. *St. Bernard Voice,* June 15, 1940, June 30, 1923; brief by Midlo, Re: Leander H. Perez, No. 35,721.
15. *St. Bernard Voice,* September 2, October 7, 1939; brief by Midlo, Re: Leander H. Perez, No. 35,721; St. Bernard Grand Jury, hearings on Treadaway shooting, in Perez Files.
16. Brief by Midlo, Re: Leander H. Perez, No. 35,721.
17. *Ibid.; St. Bernard Voice,* March 16, 1940.
18. *St. Bernard Voice,* March 16, 1940.
19. New Orleans *Times-Picayune,* March 11, 1940; editorial, Shreveport *Journal,* April 12, 1940.
20. Petition for removal from office, *Leander H. Perez* v. *J. Claude Meraux,* No. 35,755, Supreme Court of Louisiana, New Orleans.
21. David Baldwin, "Perez and Meraux Hurl Hot Charges," New Orleans *Item,* June 21, 1950; *Plaquemines Gazette,* March 16, April 6, 20, 1940; New Orleans *Times-Picayune,* March 7, 1940; *St. Bernard Voice,* April 6, 1940.
22. Baldwin, "Perez and Meraux Hurl Hot Charges"; *Plaquemines Gazette,* March 16, April 6, 20, 1940.
23. New Orleans *Times-Picayune,* June 27, 1940, April 8, 1941.
24. *Plaquemines Gazette,* July 12, 1941.
25. Baldwin, "Perez Takes Meraux's Political Scalp"; New Orleans *Times-Picayune,* August 1, 1940.
26. Baldwin, "Perez Takes Meraux's Political Scalp"; New Orleans *Times-Picayune,* January 17, 1941; *St. Bernard Voice,* January 18, 1941.
27. *St. Bernard Voice,* April 19, 1941.
28. New Orleans *Times-Picayune,* October 15, 1940, January 17, 1941; *St. Bernard Voice,* October 19, 1940, January 18, June 7, 26, July 5, 1941.
29. *St. Bernard Voice,* June 21, 1941; Sherrill, *Gothic Politics in the Deep South,* 19; New Orleans *Times-Picayune,* August 9, 1941; *Plaquemines Gazette,* August 9, 1941.
30. Baldwin, "Perez Takes Meraux's Political Scalp"; Plaquemines Parish Police Jury, resolution, August 13, 1941, Courthouse, Pointe a la Hache, La.
31. New Orleans *Times-Picayune,* September 10, 1941; *Perez* v. *Meraux,* I, 16–18.
32. Baldwin, "Perez Takes Meraux's Political Scalp."

33. *Ibid.;* New Orleans *Times-Picayune,* September 16, 1941.
34. Baldwin, "Perez Takes Meraux's Political Scalp"; New Orleans *Times-Picayune,* September 26, 1941; *Plaquemines Gazette,* October 4, 1941.
35. Judgment, *Perez* v. *Meraux;* New Orleans *Times-Picayune,* July 21, 1942, February 2, 1943.
36. New Orleans *Times-Picayune,* August 8, 15, 1942, February 2, 1943.
37. *St. Bernard Voice,* August 29, 1942.
38. Two paragraphs later the *Gazette* claimed that there was no commercial gambling in Plaquemines. *Plaquemines Gazette,* September 5, 1942.
39. *Ibid.*
40. New Orleans *Times-Picayune,* September 9, 1942; *Plaquemines Gazette,* December 12, 1942; *St. Bernard Voice,* September 12, 1942.
41. Velie, "'Democracy' in the Deep Delta," 42.
42. *St. Bernard Voice,* January 22, February 5, 1944; Perez to A. G. Stritzinger, March 21, 1944, in Perez Files.
43. Editorial, Shreveport *Journal,* January 26, 1944; *St. Bernard Voice,* March 4, 1944.
44. David Baldwin, "How Perez Tangled with Governor Jones," New Orleans *Item,* June 23, 1950; *St. Bernard Voice,* December 20, 1963.
45. *St. Bernard Voice,* October 25, 1947, January 24, February 28, July 24, 1948.
46. Carter, "Dixiecrat Boss of the Bayous," 11; Velie, "'Democracy' in the Deep Delta," 21.

CHAPTER SEVEN

1. *Henry C. Schindler, Jr., et al.* v. *Celestine Melerine et al.,* No. 5,796, Twenty-fifth Judicial District Court, St. Bernard Parish, La.; Bruce Eggler, "Plaquemines Without the Great White Father," *New Republic,* May 24, 1969, p. 12.
2. Smith, "Oil, Brimstone, and 'Judge' Perez," 151–52; Baldwin, "How Perez Got His Start in Politics"; Velie, "Kingfish of the Dixiecrats," 73.
3. Braithwaite *Challenger,* June 20, 1942.
4. Kane, *Deep Delta Country,* 207.
5. Brief of defendants, *United States* v. *Mary Ethel Fox,* No. 20,398, U.S. Fifth Circuit Court of Appeals, New Orleans, La. (district court proceedings included); editorial, Baton Rouge *Morning Advocate,* December 21, 1955; testimony of Walter Blaize, *Albert J. Tullier* v. *Frank Giordano,* No. 5,072, Twenty-fifth Judicial District Court, Plaquemines Parish, La., II, 243.
6. Blaize testimony, *Tullier* v. *Giordano,* II, 241, 243.
7. Braithwaite *Challenger,* May 16, 1942; Baldwin, "The Enormous Power of Leander Perez"; New Orleans *Item,* October 7, 1949.
8. Baldwin, "The Enormous Power of Leander Perez."
9. Kane, *Deep Delta Country,* 206–207.
10. Smith, "Oil, Brimstone, and 'Judge' Perez," 151; Sherrill, *Gothic Politics in the Deep South,* 21; Helen Fuller, "New Orleans Knows Better," *New Republic,* February 16, 1959.
11. Baldwin, "The Perez Habit of Winning Elections"; Sid Moody, "Perez Is Seen as Engaging Man Who Freely Expresses Himself," Baton Rouge *Morning Advocate,* May 3, 1964; Meyer, interview with the author.
12. New York *Times,* March 20, 1969.
13. Sherrill, *Gothic Politics in the Deep South,* 6.
14. Baldwin, "The Perez Habit of Winning Elections."
15. *Ibid.;* Moody, "Perez Is Seen as Engaging Man"; Smith, "Oil, Brimstone, and 'Judge' Perez," 151.

16. *Ibid.*
17. U.S. Senate, Judiciary Committee, *Hearings Before the Senate Judiciary Committee on S. 1564,* 89th Cong., 1st Sess., p. 550; Sherrill, *Gothic Politics in the Deep South,* 28.
18. *Ibid.*
19. *Plaquemines Gazette,* August 10, 1962.
20. *Ibid.,* August 18, 1961.
21. William F. Buckley, Jr., and Leander Perez,"The Wallace Movement," on "Firing Line," April 15, 1968 (Transcript No. 95). Baton Rouge *State-Times,* August 19, 1961.
22. Baton Rouge *State-Times,* August 13, 1966.
23. *Plaquemines Gazette,* September 3, 1965.
24. Velie, "'Democracy' in the Deep Delta," 21; Baldwin, "The Perez Habit of Winning Elections"; *Plaquemines Gazette,* September 11, 1959.
25. Buckley and Perez, "The Wallace Movement"; *Plaquemines Gazette,* November 6, 1959.
26. Braithwaite *Challenger,* June 20, 1942.
27. Cleghorn, "The Perils of Plaquemines," 9.
28. *Ibid.;* Kane, *Deep Delta Country,* 204; New Orleans *States-Item,* March 20, 1969.
29. Confidential communication.
30. Patrick Olinde, taped interview with the author, Rougon, La., February 28, 1972; New Orleans *States,* October 16, 17, 1951, January 15, 1953.
31. New Orleans *Item,* June 12, 24, 1950; Clint Bolton, "Leander's Legacy," *New Orleans,* VI (September, 1972), 55.
32. Plaquemines Parish Police Jury, resolution, February 26, 1959; Baldwin, "How Perez Got His Start in Politics."
33. Handout by Perez opponents during Sam Jones's administration, in Perez Files.
34. Joseph P. Sendker to Plaquemines Parish Commission Council, August 18, 1961, *ibid.;* Baldwin, "How Perez Got His Start in Politics."
35. James Graham Cook, *The Segregationists* (New York, 1962), 201.
36. Velie, "Kingfish of the Dixiecrats," 73; Baldwin, "The Enormous Power of Leander Perez"; Carter, "Dixiecrat Boss of the Bayous," 11–12.
37. Memorandum, James O. Eastland to Perez, August 4, 1961, in Perez Files.
38. Baldwin, "How Perez Got His Start in Politics."
39. Braithwaite *Challenger,* June 20, 1942; Bolton, "Leander's Legacy," 79.
40. Mrs. Joseph Henry and Mrs. Herbert Calhoun to Perez, June 2, 1966, in Perez Files.
41. Bolton, "Leander's Legacy," 79; Velie, "Kingfish of the Dixiecrats," 73; Meyer, interview with the author.
42. Dr. L. B. Bourg to Perez, October 1, 1957, Perez to Bourg, October 3, 1957, and other letters to Perez (names withheld by the author), all in Perez Files; Cain, interview with the author.
43. Cain, interview with the author.
44. Velie, "Kingfish of the Dixiecrats," 73; *Plaquemines Gazette* (special undated edition), November, 1967.
45. Sanford, "In His Corner of the South Few Persons Dare Talk Back to Leander (the King) Perez."
46. Smith, "Oil, Brimstone, and 'Judge' Perez," 145.
47. *Action!* (official publication of the Young Men's Business Club of Greater New Orleans), May 15, 1962; *Plaquemines Gazette,* December 4, 1959; Meyer, "Judge Leander H. Perez," 2–3; Bolton, "Leander's Legacy."
48. "The Priest and the Politician," CBS television documentary.
49. *Plaquemines Gazette,* November, 1967, June 26, 1964; Cain, interview with the author; Chalin Perez, interview with the author.

50. *Plaquemines Gazette,* November, 1967.
51. Baton Rouge *State-Times,* August 15, 1967; *Plaquemines Gazette,* August 18, 1967.
52. Carter, "Dixiecrat Boss of the Bayous," 10; Sherrill, *Gothic Politics in the Deep South,* 21.
53. Baton Rouge *Morning Advocate,* March 20, 1969; J. D. DeBlieux, taped interview with the author, Baton Rouge, La., February 22, 1972.
54. Chalin Perez, interview with the author; Meyer, interview with the author; *St. Bernard Voice,* June 26, 1937; Smith, "Oil, Brimstone, and 'Judge' Perez," 152; telegram, Wade O. Martin, Jr., to Perez, August 8, 1960, in Perez Files.
55. Cain, interview with the author.

CHAPTER EIGHT

1. Allen P. Sindler, *Huey Long's Louisiana: State Politics, 1920–1952* (Baltimore, 1956), 145.
2. *Ibid.*
3. *Ibid.,* 78, 81, 143.
4. *Ibid.,* 135–36.
5. New Orleans *Times-Picayune,* October 21, 1939.
6. Richard McCaughan, *Socks on a Rooster: Louisiana's Earl K. Long* (Baton Rouge, 1967), 87.
7. *Ibid.,* 88, 93; Sindler, *Huey Long's Louisiana,* 148–50; *Plaquemines Gazette,* February 17, 24, 1940; Perry Howard, *Political Tendencies in Louisiana* (Baton Rouge, 1971), 267, 460–61.
8. "Louisiana Repeals Its Sales Tax," *National Municipal Review,* XXIX (September, 1940), 626; "Twelve Years," *Time,* January 29, 1940, p. 24; New Orleans *Times-Picayune,* July 1, August 13, 27, 1942; "Louisiana Re-enacts Sales Tax as War Measure," *National Municipal Review,* XXXI (December, 1942), 641; *Plaquemines Gazette,* September 5, 1942.
9. Sherrill, *Gothic Politics in the Deep South,* 16.
10. Petition to the Honorable Judges of the Criminal District Court for the Parish of Orleans, State of Louisiana, No. 102,151, Docket E, New Orleans, and Reply of Respondents; New Orleans *Times-Picayune,* May 2, December 8, 1940, February 12, 1941.
11. New Orleans *Times-Picayune,* March 9, 1941, December 8, 10, 1940.
12. Sherrill, *Gothic Politics in the Deep South,* 16; New Orleans *Item,* January 20, 1941.
13. Velie, "Kingfish of the Dixiecrats," 11; *Elmer Stewart et al.* v. *Eugene Stanley,* No. 16,261, Nineteenth Judicial District Court, East Baton Rouge Parish, La.; New Orleans *Times-Picayune,* December 2, 1941.
14. *Plaquemines Gazette,* March 21, 1942.
15. *Ibid.*
16. Baldwin, "How Perez Tangled with Governor Jones"; *Walter J. Blaize* v. *Jerome A. Hayes,* 15 So.2d 217 (1943).
17. *Blaize* v. *Hayes.*
18. *Ibid.*
19. *Ibid.*
20. New Orleans *Times-Picayune,* June 12, 1943.
21. New Orleans *States,* June 9, 1943; Baldwin, "How Perez Tangled with Governor Jones."
22. New Orleans *Times-Picayune,* June 10, 1942; J. P. Cole, taped interview with the author, Baton Rouge, La., March 2, 1972; unmarked news clipping, in State

Guard Scrapbook (in possession of J. P. Cole, Baton Rouge, La.); Baton Rouge *Morning Advocate,* June 8, 1943.

23. New Orleans *Times-Picayune,* June 9, 1943; Baton Rouge *Morning Advocate,* June 8, 1943.
24. Baldwin, "How Perez Tangled with Governor Jones"; New Orleans *Times-Picayune,* June 9, 10, 11, 1943.
25. New Orleans *Times-Picayune,* June 12, 1943.
26. Baldwin, "How Perez Tangled with Governor Jones"; *Plaquemines Gazette,* July 1, 1943.
27. Baton Rouge *Morning Advocate,* June 15, 17, 1943; Baton Rouge *State-Times,* June 14, 1943; New Orleans *Times-Picayune,* June 16, 1943; editorial, Shreveport *Journal,* June 19, 1943.
28. Baldwin, "How Perez Tangled with Governor Jones"; New Orleans *Times-Picayune,* June 18, 20, 1943; Baton Rouge *Morning Advocate,* July 14, 1943; *Plaquemines Gazette,* July 1, 1943; *Blaize* v. *Hayes.*
29. *Blaize* v. *Hayes.*
30. Baton Rouge *Morning Advocate,* July 14, 1943; Baldwin, "How Perez Tangled with Governor Jones."
31. David Baldwin, "Civil War Looms as Perez Defies Jones," New Orleans *Item,* June 24, 1950; New Orleans *Times-Picayune,* October 8, 1943; telegrams, Sam Jones to Perez, undated, all in Perez Files; unmarked clipping from Lake Charles newspaper, in State Guard Scrapbook.
32. Cole, interview with the author.
33. Baldwin, "Civil War Looms as Perez Defies Jones"; Baton Rouge *State-Times,* October 7, 1943; New Orleans *Times-Picayune,* October 8, 1943.
34. New Orleans *Times-Picayune,* October 9, 1943; Baton Rouge *Morning Advocate,* October 8, 1943.
35. Baldwin, "Civil War Looms as Perez Defies Jones"; Kane, *Deep Delta Country,* 211; unmarked clipping from Lake Charles newspaper, in State Guard Scrapbook.
36. *Plaquemines Gazette,* December 11, 1943; New Orleans *Times-Picayune,* October 10, 1943; Baldwin, "Civil War Looms as Perez Defies Jones."
37. New York *Times,* October 10, 1943; New Orleans *Times-Picayune,* October 10, 1943; Cole, interview with the author; unmarked clipping, in State Guard Scrapbook.
38. New York *Times,* October 10, 1943; New Orleans *Times-Picayune,* October 10, 1943; Hermann Deutsch, "Vacancy in Sheriff's Office Started Plaquemines 'War,'" New Orleans *Times-Picayune,* May 12, 1963; affidavit of Arnold Schields, Claude C. Borne and Anthony Oddo, October 11, 1943, *Blaize* v. *Hayes;* Cole, interview with the author.
39. David Baldwin, "Perez Men Retreat in Courthouse Tiff," New Orleans *Item,* June 25, 1950; Kane, *Deep Delta Country,* 212; New York *Times,* October 10, 1943; New Orleans *Times-Picayune,* October 10, 1943; Cole, interview with the author.
40. *Ibid.*
41. Baldwin, "Perez Men Retreat in Courthouse Tiff"; New Orleans *Times-Picayune,* October 10, 1943; Shreveport *Journal,* October 9, 1943; Cole, interview with the author.
42. Affidavit of Dr. Ben R. Slater, October 9, 1943, *Blaize* v. *Hayes;* New Orleans *Times-Picayune,* October 10, 11, 1943; New York *Times,* October 10, 1943; affidavit of Mrs. Sadie M. R. Gorbach, October 15, 1943; unmarked clipping, in State Guard Scrapbook.
43. New Orleans *Times-Picayune,* October 10, 1943; Baton Rouge *Morning Advocate,* October 15, 1943.

44. Baldwin, "Perez Men Retreat in Courthouse Tiff"; New Orleans *Times-Picayune,* October 11, 1943; Shreveport *Journal,* October 11, 1943; Baton Rouge *State-Times,* October 13, 1943; Frank Nesom, taped interview with the author, Baton Rouge, La., March 10, 1972.
45. New Orleans *Times-Picayune,* October 11, 20, 1943; Baton Rouge *Morning Advocate,* October 11, 1943; *Plaquemines Gazette,* October 23, 1943; Nesom, interview with the author.
46. New Orleans *Times-Picayune,* October 11, 12, 13, 1943; Baton Rouge *Morning Advocate,* October 12, 30, 1943.
47. Baton Rouge *Morning Advocate,* October 12, 16, 1943; New Orleans *Times-Picayune,* October 13, 1943; Nesom, interview with the author; Cole, interview with the author.
48. New Orleans *Item,* October 13, 1943; Baldwin, "Perez Men Retreat in Courthouse Tiff"; New Orleans *Times-Picayune,* October 26, 1943; Velie, "'Democracy' in the Deep Delta," 44; Baton Rouge *Morning Advocate,* November 24, 1943; Nesom, interview with the author.
49. Chalin Perez, interview with the author.
50. At this hearing Slater testified that the armed guards that had been placed along parish highways were not to prevent Blaize from taking office but were merely wartime precautions. He said, "They were assigned to guard duty because this is wartime and war prisoners may break loose." New Orleans *Times-Picayune,* November 24, 1943.
51. New Orleans *Times-Picayune,* October 11, 20, 1943; *Plaquemines Gazette,* October 23, 1943.
52. *St. Bernard Voice,* November 13, 1943, January 1, 1944; New Orleans *Times-Picayune,* January 14, 1944, December 24, 1943; Baton Rouge *Morning Advocate,* October 28, 1943; brief for defendant and exceptor, *State of Louisiana ex rel Sam H. Jones* v. *Benjamin R. Slater,* No. 1,916, Twenty-fifth Judicial District Court, Plaquemines Parish, La.
53. New Orleans *Times-Picayune,* October 28, 1943, January 20, 1944; Baton Rouge *Morning Advocate,* November 28, 1943; *Plaquemines Gazette,* January 1, 1944; agreement signed by Chester Wooton and Dr. Ben R. Slater, October 15, 1943, New Orleans, La., in Perez Files.
54. New Orleans *Times-Picayune,* May 12, 1963; motion to dismiss appeal, *Benjamin Slater* v. *J. P. Cole et al.,* No. 37,573, Supreme Court of Louisiana, New Orleans, La.; *St. Bernard Voice,* October 7, 1944; unmarked New Orleans *States* editorial, in State Guard Scrapbook.

CHAPTER NINE

1. Sindler, *Huey Long's Louisiana,* 184–85; McCaughan, *Socks on a Rooster,* 96.
2. Glen Jeansonne, "Race, Religion, and the Louisiana Gubernatorial Elections of 1959-1960" (M.A. thesis, Florida State University, 1969), 126–27.
3. Sindler, *Huey Long's Louisiana,* 171–72, 183–84; editorial, Shreveport *Journal,* January 14, 1944; *Plaquemines Gazette,* December 25, 1943, January 29, 1944.
4. McCaughan, *Socks on a Rooster,* 99–100; editorial, Shreveport *Journal,* January 26, 1944; Secretary of State, *Official Returns, Democratic Primary of January 18, 1944* (Baton Rouge, 1944).
5. Baton Rouge *Morning Advocate,* January 31, 1944; *Plaquemines Gazette,* January 29, 1944.
6. McCaughan, *Socks on a Rooster,* 100; Sindler, *Huey Long's Louisiana,* 189; Cain, interview with the author.

7. Sindler, *Huey Long's Louisiana,* 189; Alexander Heard and Donald S. Strong, *Southern Primaries and Elections* (University, Ala., 1950), 72.
8. F. Edward Hebert, taped interview with the author, New Orleans, La., June 16, 1972; Cain, interview with the author.
9. Sindler, *Huey Long's Louisiana,* 192–93, 190; Baton Rouge *State-Times,* July 6, 1944.
10. Sindler, *Huey Long's Louisiana,* 197–98; "A Mayor and His City," *Newsweek,* February 17, 1958, p. 29.
11. McCaughan, *Socks on a Rooster,* 102–103; Chalin Perez, interview with the author. Chalin Perez noted that one of Jones's enemies had been posthumously indicted more than a hundred times.
12. The Old Regulars officially supported Jimmy Morrison in the first primary, causing some of the Ring leaders who favored Earl Long, such as Maestri, to resign. The Ring endorsed Long in the second primary, although Morrison himself endorsed Sam Jones. See Sindler, *Huey Long's Louisiana,* 201, 205.
13. McCaughan, *Socks on a Rooster,* 103–104; Baton Rouge *Morning Advocate,* January 3, 12, 1948. During Long's administration (1948–1952), taxes were increased by 50 percent. See Sindler, *Huey Long's Louisiana,* 200.
14. Kennon received 127,569 votes, or 19.8 percent.
15. Heard and Strong, *Southern Primaries and Elections,* 72–73; McCaughan, *Socks on a Rooster,* 117.
16. Sindler, *Huey Long's Louisiana,* 204–205; McCaughan, *Socks on a Rooster,* 117.
17. *Sam Jones* v. *Plaquemines Parish Democratic Executive Committee et al.,* No. 2,355, Twenty-fifth Judicial District Court, Plaquemines Parish, La.; Baldwin, "The Perez Habit of Winning Elections."
18. Statewide, Long received 432,528 votes to 223,971 (34.1 percent) for Jones. In Plaquemines, Long polled 3,087 votes to 291 for Jones; in St. Bernard the figures were 3,333 for Long and 265 for Jones.
19. Heard and Strong, *Southern Primaries and Elections,* 72–73; McCaughan, *Socks on a Rooster,* 118–21.
20. Velie, "'Democracy' in the Deep Delta," 42; Heard and Strong, *Southern Primaries and Elections,* 75.
21. Sindler, *Huey Long's Louisiana,* 229–30.
22. Ibid., 209–14; Irving Ferman, "Louisiana Side-Show," *New Republic,* January 21, 1952, p. 14.
23. Chicago *Daily Tribune,* August 9, 1950; Cain, interview with the author; Peltier, interview with the author; Chalin Perez, interview with the author.
24. Sindler, *Huey Long's Louisiana,* 231.
25. *Ibid.,* 231–35; McCaughan, *Socks on a Rooseter,* 140.
26. New Orleans *States,* September 14, 27, November 27, 1951; Fred Blanche, taped interview with the author, Baton Rouge, February 21, 1972.
27. New Orleans *Item,* October 16, 1951; New Orleans *Times-Picayune,* October 16, 1951.
28. New Orleans *Item,* October 1, 21, 1951.
29. New Orleans *Times-Picayune,* October 18, 1951. See also New Orleans *Item,* October 16, 18, 1951.
30. New Orleans *Item,* October 1, 21, 1951.
31. *Ibid.,* October 21, 1951.
32. *Ibid.*
33. *Ibid.;* New Orleans *States,* October 20, 1951. See also New Orleans *Times-Picayune,* October 20, 1951.
34. New Orleans *States,* November 15, 1951. See also New Orleans *Item,* November

2, 21, 1951; Sherrill, *Gothic Politics in the Deep South,* 26; New Orleans *Times-Picayune,* October 26, 1951.

35. New Orleans *Times-Picayune,* January 12, 1952, editorial, November 18, 1951; New Orleans *States,* January 11, 1952.
36. New Orleans *Item,* January 10, 1952.
37. Boggs polled 142,434 votes, or 18.7 percent.
38. *Louisiana Almanac and Fact Book, 1953–54* (Gretna, 1954), 472; DeBlieux, interview with the author; New Orleans *Item,* January 16, 1952.
39. New Orleans *States,* October 24, November 6, 1951; New Orleans *Times-Picayune,* October 25, 1951.
40. Baton Rouge *Morning Advocate,* February 13, 1952.
41. *Louisiana Almanac and Fact Book,* 473; Sindler, *Huey Long's Louisiana,* 239.
42. *St. Bernard Voice,* March 6, 13, May 1, 1953; New Orleans *States,* October 17, 1951.
43. New Orleans *States,* September 2, 1955.
44. Memorandum for file, Harry McCall, Jr., June 3, 1953, Chaffee, McCall, Tolar, and Phillips to Abbott Southall, breakdown of payments made to Bergeron for special deputies and regular deputies, July 1, 1953, all in Perez Files; *St. Bernard Voice,* October 7, September 30, 1955; New Orleans *Item,* September 29, 1955.
45. New Orleans *States,* September 9, 29, October 20, 1955; *St. Bernard Voice,* September 9, 16, 1955; New Orleans *Times-Picayune,* February 9, 1956.
46. New Orleans *States,* September 9, 10, 1955; February 9, 1956; New Orleans *Times-Picayune,* February 9, 1956.
47. New Orleans *Item,* November 16, 1955; Aaron M. Kohn to Perez, December 2, 1955, in Perez Files.
48. New Orleans *Item,* September 14, 1955; Shreveport *Times,* January 13, 1956; *St. Bernard Voice,* December 16, 1955.
49. New Orleans *States,* August 1, 7, 1956; *St. Bernard Voice,* August 10, 1956.
50. *St. Bernard Voice,* August 10, January 20, February 24, 1956.
51. McCaughan, *Socks on a Rooster,* 142; Shreveport *Times,* January 13, 1956.
52. McCaughan, *Socks on a Rooster,* 143–46; Neil R. McMillan, *The Citizens' Council: Organized Resistance to the Second Reconstruction* (Urbana, 1971), 318.
53. Howard, *Political Tendencies in Louisiana,* 288; New Iberia *Daily Iberian,* January 18, 1956; *Louisiana Almanac and Fact Book, 1961–62* (Gretna, 1962), 275.

Chapter Ten

1. Eggler, "Plaquemines Without the Great White Father," 12; Sanford, "In His Corner of the South Few Persons Dare Talk Back to Leander (the King) Perez."
2. Plaquemines produces far more oil than any other parish. Louisiana returns 25 percent of its mineral severance tax to the parish from which the mineral is extracted. The state collected more than $7,000,000 in severance taxes in Plaquemines in the fiscal year 1950–1951. See F. Edward Hebert to Robert Kennedy and Stewart Udall, August 21, 1961, and statement of Plaquemines Parish Police Jury on state revenue collected from Plaquemines Parish, 1952, both in Perez Files.
3. New Orleans *States,* August 14, 1950, April 9, 1957; Velie, "'Democracy' in the Deep Delta," 44; Perez to F. Edward Hebert, June 10, 1965, copy in Perez Files; Baton Rouge *Morning Advocate,* May 29, 1962.
4. Baton Rouge *Morning Advocate,* August 24, 1961; *St. Bernard Voice,* July 23, 1949; Frank Mayerhoff to Perez, April 6, 1950, in Perez Files; New Orleans *States,* June 13, 1950.

5. St. Bernard *Voice,* March 4, 1950; New Orleans *Item,* December 11, 1952.

6. According to Perez, the shoreline was the point where the land met the sea at low tide but the coastline was drawn from headland to headland beyond all coastal indentations.

7. Jack P. F. Gremillion, *Louisiana Tidelands: A Comprehensive Study* (Baton Rouge, 1957), 25–26; Baton Rouge *State-Times,* March 20, 1969; remark quoted by Hebert, interview with the author.

8. Jack Gremillion to the Louisiana Senate, May 28, 1962, in Perez Files; New Orleans *States,* April 9, 1957.

9. In 1973 Gremillion was sent to federal prison for perjury in connection with another case.

10. Baton Rouge *Morning Advocate,* May 29, 1962, April 11, 1964.

11. Texas and Florida, because of the historical conditions under which they had entered the Union, were awarded boundaries extending to three leagues from the undefined shoreline. See *United States* v. *Louisiana et al.,* 363 U.S. 1 (1960).

12. *Plaquemines Gazette,* December 22, 1961.

13. "The Priest and the Politician," CBS television documentary.

14. *Plaquemines Gazette,* February 21, 1964. See also Baton Rouge *Morning Advocate,* April 12, 1956; editorial, Shreveport *Times,* June 17, 1956; Reed Larson to Perez, March 4, 1960, Louis P. Niklaus to Perez, March 7, 1960, annotated copies of House Bill 402, 1968, and proposed amendments, all in Perez Files.

15. Federation for Constitutional Government newsletter, undated, John U. Barr to F. Edward Hebert, May 10, 1955, Washington *Daily News* clipping, February 16, 1956, minutes of meeting held at Jackson, Miss., January 21–22, 1955, federation letter to "Friends," May 9, 1956, including reprint of Williams speech, and John U. Barr to Claude Harrison, May 10, 1955, all in Perez Files.

16. Washington *Daily News* clipping, February 16, 1956, *ibid.*

17. Chalin Perez, interview with the author.

18. *Thunderbolt* (special undated New Orleans edition), September, 1960.

19. Sanford, "In His Corner of the South Few Persons Dare Talk Back to Leander (the King) Perez."

20. New York *Times,* January 25, 1950.

21. *States' Righter,* May 15, 1950. See also Perez testimony before Senate Foreign Relations Committee, *Congressional Digest,* XXIX (December, 1950), 318.

22. U.S. Senate, Judiciary Committee, *Hearings Before Senate Judiciary Subcommittee on S.1725 and S.1734,* 81st Cong., 1st Sess.

23. "Discussions Unlimited" letter on Connally Amendment, and invitation to discussion and coffee, undated, both in Perez Files; Perez testimony on genocide treaty, *Congressional Digest,* 316–18; New Orleans *States,* May 13, 1955.

24. New Orleans *Times-Picayune,* March 20, 1969.

25. Perez's correspondence documents contributions to all of the above. See Perez Files.

26. The totals were: FDR, 1,918, and Hoover, 38, in 1932; FDR, 2,209, and Alf Landon, 93, in 1936; FDR, 1,979, and Wendell Wilkie, 204, in 1940; and FDR, 1,755, and Dewey, 335, in 1944. See Secretary of State, *Official Returns, 1944* (Baton Rouge, 1945).

27. *St. Bernard Voice,* January 23, 1937.

28. Numan V. Bartley, *The Rise of Massive Resistance: Race and Politics in the South During the 1950's* (Baton Rouge, 1969), 29; Secretary of State, *Official Returns, 1944.*

29. *States' Righter,* May 15, 1950.

30. L. Vaughn Howard and David R. Deener, *Presidential Politics in Louisiana, 1952* (New Orleans, 1954), 54–58.

31. Minutes of States' Rights Democratic Campaign Committee, June 8, 1948, and George C. Wallace to Perez, May 18, 1950, both in Perez Files.
32. *Ibid.*
33. Certified copy of resolution adopted at Mississippi state Democratic convention, June 22, 1948, *ibid.;* Howard and Deener, *Presidential Politics in Louisiana,* 59.
34. "War Between the Democrats," *Newsweek,* July 26, 1948, p. 21.
35. "Southern Revolt," *Time,* October 11, 1948, pp. 24–27; "The Pot Boils," *Time,* October 4, 1948, p. 22; Sarah McCulloh Lemmon, "The Ideology of the 'Dixiecrat' Movement," *Social Forces,* XXX (December, 1951), 170.
36. George M. Wallace to Perez, May 18, 1950, in Perez Files; *St. Bernard Voice,* August 21, 1948.
37. *Plaquemines Gazette,* August 14, 1948; Dixiecrat handout including reprint of Thurmond acceptance speech, in Perez Files; *St. Bernard Voice,* August 21, 1948.
38. Howard and Deener, *Presidential Politics in Louisiana,* 61.
39. Lemmon, "The Ideology of the 'Dixiecrat' Movement," 170.
40. Howard and Deener, *Presidential Politics in Louisiana,* 61–62.
41. *Athan Coe et al.* v. *Wade O. Martin et al.,* No. 30,345, Nineteenth Judicial District Court, Division C, East Baton Rouge Parish, La.; New Orleans *Item,* August 30, 1949; "Conversation Carte Blanche," tape of WDSU (New Orleans) radio debate between Leander Perez and Victor Bussie, April 10, 1964.
42. Resolutions 2, 3, and 5 by Perez, Democratic State Central Committee, September 10, 1948, all in Perez Files; Howard and Deener, *Presidential Politics in Louisiana,* 61–62; Washington *Post,* September 11, 1948.
43. *Athan Coe et al.* v. *Wade O. Martin et al.,* No. 39,168, Supreme Court of Louisiana, New Orleans, La.; Howard and Deener, *Presidential Politics in Louisiana,* 63.
44. Washington *Evening Star,* September 11, 1948.
45. "Conversation Carte Blanche"; New Orleans *Item,* February 14, 1950; Howard, *Political Tendencies in Louisiana,* 306.
46. Howard and Deener, *Presidential Politics in Louisiana,* 62–63.
47. *Ibid.;* New Orleans *States,* October 2, 5, 1948; New Orleans *Times-Picayune,* October 2, 1948; Sindler, *Huey Long's Louisiana,* 221–22.
48. New York *Times,* October 14, 1948; Dixiecrat handout, in Perez Files; *Plaquemines Gazette,* October 14, 1950; Sindler, *Huey Long's Louisiana,* 220.
49. Mordaunt Thompson to Perez, September 12, 1948, in Perez Files. See also Des Moines *Tribune* clipping, October 22, 1948, Merrit H. Gibson to Palmer Bradley, October 5, 1948, and Perez to W. W. Wright, August 30, 1948, all in Perez Files; Howard and Deener, *Presidential Politics in Louisiana,* 64.
50. Secretary of State, *Official Returns, 1948* (Baton Rouge, 1949); Howard, *Political Tendencies in Louisiana,* 306; New York *Times,* January 20, 1951.
51. New Orleans *States,* August 9, 1950. See also New Orleans *States,* August 24, 1949; New Orleans *Item,* August 24, 1949; New York *Times,* August 25, 1949; Chicago *Daily Tribune,* August 9, 1950; Anderson, interview with the author.
52. Merritt H. Gibson to Perez, October 26, 1948, with copy of resolution and list of committee on organization members enclosed, in Perez Files.
53. Typescript of speech by Harry F. Klinefelter, December 8, 1948, Baltimore, Md., and George M. Wallace to Perez, May 18, 1950, both in Perez Files; New Orleans *States,* February 7, 1949; New Orleans *Times-Picayune,* January 29, 1949.
54. Emile Bertrand Ader, *The Dixiecrat Movement* (Washington, D.C., 1955), 16–17; George M. Wallace to Perez, May 18, 1950, and constitution and declaration of principles of the National States' Rights Committee, 1949, both in Perez Files.
55. New Orleans *Times-Picayune,* January 29, 1949; Frank Dixon to Wallace Wright, August 27, 1949, copy in Perez Files; Carter, "Dixiecrat Boss of the Bayous," 12.

56. Perez to Frank Mayerhoff, April 13, 1950, Perez to George M. Wallace, November 10, 1949, Frank Dixon to Wallace Wright, August 27, 1949, Dixon to Wright, April 25, 1949, budget of National States' Rights Committee Washington office, April 19, 1950; memo on Pope Haley phone call to Perez, May 22, 1951, Perez to Justice B. Detwiler, May 23, 1951, Perez to Thomas Sunderland, May 23, 1951, and Detwiler to Perez, April 4, 1951, all in Perez Files.

57. *States' Righter,* May 15, 1950; Bartley, *The Rise of Massive Resistance,* 36; Perez to H. R. Cullen, April 3, 12, 1951, Cullen to Perez, April 9, 1951, telegram, Pope Haley to Perez, March 21, 1951, Perez to Haley, March 22, 1951, September 12, 1952, Haley to Perez, August 15, September 10, 1952, all in Perez Files.

58. New York *Times,* January 20, 1951; Strom Thurmond to Perez, March 20, 1952, in Perez Files.

59. New Orleans *Item,* October 3, 1951. See also Bartley, *The Rise of Massive Resistance,* 52–53; E. M. Clinton, "Perez Proposal to Change Electoral Plan Defeated," New Orleans *Times-Picayune,* October 3, 1951.

60. Minutes of Democratic State Central Committee meeting, August 20, 1952, and minutes of First Congressional District Democratic Committee of Louisiana meeting, March 18, 1952, both in Perez Files.

61. Howard and Deener, *Presidential Politics in Louisiana,* 75. See also minutes of Democratic State Central Committee meeting, August 20, 1952, in Perez Files.

62. Howard and Deener, *Presidential Politics in Louisiana,* 74–78; minutes of Democratic State Central Committee meeting, August 20, 1952, in Perez Files; Shreveport *Times,* August 5, 1952; H. E. Linam to editor, Shreveport *Journal,* December 16, 1959.

63. New Orleans *Times-Picayune,* August 20, 1952.

64. New Orleans *States,* July 25, 1952.

65. New Orleans *Item,* July 25, 1952.

66. New Orleans *Times-Picayune,* August 6, 1952.

67. Howard and Deener, *Presidential Politics in Louisiana,* 83, 84; minutes of Democratic State Central Committee meeting, August 20, 1952, in Perez Files.

68. New Orleans *Times-Picayune,* July 28, August 24, 1952; Bartley, *The Rise of Massive Resistance,* 51.

69. New Orleans *Item,* September 8, 1952; Howard and Deener, *Presidential Politics in Louisiana,* 86–92; E. Herman Guillory to Charles Perlitz, November 29, 1954, in Perez Files.

70. Sherrill, *Gothic Politics in the Deep South,* 20. For election statistics see Secretary of State, *Official Returns, 1952* (Baton Rouge, 1953); Bartley, *The Rise of Massive Resistance,* 50; Howard and Deener, *Presidential Politics in Louisiana,* 91–93.

71. Howard, *Political Tendencies in Louisiana,* 329.

72. New York *Times,* June 2, 1954; *Hearings Before the Senate Judiciary Committee on S. 1564,* 554.

73. Richard M. Scammon (comp.), *America Votes: A Handbook of Contemporary American Election Statistics* (Pittsburgh, 1959), III, 154; *St. Bernard Voice,* November 9, 1956.

CHAPTER ELEVEN

1. New Orleans *Item,* August 8, 1950.

2. New Orleans *Times-Picayune,* June 18, 1956.

3. New Orleans *States,* February 20, 1958.

4. Cain, interview with the author.

5. New Orleans *Times-Picayune,* June 18, 1956.

6. Sherrill, *Gothic Politics in the Deep South,* 29.

7. Alex Vuillemot, "Perez Dynasty Fights for Life," New Orleans *States*, August 3, 1957.
8. *St. Bernard Voice*, July 12, 1957.
9. Vuillemot, "Perez Dynasty Fights for Life."
10. *St. Bernard Voice*, August 23, 1957.
11. *Ibid.*, September 6, 1957; *Schindler* v. *Melerine*.
12. New Orleans *Times-Picayune*, August 7, 1957.
13. Vuillemot, "Perez Dynasty Fights for Life."
14. *St. Bernard Voice*, August 26, 1956.
15. According to state law, the governor could remove parish registrars, but only the police jury could appoint them.
16. A large company that sold supplies to trappers in the Delacroix Island area.
17. New Orleans *Times-Picayune*, August 21, 1956.
18. *Ibid.*, January 11, 1958.
19. *Ibid.*, August 24, 28, 1956.
20. *Ibid.*, August 24, September 19, 20, 1956, February 18, March 5, 1958; *St. Bernard Voice*, October 25, 1957, February 21, 1958; *State of Louisiana ex rel Board of Commissioners of Lake Borgne Basin Levee District* v. *Lawrence Bergeron et al.*, No. 43,917, Supreme Court of Louisiana, New Orleans; *State of Louisiana ex rel Board of Commissioners for the Lake Borgne Basin Levee District* v. *William J. Dodd et al.*, No. 44,015, Supreme Court of Louisiana, New Orleans; *State of Louisiana ex rel Lake Borgne and Chalmette Levee Districts* v. *Dr. Nicholas P. Trist*, Nos. 43,932, 43,952, 43,953, Supreme Court of Louisiana, New Orleans.
21. New Orleans *States*, September 6, 1956.
22. Baton Rouge *State-Times*, July 7, 1956.
23. New Orleans *States*, July 5, 1956.
24. *Ibid.*, September 21, 1956.
25. *Ibid.*
26. *Ibid.*, September 5, 1956.
27. New Orleans *States-Item*, June 13, 1960.
28. New Orleans *Times-Picayune*, July 7, 1956, May 3, 1957; *Board of Commissioners of the Buras Levee District* v. *Police Jury of Plaquemines Parish et al.*, No. 351-967, Civil District Court, Orleans Parish, La.
29. New Orleans *Times-Picayune*, June 18, 1956; New Orleans *Item*, June 18, 1956; Baton Rouge *Morning Advocate*, July 7, 1956; Baton Rouge *State-Times*, July 3, 1956.
30. New Orleans *States*, August 31, 1958; motion to have district attorney recused, *State of Louisiana* v. *Celestine Melerine and James Licciardi*, No. 4,634, Twenty-fifth Judicial District Court, St. Bernard Parish, La.; *St. Bernard Voice*, October 25, September 6, 1957.
31. Transcript of Proceedings in Open Hearing Before the Honorable Richard Rees, April 3, 1958, in Perez Files; New Orleans *States*, April 4, 1958; *St. Bernard Voice*, February 21, 1958.
32. No suit should have been necessary, because the police jury and levee board records are public documents. In dismissing the suit, Nunez upheld exceptions of no right of action filed by Perez, maintaining that the four had sued as representatives of the Chalmette Civic Improvement Association, which was a nonentity under law. The indignant residents claimed that they had filed suit only in their capacity as private citizens. See *St. Bernard Voice*, November 11, 1955, January 6, February 10, 1956.
33. New Orleans *Times-Picayune*, April 12, 1958; Transcript of Proceedings in Open Hearing Before the Honorable Richard Rees, April 3, 1958, in Perez Files.

34. Transcript of Proceedings in Open Hearing Before the Honorable Richard Rees, April 3, 1958, in Perez Files.
35. New Orleans *Times-Picayune,* April 4, 8, 1958.
36. *St. Bernard Voice,* April 10, 1959, August 22, 1958; New Orleans *Times-Picayune,* November 13, 1959.
37. New Orleans *Times-Picayune,* April 1, 1959.
38. *Ibid.,* May 28, 1958, April 14, 1959; *Leander Perez* v. *James Licciardi,* No. 6,192, Twenty-fifth Judicial District Court, St. Bernard Parish, La.; *Leander Perez* v. *Celestine Melerine,* No. 6,193, Twenty-fifth Judicial District Court, St. Bernard Parish, La.; *St. Bernard Voice,* May 8, June 5, 26, 1959.
39. Baton Rouge *State-Times,* February 5, 1959; New Orleans *Times-Picayune,* February 20, 1959; *Mrs. Una M. Vullo* v. *Plaquemines Parish Police Jury et al.,* No. 44,535, Supreme Court of Louisiana, New Orleans; *Plaquemines Gazette,* February 13, November 20, 1959, August 11, 1961.
40. New Orleans *Times-Picayune,* February 20, 1959.
41. A. J. Liebling, *The Earl of Louisiana* (New York, 1960), 17–21.
42. *Ibid.,* 30; Jeansonne, "Race, Religion, and the Louisiana Gubernatorial Elections of 1959–1960," 20–22.
43. Jeansonne, "Race, Religion, and the Louisiana Gubernatorial Elections of 1959–1960," 22.
44. Liebling, *The Earl of Louisiana,* 30.
45. Baton Rouge *Morning Advocate,* May 27, 1959.
46. Jeansonne, "Race, Religion, and the Louisiana Gubernatorial Elections of 1959–60," 22–23, 29.
47. *Ibid.,* 25–27, 30–38.
48. Leslie Scobel, form letter to parish voters, November 30, 1959, in Perez Files; New Orleans *Times-Picayune,* September 30, 1959.
49. New Orleans *Times-Picayune,* November 19, 21, 1959; New Orleans *States-Item,* November 18, 1959; Leslie Scobel, form letter to parish voters, November 30, 1959, in Perez Files.
50. *Plaquemines Gazette,* December 11, 18, 1959, June 10, 1960.
51. *St. Bernard Voice,* September 18, December 11, 1959; Bryan T. Petitfuls campaign handout and notes taken by Perez representative at AFL-CIO political rally, November 14, 1959, both in Perez Files.
52. Rowley campaign handout, in Perez Files.
53. *St. Bernard Voice,* September 11, 1959.
54. *Charles A. Leon* v. *St. Bernard Democratic Committee and Edward L. Jeanfreau,* No. 7,249, Twenty-fifth Judicial District Court, St. Bernard Parish, La.; *St. Bernard Voice,* January 15, 1960.
55. *St. Bernard Voice,* January 22, 1960, February 10, 1961, May 27, 1960.
56. New Orleans *Times-Picayune,* March 23, 1960; "A Sordid Case: Melerine and Licciardi," typescript of WDSU-TV and WDSU radio editorial, March 23, 1960, New Orleans, La.; *St. Bernard Voice,* March 25, 1960.
57. Jeansonne, "Race, Religion, and the Louisiana Gubernatorial Elections of 1959–1960," 60.
58. *Ibid.,* 128–30; James H. Davis, taped interview with the author, Baton Rouge, La., July 8, 1969.
59. *Plaquemines Gazette,* December 4, 1959.
60. Jeansonne, "Race, Religion, and the Louisiana Gubernatorial Elections of 1959–60," 107.
61. *Ibid.,* 146–55; William J. Dodd, taped interview with the author, Baton Rouge, La., June 30, 1969; Davis, interview with the author.

62. Jeansonne, "Race, Religion, and the Louisiana Gubernatorial Elections of 1959–1960," 180–85.
63. *Ibid.,* 196–97, 216.
64. *Ibid.,* 207–209; Davis, interview with the author.
65. Jeansonne, "Race, Religion, and the Louisiana Gubernatorial Elections of 1959–1960," 215–16.
66. *St. Bernard Voice,* July 8, August 5, 12, 1960; *Plaquemines Gazette,* August 12, 1960, February 3, 1961; House Bill 287, regular session of 1960, in Perez Files.

CHAPTER TWELVE

1. Baldwin, "Perez—Tough, Able Political Boss"; nonresident bull moose permit issued to Perez, August 16, 1956, by Wyoming Game and Fish Commission, in Perez Files.
2. Anderson, interview with the author; Mrs. John Barton, taped interview with the author, Baton Rouge, La., February 9, 1972; "The Priest and the Politician," CBS television documentary.
3. Anderson, interview with the author; Barton, interview with the author.
4. Singelmann, interview with the author; Hebert, taped interview with the author.
5. In Perez Files.
6. New Orleans *States,* December 13, 1954.
7. See, for example, Perez correspondence with the segregationists cited and with Senators James O. Eastland and Allen Ellender, all in Perez Files.
8. Cook, *The Segregationists,* 204.
9. "The Segregationists' Segregationist," Washington *Post,* April 1, 1965; *Congressional Record,* 89th Cong., 2nd Sess., 12,015.
10. "Racist Leader," 21.
11. See the *Thunderbolt,* May, 1968.
12. Reese Cleghorn, "The Segs," *Esquire,* LXI (January, 1964), 133.
13. *Ibid.* On the matter of racial intelligence, a standard anthropology text admits the possibility of inherent differences existing in the structure and functioning of the nervous systems of various races and proposes three avenues toward empirical verification of them: "(1) neurological analysis of the anatomy and physiochemical functioning of the nervous systems of different races, which, unfortunately, calls for a refinement of laboratory technique far beyond that yet developed by neurologists; (2) controlled psychological experimentation, in which the cultural and environmental factors are held constant or eliminated, so that the inherent functional capacities of different races may be measured; and (3) anthropological analysis of the cultural accomplishments of different races." Any investigative regimen of the sort described here would of course be beyond the scope of the type of research undertaken by Perez and Singelmann or the editorial staff of the *Thunderbolt.* See E. Adamson Hoebel, *Anthropology: The Study of Man* (3rd ed.; New York, 1966), 226–27.
14. Cleghorn, "The Segs," 133.
15. Cook, *The Segregationists,* 204.
16. Baton Rouge *Morning Advocate,* April 29, 1959.
17. Cleghorn, "The Segs," 133. See also *ibid.*
18. Letter to Perez, September 20, 1963, in Perez Files.
19. *Plaquemines Gazette,* October 4, 1963.
20. Perez statewide television address, "The Unconstitutionality of the 'Federal Voting Rights Bill of 1965,'" April 6, 1965, typescript in Perez Files. See also Cleghorn, "The Segs," 133; Perez address, "The Challenge to the South and How

It Must Be Met," Biloxi, Miss., July 21, 1960, typescript in Perez Files; Cook, *The Segregationists,* 195.

21. U.S. Senate, Judiciary Committee, Hearings Before the Senate Subcommittee on Constitutional Rights of the Senate Judiciary Committee, 86th Cong., 1st Sess., Pt. 2, p. 808.
22. *Ibid.,* 946; Moody, "Perez Is Seen as Engaging Man"; Cleghorn, "The Segs," 133; New Orleans *States-Item,* June 29, 1962.
23. *Hearings Before the Senate Subcommittee on Constitutional Rights,* 793–94.
24. New Orleans *States-Item,* September 1, 2, 1960; New Orleans *Times-Picayune,* September 1, 1960.
25. Cleghorn, "The Segs," 133.
26. Letter to Perez, March 16, 1961, in Perez Files.
27. Cleghorn, "The Segs," 133.
28. New York *Herald-Tribune,* March 30, 1962.
29. So named for the party's SS-type lightning bolt insignia.
30. Letter to Perez, December 27, 1960, and typescript of Perez speech to Little Rock Citizens' Council, January 29, 1959, both in Perez Files; *Thunderbolt* (special undated New Orleans edition), September, 1960; Cook, *The Segregationists,* 203.
31. Smith, "Oil, Brimstone, and 'Judge' Perez," 146. See also *Plaquemines Gazette,* February 27, 1959.
32. *Brown* v. *Board of Education,* 347 U.S. 483 (1954).
33. "The Challenge to the South and How It Must Be Met," in Perez Files. See also New Orleans *Times-Picayune,* May 12, 1959.
34. Perez speech to Little Rock Citizens' Council, January 29, 1959, in Perez Files.
35. *Ibid.*
36. *Hearings Before the Senate Subcommittee on Constitutional Rights,* 790, 953.
37. *Plaquemines Gazette,* February 13, 1959.
38. "The Challenge to the South and How It Must Be Met," in Perez Files.
39. Buckley and Perez, "The Wallace Movement." See also Leander H. Perez, "Racial Integration by Court Decree," (speech before Young Men's Business Club, New Orleans, La., December 29, 1954, p. 5), copy in Perez Files; Cook, *The Segregationists,* 198–99.
40. Perez, "Racial Integration by Court Decree," 5.
41. *Hearings Before the Senate Subcommittee on Constitutional Rights,* 805. According to Perez, Myrdal endorsed racial integration because "he held there is no such thing as race." The Judge, in fact, had a special dislike for social scientists who deemphasized racial differences. One such was the eminent ethnologist Franz Boas, whom he considered a chief apologist for the Negro race and blamed for the popular theory that environment was more crucial than heredity in determining the relative intelligence and cultural attainment of different peoples. Perez was much more comfortable with the theories of such southern scholars as Virginia-born Henry E. Garrett, Boas' colleague at Columbia and onetime head of the psychology department there. Garrett made a study of intelligence evaluation tests administered in schools and in the military and concluded "that Negro-white differences . . . are so regular and persistent as strongly to suggest a genetic basis." See Henry E. Garrett, "The S.P.S.S.I. and Race Differences," *American Psychologist,* XVII(May, 1962). An unpaginated reprint is in the Perez Files.

Perez also admired the work of Dr. Wesley C. George, a former chairman of the anatomy department at the University of North Carolina. George did a good deal of research on inherited emotional and mental qualities. He remarked the differences in breeds of animals of the same species and concluded that "the leopard cannot change his spots, nor can the Ethiopian change his skin or his genetic constitution." Adopting a quasi-biblical approach in his writings on the subject, he believed, among other things, that criminality and capacity for civilization are heritable and probably race linked. He concluded that the Negro could not be considered "genetically acceptable" for breeding with whites and warned of the consequences of intermarriage: "There is enough stupidity, indolence, slovenliness and criminality already in the white race without the absorption of 13,000,000 Negroes in whom these qualities appear to be present in still higher degree." See W. C. George, *The Race Problem from the Standpoint of One Who Is Concerned About the Evils of Miscegenation* (Birmingham: American States' Rights Assn., Inc., 1955). A copy is in the Perez Files.

Another scientist whose work Perez occasionally drew upon was former London University professor Ruggles Gates, whose book *Human Ancestry* was published by the Harvard University Press in 1948. Gates was convinced that the Negro belonged to a different species from the white man (*Homo africanus,* as opposed to *Homo caucasius*) and "that the negro is closer to the anthropoid ape from which he sprung." Perez noted smugly, "That is a genetic question for the Harvard Press and the N.A.A.C.P. to debate." See Perez, "Racial Integration by Court Decree," 6.

Perez himself was no theorist; he simply relied on the findings of others to buttress his fixed ideas. The extent of his own thought on the subject is expressed in his question, "If He didn't intend him to be inferior, why did God make the black man?" See Smith, "Oil, Brimstone, and 'Judge' Perez," 146.

42. L. H. Perez, *The Unconstitutionality of the Fourteenth Amendment* (Belle Chasse, La., n.d.); New Orleans *Times-Picayune,* January 6, 1961; letters to Perez requesting copies of treatise, in Perez Files. Perez had sound historical grounds for maintaining that the amendment had been pushed through by extralegal methods during the turbulent era of Reconstruction. However, every time he brought up the issue in court, the judges held that it was the duty of Congress, not the courts, to rule on the validity of the ratification of constitutional amendments.

43. McMillan, *The Citizens' Council,* 159.

44. Earleen Mary McCarrick, "Louisiana's Official Resistance to Desegregation" (Ph.D. dissertation, Vanderbilt University, 1964), 26; House Bill 1139, in Perez Files.

45. Collins, who had been a fiscal official in the Harding and Coolidge administrations, had an impressive academic background. Although born in Alabama, he had spent most of his adult years as an attorney and government official in Washington, D.C. He had studied archeology at Chicago and economics at Harvard and had written a number of scholarly works on constitutional and banking law, as well as having drafted the Budget and Accounting Act of 1921. Since his retirement he had authored several pamphlets on the race question, which Perez had thoroughly digested. The Judge routinely referred to him as a "noted historian" and frequently quoted him in support of his views. During a televised debate with William Buckley, Perez quoted a passage from one of Collins' little books to support his contention that he (Perez) was not a racist. When Buckley suggested that the Judge certainly fit Webster's definition of a racist, Leander denied it and declared, "I quote from a noted historian, and I stand on that." Buckley replied, "Noted historians have been racists, haven't they?" See Buckley and Perez, "The Wallace Movement," and "Charles Wallace Collins," *National Cyclopedia of American Biography* (New York, 1969), LI, 297–98.

46. Perez to Charles Wallace Collins, August 17, 23, 1954, both in Perez Files.

47. Collins to Perez, August 30, 1954, *ibid.*

48. McCarrick, "Louisiana's Official Resistance to Desegregation," 26, 32–34; McMillan, *The Citizens' Council*, 61–63; Singelmann, interview with the author.

49. Joint Legislative Committee on Segregation, *Explanation of Segregation Bills Passed by Louisiana Legislature, General Session, 1954;* James W. Vander Zanden, "The Southern White Resistance Movement to Integration" (Ph.D. dissertation, University of North Carolina, 1957), 179, 182; New York *Times,* November 7, 1954.

50. Joint Legislative Committee on Segregation, *Special Report, March 8, 1955;* Vander Zanden, "The Southern White Resistance Movement to Integration," 180.

51. *Brown* v. *Board of Education,* 349 U.S. 294 (1955).

52. New Orleans *States,* August 8, 1956. See also Joint Legislative Committee on Segregation, *Explanation of Segregation Bills Passed by the Regular Session of the Louisiana Legislature, 1956;* Vander Zanden, "The Southern White Resistance Movement to Integration," 184–85.

53. Vander Zanden, "The Southern White Resistance Movement to Integration," 184; Baton Rouge *Morning Advocate,* April 12, 1956.

54. Joint Legislative Committee on Segregation, *Explanation of Segregation Measures Passed by the Regular Session of the Louisiana Legislature, 1958.*

55. Martin, *Dynasty: The Longs of Louisiana,* 201.

56. McMillan, *The Citizens' Council,* 59; Sam B. Short to Perez, January 27, 1960, Perez to Short, December 21, 1964, Perez to J. Y. Sanders, Jr., February 11, 1960, and Sanders to Perez, February 12, 17, 1960, all in Perez Files.

57. McMillan, *The Citizens' Council,* 62–68; minutes of board of directors meeting, Association of Citizens' Councils of Louisiana, Inc., April 5, 1959, Association of Citizens' Councils of Louisiana to Perez, August 5, 1957, William M. Rainach to Perez, October 15, 1956, Paul R. Davis to Perez, January 6, 1958, Educational Fund of the Citizens' Councils of Louisiana, Inc., circular letter, December 20, 1957, Perez to Davis, December 31, 1957, January 2, 1958, and John S. Garrett to Perez, February 23, 1960, all in Perez Files.

58. McMillan, *The Citizens' Council,* 64–67; Singelmann, interview with the author; *Plaquemines Gazette,* May 15, 1959.

59. McMillan, *The Citizens' Council,* 34; New Orleans *Times-Picayune,* March 1, 1961; letter to Perez, September 7, 1960, in Perez Files.

60. Letter to Perez, November 16, 1960, in Perez Files. Perez also received numerous letters applauding his position, including one from a man who enclosed a copy of a letter he had mailed to the New Orleans *States-Item* under an assumed name. The writer claimed that Judaism had been invented by Pope Leo X in 1530 and concluded, "Every Jew is pro-communist and anti-American." (letter to Perez, October 2, 1960).

61. New Orleans *Times-Picayune,* May 4, 1962; copy of Citizens' Council petition to Governor Davis and the legislature to abolish welfare payments to illegitimate children, and copy of extract from Louisiana Board of Health, Division of Public Health Statistics, Tabulation and Analysis Section, January 18, 1961, showing that illegitimate birth and syphilis rates in New Orleans and in the whole state were much higher among nonwhites than among whites, both in Perez Files.

62. New Orleans *States,* February 5, 27, 1960; *Plaquemines Gazette,* May 20, 1960.

63. "God Bless You, Now," *Newsweek,* May 7, 1962, p. 33. See also "What It Shows," *Nation,* May 5, 1962, p. 391; McMillan, *The Citizens' Council,* 230–31; New York *Times,* April 29, 1962; Singelmann, interview with the author.

64. New York *Times,* April 20, 22, 24, 28, May 12, 1962.

65. Cal Brumley, "A Visit to Hyannis," *Wall Street Journal,* June 15, 1962; New York *Times,* July 8, 9, 11, December 4, 1962; *Plaquemines Gazette,* December 7, 1962; McMillan, *The Citizens' Council,* 231.

66. Singelmann, interview with the author; New York *Times,* April 24, 25, 27, May 10, 25, December 8, 1962; Brumley, "A Visit to Hyannis."

67. Cook, *The Segregationists,* 61; McMillan, *The Citizens' Council,* 118–19, 122, 152–53, 351, 362; Bartley, *The Rise of Massive Resistance,* 122–25.

68. C. E. Vetter to Citizens' Council of Greater New Orleans, January 1, 1964, in Perez Files.

69. New Orleans *Times-Picayune,* March 27, 1959; James O. Eastland to Perez, May 23, 1956, in Perez Files; "Civil Rights Bill," *Time,* May 6, 1957, p. 26; McMillan, *The Citizens' Council,* 220. In 1956, about the time that he was testifying on the administration's civil rights bill before the Eastland committee, Perez was also offered the job of chief counsel for a congressional subcommittee that was planning to investigate the Washington, D.C., school system. His name was later withdrawn from consideration, according to him, at his own request. Reports about Washington, however, claimed that Sam Rayburn of Texas, the speaker of the House, and Governor Earl Long had intervened to quash the appointment. See New Orleans *Times-Picayune,* July 5, 6, 1956.

70. *Hearings Before the Senate Subcommittee on Constitutional Rights,* 919; Cook, *The Segregationists,* 297–301; Baton Rouge *State-Times,* May 15, 1959; New Orleans *Times-Picayune,* April 1, 1960; New Orleans *States-Item,* April 1, 1960.

71. James O. Eastland to Perez, February 14, 1962, in Perez Files; *Plaquemines Gazette,* March 27, September 4, 1964.

72. *Hearings Before the Senate Judiciary Committee on S. 1564,* 324.

73. *Ibid.,* 544. Perez claimed that the majority of Plaquemines whites, in contrast to the blacks, were conscientious citizens, though there were some exceptions. "Some of them are romantic, I would say" (547).

74. Perez told William Buckley that the 1965 Voting Rights Act had been "drawn practically in full by the legal staff of the Communist Party U.S.A. prior to December, 1956," and that this had been exposed by a former United States ambassador to Switzerland in the *Star,* a small, conservative newspaper in Texas. Tongue firmly in cheek, Buckley wondered aloud how such a scoop could have been missed by the major dailies. See Buckley and Perez, "The Wallace Movement."

75. *Hearings Before the Senate Judiciary Committee on S. 1564,* 540–47, 325–54; New York *Times,* March 31, 1965; New Orleans *States-Item,* March 30, 1965; Baton Rouge *Morning Advocate,* March 31, 1965; Baton Rouge *State-Times,* March 31, 1965.

76. *United States* v. *Fox.*

77. Ignis fatuus, bits of marsh gas that form balls and bounce through the swamp; also known as will-o'-the-wisps.

78. *Victor Ragas et al.* v. *Frank Giordano,* No. 4,182, U.S. District Court, New Orleans, La.

79. U.S. Civil Rights Commission, *Hearings Before the United States Commission on Civil Rights Held in New Orleans, 1960–61* (Washington, D.C., 1961).

80. *Hearings Before the Senate Judiciary Committee on S. 1564;* 1965; *United States* v. *Fox.*

81. Baton Rouge *Morning Advocate,* September 28, 1960; Public Affairs Research Council of Louisiana, *A Statistical Profile of Plaquemines Parish* (Baton Rouge, 1964), 1.

82. New Orleans *Times-Picayune,* September 28, 1960.

83. Baton Rouge *Morning Advocate,* September 28, 1960.

84. *Ragas* v. *Giordano.*

85. *United States* v. *Fox.*

86. U.S. Civil Rights Commission, *Hearings Held in New Orleans, 1960–61.*
87. When the rolls were frozen in 1954, there were fewer than fifty blacks registered to vote in Plaquemines Parish.
88. *United States* v. *Fox;* New York *Times,* October 17, 1961.
89. Here are two of the more difficult questions: "Prescription shall not run against the state in any civil matter" and "Perpetual franchises or privileges shall not be granted to any person or corporation by the state or by any political subdivision there of." See the appendices to brief for appellant, *United States* v. *Fox.* Also included are graphs showing the distribution of constitutional test cards to white and Negro applicants before September 27, 1960, tables comparing interpretations of test questions given by white applicants, and a comparison of the application cards of rejected Negroes and accepted whites.
90. *United States* v. *Fox; United States* v. *State of Louisiana,* No. 2,548, U.S. District Court, Baton Rouge, La.
91. New Orleans *Times-Picayune,* September 27, 1960.
92. U.S. Civil Rights Commission, *Hearings Held in New Orleans, 1960–61.*
93. *Hearings Before the Senate Judiciary Committee on S. 1564;* New Orleans *States-Item,* November 9, 1961.
94. *United States* v. *Fox.*
95. *Ibid.;* Singelmann, interview with the author.
96. *United States* v. *Fox.*
97. *Ibid.*
98. Undated clipping, Baton Rouge *Morning Advocate,* and Perez memorandum on new registration, both in Perez Files. The proposal was introduced as House Bill No. 958, in the 1964 regular session.
99. New Orleans *Times-Picayune,* March 20, 1969; *Plaquemines Gazette,* September 3, 1965; Baton Rouge *Morning Advocate,* August 28, 1965.

CHAPTER THIRTEEN

1. Louisa Dulcher, "Time of Worry in 'The City Care Forgot,'" *Reporter,* March 8, 1956, p. 17.
2. J. W. Peltason, *Fifty-eight Lonely Men: Southern Federal Judges and School Desegregation* (Urbana, 1961), 126–27; Louisiana State Advisory Committee on Civil Rights, *The New Orleans School Crisis* (Washington, D.C., 1961), 182.
3. *Ibid.*
4. Peltason, *Fifty-eight Lonely Men,* 221–22.
5. McMillan, *The Citizens' Council,* 285–86.
6. *Ibid.;* Tom P. Brady to Ross Barnett, undated telegram, 1960, and Barnett to Brady, undated telegram, 1960, both in Perez Files.
7. J. Y. Sanders, Jr., to Perez, February 12, 17, 1960, and Perez file of legislation from other states, all in Perez Files.
8. McCarrick, "Louisiana's Official Resistance to Desegregation," 126–29; Louisiana State Advisory Committee, *The New Orleans School Crisis,* 187; *Bush* v. *Orleans Parish School Board et al.,* Civil Action No. 3,630, U.S. District Court, New Orleans, La.; *Harry K. Williams* v. *Jimmie Davis et al.,* Civil Action No. 10,329, U.S. District Court, New Orleans, La. (temporary injunction).
9. Louisiana State Advisory Committee, *The New Orleans School Crisis,* 187.
10. New Orleans *States,* October 10, 1960; New Orleans *Times-Picayune,* October 26, 1960; "Integration in the South," *Life,* November 28, 1960, p. 49.
11. Louisiana State Advisory Committee, *The New Orleans School Crisis,* 188–90.
12. Morton Inger, *Politics and Reality in an American City: The New Orleans School*

Crisis of 1960 (New York, 1969), 50–51; Edward L. Pinney and Robert S. Fried-man, *Political Leadership and the School Desegregation Crisis in Louisiana* (New York, 1963), 18; editorial, Chicago *Daily Tribune,* November 22, 1960.

13. Louisiana State Advisory Committee, *The New Orleans School Crisis,* 182, 190–92; New Orleans *States-Item,* November 4, 1960; Acts 1–29, 1st Special Sess. Louisiana legislature, 1960.

14. In ruling the interposition act unconstitutional, a three-judge federal panel called it "a preposterous perversion of Article V of the constitution." The opinion further stated, "If taken seriously, it is illegal defiance of constitutional authority. Otherwise it amounts to no more than a protest, an escape valve through which the legislators blow off steam to relieve their tensions."

15. Act 2, 1st Special Sess., Louisiana legislature, 1960; Leander H. Perez, "Interposition: What Is It?", address to the Seventy-ninth Annual Meeting of the American Bar Association, Dallas, Texas, August 27, 1956, in Perez Files.

16. Louisiana State Advisory Committee, *The New Orleans School Crisis,* 190; McCarrick, "Louisiana's Official Resistance to Desegregation," 153–57.

17. New Orleans *Times-Picayune,* November 15, 1960; McCarrick, "Louisiana's Official Resistance to Desegregation," 161–62; Pinney and Friedman, *Political Leadership and the School Desegregation Crisis in Louisiana,* 13–14; Inger, *Politics and Reality in an American City,* 50–51.

18. New Orleans *Times-Picayune,* November 16, 1960.

19. Lillian Smith, "The Ordeal of Southern Women," *Redbook,* CXVII (May, 1961), 82–83.

20. Inger, *Politics and Reality in an American City,* 50–51; McMillan, *The Citizens' Council,* 289; New Orleans *Times-Picayune,* November 16, 1960. Following the November 15 rally, Perez received numerous letters praising him for his efforts to maintain segregation. A Texas man commended him for fingering the Jew as the cause of integration and suggested that Leander organize the white Christians to march through New Orleans denouncing Jewish merchants as the cause of integration and threatening to boycott them. See Tony D'Amico to Perez, November 16, 1960, in Perez Files.

21. Louisiana State Advisory Committee on Civil Rights, *Report to the United States Commission on Civil Rights* (New Orleans, 1961), 191.

22. New Orleans *Times-Picayune,* November 17, 1960; Pinney and Friedman, *Political Leadership and the School Desegregation Crisis in Louisiana,* 51–52; McCarrick, "Louisiana's Official Resistance to Desegregation," 165–66.

23. New York *Times,* November 27, 1960. Morrison was often criticized by the out-of-state press for not taking a stronger stand for court-ordered integration. In his own area, however, the most frequent charge was that he was not staunch enough in defending segregation and did not attend a single Citizens' Council meeting. An outright endorsement of integration would have been political suicide for Morrison in New Orleans at that time.

24. Pinney and Friedman, *Political Leadership and the School Desegration Crisis in Louisiana,* 15–16; Inger, *Politics and Reality in an American City,* 52–54; New York *Times,* November 27, 1960.

25. Peltason, *Fifty-eight Lonely Men,* 233–34.

26. Louisiana State Advisory Committee, *The New Orleans School Crisis,* 190–91; Smith, "The Ordeal of Southern Women," 81–83.

27. Inger, *Politics and Reality in an American City,* 51–52; WDSU-TV and radio editorial, December 8, 1960, New Orleans, La.; Louisiana State Advisory Committee, *The New Orleans School Crisis,* 193.

28. Louisiana State Advisory Committee, *The New Orleans School Crisis,* 192; New

York *Times,* September 6, 1961; Sidney W. Provensal, Jr., to Perez, November 28, 1961, in Perez Files; Singelmann, interview with the author.

29. Louisiana State Advisory Committee, *The New Orleans School Crisis,* 186–87; New Orleans *Times-Picayune,* September 27, October 6, 1960. In their desperation, proponents of private schools for whites were ready to resort to almost any expedient. One militant segregationist wrote Perez to suggest that he look into the possibility of renting or buying old buses, which could be hauled to a central location, set up on blocks, and used as classrooms. The students could sit in the passengers' seats, and the teacher could occupy the driver's seat. Books could be stored under the seats, and the windshield could be converted into a blackboard. Parking space and toilet facilities could be made available by neighboring residents. See John L. Dorsa to Perez, December 13, 1960, in Perez Files.

30. Peltason, *Fifty-eight Lonely Men,* 243.

31. New Orleans *Times-Picayune,* February 11, 1961.

32. Peltason, *Fifty-eight Lonely Men,* 243; WDSU-TV and radio editorial, January 3, 17, 1961, New Orleans, La.; Louisiana State Advisory Committee, *The New Orleans School Crisis,* 196.

33. New Orleans *Times-Picayune,* August 25, 1960; "Where's Jimmie?" *Newsweek,* August 29, 1960, pp. 30–31.

34. *St. Bernard Voice,* September 9, 1960; New Orleans *Times-Picayune,* December 19, 1960; Gus and Carries[?] to Perez, December 19, 1960, and Charles L. Gambel to Perez, December 18, 1960, both in Perez Files. One woman suggested to Perez that Governor Davis had given up the segregation fight too easily and might be impeached for not standing fast. She indicated that she did not want to impeach Davis right away but did want to impeach Chief Justice Earl Warren. See Mrs. E. Perez to Perez, March 16, 1961, in Perez Files.

35. McMillan, *The Citizens' Council,* 293; McCarrick, "Louisiana's Official Resistance to Desegregation," 193–95; Hedrick Smith, "Integration Gain at New Orleans," New York *Times,* September 9, 1962.

36. New York *Times,* August 20, 1961.

37. Edward Hoag, "New Orleans Looking Forward," *Ave Maria,* June 2, 1962, p. 14; New York *Times,* November 9, 1964; Cook, *The Segregationists,* 235–36; New Orleans *Times-Picayune,* August 23, 1960; *Plaquemines Gazette,* August 26, 1960.

38. Hoag, "New Orleans Looking Forward," 9–10.

39. *Ibid.;* Mrs. B. J. Gaillot, Jr., *God Gave the Law of Segregation to Moses on Mount Sinai* (New Orleans, 1960); Mrs. B. J. Gaillot to Perez, June 19, 1962, in Perez Files.

40. Joseph Francis Rummel to Mrs. B. J. Gaillot, March 31, 1962, in Perez Files.

41. New Orleans *Times-Picayune,* April 17, 1962.

42. New Orleans *States-Item,* April 6, 7, 1962; New York *Times,* April 3, 1962.

43. New York *Times,* April 17, 1962; New York *Daily News,* April 17, 1962.

44. "Satan and Segregation," *Newsweek,* April 30, 1962, pp. 66–67; New York *Times,* April 18, 1962.

45. *Plaquemines Gazette,* May 4, 1962.

46. Baton Rouge *Morning Advocate,* April 26, 1962.

47. New Orleans *Times-Picayune,* April 24, 1962; Moody, "Perez Is Seen as Engaging Man."

48. Bill Crider, "Three Segregationists Relate Feelings About Their Excommunication," Baton Rouge *State-Times,* September 13, 1963; New York *Times,* April 27, 29, 1962; Mrs. B. J. Gaillot to Perez, undated [1968], in Perez Files.

49. New Orleans *States-Item,* August 28, 29, 1962; New York *Times,* August 20, 1962; "The Priest and the Politician," CBS television documentary.
50. "The Priest and the Politician," CBS television documentary.
51. *Ibid.*
52. *Ibid.;* New Orleans *States-Item,* August 29, 1962.
53. "The Priest and the Politician," CBS television documentary.
54. New Orleans *States-Item,* August 30, 1962; New Orleans *Times-Picayune,* August 31, 1962.
55. Sanford, "In His Corner of the South Few Persons Dare Talk Back to Leander (the King) Perez"; "The Priest and the Politician," CBS television documentary.
56. New Orleans *States-Item,* August 31, September 1, 1962; "The Priest and the Politician," CBS television documentary.
57. The New Orleans *States-Item,* September 7, 1962; "The Priest and the Politician," CBS television documentary; New York *Times,* November 18, 1962.
58. "The Priest and the Politician," CBS television documentary.
59. New York *Times,* August 28, 1963; Baton Rouge *State-Times,* July 22, 1966.
60. See, for example, John C. Hoffman to Perez, September 20, 1963, Mrs. C. M. Arwood to Perez, September 23, 1963, and James W. Morgan to Perez, September 20, 1963, all in Perez Files.
61. New York *Times,* September 5, October 7, 1962; New Orleans *Times-Picayune,* September 9, 1962; list of integrated Catholic schools in Orleans Parish, October 21, 1964, in Perez Files.

CHAPTER FOURTEEN

1. New Orleans *States,* August 28, 1962.
2. The commission council had replaced the police jury as the parish governing body under a new charter written by Perez and adopted in 1961.
3. *Plaquemines Gazette,* March 27, 1964.
4. See, for example, the case of Gary Duncan, in Baton Rouge *State-Times,* November 20, 1968; Baton Rouge *Morning Advocate,* June 15, 1971.
5. *Plaquemines Gazette,* February 19, 1965. See also *Plaquemines Gazette,* December 22, 1961, November 1, 1963, March 27, 1964, February 19, 1965; Edward J. Cocke, "Judge Warns Officials in Plaquemines," Baton Rouge *State-Times,* August 31, 1966.
6. Moody, "Perez Is Seen as Engaging Man."
7. New Orleans *States-Item,* April 24, 1963. See also New Orleans *Times-Picayune,* April 24, 1963.
8. *Plaquemines Gazette,* July 10, 28, 1963.
9. Cleghorn, "The Perils of Plaquemines," 10; New York *Times,* July 27, 1963; New Orleans *Times-Picayune,* August 30, 1963.
10. *Plaquemines Gazette,* August 23, September 6, 1963; New Orleans *Times-Picayune,* August 30, 1963.
11. *Plaquemines Gazette,* August 16, 1963; New York *Times,* August 10, 1963.
12. New Orleans *Times-Picayune,* August 30, 1963; editorial, *Plaquemines Gazette,* September 27, 1963.
13. New Orleans *States-Item,* September 6, 1963; Houston *Press,* August 10, 1963.
14. New Orleans *States-Item,* August 17, 1963; *Plaquemines Gazette,* August 23, 1963.
15. Cleghorn, "The Perils of Plaquemines," 10; New Orleans *Times-Picayune,* August 10, 1963; Baton Rouge *Morning Advocate,* August 15, 1963.
16. New Orleans *States-Item,* September 6, 1965.
17. Cleghorn, "The Perils of Plaquemines," 10.

18. Letter to Perez, August 10, 1963, in Perez Files.
19. Letters to Perez, September 24, October 7, 1963, both *ibid.*
20. *Plaquemines Gazette,* November 8, 1963.
21. New Orleans *States-Item,* October 11, 1963; Sanford, "In His Corner of the South Few Persons Dare Talk Back to Leander (the King) Perez."
22. Bill Crider, "Perez's Fort St. Philip Prison Is Uncomfortable," Baton Rouge *Morning Advocate,* October 24, 1963.
23. New Orleans *States-Item,* April 18, 1964.
24. *Ibid.*
25. *Ibid.,* October 11, 1963; I. J. Vidacovich, "Leander Perez Leads Tour Around His Prison Fortress," Baton Rouge *Morning Advocate,* April 18, 1964.
26. Vidacovich, "Leander Perez Leads Tour Around His Prison Fortress"; New Orleans *States-Item,* April 18, 1964.
27. "Prison Perez Style: Ready for Race Demonstrators," *U.S. News & World Report,* November 4, 1963, p. 16.
28. *Plaquemines Gazette,* April 3, 1964.
29. Baton Rouge *State-Times,* March 31, 1964.
30. New Orleans *Times-Picayune,* July 11, 1964; New Orleans *States-Item,* July 10, 1964.
31. *Ibid.*
32. Letters to Perez, October 30, 29, 25, 1963, all in Perez Files.
33. *Plaquemines Gazette,* May 1, 1964.
34. Vidacovich, "Leander Perez Leads Tour Around His Prison Fortress."
35. *Plaquemines Gazette,* February 3, August 9, 1963; Baton Rouge *Morning Advocate,* January 16, 1965.
36. Baton Rouge *Morning Advocate,* January 21, 1965; Perez to John J. McKeithen, February 23, 1965, in Perez Files.
37. Baton Rouge *State-Times,* May 20, 1966; New York *Times,* July 3, 1966.
38. New York *Times,* July 22, 1966. See also New Orleans *States-Item,* July 21, 1966.
39. *United States* v. *Plaquemines Parish School Board,* No. 66-71, Section A, U.S. District Court, New Orleans, La. This important case involved numerous hearings stretching over many months and resulted in a myriad of bound volumes of testimony.
40. *Ibid.*
41. During a hearing on the matter, the school board attorney claimed that the reason Guidroz had asked Anderson during their conversation if there was something wrong with Phoenix School was because it was his job to correct deficiencies in the parish schools. *United States* v. *Plaquemines.*
42. Baton Rouge *Morning Advocate,* August 4, 1966. See also *United States* v. *Plaquemines.*
43. *United States* v. *Plaquemines.*
44. *Ibid.*
45. *Ibid.*
46. *Plaquemines Gazette,* July 29, 1966.
47. *United States* v. *Plaquemines.*
48. *Ibid.;* Sidney W. Provensal, Jr., taped interview with the author, New Orleans, La., July 25, 1972; Luke Petrovitch, taped interview with the author, New Orleans, La., July 17, 1972.
49. *United States* v. *Plaquemines;* Baton Rouge *Morning Advocate,* August 13, 1966.
50. *United States* v. *Plaquemines.*
51. Presumably, boats or helicopters would have been sent to transport students who indicated that they wanted to attend classes on the mainland.
52. *United States* v. *Plaquemines;* Baton Rouge *State-Times,* August 12, 1966.

53. Perez to James O. Eastland, August 19, 1966, in Perez Files; Bill Crider, "Plaquemines Plan Stymied," Baton Rouge *State-Times,* August 6, 1966.
54. *United States* v. *Plaquemines.*
55. Paul Freeman, "Threaten Perez with Contempt," Baton Rouge *State-Times,* August 5, 1966; Baton Rouge *Morning Advocate,* August 27, 1966; Roy Reed, "Negro Pupils Sign in Perez's Parish," New York *Times,* September 1, 1966.
56. Baton Rouge *Morning Advocate,* August 30, 1966.
57. Leander Perez, taped interview on school desegregation order, August 27, 1966, in Perez Files (copy in possession of the author).
58. Cocke, "Judge Warns Officials in Plaquemines"; Ed McCusker, "Plaquemines' White Pupils Stage Boycott," Baton Rouge *Morning Advocate,* September 1, 1966; photograph of FBI agent, in Perez Files.
59. New York *Times,* September 17, 1966; John M. Pearce, "Plaquemines Economy Is Oil, Gas; Society Is Segregation," Baton Rouge *Morning Advocate,* September 11, 1966; *United States* v. *Plaquemines; Plaquemines Gazette,* October 21, November 11, 1966.
60. *United States* v. *Plaquemines.*
61. Baton Rouge *Morning Advocate,* April 20, 1967.
62. The salaries of Plaquemines public school teachers remained lower than those in surrounding parishes, although some fringe benefits were provided.
63. *United States* v. *Plaquemines.*
64. *Ibid.*
65. On October 20, Tinsley testified that he had only attended one school board meeting before becoming superintendent and that in the four weeks that he had been superintendent, the board had not held a single meeting. See *ibid.*
66. In response to this testimony, the *Plaquemines Gazette,* April 28, 1967, reported that the principal of the boy's school said that his students had all the books they needed but were often careless and lost them.
67. *United States* v. *Plaquemines;* Baton Rouge *Morning Advocate,* April 19, 20, 1967; Baton Rouge *State-Times,* April 24, 1967.
68. *United States* v. *Plaquemines;* list of key members attending second meeting of Save Our Public Schools, September 26, 1966, in Perez Files; *Plaquemines Gazette,* December 16, 1966.
69. *Plaquemines Gazette,* September 16, October 7, 1966, April 28, 1967; *United States* v. *Plaquemines.*
70. Alba Guidroz, interview with the author, New Orleans, La., July 22, 1972.
71. *Plaquemines Gazette,* May 12, 1967.
72. New Orleans *Times-Picayune,* March 20, 1969; *United States* v. *Plaquemines.*
73. *United States* v. *Plaquemines.*
74. *Plaquemines Gazette,* September 9, 23, 1966; Baton Rouge *Morning Advocate,* September 30, 1966; McMillan, *The Citizens' Council,* 296.
75. Meyer, interview with the author.
76. After WDSU-TV broadcast an editorial sponsored by Esso asserting that the Plaquemines private schools provided only a "third-rate" education, many parish whites mailed in their Esso credit cards for cancellation. See *Plaquemines Gazette,* September 30, 1966.
77. *Ibid.,* September 16, 23, 30, October 7, 21, November 11, 1966; Baton Rouge *State-Times,* March 20, 1968; *United States* v. *Plaquemines.*
78. *Plaquemines Gazette,* October 21, November 11, 1966.
79. *Ibid.,* September 30, October 21, November 11, 1966, April 7, June 9, 1967.
80. Motion to affirm, *Louisiana Education Commission for Needy Children et al., Appellants* v. *Bryan Poindexter et al.,* No. 284, U.S. Supreme Court, October term, 1968, Washington, D.C.

81. New Orleans *Times-Picayune,* December 1, 1960.
82. *Plaquemines Gazette,* November 4, 1966; *Bryan Poindexter et al.* v. *Louisiana Education Commission for Needy Children,* Civil Action No. 14,683, U.S. District Court, New Orleans, La.
83. New York *Times,* September 15, 1962; *Plaquemines Gazette,* May 26, June 2, 9, 1967; *Poindexter* v. *Louisiana.*
84. *Poindexter* v. *Louisiana.*
85. The others were Robert A. Ainsworth, Jr., and John Minor Wisdom.
86. *Poindexter* v. *Louisiana; Plaquemines Gazette,* September 29, November 3, 1967; Baton Rouge *Morning Advocate,* October 27, 1967.
87. *Ibid.*
88. *Poindexter* v. *Louisiana.*
89. *St. Bernard Voice,* September 16, 1966; New York *Times,* September 15, 17, 1966.
90. *United States* v. *Plaquemines; Plaquemines Gazette,* July 7, 1967; *Plaquemines Parish Commission Council et al.* v. *United States,* No. 24,009, U.S. Fifth Circuit Court of Appeals, New Orleans, La.
91. Baton Rouge *Morning Advocate,* September 1, 1967; *Plaquemines Gazette,* September 8, 1967.
92. Elementary and secondary school civil rights survey, U.S. Department of Health, Education, and Welfare, October, 1971, in Perez Files.

CHAPTER FIFTEEN

1. New Orleans *States-Item,* October 29, 1960.
2. New Orleans *Times-Picayune,* June 19, 20, 1960; New York *Times,* July 8, 9, 1960; *St. Bernard Voice,* June 3, 1960; WDSU-TV and radio editorial, June 23, 1960, New Orleans, La.
3. New Orleans *Times-Picayune,* August 16, 1960.
4. *Ibid.,* September 23, 1960.
5. New Orleans *States-Item,* October 11, 1960.
6. *Plaquemines Gazette,* October 21, 1960.
7. Leander H. Perez, "The Challenge to the South and How It Must Be Met," speech delivered at Edgewater Gulf Hotel, Biloxi, Miss., July 21, 1960, copy in Perez Files.
8. *Ibid.;* New Orleans *Times-Picayune,* September 23, 1960; New Orleans *States-Item,* October 11, 1960.
9. Perez, "The Challenge to the South and How It Must Be Met."
10. New Orleans *States-Item,* September 5, 1961.
11. J. Y. Sanders, Jr., to editor, Baton Rouge *State-Times,* September 19, 1960; New Orleans *States-Item,* October 24, 1960.
12. Letter to the editor, New Orleans *States-Item,* October 10, 1960.
13. See C. Vann Woodward, *Reunion and Reaction: The Compromise of 1877 and the End of Reconstruction* (Boston, 1966).
14. W. F. Minor, "Free Electors Urged by Perez," New Orleans *Times-Picayune,* July 22, 1960.
15. New Orleans *Times-Picayune,* August 4, 1960; Baton Rouge *Morning Advocate,* August 3, 1960. Gravel, white and a former Democratic national committeeman, had been heavily criticized for his moderate position on the racial issue. Tureaud was a black New Orleans attorney prominent in the civil rights movement.
16. New Orleans *Times-Picayune,* August 3, 1960.
17. John F. Kennedy and Lyndon B. Johnson, telegram to Perez, August 11, 1960, in Perez Files; Baton Rouge *Morning Advocate,* September 23, 1960.

18. Walter J. Suthon to Paulsen Spence, September 2, 1960, Perez solicitation letter to voters, October 17, 1960, and David Treen to Perez, October 12, 1960, all in Perez Files.
19. McMillan, *The Citizens' Council,* 331; New Orleans *Times-Picayune,* October 15, 1960; *Plaquemines Gazette,* October 28, 1960; *St. Bernard Voice,* October 28, 1960; New Orleans *States-Item,* October 20, 1960.
20. Paulsen Spence to David Treen, October 14, 1960, copy in Perez Files.
21. New Orleans *States-Item,* October 5, 1960.
22. New Orleans *Times-Picayune,* October 6, 1960; *Plaquemines Gazette,* September 30, 1960.
23. New Orleans *States-Item,* October 22, 27, 1960.
24. Perez speech on presidential election of 1960, undated, copy in Perez Files.
25. Scammon (comp.), *America Votes* (Pittsburgh, 1962), IV, 1, 155; McMillan, *The Citizens' Council,* 332–33.
26. McMillan, *The Citizens' Council,* 332–33; New Orleans *Times-Picayune,* December 16, 1960; editorial, Shreveport *Journal,* November 22, 1960.
27. McMillan, *The Citizens' Council,* 332; Perez to Ed Gossett, January 13, 1965, in Perez Files.
28. Perez to Gossett, February 23, 1966, and electoral reform memorandum by John Rau, state representative from Jefferson Parish, both in Perez Files.
29. Perez to Gossett, January 13, 1965, *ibid.*
30. Edwin C. Johnson to Perez, undated, American Good Government Society bulletin, undated, J. Harvie Williams, memorandum on electoral reform, undated, Albert R. Russell to Perez, December 28, 1962, Ed Gossett to Perez, August 7, 1963, November 14, 1967, H. L. Hunt, letter to editor for selected newspapers, April 6, 1967, Albert Russell, memorandum to electoral college reform advocates, November 29, 1962, and H. L. Hunt to Perez, March 3, 1962, April 19, 1967, all in Perez Files; New Orleans *States-Item,* March 28, 1963; New York *Times,* June 29, 1965; Singelmann, interview with the author.
31. "Conversation Carte Blanche"; Singelmann, interview with the author.
32. Editorial, *Plaquemines Gazette,* June 14, 1963; Baton Rouge *Morning Advocate,* September 13, 1963.
33. Baton Rouge *Morning Advocate,* September 13, 1963; Jackson (Miss.) *Clarion-Ledger,* September 8, 1963.
34. "Conversation Carte Blanche."
35. New Orleans *Times-Picayune,* September 8, 1963; Baton Rouge *Morning Advocate,* September 13, 1963.
36. Claude Sitton, "Democrats Plan Louisiana Fight," New York *Times,* April 13, 1964; New Orleans *Times-Picayune,* April 12, 1964; tape of Louisiana Democratic State Central Committee meeting, April 11, 1964, in Perez Files.
37. *Ibid.*
38. Bill Jones, *The Wallace Story* (Northport, Ala., 1966), 20–21; Singelmann, interview with the author.
39. Baton Rouge *Morning Advocate,* January 15, 1963.
40. Los Angeles *Times,* September 17, 1968; editorial, Shreveport *Times,* April 26, 1964; Perez to John C. McLaurin, April 15, 1964, in Perez Files.
41. Minutes of the Democratic State Central Committee meeting, May 22, 1964, in Perez Files; New York *Times,* May 23, 1964.
42. Baton Rouge *Morning Advocate,* July 25, 1964; judgment, *Francis Ralston McLavy, Sr., et al.* v. *Wade O. Martin, Jr., Secretary of State,* No. 101,315, Nineteenth Judicial District Court, East Baton Rouge Parish, La.; judgment, *Francis Ralston McLavy, Sr., et al.* v. *Wade O. Martin, Jr., Secretary of State,* No. 6,335, First Circuit Court of Appeals, Baton Rouge, La.; Richard Cadwallader to

Perez, September 24, 1964, and Perez to Cadwallader, September 30, 1964, both in Perez Files.

43. Jones, *The Wallace Story,* 321.
44. Leander Perez, taped interview on 1964 presidential election, undated, in Perez Files.
45. Baton Rouge *Morning Advocate,* September 13, 1964.
46. *Ibid.;* New Orleans *Times-Picayune,* September 13, 1964; *Plaquemines Gazette,* September 18, 1964.
47. *Plaquemines Gazette,* August 21, 1964.
48. Perez interview on 1964 presidential election.
49. *Plaquemines Gazette,* October 16, 1964.
50. *Ibid.,* August 21, 1964.
51. *Ibid.,* October 2, 1964.
52. New Orleans *Times-Picayune,* October 27, 1964.
53. Perez to Republican National Finance Committee, October 14, 1964, and Goldwater to Perez, telegram, October 29, 1964, both in Perez Files; Singelmann, interview with the author.
54. *Plaquemines Gazette,* September 25, 1964; New York *Times,* September 18, 1964.
55. Scammon (comp.), *America Votes* (Washington, D.C., 1966), VI, 1, 158.
56. Perez to D. Bruce Evans, executive director, United Republicans of America, June 22, 1965, in Perez Files. See also Baton Rouge *State-Times,* September 30, 1966.
57. Margaret Dixon, "Top Candidates May Not Appear on State Ballots," Baton Rouge *Morning Advocate,* June 11, 1966; Margaret Dixon, "State Democrats Head Down Path Already Trodden," Baton Rouge *Morning Advocate,* June 12, 1966; minutes of the Democratic State Central Committee meeting, June 14, 1968, in Perez Files.
58. Baton Rouge *State-Times,* June 10, December 15, 1966; DeBlieux, interview with the author.
59. Marion Guyton Simpson to Perez, October 13, 16, 1967, and unsigned circular letter, undated, urging election of conservative candidates and listing all Negroes running for office, both in Perez Files; Baton Rouge *Morning Advocate,* August 12, 1967; F. E. Shephard, "Fight Within State Central Demo Body Almost Unnoticed," Baton Rouge *State-Times,* October 19, 1967.
60. Baton Rouge *Morning Advocate,* August 12, November 6, 1967, January 4, 1968; Simpson to Perez, October 13, 1967, in Perez Files; Jack Lord, "Perez Forces Name Democratic Group Head," Baton Rouge *State-Times,* December 19, 1967.
61. Buckley and Perez, "The Wallace Movement"; New Orleans *Clarion Herald,* April 19, 1968.
62. Minutes of Democratic State Central Committee meeting, May 11, 1968, Act 194 of 1968, and Perez to Arthur Watson, August 22, 1968, all in Perez Files.
63. Minutes of Democratic State Central Committee meeting, June 14, 1968, *ibid.*
64. *Plaquemines Gazette,* July 26, 1968.
65. *Ibid.,* April 5, 1968; Baton Rouge *State-Times,* August 7, 1968.
66. *Plaquemines Gazette,* April 5, 1968.
67. Quote from New Orleans *States-Item,* September 4, 1968. See also Margaret Dixon, "McKeithen Quits as Favorite Son," Baton Rouge *State-Times,* August 26, 1968; telegram, Perez to John J. McKeithen, July 29, 1968, in Perez Files; Shreveport *Times,* September 4, 1968.
68. New York *Times,* October 24, 1968; *Daily Reveille* (LSU student newspaper), October 16, 1968.
69. *George Soule et al.* v. *Wade O. Martin, Jr.,* No. 49,514, Louisiana Supreme Court, New Orleans; Gerald Moses, "Wallace Supporters Obtain Court Order in Rooster

Battle," Baton Rouge *Morning Advocate,* September 1, 1968; Gibbs Adams, "Cole Decision on Rooster Set Thursday," Baton Rouge *Morning Advocate,* September 26, 1969; Baton Rouge *Morning Advocate,* September 19, October 5, 1968.

70. Chalin Perez, interview with the author; editorial, Shreveport *Times,* September 15, 1968.
71. Baton Rouge *Morning Advocate,* April 19, October 3, 1968; *Daily Reveille,* October 16, 1968; George Soule to Perez, December 20, 1968, in Perez Files; *Plaquemines Gazette,* November 1, 1968.
72. Mrs. Josie Ames to Perez, August 23, 1968, in Perez Files; New Orleans *Jewish Civic Press,* September, 1968; Buckley and Perez, "The Wallace Movement."
73. New York *Times,* October 24, 1968; Buckley and Perez, "The Wallace Movement"; Perez to Wallace staff, October 14, 1968, and telegram, Perez to Wallace, October 24, 1968, both in Perez Files.
74. *Daily Reveille,* October 16, 1968.
75. Jean Graves, "Tempers Flare as Liberals Ridicule Perez," Baton Rouge *Morning Advocate,* October 23, 1968.
76. Ville Platte *Gazette,* September 19, 1968.
77. Perez to Wallace campaign headquarters, October 28, 1968, and Richard Smith to Perez, November 18, 1968, both in Perez Files.
78. *Plaquemines Gazette,* November 1, 1968; Wallace-for-president form letter, undated, in Perez Files.
79. Baton Rouge *State-Times,* October 30, 1968; New York *Times,* October 30, 1968; list of contributors to Wallace campaign, file of Sas-Jaworsky expenditures paid by Perez, and Sas-Jaworsky form letter, October 20, 1968, all in Perez Files.
80. Scammon (comp.), *America Votes* (Washington, D.C., 1968), VII, 1, 161; *Plaquemines Gazette,* November 15, 1968.
81. McMillan, *The Citizens' Council,* 354.

CHAPTER SIXTEEN

1. Anderson, interview with the author; Foret, interview with the author; Barton, interview with the author; Cain, interview with the author.
2. *Plaquemines Gazette,* February 17, 1967; Foret, interview with the author; Anderson, interview with the author; Cain, interview with the author.
3. Chalin Perez, interview with the author; Anderson, interview with the author; Baton Rouge *Morning Advocate,* March 20, 1969.
4. New Orleans *Times-Picayune,* September 3, 1960.
5. *Ibid.,* June 27, 1960.
6. Carlton F. Wilson, "Perez Praised by Many at Testimonial Dinner," Baton Rouge *State-Times,* December 6, 1960; *Plaquemines Gazette,* December 9, 1960.
7. *St. Bernard Voice,* April 12, 1963; *Plaquemines Gazette,* March 31, May 5, 1961; Proclamation of election returns by police jury, May 15, 1961, in Perez Files.
8. Plaquemines Parish charter, Courthouse, Pointe a la Hache, La.; editorial, New Orleans *Times-Picayune,* May 7, 1961.
9. Plaquemines Parish charter.
10. *Ibid.;* editorial, New Orleans *Times-Picayune,* May 7, 1961.
11. New Orleans *Times-Picayune,* June 3, 1961; New Orleans *States-Item,* July 8, 14, 1961.
12. Cleghorn, "The Perils of Plaquemines."
13. *Plaquemines Gazette,* August 11, September 8, 1961, October 26, 1962.
14. *Ibid.,* September 8, 1961, March 15, September 20, 1963.
15. *St. Bernard Voice,* June 8, July 20, 1962; New Orleans *States-Item,* August 1, 1962.

16. New Orleans *States-Item,* August 1, 1962.
17. *St. Bernard Voice,* August 17, 1962.
18. *Ibid.,* August 31, September 7, 1962, December 13, 1963; Cain, interview with the author.
19. *Plaquemines Gazette,* June 28, 1963.
20. New Orleans *Times-Picayune,* December 1, 7, 1963; Charles W. Tapp, "The Gubernatorial Election of 1964: An Affirmation of Political Trends," *Louisiana Academy of Science Proceedings,* XXVII (1964), 80.
21. *Plaquemines Gazette,* November 22, 1963.
22. *Ibid.,* December 6, 1963.
23. Secretary of State, *Primary Election Returns, December 7, 1963, and January 11, 1964* (Baton Rouge, 1964); Howard, *Political Tendencies in Louisiana,* 362.
24. *Plaquemines Gazette,* December 27, 1963.
25. Circular entitled *Do You Want Benefits Like These????,* in Perez Files.
26. *Plaquemines Gazette,* January 17, February 28, 1964; telegram, Perez to John J. McKeithen, March 4, 1964, in Perez Files; Howard, *Political Tendencies in Louisiana,* 367.
27. *Plaquemines Gazette,* September 17, October 8, 1965, and annual progress issue, June, 1966.
28. *Ibid.,* June, 1966; Saul Friedman, "Boss Perez of Plaquemines Running into Discontent," Houston *Chronicle,* September 16, 1965.
29. Baton Rouge *Morning Advocate,* October 6, 1965.
30. *Plaquemines Gazette,* September 24, October 8, 15, 1965, April 22, May 6, 1966; Baton Rouge *Morning Advocate,* October 8, 1965.
31. *Plaquemines Gazette,* September 24, October 8, 1965; New Orleans *States-Item,* November 17, 1967.
32. *Plaquemines Gazette,* February 17, 1967; Anderson, interview with the author; Harold Asevedo, taped interview with the author, New Orleans, La., June 30, 1972.
33. Eggler, "Plaquemines Without the Great White Father," 12; brief of defendants, *Richard B. Sobol* v. *Leander Perez, Sr., et al.,* No. 67,243, U.S. Fifth Circuit Court of Appeals, New Orleans, La.; Baton Rouge *Morning Advocate,* February 23, 1967, January 24, 1968; Baton Rouge *State-Times,* January 30, 31, February 8, 1968.
34. Baton Rouge *State-Times,* August 15, 1967; *Plaquemines Gazette,* August 18, 1967; New Orleans *States-Item,* August 11, 1967.
35. *Ernest Hingle* v. *Plaquemines Parish Democratic Executive Committee et al.,* No. 10,422, Twenty-fifth Judicial District Court, Plaquemines Parish, La.; Perez to Leon Scobel, November 17, 1967, Perez to Walter Blaize, November 17, 1967, and minutes of a meeting of the Plaquemines Parish Democratic Executive Committee, November 9, 1967, all in Perez Files; *Plaquemines Gazette,* September 1, 1967.
36. *Lawrence J. Rousselle, Jr.* v. *Leander Perez et al.,* No. 68-1433, U.S. District Court, New Orleans, La.; John S. Lang, "Perez Says Group Involved in Plot to Take His Life," Baton Rouge *State-Times,* August 1, 1967; John S. Lang, "Plaquemines D.A. Won't Tell Charge Against Plot Suspect," Baton Rouge *State-Times,* August 2, 1967; John S. Lang, "Rousselle Bonded, Charges Arrest Is Perez Retaliation," New Orleans *Times-Picayune,* August 1, 1967.
37. Baton Rouge *Morning Advocate,* August 2, 1967.
38. *Rousselle* v. *Perez.*
39. John S. Lang, "Five Men Testify to Hearing Perez Threatened by Lawrence Rousselle," Baton Rouge *Morning Advocate,* August 5, 1967.
40. Baton Rouge *Morning Advocate,* August 5, 1967.

41. *Plaquemines Gazette,* August 18, September 1, 1967.
42. *Ibid.,* September 8, November 10, 1967.
43. Baton Rouge *Morning Advocate,* February 24, August 14, 29, 1968; G. Michael Harmon, "Perez Opposes Special Meet," Baton Rouge *State-Times,* October 15, 1968; Baton Rouge *State-Times,* March 20, 1969.
44. *Plaquemines Gazette,* December 8, 1967.
45. *Ibid.*
46. *Ibid.,* July 12, 1968.
47. Chalin Perez, interview with the author; Asevedo, interview with the author.
48. *Plaquemines Gazette,* January 17, 1969; Asevedo, interview with the author.
49. Foret, interview with the author; Asevedo, interview with the author.
50. Unidentified clipping, March 21, 1969, in Perez File, Tulane University Archives.
51. Unidentified clipping, March 22, 1969, *Ibid.; Plaquemines Gazette,* March 28, 1969; Baton Rouge *Morning Advocate,* March 22, 1969.
52. *Plaquemines Gazette,* March 28, 1969; New Orleans *States-Item,* March 20, 1969; Baton Rouge *Morning Advocate,* March 22, 1969; Baton Rouge *State-Times,* March 21, 1969; unidentified clippings, March 21, 1969, all in Perez File, Tulane University Archives.
53. Baton Rouge *State-Times,* March 21, 1969; *Plaquemines Gazette,* March 28, 1969; unidentified clipping, March 22, 1969, in Perez File, Tulane University Archives.
54. Baton Rouge *Morning Advocate,* March 22, 1969; unidentified clipping, March 22, 1969, in Perez File, Tulane University Archives.
55. Unidentified clipping, March 22, 1969, in Perez File, Tulane University Archives.
56. Baton Rouge *State-Times,* March 20, 1969.
57. *Ibid.*
58. *Ibid.*
59. New Orleans *States-Item,* March 20, 1969.
60. *Ibid.*
61. Eggler, "Plaquemines Without the Great White Father," 11; *Plaquemines Gazette,* April 4, 1969.
62. Eggler, "Plaquemines Without the Great White Father," 11; Baton Rouge *Morning Advocate,* April 26, 1969; Baton Rouge *State-Times,* April 26, 1969.
63. David Snyder, "Speech Won Forgiveness for Perez," New Orleans *States-Item,* March 25, 1969.
64. *Ibid.;* Bennett M. Bolton, "Absolution for Perez Described," Baton Rouge *State-Times,* March 28, 1969.
65. *Plaquemines Gazette,* November 27, 1970; Bert Hyde, "'Plaquemines Fine Place to Live; We Intend Keeping It That Way,'" New Orleans *States-Item,* November 30, 1970.
66. Hyde, "'Plaquemines Fine Place to Live,'"
67. New Orleans *Times-Picayune,* April 18, March 4, 1972.
68. *Ibid.,* January 24, 1972.
69. Hyde, "'Plaquemines Fine Place to Live.'"
70. *Ibid.*
71. New Orleans *Times-Picayune,* June 8, 1973.
72. Chalin O. Perez, Jr., interview with the author, New Orleans, La.
73. Meyer, interview with the author.

EPILOGUE

1. Smith, "Oil, Brimstone, and 'Judge' Perez," 145.
2. Anderson, interview with the author.

3. Gordon W. Allport, *The Nature of Prejudice* (New York, 1954), 8.
4. *Ibid.,* 388, 223.
5. Foret, interview with the author.
6. Tom P. Brady to Perez, January 2, 1969, in Perez Files.
7. Ray Ginger (ed.), *The Nationalizing of American Life, 1877–1900* (New York, 1965), 248.
8. Baton Rouge *State-Times,* December 8, 1954.
9. Buckley and Perez, "The Wallace Movement"; Gelpi, interview with the author; Foret, interview with the author.
10. Allport, *The Nature of Prejudice,* 284.
11. *Ibid.,* 374, 361.
12. *Ibid.,* 357–60; confidential communication.
13. Gordon W. Allport, *Personality: A Psychological Interpretation* (New York, 1937), 173; Allport, *The Nature of Prejudice,* 352.
14. Allport, *The Nature of Prejudice,* 354.
15. *Ibid.,* 341.

Bibliography

PRIMARY SOURCES

PAMPHLETS AND DOCUMENTS

Acts 1–29, 1st Special Sess., Louisiana Legislature, 1960.

Certificate of Marriage, Mater Dolorosa Church, New Orleans.

Certified copy of resolution adopted at the Mississippi State Democratic Convention at Jackson, Miss., June 22, 1948.

Civil Rights Commission. *Hearings Before the United States Commission on Civil Rights Held in New Orleans, 1960–61*. Washington, D.C.: Government Printing Office, 1961.

Extract from the Minutes of a Meeting of the Board of Commissioners for the Buras Levee District Held at Buras, September 8, 1928. Plaquemines Parish Conveyance Original Book, fol. 266.

Gaillot, Mrs. B. J., Jr. *God Gave the Law of Segregation to Moses on Mount Sinai*. New Orleans: n.p., 1960.

Gremillion, John Berton. *Plaquemines Parish*. Baton Rouge: n.p., 1963.

Inger, Morton. *Politics and Reality in an American City: The New Orleans School Crisis of 1960*. New York: Center for Urban Education, 1969.

Joint Legislative Committee on Segregation. *Explanation of Segregation Bills Passed by Louisiana Legislature, General Session, 1954*.

———. *Explanation of Segregation Bills Passed by the Regular Session of the Louisiana Legislature, 1956*.

———. *Explanation of Segregation Measures Passed by the Regular Session of the Louisiana Legislature, 1958*.

———. *Special Report*, March 8, 1955.

Lease, Board of Commissioners for the Buras Levee District to Creole Oil Co., Inc., February 6, 1937. Plaquemines Parish Conveyance Original Book, 83, fol. 510.

Louisiana Almanac and Fact Book, 1953–54. Gretna: Pelican Publishing Co., 1954.

Louisiana Almanac and Fact Book, 1961–62. Gretna: Pelican Publishing Co., 1962.

Louisiana State Advisory Committee on Civil Rights. *The New Orleans School Crisis.* Washington, D.C.: Government Printing Office, 1961.

————. *Report to the United States Commission on Civil Rights.* New Orleans: Louisiana State Advisory Committee, 1961.

Minutes of States' Rights Democratic Campaign Committee, Jackson, Miss., June 8, 1948. In Leander Perez Files.

Minutes of Meeting of the Democratic State Central Committee, Held in Baton Rouge, August 20, 1952, May 22, 1964, May 11, 1968, June 14, 1968. In Leander Perez Files.

Minutes of a Meeting of the Plaquemines Parish Democratic Executive Committee, November 9, 1969. In Leander Perez Files.

Official Journal of the Senate of the State of Louisiana Sitting as a Court of Impeachment for the Trial of Huey P. Long, Governor of the State of Louisiana, May 16, 1929. Special Sess., March 20–April 6, 1929.

Official transcript of Leander H. Perez, Louisiana State University, Baton Rouge.

Overriding Royalty Agreement Between Gulf Refining Co. of Louisiana and Robert J. Lobrano. Plaquemines Parish Conveyance Original Book, fol. 407.

Perez, Leander H., statement of service. United States General Services Administration, Washington, D.C.

————. *The Unconstitutionality of the Fourteenth Amendment.* Belle Chasse, La.: Plaquemines Gazette, Inc., n.d.

Pinney, Edward L., and Robert S. Friedman. *Political Leadership and the School Desegregation Crisis in Louisiana.* New York: Eagleton Institute, 1961.

Plaquemines Parish Charter. Courthouse, Point a la Hache., La.

Public Affairs Research Council of Louisiana. *A Statistical Profile of Plaquemines Parish.* Baton Rouge: Public Affairs Research Council, 1964.

Secretary of State. Compilations Under Various Title of Primary Election and General Election Returns for 1921, 1924, 1928, 1930, 1932, 1936, 1944, 1948, 1952, 1963, 1964. Baton Rouge: Secretary of State's Office.

Testimony of genocide treaty. *Congressional Digest,* XXIX (December, 1950), 316, 318.

Transcript of Proceedings in Open Hearing Before the Honorable Richard Rees, April 3, 1958. In Leander Perez Files.

U.S. Department of Health, Education, and Welfare, Office for Civil Rights. *Elementary and Secondary School Civil Rights Survey.* Washington, D.C.: Government Printing Office, 1971.

U.S. Senate, Judiciary Committee. *Hearings before the Senate Judiciary Subcommittee on S. 1725 and S. 1734.* 81st Cong., 1st Sess.

————. *Hearings Before the Senate Subcommittee on Constitutional Rights of the Senate Judiciary Committee on S. 435, S. 456, S. 810, S. 958-60, S. 1084, S. 1199, S. 1277, S. 1848, S. 1998, S. 2001, S. 2002, S. 2003, and S. 2041.* 86th Cong., 1st Sess.

————. *Hearings Before the Senate Judiciary Committee on S. 1564.* 89th Cong., 1st Sess.

YEARBOOKS

Gumbo, 1911. Louisiana State University yearbook.
Gumbo, 1912. Louisiana State University yearbook.
Holy Cross College Yearbook, 1904–1905.
Holy Cross College Yearbook, 1905–1906.
Jambalaya, 1914. Tulane University yearbook.

LEGAL CASES

Walter J. Blaize v. Jerome A. Hayes. 15 So. 2d 217 (1943).
Board of Commissioners of the Buras Levee District v. Police Jury of Plaquemines Parish et al. No. 351–967. Civil District Court, Orleans Parish, La.
Bush v. Board of Education. 357 U.S. 483 (1954).
Brown v. Board of Education. 349 U.S. 294 (1955).
Athan Coe et al. v. Wade O. Martin et al. No. 30, 345. Nineteenth Judicial District Court, Division C, East Baton Rouge Parish, La.
Athan Coe et al. v. Wade O. Martin et al. No. 39,168. Supreme Court of Louisiana, New Orleans.
Sam Jones v. Plaquemines Parish Democratic Executive Committee et al. No. 2,355. Twenty-fifth Judicial District Court, Plaquemines Parish, La.
Ernest Hingle v. Plaquemines Parish Democratic Executive Committee et al. No. 10,422. Twenty-fifth Judicial District Court, Plaquemines Parish, La.
Charles A. Leon v. St. Bernard Democratic Committee and Edward L. Jeanfreau. No. 7,249. Twenty-fifth Judicial District Court, St. Bernard Parish, La.
Philip R. Livaudais v. Leander H. Perez. No. 26,307. Supreme Court of Louisiana, New Orleans.
Louisiana Education Commission for Needy Children et al. v. Bryan Poindexter et al. No. 284, U.S. Supreme Court, October term, 1968, Washington, D.C.
Louisiana Muskrat Ranch v. Manuel Molero et al. No. 18,560. U.S. District Court, New Orleans.

Francis Ralston McLavy, Sr., et al. v. *Wade O. Martin, Jr., Secretary of State.* No. 6,335. First Circuit Court of Appeals, Baton Rouge, La.

Francis Ralston McLavy, Sr., et al. v. *Wade O. Martin, Jr., Secretary of State.* No. 101,315. Nineteenth Judicial District Court, East Baton Rouge Parish, La.

Leander Perez v. *Celestine Melerine.* No. 6,193. Twenty-fifth Judicial District Court, St. Bernard Parish, La.

Leander H. Perez v. *J. Claude Meraux.* No. 35,755. Supreme Court of Louisiana, New Orleans.

Leander Perez v. *James Licciardi.* No. 6,192. Twenty-fifth Judicial District Court, St. Bernard Parish, La.

Miguel Perez v. *Canadian Land and Fur Co., Inc.* No. 18,457. U.S. District Court, New Orleans, La.

Petition to the Honorable Judges of the Criminal District Court for the Parish of Orleans, State of Louisiana. No. 102,151. Docket E, New Orleans.

Plaquemines Parish Commission Council et al. v. *United States.* No. 24,009. U.S. Fifth Circuit Court of Appeals, New Orleans, La.

Bryan Poindexter et al. v. *Louisiana Education Commission for Needy Children.* Civil Action No, 14,683. U.S. District Court, New Orleans, La.

Re: Leander H. Perez, District Attorney for the Parishes of Plaquemines and St. Bernard, State of Louisiana. No. 1,558. Twenty-fifth Judicial District Court, Plaquemines Parish, La.

Re: Leander H. Perez, District Attorney for the Parishes of Plaquemines and St. Bernard. No. 35,721. Supreme Court of Louisiana, New Orleans.

Richardson and Bass v. *Board of Levee Commissioners of Orleans Levee District.* No. 42,057. Supreme Court of Louisiana, New Orleans.

Lawrence J. Rousselle, Jr. v. *Leander Perez et al.* No. 68-1433. U.S. District Court, New Orleans, La.

Percy Saint v. *Harry W. Fisher, Registrar of Voters, and Parish Democratic Executive Committee for the Parish of St. Bernard.* No. 31,656. Supreme Court of Louisiana, New Orleans.

St. Bernard Trappers' Association v. *Anthony Alonzo et al.* Twenty-fifth Judicial District Court, St. Bernard Parish, La.

St. Bernard Trappers' Association v. *J. Walter Michel.* No. 28,264. Supreme Court of Louisiana, New Orleans.

Henry C. Schindler, Jr., et al. v. *Celestine Melerine et al.* No. 5,796. Twenty-fifth Judicial District Court, St. Bernard Parish, La.

Benjamin Slater v. *J. P. Cole et al.* No. 37,573. Supreme Court of Louisiana, New Orleans.

Richard B. Sobol v. *Leander Perez, Sr., et al.* No. 67,243. U.S. Fifth Circuit Court of Appeals, New Orleans, La.

George Soule et al. v. *Wade O. Martin, Jr.* No. 49,514. Louisiana Supreme Court, New Orleans.

State ex rel Philip R. Livaudais, District Attorney v. *L. H. Perez, Judge.* No. 26,174. Supreme Court of Louisiana, New Orleans.

State ex rel Leander H. Perez v. *H. C. Cage, Judge.* No. 23,844. Supreme Court of Louisiana, New Orleans.

State of Louisiana v. *John Dymond, Jr.* No. 386. Twenty-ninth Judicial District Court, Plaquemines Parish, La.

State of Louisiana v. *William Dymond.* Nos. 389, 420, 421. Twenty-ninth Judicial District Court, Plaquemines Parish, La.

State of Louisiana v. *Emile Martin.* No. 383. Twenty-ninth Judicial District Court, Plaquemines Parish, La.

State of Louisiana v. *Celestine Melerine and James Licciardi.* No. 4,634. Twenty-fifth Judicial District Court, St. Bernard Parish, La.

State of Louisiana ex rel Board of Commissioners for the Lake Borgne Basin Levee District v. *William J. Dodd et al.* No. 44,015. Supreme Court of Louisiana, New Orleans.

State of Louisiana ex rel Board of Commissioners of Lake Borgne Basin Levee District v. *Lawrence Bergeron et al.* No. 43,917. Supreme Court of Louisiana, New Orleans.

State of Louisiana ex rel Lake Borgne and Chalmette Levee Districts v. *Dr. Nicholas P. Trist.* Nos. 43,932, 43,952, 43,953. Supreme Court of Louisiana, New Orleans.

State of Louisiana ex rel Sam H. Jones v. *Benjamin R. Slater.* No. 1,916. Twenty-fifth Judicial District Court, Plaquemines Parish, La.

Elmer Stewart et al. v. *Eugene Stanley.* No. 16,261. Nineteenth Judicial District Court, East Baton Rouge Parish, La.

Succession of Roselius E. Perez and Gertrude Solis. No. 1,953. Twenty-fifth Judicial District, Plaquemines Parish, La.

Trappers v. *Michel.* 110 So. 617 (1926).

Albert J. Tullier v. *Frank Giordano.* No. 5,072. Twenty-fifth Judicial District Court, Plaquemines Parish, La.

United States v. *Mary Ethel Fox.* No. 20,398. U.S. Fifth Circuit Court of Appeals, New Orleans, La.

United States v. *Plaquemines Parish School Board.* No. 66-71. Section A, U.S. District Court, New Orleans, La.

United States v. *Louisiana et al.* 363 U.S. 1 (1960).

United States v. *State of Louisiana.* No. 2,548. U.S. District Court, Baton Rouge, La.

Mrs. Una M. Vullo v. *Plaquemines Parish Police Jury et al.* No. 44,535. Supreme Court of Louisiana, New Orleans.

Harry K. Williams v. *Jimmie Davis et al.* Civil Action No. 10,329. U.S. District Court, New Orleans, La.

Collections and Srapbooks

Meyer, J. Ben. "Judge Leander H. Perez: Hi Lites of His Life." Typescript in possession of the author.
——. Scrapbook.
Perez, Leander H. Files. New Orleans, La.
Perez File. Tulane University Archives, New Orleans, La.
State Guard Scrapbook. In possession of J. P. Cole, Baton Rouge, La.

Newspapers

Baton Rouge *Morning Advocate,* 1925–69.
Baton Rouge *State-Times,* 1919–69.
Braithwaite *Challenger,* scattered editions.
Daily Reveille (LSU student newspaper), scattered runs.
Dalcour Times, scattered editions.
Lower Coast Gazette (Pointe a la Hache, La.), 1913–14.
New Orleans *Item,* 1919–58.
New Orleans *Morning Tribune,* scattered editions.
New Orleans *States,* 1919–58.
New Orleans *States-Item,* 1958–69.
New Orleans *Times-Picayune,* 1919–69.
New York *Times,* 1919–69.
Plaquemines Gazette (Belle Chase, La.), scattered earlier editions available. Published in Point a la Hache until 1940s.
Plaquemines Protector (Pointe a la Hache, La.), 1912–16.
Shreveport *Journal,* scattered runs.
Shreveport *Times,* scattered runs.
St. Bernard Voice (Arabi, La.), 1919–69.

Speeches

Buckley, William F., Jr., and Leander Perez. "The Wallace Movement" on "Firing Line," April 15, 1968. Transcript No. 95.
Long, Earl. Typescript of radio and television address, 1959. Copy in Leander Perez Files.
Perez, Leander H. "The Challenge to the South and How it Must be Met." Speech delivered at Edgewater Gulf Hotel, Biloxi, Miss., July 21, 1960. Copy in Leander Perez Files.
——. "Interposition: What Is It?" Speech delivered at the Seventy-ninth Annual Meeting, American Bar Association, Dallas, Texas, August 27, 1956.
——. "Racial Integration by Court Decree." Speech before Young Men's Business Club, New Orleans, La., December 29, 1954. Copy in Leander Perez Files.

————. Speech on presidential election of 1960, undated. Copy in Leander Perez Files.
————. Speech to Little Rock Citizens' Council, Little Rock, Ark., January 29, 1959. Copy in Leander Perez Files.

TAPED INTERVIEWS WITH LOUISIANIANS

Anderson, Mrs. W. E., Baton Rouge, February 9, 1972.
Asevedo, Harold, New Orleans, June 30, 1972.
Barton, Mrs. John W., Baton Rouge, February 9, 1972.
Blanche, Fred, Baton Rouge, February 21, 1972.
Cain, A. S., Jr., New Orleans, July 19–20, 1972.
Carrere, Mrs. Richard J., New Orleans, March 13, 1972.
Cole, J. P., Baton Rouge, March 2, 1972.
Davis, James H., Baton Rouge, July 8, 1969.
DeBlieux, J. D., Baton Rouge, February 22, 1972.
Dodd, William J., Baton Rouge, June 30, 1969.
Foret, Mrs. Claude P., New Orleans, March 13, 1972.
Francioni, Dr. J. B., Baton Rouge, February 17, 1972.
Gelpi, Mrs. Chester, New Orleans, March 13, 1972.
Gottlieb, Lewis, Baton Rouge, March 1, 1972.
Haspel, Edward, New Orleans, July 27, 1972.
Herbert, F. Edward, New Orleans, July 16, 1972.
Meyer, J. Ben, Promised Land, June 19, 1970.
Moyse, Hermann, Baton Rouge, March 1, 1972.
Nesom, Frank, Baton Rouge, March 10, 1972.
Olinde, Patrick, Rougon, February 28, 1972.
Peltier, Harvey, Thibodaux, September 18, 1972.
Perez, Chalin O., New Orleans, June 21, 1972.
Petrovitch, Luke, New Orleans, July 17, 1972.
Provensal, Sidney W., Jr., New Orleans, July 25, 1972.
Singelmann, George, New Orleans, March 15, 1972.
Stern, Percival H., New Orleans, July 28, 1972.

OTHER TAPES

"Conversation Carte Blanche." WDSU (New Orleans) radio debate between Leander Perez and Victor Bussie, April 10, 1964.
Perez, Leander. Taped interview on desegregation order, August 27, 1966. In Leander Perez Files. Copy in possession of the author.
"The Priest and the Politician." CBS television documentary, September 18, 1963.
"A Sordid Case: Melerine and Licciardi." WDSU-TV and radio editorial, March 23, 1960, New Orleans, La.

WDSU-TV and radio editorial, December 8, 1960, New Orleans, La.
WDSU-TV and radio editorial, June 23, 1960, New Orleans, La.

SECONDARY SOURCES

BOOKS

Ader, Emile Bertrand. *The Dixiecrat Movement*. Washington, D.C.: Public Affairs Press, 1955.
Allport, Gordon W. *The Nature of Prejudice*. New York: Addison-Wesley, 1954.
———. *Personality: A Psychological Interpretation*. New York: Henry Holt, 1937.
Bartley, Numan V. *The Rise of Massive Resistance: Race and Politics in the South During the 1950's*. Baton Rouge: Louisiana State University Press, 1969.
Conaway, James. *Judge: The Life and Times of Leander Perez*. New York: Alfred A. Knopf, 1973.
Cook, James Graham. *The Segregationists*. New York: Appleton-Century-Crofts, 1962.
Ginger, Ray, ed. *The Nationalizing of American Life, 1877–1900*. New York: Free Press, 1965.
Gremillion, Jack P. F. *Louisiana Tidelands: A Comprehensive Study*. Baton Rouge: Louisiana Department of Justice, 1957.
Heard, Alexander, and Donald S. Strong. *Southern Primaries and Elections*. University, Ala.: University of Alabama Press, 1950.
Hoebel, E. Adamson. *Anthropology: The Study of Man*. 3rd ed. New York: McGraw-Hill, 1966.
Howard, L. Vaughn, and David R. Deener. *Presidential Politics in Louisiana, 1952*. New Orleans: Tulane University, 1954.
Howard, Perry. *Political Tendencies in Louisiana*. Baton Rouge: Louisiana State University Press, 1971.
Jones, Bill. *The Wallace Story*. Northport, Ala.: American Southern Publishing Co., 1966.
Kane, Harnett T. *Deep Delta Country*. New York: Duell, Sloan, and Pearce, 1944.
Liebling, A. J. *The Earl of Louisiana*. New York: Ballantine Books, 1960.
McCaughan, Richard. *Socks on a Rooster: Louisiana's Earl K. Long*. Baton Rouge: Claitor's Book Store, 1967.
McMillan, Neil R. *The Citizens' Council: Organized Resistance to the Second Reconstruction*. Urbana: University of Illinois Press, 1971.
Martin, Thomas. *Dynasty: The Longs of Louisiana*. New York: G. P. Putnam's Sons, 1960.
Peltason, J. W. *Fifty-eight Lonely Men: Southern Federal Judges and School Desegregation*. Urbana: University of Illinois Press, 1961.

Scammon, Richard M., comp. *America Votes: A Handbook of Contemporary American Election Statistics.* 7 vols. New York: Congressional Quarterly, Inc., 1956, 1958; Pittsburgh: Congressional Quarterly, Inc., 1959, 1962, 1964; Washington, D.C.: Congressional Quarterly, Inc., 1966, 1968.
Sherrill, Robert. *Gothic Politics in the Deep South.* New York: Ballantine Books, 1969.
Sindler, Allan P. *Huey Long's Louisiana: State Politics, 1920–1952.* Baltimore: Johns Hopkins Press, 1956.
Williams, T. Harry. *Huey Long.* New York: Knopf, 1969.
Woodward, C. Vann. *Reunion and Reaction: The Compromise of 1877 and the End of Reconstruction.* Boston: Little, Brown, 1966.

THESES AND DISSERTATIONS

Jeansonne, Glen. "Race, Religion, and the Louisiana Gubernatorial Elections of 1959–1960." M.A. thesis, Florida State University, 1969.
McCarrick, Earleen Mary. "Louisiana's Official Resistance to Desegregation." Ph.D. dissertation, Vanderbilt University, 1964.
Vander Zanden, James W. "The Southern White Resistance Movement to Integration." Ph.D. dissertation, University of North Carolina, 1957.

ARTICLES

Barrios, Etienne. "King of the River People?" *Commonweal,* June 6, 1962, pp. 365–66.
Beals, Carleton, and A. Plenn. "Louisiana Skin Game: Independent Fur Trappers Starving." *Nation,* December 25, 1935, pp. 738–40.
Bolton, Clint. "Leander's Legacy." *New Orleans,* VI (September, 1972), 52–55.
Brumley, Cal. "A Visit to Hyannis." *Wall Street Journal,* June 15, 1962.
Carter, Hodding. "Dixiecrat Boss of the Bayous." *Reporter,* January 17, 1950.
"Civil Rights Bill." *Time,* May 6, 1957, p. 26.
Cleghorn, Reese. "The Perils of Plaquemines." *New Republic,* September 21, 1963, pp. 8–10.
———. "The Segs." *Esquire,* LXI (January, 1964), 71–76, 133–36.
"Collins, Charles Wallace." *National Cyclopedia of American Biography.* New York: University Microfilms, 1969.
Dietz, Lew. "Trembling Prairie." *Field and Stream.* LXIX (February, 1965), 57–59, 98.
Dulcher, Louisa. "Time of Worry in 'The City Care Forgot.'" *Reporter,* March 8, 1956, p. 17.
Eggler, Bruce. "Plaquemines Without the Great White Father." *New Republic,* May 24, 1969, pp. 11–12.

Ferman, Irving. "Louisiana Side-Show." *New Republic,* January 21, 1952, pp. 13–14.

Fuller, Helen. "New Orleans Knows Better." *New Republic,* February 16, 1959, 14–17.

"God Bless You, Now." *Newsweek,* May 7, 1962, p. 30–33.

Hoag, Edward. "New Orleans Looking Forward." *Ave Maria,* June 2, 1962, p. 14.

"Integration in the South." *Life,* November 28, 1960, p. 49.

Lemmon, Sarah McCulloh. "The Ideology of the 'Dixiecrat' Movement." *Social Forces,* XXX (December, 1951).

"Louisiana Re-enacts Sales Tax and War Measure." *National Municipal Review,* XXXI (December, 1942), 641.

"Louisiana Repeals Its Sales Tax." *National Municipal Review,* XXIX (September 1940), 626.

"A Mayor and His City," *Newsweek,* February 17, 1958, pp. 29–30.

"Perez, Leander Henry." *Who's Who in Government.* New York: Biographical Research Bureau, Inc., 1930.

"The Pot Boils," *Time,* October 4, 1948, p. 22.

"Prison Perez Style: Ready for Race Demonstrators." *U.S. News & World Report,* November 4, 1963, p. 16.

"Racist Leader,' *Time,* December 12, 1960, p. 21.

Ramsey, Carolyn. "Louisiana's Fabulous Muskrat Marshland." *Reader's Digest,* XLVI (March, 1945), 77.

———. "Rats to Riches." *Saturday Evening Post,* May 8, 1943.

Sanford, Robert K. "In His Corner of the South Few Persons Dare Talk Back to Leander (the King) Perez." Kansas City *Star,* January 26, 1964.

Smith, Lillian. "The Ordeal of Southern Women." *Redbook,* CXVII (May, 1961).

Smith, Richard Austin. "Oil, Brimstone, and 'Judge' Perez." *Fortune,* LVII (March, 1958), 143–46.

"Southern Revolt." *Time,* October 11, 1948, pp. 24–27.

Tapp, Charles W. "The Gubernatorial Election of 1964: An Affirmation of Political Trends." *Louisiana Academy of Sciences Proceedings,* XXVII (1964), 80.

"Twelve Years." *Time,* January 29, 1940, pp. 23–24, March 4, 1940, pp. 15–16.

Velie, Lester. "'Democracy' in the Deep Delta." *Collier's,* December 24, 1949, pp. 21, 42–43.

———. "Kingfish of the Dixiecrats." *Collier's,* December 17, 1949, pp. 9–11, 21.

"War Between the Democrats." *Newsweek,* July 26, 1948, p. 21.

"What It Shows." *Nation,* May 5, 1962, p. 391.

"Where's Jimmie?" *Newsweek,* August 29, 1960, pp. 30–31.

Index

Alvin Callender Naval Air Station: desegregation of, 274–77
Association of Citizens' Councils: Perez's support of, 235–36, 240; decline of, 240; and its Project Perez, 301

Battle, John S., 190, 191
Bergeron, Lawrence, 159
Blaize, Walter: and the "little war of 1943," pp. 128–41; mentioned, 104, 211
Boggs, T. Hale, 152, 153, 158
Booth, Harry, 311
Bootlegging, 22–23
Broussard, Edwin S., 72
Brown vs. *Board of Education,* 227, 228–29
Buckley, William F., 337
Bush v. *Orleans Parish School Board,* 253
Bussie, Victor, 327

Cain, A. S.: as Perez law partner, 79; as dummy candidate in gubernatorial election, 148; characterizes Earl Long, 197
Caldwell, Sam, 143
Chapman, Oscar, 167
Chiapetta, Salvador: and attempt to register, 104–105; appointed a Plaquemines police juror, 202
Christenberry, Herbert W., 290–93
Citizens' Council of Greater New Orleans: and Perez's support of, 236, 237; and Freedom Rides North, 238–40; and desegregation, 255–56, 259; and unpledged-elector ticket, 319
Clements, Ernest, 142, 143
Cole, J. Perry, 130
Collins, Charles Wallace, 230, 230*n,* 231

Congress of Racial Equality: and racial demonstrations in Plaquemine (Iberville Parish), 278–79

Dauterive, Louis D., 127
Dauterive, Wilson, 131
Davis, Jimmie: as governor, 143, 144, 145, 214–16; repeals anti-Perez legislation, 216–17; and segregation, 257–58, 259–60, 262; mentioned, 142, 311, 317
Davis, Malcolm, Jr., 292
Debaillon, Paul: and Plaquemines juries, 92–93; and St. Bernard grand jury, 94–95; dismisses case against Perez, 95
DeBlieux, J. D.: leads opposition to Perez plan, 328; mentioned, 332
Delacroix Island, 55–59
Delesdernier, George, 67
Delta Development Company, 80–82
Democratic National Convention: in 1948, pp. 176–77; in 1952, pp. 189–191, 195
Democratic State Central Committee: rules on Hale Bogg's gubernatorial candidacy, 153–55; committee members' suit to permit only Truman and Barkley on Louisiana ballot, 180; dismisses W. H. Talbot, 184; committee actions, 1952 meeting, 193; in free-elector strategy conference, 316; its motion to rescind Perez plan, 328 330; its two slates of electors, 330; awards rooster to Lyndon Johnson, 330; Perez's suit against, 330–31; on electing presidential electors prior to general election, 335; its May 11 and June 14, 1968, meetings and work, 337–38; use of rooster and donkey symbols, 340

435